Elliott Carter

COMPOSER RESOURCE MANUALS
VOLUME 52
GARLAND REFERENCE LIBRARY OF THE HUMANITIES
VOLUME 2003

ELLIOTT CARTER
A GUIDE TO RESEARCH

JOHN F. LINK

GARLAND PUBLISHING, INC.
NEW YORK & LONDON
2000

Published in 2000 by
Garland Publishing, Inc.
29 West 35th Street
New York, NY 10001

Garland is an imprint of the Taylor & Francis Group.

Copyright © 2000 by John F. Link

All rights reserved. No part of this book may be reprinted or reproduced or utilized in any form or by any electronic, mechanical, or other means, now known or hereafter invented, including photocopying and recording, or in any information storage or retrieval system, without permission in writing from the publisher.

10 9 8 7 6 5 4 3 2 1

Library of Congress Cataloging-in-Publication Data

Link, John F.
    Elliott Carter : a guide to research / John F. Link.
       p. cm. — (Composer resource manuals ; v. 52) (Garland reference library of the humanities ; v. 2003)
    Includes index.
    ISBN 0-8153-2432-4 (alk. paper)
    1. Carter, Elliott, 1908– —Bibliography. I. Title.

ML134.C19 L56 2000
016.780'92 21—dc21   99-042718

Cover: Photograph copyright © 2000 by John F. Link.

Printed on acid-free, 250-year-life paper
Manufactured in the United States of America

In memory of Jonathan Raz

COMPOSER RESOURCE MANUALS

In response to the growing need for bibliographic guidance to the vast literature on significant composers, Garland is publishing an extensive series of research guides. This ongoing series encompasses more than fifty composers; they represent Western musical tradition from the Renaissance to the present century.

Each research guide offers a selective, annotated list of writings, in all European languages, about one or more composers. There are also lists of works by the composers, unless these are available elsewhere. Biographical sketches and guides to library resources, organizations, and specialists are presented. As appropriate to the individual composer, there are maps, photographs, or other illustrative matter, glossaries, and indexes.

Contents

Preface	xi
Acknowledgments	xiii
An Elliott Carter Chronology	1
Abbreviations	9
Elliott Carter's Compositions	13
I. Works Presumed Lost or Destroyed	13
II. Juvenilia and Unpublished Works in Manuscript	16
III. Published Works	20
Discography of Commercial Recordings of Elliott Carter's Compositions	65
Annotated Bibliography of Carter Studies	161
I. Sources Written by Elliott Carter	161
Collections	161
Other Sources	162
II. Interviews and Panel Discussions with Elliott Carter as a Participant	215
Collections	215
Panel Discussions	215
Interviews	217

III. Sources on Elliott Carter and His Music by
       Other Authors   225
       Bibliographies and Discographies   225
       Books and Articles   227
       Films and Video Recordings   286
       Doctoral Dissertations   288
       Related Writings about Music   294

Appendix 1: A Chronology of Elliott Carter's Compositions   299
Appendix 2: A Note about Primary Sources   305
Index   307

Preface

This volume contains a complete list of Elliott Carter's compositions, a discography of commercial recordings of his works, and an annotated bibliography. The list of compositions spans Carter's entire output, from his earliest student efforts (many of which are now lost or destroyed) to the song cycle *Tempo e tempi,* which Carter had not yet finished at the time of this writing. The discography contains every commercially released recording of Carter's music I could find through the end of 1998, with the exception of reissues found in anthologies produced for classroom use. Although I have tried to be as comprehensive as possible, the reader should be aware that Carter is one of the most frequently recorded contemporary composers and that new recordings that postdate my discography will certainly appear. I have included one noncommercial release (item 112) because it is currently the only recording of *A 6 Letter Letter.* The interested listener will find many other noncommercial recordings, including those of many premiere performances of Carter's works, among the holdings of the research institutions mentioned in Appendix 2.

The bibliography includes the most important writings on Carter and his music that have appeared in America and Western Europe from the 1940s—when Carter's music first began to attract attention—to 1998, when the bibliography was completed. Although every effort has been made to include the most significant writings in English, French, German, Italian, and Spanish, some qualifications are in order. Newspaper articles, articles in popular magazines, concert announcements and reviews, acceptance speeches, and entries in biographical dictionaries and textbooks have been omitted. I have made exceptions, however, for popular sources written by Carter himself, for those that include substantial interviews with him that are not to be found elsewhere, and for Andrew Porter's eloquent critiques, which first appeared in *The New Yorker*. No effort has been made to include the thousands of brief interviews Carter has given to newspapers over the years. Dissertations have been included; master's theses have not. Book reviews—which provide an important context for scholarly discussion—also have been included, while reviews of recordings—which tend to gloss over both music and performance practice—have been omitted. In a few cases I have included record reviews that contain substantive analyses of one or more of Carter's compositions. An example is George Rochberg's review of the Composers String Quartet recording of the *String Quartet No. 1* (item 749), an unusually balanced critique of Carter's work by a notable contemporary.

This is a particularly exciting time for Carter studies. Past the age of 90, Carter himself is in the midst of the most productive period of his career, and his music continues to inspire a growing number of performers, listeners, and scholars around the world. It is my hope that this book will be a helpful resource, and that it will encourage the reader to further explore some of the most wonderful music of our time.

The author would welcome reader reports of omissions and/or errata, which may be sent to link@wpunj.edu. Corrections will be posted on the author's web site: <www.wpunj.edu/coac/music/link/index.html>.

Acknowledgments

All bibliographers are indebted to their predecessors. The bibliographies, discographies, works lists, and collections of writings compiled by Jonathan W. Bernard (item 402), William T. Doering (item 609), Richard Franko Goldman (item 668), Richard Jackson, Pamela S. Berlin, and John Shepard (item 610), David Schiff (item 769), Abraham Skulsky (item 789), Else Stone and Kurt Stone (item 399), Jerome F. Weber (item 611), and Harold Whipple (item 612) were all of great assistance. A fellowship from the Paul Sacher Foundation allowed me to study Carter's manuscripts in the summer of 1991 and again in the summer of 1995. Hilda Raz got this project going by putting me in touch with Garland Press. Jeffrey Herman, at Boosey & Hawkes, generously helped me to track down and resolve a number of inconsistencies. The librarians and staff at the New York Public Library for the Performing Arts answered hundreds of questions. Barb, at Hal Leonard Corp., Richard Brundage, at G. Schirmer, James Ginsburg, president of Cedille Records, and Wayne Wadhams, owner of Boston Skyline Records, provided helpful responses to my queries. Jonathan Bernard provided a detailed critique of an early outline of this book. Frederick M. Link made many helpful suggestions for improving my first draft. David Schiff asked me to compile the bibliography and discography for the second edition of his *The Music of Elliott Carter* (item 769), a task that contributed to this book as well. Chris Mullis generously provided access to the CD collection of WKCR-FM in New York. Fina Modesto was my essential source for help with articles in Italian. Leo Balk, Guy Marco, and Soo Mee

Kwon were conscientious and patient editors. Maria Schoenhammer, my partner in all things, gave me excellent advice about a wide variety of matters. Finally, this volume could never have been written without the encouragement and generous assistance of Helen and Elliott Carter. To all who helped I offer my thanks; the errors that remain are mine alone.

Elliott Carter

An Elliott Carter Chronology

1908   Born 11 December, West 95th Street, New York, NY, to Elliott Cook Carter Sr. and Florence Doris Chambers.

1920–26   Attends Horace Mann High School, studying music with Clifton Furness.

1924   Introduced to Charles Ives by Furness.

1926–30   Attends Harvard University, majoring in English literature (B.A., 1930). Member, Harvard Glee Club.
    Studies piano with Newton Swift and solfège with Hans Ebell at the Longy School, Cambridge, MA.

1927   Spends the summer transcribing Arabic music in Tunisia for the Baron Rudolphe d'Erlanger. Stays at the home of Laura Williams, to whom he dedicated *My Love Is in a Light Attire* (item 30).

1930–32   Graduate study at Harvard University; teachers include A. T. Davison (choral composition), Edward Burlingame Hill (music history), visiting professor Gustav Holst (composition), and Walter Piston (harmony and counterpoint); M.A., 1932.

1932–35   At Piston's urging, goes to Paris to study composition privately with Nadia Boulanger and attend her classes at

	the École Normale de Musique. Sings in a madrigal group directed by Henri Expert. Graduates from the École Normale with a *Licence de contrepoint*.
1935	Returns to Cambridge, MA.
1936	Returns to New York.
1937–39	Music director of Lincoln Kirstein's Ballet Caravan.
1937–46	Contributor to *Modern Music*.
1938	*To Music* (item 103) wins Choral Contest sponsored by the WPA Federal Music Project in conjunction with the Columbia Broadcasting System and Columbia Records.
1939	Marries Helen Frost-Jones, sculptor and art critic, on 6 July.
1939–50	Board member of the American Composers Alliance.
1939–52	Board member of the League of Composers.
1940	*Pocahontas* (item 81) wins Juilliard Publication Award.
1940–42	Teaches music, Greek, and mathematics at St. John's College, Annapolis, MD.
1943	Son, David Chambers Carter, born on 4 January.
1943–45	Music consultant to the Office of War Information.
1945	*Holiday Overture* (item 67) wins first prize in the Independent Music Publishers Contest. *Canonic Suite* (item 45) for four alto saxophones wins BMI Publication Prize. Guggenheim Fellowship.
1946–48	Professor of Composition, Peabody Conservatory, Baltimore, MD.

An Elliott Carter Chronology

1946–52 Board member of the U.S. section of the International Society for Contemporary Music.

1948 Music Library Association cites Carter's *Piano Sonata* (item 80) as best American work for piano published in 1948.

1948–50 Professor of Composition, Columbia University.

1950 Guggenheim Fellowship.
Grant from the National Institute of Arts and Letters.

1952 President of U.S. section of the International Society for Contemporary Music.

1953 *String Quartet No. 1* (item 88) is awarded first prize in the Concours international de quatuors à cordes, Liège, Belgium. Carter must renounce the prize because the first performance had already been given.
Awarded Prix de Rome.

1953–54 Fellow of the American Academy in Rome.

1955 Vice president, International Society for Contemporary Music.

1955–56 Professor of Composition, Queens College, New York, NY.

1956 *Sonata for Flute, Oboe, Cello, and Harpsichord* (item 86) wins Walter W. Naumburg Musical Foundation Award.
Elected to membership in the National Institute of Arts and Letters.

1957 Teaches at the Dartington School in England.

1958 Instructor, Salzburg Seminars.

1960 *String Quartet No. 2* (item 89) wins Pulitzer Prize.

String Quartet No. 2 (item 89) wins New York Music Critics' Circle Award.

1960–62 Professor of Composition, Yale University.

1961 *String Quartet No. 2* (item 89) wins UNESCO Prize for Outstanding Musical Work of 1961.
Double Concerto (item 51) wins New York Music Critics' Circle Award.
Awarded Sibelius Medal for Music.
Honorary Doctorate from New England Conservatory of Music.
American delegate to East-West Encounter, Tokyo, Japan.

1962 Elected to membership in the American Academy of Arts and Letters.

1963 Composer-in-residence at the American Academy in Rome.
Elected to membership in the American Academy of Arts and Sciences.

1964 Composer-in-residence in Berlin, under the auspices of the Ford Foundation.

1964–84 Professor of Composition, Juilliard School of Music.

1965 Honorary doctorate from Swarthmore College.
Creative Arts Award from Brandeis University.

1966 Ward Lucas Visiting Professor of Music at Carleton College.
Professor of Composition, the Massachusetts Institute of Technology.

1967 Harvard Glee Club Medal.
Honorary doctorate from Princeton University.

1967–68 A. D. White Professor-at-Large, Cornell University.

1968 Composer-in-residence at the American Academy in Rome.
Honorary doctorate from Ripon College.

1969 Premio delle Muse, "Polimnia," awarded by the Associazione Artistico Letteraria Internationale, Florence, Italy.

1970 Elected to membership in the American Academy of Arts and Letters.
Elected honorary member of the Akademie der Küste, Berlin.
Honorary doctorate from Boston University.
Honorary doctorate from Harvard University.
Honorary doctorate from Oberlin College.
Honorary doctorate from Yale University.

1971 Awarded Gold Medal for Eminence in Music from the National Institute of Arts and Letters.
Elected member of the National Institute of Arts and Sciences.

1973 *String Quartet No. 3* (item 90) wins Pulitzer Prize.

1973–74 Exhibition of sketches and scores in manuscript in the Vincent Astor Gallery of the Library and Museum of the Performing Arts, the New York Public Library at Lincoln Center, in honor of Carter's sixty-fifth birthday.

1974 Composer-in-residence, Aspen Center for Compositional Studies.
Honorary doctorate from the Peabody Conservatory of Music.

1978 Awarded Handel Medallion, New York City's highest cultural award.

1979 Composer-in-residence, American Academy in Rome.

1981 First American composer to be awarded the Ernst-von-Siemens Prize, Munich.

1983   Honorary doctorate from Cambridge University.
        Awarded Edward MacDowell Medal for lifetime achievement in music.
        Elliott Carter Festival, Los Angeles, CA.

1984   George Peabody Medal.

1985   Awarded National Medal of Arts.

1987   Awarded rank of Commandeur dans l'Ordre des Arts et des Lettres from the French Ministry of Culture.

1988   Elliott Carter Festival in Turin.

1990   Composer-in-residence at the Royal Academy of Music's American Music Festival.

1991   "Compositeur invité" at the Centre Acanthes festival, Avignon, France, and professor at Chartreuse de Villeneuve lez Avignon.
        Awarded rank of Commendatore in the Order of Merit of the Republic of Italy.

1992   "Compositeur invité," Archipel festival, Geneva, 18–29 March.
        Composer-in-residence at the Getty Center in Santa Monica, CA.
        Receives National Music Council's American Eagle Award.

1993   Composer of the Year, *Musical America Directory*.
        Violin Concerto (item 107) wins *Gramophone* Award for Best Contemporary Composition.

1996   Awarded Royal Philharmonic Society Gold Medal.

1997   Royal Philharmonic Society Music Award.
        International Society for the Performing Arts "Tiffany Award."

1998 *Allegro scorrevole* (item 93.3) awarded Lauréat du Prix de Composition Musicale 1998, by a jury led by Henri Dutilleux.

Allegro scorrevole (item 93.3) awarded 1998 Award for Musical Composition of the Prince Pierre of Monaco Foundation.

Abbreviations

EC   *Elliott Carter: edizione italiana aggiornata dall'Autore* (item 401)
EEC   *Entretiens avec Elliott Carter* (item 575)
CARTER   *Carter* (item 400)
CEL   *Collected Essays and Lectures, 1937–1995* (item 402)
WEC   *The Writings of Elliott Carter* (item 399)

Woodwinds

fl	flute
picc	piccolo
afl	alto flute
ob	oboe
eh	English horn (cor Anglais)
cl	clarinet
bcl	bass clarinet
cbcl	contrabass clarinet
e♭cl	clarinet in E♭
bn	bassoon
cbn	contrabassoon
ssax	soprano saxophone
asax	alto saxophone
tsax	tenor saxophone
bsax	baritone saxophone

Brass

hn	horn
tpt	trumpet
c tpt	trumpet in C
tb	trombone
tbtb	tenor-bass trombone
btb	bass trombone

Percussion

perc	percussion
mar	marimba
vib	vibraphone
xyl	xylophone

Keyboards, Harp, and Guitar

cel	celesta
pno	piano
hps	harpsichord
hp	harp
gui	guitar

Voices

sop	soprano
ms	mezzo-soprano
ten	tenor
bar	baritone
bbar	bass-baritone
b	bass

Strings

vn	violin
va	viola
vc	cello
db	double bass (contrabass)

Other

arr arranger
cond conductor

Standard order of instrumentation:

fl, ob, cl, bn – hn, tpt, tb, tuba – perc – other – vn I, vn II, va, vc, db

Elliott Carter's Compositions

I. Works Presumed Lost or Destroyed

The principal source for Carter's lost or destroyed works is a list Carter provided for Claire Reis's *Composers in America* (item 748), p. 57. This list was reproduced in the first edition of Schiff, *The Music of Elliott Carter* (item 769, 1st ed.), p. 72, together with Schiff's annotations, made in consultation with Carter, indicating the status of each work. The annotations are currently the only authority for the status of these works. Thus, it is possible that some may still exist in manuscript.

1. *Bombs in the Ice-Box*

    ca. 1937
    Ballet
    Scenario by James Agee
    Listed as "scheduled for performance next Fall" in the contributors' notes for *Modern Music* 14, no. 3 (March–April 1937)

2. *Concerto for English Horn and Orchestra*

    1937
    "Never completed—destroyed" (Schiff, item 769, 1st ed., p. 72)

3. *First String Quartet*

   1935
   ca. 25:00
   "Destroyed" (Schiff, item 769, 1st ed., p. 72) but see *String Quartet in C* (item 34)

4. *Flute Sonata*

   1934
   for flute and piano
   ca. 14:00
   "Destroyed" (Schiff, item 769, 1st ed., p. 72)

5. *Incidental music and choruses for Shakespeare's* Much Ado About Nothing

   1937
   for women's chorus, two violas, and two cellos
   Text by William Shakespeare
   ca. 20:00
   "Project?" (Schiff, item 769, 1st ed., p. 72)

6. *Madrigal Book*

   1937
   Twelve madrigals for mixed voices, three, four, five, six, eight parts
   Listed as "recently completed" in contributors' notes to *Modern Music* 15, no. 1 (November–December 1937)
   "Mostly destroyed" (Schiff, item 769, 1st ed., p. 72) but see *To Music* (item 103)

7. *Music Portrait of Prince Obolensky*

   ca. 1938
   "[Carter] was commissioned to write a music portrait of Prince Obolensky for the April evening of the High-Low concerts." (Contributors' note to *Modern Music* 15, no. 4 [May–June 1938])

8. *One-Act Opera*

   1937

   "Project?" (Schiff, item 769, 1st ed., p. 72)

9. *Oratorio—Setting of Hart Crane's "The Bridge"*

   1937

   "Project" (Schiff, item 769, 1st ed., p. 72)

10. *Piano Sonata*

    ca. 1920s

    "Carter has spoken of a 'very advanced and complicated piano sonata, as well as some simpler settings of Joyce's Chamber Music' [see item 12], which he wrote in the 1920s and showed to Charles Ives." (Schiff, item 769, 1st ed., p. 73)

11. *Second String Quartet*

    1937

    ca. 16:00

    "Destroyed" (Schiff, item 769, 1st ed., p. 72) but see *String Quartet in C* (item 34)

12. *Settings of Joyce's* Chamber Music

    Before 1928

    "One of the Joyce songs ["My Love Is in a Light Attire," item 30] accidentally survived because it was sent to Henry Cowell in 1928 with hopes of publication in *New Music*. Cowell never published it, but also did not return it until a few months before his death in 1965." (Schiff, item 769, 1st ed., p. 73)

13. *Short Symphony*

    ca. 1939

    Listed as "recently completed" in the contributors' notes to *Modern Music* 17, no. 2 (January–February 1940)

14. *String Quartet*

   ca. 1920s
   "[Carter's] letters to Ives reveal the one-time existence of yet another early string quartet, number 'minus three.'" (Schiff, item 769, 1st ed., p. 72)

15. *Symphony*

   1937
   for orchestra
   ca. 20:00
   "Destroyed" (Schiff, item 769, 1st ed., p. 72)

16. *Tom and Lily*

   1934
   Comic opera in one act
   for four solo voices, small mixed chorus, and chamber orchestra
   ca. 30:00
   "Destroyed" (Schiff, item 769, 1st ed., p. 72)

II. Juvenilia and Unpublished Works in Manuscript

Much of Carter's unpublished work is now in the collections of the Paul Sacher Foundation and the Library of Congress (see Appendix 2). What follows should be taken as a provisional list until a more comprehensive catalog of Carter's manuscripts becomes available.

17. *The Ball Room Guide*

   1937–38
   Ballet suite
   Written for Lincoln Kirstein
   Unfinished (planned to be ca. 40:00)
   a. for two pianos
      1. Galop (sketches only)
      2. Polka
   b. *Prelude, Fanfare and Polka*

for flute, oboe, bass clarinet, alto saxophone, tenor saxophone, and strings
ca. 10:00
1. Prelude
2. Fanfare and Polka
Autograph materials: Paul Sacher Foundation
Bibliography: Items 597, 769 1st ed.

18. *Canon* from *Easy Piano Pieces*

ca. 1940
for piano
ca. 1:00
Autograph materials: Paul Sacher Foundation

19. [*Counterpoint Exercises*]

ca. 1933–35
Written during Carter's study with Nadia Boulanger
Autograph materials: Library of Congress

20. *The Difference*

1944
for soprano, baritone, and piano
Text by Mark Van Doren
ca. 10:00
Autograph materials: Paul Sacher Foundation
Bibliography: Item 769 1st ed.

21. *Double Piano Sonata*

Date unknown
for two pianos
Sketches only
Autograph materials: Paul Sacher Foundation

22. *Five Fanfares*

ca. 1940s?
for brass ensemble and percussion
Autograph materials: Paul Sacher Foundation

23. *Folk Dance No. 2*

   Date unknown
   for orchestra
   Autograph materials: Paul Sacher Foundation

24. *I Am Rose, My Eyes Are Blue*

   Date and instrumentation unknown
   Text by [author unknown]
   Sketches only
   Autograph materials: Paul Sacher Foundation

25. *Incidental music and choruses for Plautus's* Mostellaria

   1936
   for baritone, tenor, men's chorus, and ten-piece chamber orchestra
   Texts by Plautus, *Mostellaria*; Ovid, *Fasti*
   ca. 20:00
   Commissioned by the Harvard Classical Club
   Premiere: 15 April 1936, Sanders Theatre, Harvard University, Cambridge, MA; Harvard Classical Club
   Autograph materials: Paul Sacher Foundation
   Finale arranged as *Tarantella* (item 97)
   Bibliography: Items 597, 769 1st ed., 769 2nd ed.

26. *Incidental music and choruses for Sophocles'* Philoctetes

   1931
   for baritone, tenor, men's chorus, and chamber orchestra
   According to Schiff, the ensemble includes "offstage oboe, onstage drum (a dharbhouka is specified) and unison chorus." (Schiff, item 769, 1st ed., p. 74)
   Text by Sophocles
   ca. 30:00
   Commissioned by the Harvard Classical Club
   Premiere: 15 March 1933, Sanders Theatre, Harvard University, Cambridge, MA; Harvard Classical Club: Harry Levin (Odysseus), Robert Fitzgerald (Philoctetes), Milman Parry (director)
   Autograph materials: Paul Sacher Foundation
   Bibliography: Items 597, 769 1st ed., 769 2nd ed.

27. *Invention on Prout's Subject*

   ca. 1933–35?
   Autograph materials: Paul Sacher Foundation

28. *Labyrinth*

   ca. 1933–35
   for four trumpets or four horns
   "4-part canon at unison written in Paris" (Carter's note)
   Autograph materials: Paul Sacher Foundation

29. *Musical Studies Nos. 1–4.* See *Canonic Suite* (item 45)

30. *My Love Is in a Light Attire*

   1928
   for voice and piano
   Text by James Joyce
   Dedication: Laura Williams "at whose house in Tunisia Carter transcribed Arabic music during the summer of 1927" (Schiff, item 769, 1st ed., p. 73).
   Premiere: 15 March 1933, Harvard Classical Club
   Autograph materials: Paul Sacher Foundation
   Also see item 12
   Bibliography: Items 597, 769 1st ed.

31. *Piano Trio*

   Date unknown
   for violin, cello, and piano
   Unfinished
   Autograph materials: Paul Sacher Foundation

32. *Prelude, Fanfare and Polka.* See *The Ball Room Guide* (item 17)

33. *Sonatina*

   Date unknown
   for oboe and harpsichord
   Unfinished
   Autograph materials: Paul Sacher Foundation

34. *String Quartet in C.*

> Date unknown
> Autograph materials: Paul Sacher Foundation
> Unclear whether this forty-seven-page score has any relationship to the *First String Quartet* (item 3) or *Second String Quartet* (item 11)

35. *Symphony No. 2*

> Date unknown
> for orchestra
> Sketches only
> Autograph materials: Paul Sacher Foundation

36. *Trio*

> ca. 1933–35
> for flute, clarinet, and bassoon
> Sketches only
> Autograph materials: Paul Sacher Foundation

37. *Trio*

> Date unknown
> for clarinet, violin, and cello
> Unfinished
> Autograph materials: Paul Sacher Foundation

III. Published Works

38. *A 6 Letter Letter to Paul Sacher for His 90th Birthday*

> 1996
> for English horn
> ca. 3:00
> Hendon Music (Boosey & Hawkes) M051660735, in preparation
> Dedication: Paul Sacher
> Premiere: 27 April 1996, Concert Hall of the Stadt-Casinos, Basel, Switzerland; Heinz Holliger (eh)
> Autograph materials: Paul Sacher Foundation
> Bibliography: Item 769 2nd ed.

39. *90+*

"composed in March of 1994"
for piano
ca. 5:30
Hendon Music (Boosey & Hawkes) M051285037 (PIB 503), 1994
Dedication: "mille e novanta auguri a caro Goffredo [Petrassi]" (a thousand and ninety good wishes to dear Goffredo)
Premiere: 11 June 1994, Pontino Music Festival, Pontino, Italy; Giuseppe Scotese (pno)
Autograph materials: Paul Sacher Foundation
Bibliography: Item 769 2nd ed.

Across the Yard: La Ignota

See *In Sleep, in Thunder* (item 68)

Adagio

See *Eight Pieces for Four Timpani* (item 54)

Adagio for Cello and Piano

See *Elegy* (item 55)

Adagio tenebroso

See *Symphonia—Sum Fluxae Pretiam Spei* (item 93)

Adagio for Viola and Piano

See *Elegy* (item 55)

Allegro scorrevole

See *Symphonia—Sum Fluxae Pretiam Spei* (item 93)

Am Klavier (at the Piano)

See *Of Challenge and of Love* (item 76)

Anaphora

See *A Mirror on Which to Dwell* (item 72)

Anniversary

See *Three Occasions for Orchestra* (item 100)

Argument

See *A Mirror on Which to Dwell* (item 72)

40. *Birthday Fanfare*

   1978
   for three trumpets, vibraphone, and chimes
   Unpublished
   Dedication: "For Sir William Glock's 70th"
   Premiere: 3 May 1978, London
   Autograph materials: Paul Sacher Foundation
   Bibliography: Items 769 1st ed., 769 2nd ed.

41. *Birthday Flourish*

   composed 4 July 1988
   a. for five trumpets
      Premiere: 14 September 1988; members of the San Francisco Symphony, Herbert Blomstedt (cond)
   b. for two trumpets, horn, and two trombones
      Premiere: 20 January 1989; members of the Cincinnati Symphony Orchestra, Jesus Lopez-Cobos (cond)
   ca. 1:00
   Hendon Music (Boosey & Hawkes) M051103348 (ENB 334), score and parts, 1993
   Dedication: "For Helen [Carter]"
   Autograph materials: Paul Sacher Foundation
   Bibliography: Item 769 2nd ed.

42. *Brass Quintet*

   15 May–29 August 1974, Aspen, CO, and Waccabuc, NY
   for two B♭ trumpets, horn, tenor trombone, and tenor-bass trombone
   ca. 17:00
   AMP 7521, 1976; "1993 edition," distributed by Hal Leonard, HL50226320, ISBN 0-7935-2512-8 (score and parts), HL50238490 (study score)
   Commissioned by the American Brass Quintet

Dedication: "For the American Brass Quintet"
Premiere: 20 October 1974, a Charles Ives Festival broadcast by the BBC from London, England; American Brass Quintet: Raymond Mase (tpt), Louis Ranger (tpt), Edward Birdwell (hn), Robert Biddlecome (tb), Herbert Rankin (btb)
Autograph materials: Paul Sacher Foundation
Bibliography: Items 410, 615, 703, 733, 766, 769 1st ed., 769 2nd ed.

Canaries

See *Eight Pieces for Four Timpani* (item 54)

43. *Canon for 3: In Memoriam Igor Stravinsky*

1971
for three equal instrumental voices
ca. 1:00
Supplement ("In Memoriam Igor Stravinsky; Canons & Epitaphs Set 2") to *Tempo* 98 (1972): n.p.; AMP 7203, 1972, "1992 printing," distributed by Hal Leonard, HL50235490, ISBN 0-7935-1432-0; *Elliott Carter: Sketches and Scores in Manuscript* (New York: The New York Public Library and Readex Books, 1973), 60. *Winds Quarterly* 1 (Fall 1980): 7–8. *Indiana Theory Review* 4, no. 1 (Fall 1980): 2–3.
Composed "at the request of David Drew," the editor of *Tempo*
Dedication: "In Memoriam Igor Stravinsky"
Premiere: 23 January 1972, Alice Tully Hall, New York, NY; Joel Timm (ob), Alan Blustine (cl), James Stubb (tpt)
Autograph materials: Paul Sacher Foundation
Bibliography: Items 637, 643, 646, 769 1st ed., 769 2nd ed.

44. *Canon for 4*

Completed 19 April 1984
for flute, bass clarinet, violin, and cello
ca. 4:00
Hendon Music (Boosey & Hawkes) M051209842 (HPS 984), study score, 1986; M051102594 (ENB 259), score and parts, 1986

Dedication: "for the occasion of Sir William Glock's retirement from the Bath Festival which rose to such eminence under his leadership"
Premiere: 3 June 1984, Bath Festival, Bath, England; members of the London Sinfonietta
Autograph materials: Paul Sacher Foundation
Bibliography: Items 742, 769 2nd ed.

45. *Canonic Suite*
    a. *Musical Studies Nos. 1–4*
       ca. 1932–35
       1. *Fanfare*
       2. *Nocturne*
       3. *Tarantella*
       4. *Andante Espressivo*
       for unspecified instrumentation
       Unpublished
       Autograph materials: Paul Sacher Foundation
    b. *Suite for Quartet of Alto Saxophones*
       renamed *Canonic Suite for Quartet of Alto Saxophones*
       1939; rev. 1981
       1. *Fanfare*, ca. 1:00
       2. *Nocturne*, ca. 3:00
       3. *Tarantella*, ca. 2:00
       Revision of *a*
       BMI, 1945; AMP 7904-4, 1984; reprint, distributed by Hal Leonard, HL50228360 (score and parts)
       Awarded: BMI Publication Prize, sponsored jointly by American Composers Alliance and Broadcast Music Inc., 1945
       Autograph materials: Paul Sacher Foundation has most materials; Library of Congress has a printed score with corrections from 1954
    c. *Canonic Suite for Four Clarinets in B♭*
       1955–56
       arrangement of *b*
       AMP 95736-10, 1957; reprint, distributed by Hal Leonard, HL50237310 (score), HL50234860 (parts)
       Autograph materials: Paul Sacher Foundation
       Bibliography: Items 769 1st ed., 769 2nd ed.

Canto

See *Eight Pieces for Four Timpani* (item 54)

Careless Night

See *In Sleep, in Thunder* (item 68)

A Celebration of Some 100 × 150 Notes

See *Three Occasions for Orchestra* (item 100)

Cello Sonata

See *Sonata for Violoncello and Piano* (item 87)

46. *Changes*

    Completed 8 September 1983, Waccabuc, NY
    for guitar
    ca. 7:00
    Hendon Music (Boosey & Hawkes) M051390151 (SRB 15), 1986
    "Dedicated to David Starobin who commissioned it and generously gave me advice about the guitar"*
    Premiere: 11 December 1983, 92nd St. Y, New York, NY; David Starobin (gui)
    Autograph materials: Paul Sacher Foundation
    Bibliography: Items 597, 684, 693, 741, 769 2nd ed., 772, 849

    *Numerous letters by Carter and Starobin in the collection of the Paul Sacher Foundation document this collaboration.

47. *Clarinet Concerto*

    1996
    for clarinet and orchestra
    1,2(2 eh),0,1 – 1,1,1,1 – perc(3) – harp – pno – str (1,1,1,1,1 or 10,8,6,4,3)
    ca. 18:00
    Hendon Music (Boosey & Hawkes), in preparation
    Commissioned by the Ensemble InterContemporain
    Premiere: 10 January 1997, Cité de la Musique, Paris; Alain Damiens (cl), Ensemble InterContemporain, Pierre Boulez (cond)

Autograph materials: Paul Sacher Foundation
Bibliography: Items 769 2nd ed., 817

48. *Con leggerezza pensosa*

    Omaggio a Italo Calvino
    "written in June 1990"
    for B♭ clarinet, violin, and cello
    ca. 5:00
    Hendon Music (Boosey & Hawkes) M051211678 (HPS 1167), study score, 1991; M051103218 (ENB 321), score and parts, 1991
    Commissioned by the Istituto di Studi Musicali in Latina, Italy
    Premiere: 29 September 1990, Istituto di Studi Musicali, Latina, Italy; Ciro Scarponi (cl), Jorge Risi (vn), Luigi Lanzillotta (vc)
    Autograph materials: Paul Sacher Foundation
    Bibliography: Item 769 2nd ed.

Concerto for Clarinet

See *Clarinet Concerto* (item 47)

Concerto for Oboe

See *Oboe Concerto* (item 75)

49. *Concerto for Orchestra*

    1969
    3(2 picc),3(eh),3(e♭cl, bcl),3(cbn) – 4,3(tpt in D),3,1 – timp – perc(6–8) – harp – pno – str
    Composed while Carter was composer-in-residence at the American Academy in Rome. "The Adagio movement was written at Villa Serbellni, Bellagio, where Carter was invited for a month by the Rockefeller Foundation." (Schiff, item 769, 1st ed., p. 243)
    ca. 20:00
    AMP 7011, 1972; reprint, distributed by Hal Leonard, HL50225800
    Commissioned by the New York Philharmonic Symphony Society to celebrate its 150th anniversary

Premiere: 5 February 1970, Philharmonic Hall, New York, NY; New York Philharmonic, Leonard Bernstein (cond)
Autograph materials: Paul Sacher Foundation has most materials; Library of Congress has ca. two hundred pages of sketches, a photocopy of the score with corrections, and ca. twenty rejected pages
Bibliography: Items 422, 485, 514, 580, 584, 586, 597, 615, 621, 622, 673, 677, 730, 758, 763, 769 1st ed., 769 2nd ed., 824, 887

Concerto for Piano

See *Piano Concerto* (item 79)

Concerto for Violin

See *Violin Concerto* (item 107)

50. *The Defense of Corinth*
1941
for speaker, men's chorus (TTBB), and piano four hands
ca. 15:00
Text by François Rabelais, Prologue to Book III of *Pantagruel* (trans. Urquhart and Motteux)
Merrymount Music Press, published by Mercury Music Corporation (Theodore Presser), MC 148, by special arrangement, 1950
Commissioned by the Harvard Glee Club
Dedication: G. Wallace Woodworth and the Harvard Glee Club
Premiere: 12 March 1942, Cambridge, MA; Harvard Glee Club, G. Wallace Woodworth (cond)
Autograph materials: Library of Congress has a holograph score; Paul Sacher Foundation has a holograph score
Bibliography: Items 597, 668, 769 1st ed., 769 2nd ed., 789

Dies Irae

See *In Sleep, in Thunder* (item 68)

Dolphin

See *In Sleep, in Thunder* (item 68)

51. *Double Concerto*

for harpsichord and piano with two chamber orchestras
Completed August, 1961
1(picc),1,1(e♭cl),1 – 2,1,1,0 – perc(4) – 1,0,1,1,1
Orchestra 1: fl(picc), hn, tpt, tb, perc(2), hps, vla, db
Orchestra 2: ob, cl(e♭cl), bn, hn, perc(2), pno, vn, vc
Completed August 1961, Waccabuc, NY
ca. 24:00
AMP 8075, 1964, also issued as AMP 96139-168; "1994 Printing," distributed by Hal Leonard, HL50237800, ISBN 0-7935-3415-1
Commissioned by the Fromm Music Foundation
Dedicated to Paul Fromm
Premiere: 6 September 1961, Grace Rainey Rogers Auditorium, New York, NY; Ralph Kirkpatrick (hps), Charles Rosen (pno), Gustav Meier (cond). The premiere took place at the concert of New American Music presented by the Fromm Music Foundation at the Eighth Congress of the International Society for Musicology.
Awarded: New York Music Critics' Circle Award, 1961
Autograph materials: Library of Congress has most materials; Paul Sacher Foundation has fifty-five pages of sketches, several rejected score pages, and a photocopy of the score with autograph corrections
Bibliography: Items 485, 503, 516, 558, 581, 597, 600, 616, 647, 670, 673, 677, 682, 713, 729, 732, 754, 758, 763, 769 1st ed., 769 2nd ed., 795, 796, 810, 823, 827

52. *Duo for Violin and Piano*

Begun ca. 1972; completed 27 April 1974
ca. 21:00
AMP 7547, 1976; "1993 edition" distributed by Hal Leonard, HL50226350, ISBN 0-7935-2062-2
Commissioned by the McKim Fund in the Library of Congress
Dedication: "For Helen [Carter]"
Premiere: 21 March 1975, New York Philharmonic Prospective Encounter Concert, Cooper Union, New York, NY; Paul Zukofsky (vn), Gilbert Kalish (pno)

Autograph materials: Paul Sacher Foundation
Bibliography: Items 503, 597, 623, 648, 734, 769 1st ed., 769 2nd ed.

Dust of Snow

See *Three Poems of Robert Frost* (item 101)

Ed è subito sera

See *Tempo e tempi* (item 99)

53. Eight Etudes and a Fantasy
    1949–1950
    for flute, oboe, clarinet, and bassoon
    ca. 23:00
    AMP 95825-42, 1959; reprint, distributed by Hal Leonard, HL50237430 (score), HL50235020 (parts)
    Dedication: "for Richard Franko Goldman"
    Premiere: 28 October 1952, American Composers Alliance Concert, Museum of Modern Art, New York, NY; New York Woodwind Quintet: Murray Panitz (fl), Jerome Roth (ob), David Glazer (cl), Bernard Garfield (bn)
    Autograph materials: Library of Congress has sketches and a photocopy of the score with corrections; Paul Sacher Foundation has a score and parts, both with corrections
    Bibliography: Items 420, 485, 597, 636, 687, 766, 769 1st ed., 769 2nd ed., 789

54. Eight Pieces for Four Timpani

    a. *Suite for Timpani* (also known as *Six Pieces for Kettledrums*)
       1950
       1. *Saëta*, ca. 4:30; dedicated to Al Howard
       2. *Moto Perpetuo*, ca. 2:00; to Paul Price
       3. *Recitative*, ca. 3:30; to Morris Lang
       4. *Improvisation*, ca. 3:00; to Paul Price
       5. *Canaries*, ca. 3:30; to Raymond DesRoches
       6. *March*, ca. 3:00; to Saul Goodman
       Unpublished

Premiere: 6 May 1952, Museum of Modern Art, New York, NY; Al Howard (timp)
b. *Recitative and Improvisation for Four Kettledrums (one player)*
revised excerpt of *a*
AMP 9601-6, 1960 (missing the indications of where to strike the drumhead)
c. *Eight Pieces for Four Timpani*
1950; rev. 1966
1. *Saëta* (1950), ca. 4:30; dedicated to Al Howard
2. *Moto Perpetuo* (1950), ca. 2:00; to Paul Price
3. *Adagio* (1966), ca. 2:30; to Jan Williams
4. *Recitative* (1950), ca. 3:30; to Morris Lang
5. *Improvisation* (1950), ca. 3:00; to Paul Price
6. *Canto* (1966), ca. 3:30; to Jan Williams
7. *Canaries* (1950), ca. 3:30; to Raymond DesRoches
8. *March* (1950), ca. 3:00; to Saul Goodman
AMP 6820, 1968; reprint, distributed by Hal Leonard, HL50234240, ISBN 0-7935-4848-9
Revision of *a* with two new pieces added
Autograph materials: Paul Sacher Foundation has most materials; Library of Congress has holograph scores on transparencies of the *Improvisation, Recitative,* and *March*
Bibliography: Items 485, 597, 606, 698, 705, 712, 763, 769 1st ed., 769 2nd ed., 786, 805, 829, 846

55. Elegy
ca. 4:00
a. *Adagio for Cello and Piano*
ca. 1943–44*
Unpublished
b. *Adagio for Viola and Piano*
ca. 1943–44*
Unpublished
c. *Elegy*
1946
for string quartet
Peer International Corporation, 1958
Premiere: 21 August 1946, Eliot, ME; Lanier String Quartet

Elliott Carter's Compositions 31

>Dedication: The Lanier String Quartet
>Arrangement of *b*
>
>d. *Elegy*
>1952
>for string orchestra
>Peer International Corporation, 1957
>Premiere: 1 March 1953, "Music in the Making," Cooper Union, New York, NY; uncredited string orch, David Broekman (cond)
>Arrangement of *c*
>
>e. *Elegy*
>1961
>for viola and piano
>Peer International Corporation, 1964
>Premiere: 16 April 1963, Cambridge, MA; George Humphrey (va), Alice Canady (pno)
>Revision of *b*
>Autograph materials: Paul Sacher Foundation has most materials; Library of Congress has a holograph score and viola part on transparencies of *b* and two holograph scores and one set of parts on transparencies of *c*
>Bibliography: Items 769 1st ed., 769 2nd ed.

*It is unclear whether *a* or *b* was the original version. According to the Library of Congress catalog, one note in Carter's hand describes *a* as "arranged from *Adagio for Viola and Piano*," while another describes *a* as "Original piece—later transcribed for: a) viola and piano, b) string quartet, c) string orchestra, d) rewritten for viola (1961?) E.C." Carter now says he thinks *a* was the original version (conversation with the author, June 1998).

56. *Emblems*

>Completed "Dorset, Vt. Sept., 1947"
>for men's chorus (TTBB) and piano
>ca. 15:00
>Music Press, MP 120, 1949; reprinted as Mercury Music Corporation (Theodore Presser) 352-00119 (title page), 352-00120 (cover)
>Text by Allen Tate
>Commissioned by the Harvard Glee Club
>Dedication: "To: G. Wallace Woodworth and Harvard Glee Club"

Premiere: Part II only: 3 April 1951, New York; Harvard Glee Club, G. Wallace Woodworth (cond). First complete performance: Summer 1952; Colgate College Singers
Autograph materials: Library of Congress has most materials; Paul Sacher Foundation has a photocopy of the holograph score with corrections and a typescript of the text
Bibliography: Items 668, 769 1st ed., 769 2nd ed., 789

57. *Enchanted Preludes*

Completed 13 February 1988, New York
for flute and cello
ca. 6:00
Hendon Music (Boosey & Hawkes) M051211210 (HPS 1121), study score, 1989; M051102785 (ENB 278), parts, 1989
Commissioned by Harry Santen
Dedication: "for Ann Santen's [50th] birthday"*
Premiere: 16 May 1988, New York, NY, at a concert of the Da Capo Chamber Players; Patricia Spencer (fl), André Emelianoff (vc)
Autograph materials: Paul Sacher Foundation
Bibliography: Items 769 2nd ed., 772, 815, 817a

*Ann Santen served as musical director of Cincinnati's public radio station WGUC.

End of a Chapter

See *Of Challenge and of Love* (item 76)

58. *Esprit rude/Esprit doux*

Completed 2 November 1984, Waccabuc, NY
for flute and B♭ clarinet
ca. 4:00
Hendon Music (Boosey & Hawkes) M051102518 (ENB 251), 1985
Dedication: "pour Pierre Boulez en célébration de son soixantième anniversaire" (for Pierre Boulez in celebration of his sixtieth birthday)

Premiere: 31 March 1985, Südwestfunk, Baden-Baden, Germany; Ensemble InterContemporain: Lawrence Beauregard (fl), Alain Damiens (cl)
Autograph materials: Paul Sacher Foundation
Bibliography: Items 597, 769 2nd ed., 772, 804, 814

59. *Esprit rude/Esprit doux II*
1994
for flute, B♭ clarinet, and marimba
ca. 5:00
Hendon Music (Boosey & Hawkes) M051104369 (ENB 436), score and parts, 1994; M051096305 (full score), in preparation
Dedication: "pour Pierre Boulez en célébration de son soixante-dixième anniversaire avec profonde admiration et amitié affectueuse" (for Pierre Boulez in celebration of his seventieth birthday with deep admiration and affectionate friendship)
Premiere: 30 March 1995, Grainger Ballroom, Orchestra Hall, Chicago, IL; members of Chicago Pro Musica: Richard Graef (fl), John Bruce Yeh (cl), Patricia Dash (mar)
Autograph materials: Paul Sacher Foundation
Bibliography: Item 769 2nd ed.

Fantasy—Remembering Roger

See *Three Recollections* (item 102)

60. *A Fantasy About Purcell's* Fantasia upon One Note
1974
for 2 B♭ trumpets, horn, alto or tenor trombone, and bass trombone
ca. 3:00
AMP 7546, 1977; reprint, distributed by Hal Leonard, HL50238540 (score), HL50226490 (parts)
Dedication: "A Christmas Present for the American Brass Quintet"
Premiere: 13 January 1975, Carnegie Recital Hall, New York, NY; American Brass Quintet: Raymond Mase (tpt), Louis

Ranger (tpt), Edward Birdwell (hn), Robert Biddlecome (tb), Herbert Rankin (tb)
Autograph materials: Paul Sacher Foundation
Bibliography: Items 769 1st ed., 769 2nd ed.

61. *Figment*

1994
for cello
ca. 5:00
Hendon Music (Boosey & Hawkes) M051371549 (SCB 154), 1995
Commissioned by Thomas Demenga
Dedication: Thomas Demenga
Premiere: 8 May 1995, Merkin Hall, New York, NY; Thomas Demenga (vc)
Autograph materials: Paul Sacher Foundation
Bibliography: Items 769 2nd ed., 817

62. *Fragment*

1994
for string quartet
ca. 4:00
Musical supplement in *Tempo* 192 (April 1995): n.p.; Hendon Music (Boosey & Hawkes) M051104376 (score and parts), M051212576 (study score)
Dedication: "David Huntley In Memoriam"
Premiere: 13 October 1994, Merkin Concert Hall, New York, NY; The Kronos String Quartet: David Harrington (vn I), John Sherba (vn II), Hank Dutt (va), Joan Jeanrenaud (vc)
Autograph materials: Paul Sacher Foundation
Bibliography: Item 769 2nd ed.

Godimento

See *Tempo e tempi* (item 99)

63. *Gra*

"NY Feb. 26 [/] March 7" 1993
ca. 5:00

a. for B♭ clarinet
Hendon Music (Boosey & Hawkes) M051581993 (WCB 199), 1994
Commissioned by the Pontino Festival for Witold Lutosławski's eightieth birthday.
Dedication: "For Witold Lutosławski's 80th birthday with admiration and affection"
Premiere: 4 June 1993, Pontino Music Festival, Sermoneta, Italy; Roland Diry (cl)

b. for trombone (transcribed by Benny Sluchin)
Hendon Music (Boosey & Hawkes) M051050345 (BTB 34), 1995
Autograph materials: Paul Sacher Foundation
Bibliography: Items 628, 631, 769 2nd ed., 817

64. *The Harmony of Morning*

1944
for women's chorus (SSAA) and chamber orchestra
1,1,1,1 – 1,0,0,0 – pno – str
ca. 8:30
AMP A-196, 1955 (vocal score); AMP 7955-7, 1986 (full score); reprint, distributed by Hal Leonard, HL50481102 (vocal score), HL50480198 (full score)
Text by Mark Van Doren, *Another Music*
Commissioned by Temple Emanu-El
Dedication: "To the Congregation EMANU-EL of New York City on the occasion of its Hundredth Anniversary"
Premiere: 25 February 1945, New York, NY; Temple Emanu-El Choir, Lazare Saminsky (cond)
Autograph materials: Paul Sacher Foundation
Bibliography: Items 597, 668, 764, 769 1st ed., 769 2nd ed., 789

Harriet

See *In Sleep, in Thunder* (item 68)

65. *Harvest Home*

1937
for mixed chorus (SATB) a cappella

Text by Robert Herrick
ca. 4:20
Hendon Music (Boosey & Hawkes) M051470921 (OCTB 7092), 1998
Premiere: Spring 1938, New York; Lehman Engel Madrigal Singers, Lehman Engel (cond)
Autograph materials: Paul Sacher Foundation
Bibliography: Items 597, 760, 769 1st ed., 769 2nd ed.

66. *Heart Not So Heavy As Mine*

1938

for mixed chorus (SATB) a cappella

ca. 5:00

Arrow Music Press; AMP A-273, 1939, also issued as AMP 95824-6; reprint, distributed by Hal Leonard, HL50229310, ISBN 0-7399-9293-104

Text by Emily Dickinson

Commissioned by the Temple Emanu-El

Dedication: "To Lazare Saminsky"

Premiere: 31 March 1939, Fourth Annual Three Choir Festival, Temple Emanu-El, New York, NY; Temple Emanu-El Choir, Lazare Saminsky (cond)

Autograph materials: Paul Sacher Foundation

Bibliography: Items 764, 769 1st ed., 769 2nd ed.

High on Our Tower

See *Of Challenge and of Love* (item 76)

67. *Holiday Overture*

Completed August 1944, Saltaire, Long Island; revised 1960–61

for orchestra

3,3,3,3 – 4,3,3,1 – timp – perc – pno – str

ca. 10:00

Arrow Music Press, 1946; revised version AMP 96119-68, 1962; reprint, distributed by Hal Leonard, HL50237590, ISBN 0-7935-7289-4

Premiere: 1946, Frankfurt, Germany; Frankfurt Symphony Orchestra, Hans Blumer (cond)

Elliott Carter's Compositions

Awarded: First prize ($500 and publication), Independent Music Publishers Contest, 1945. The judges were Serge Koussevitzky, Nicolai Berezowsky, and Aaron Copland

Autograph materials: Paul Sacher Foundation has most materials; Library of Congress has a holograph score, and one page of corrections for mm. 31–38

Bibliography: Items 516, 584, 616, 668, 697, 769 1st ed., 769 2nd ed., 789, 824

Improvisation

See *Eight Pieces for Four Timpani* (item 54)

In Genesis

See *In Sleep, in Thunder* (item 68)

Inner Song

See *Trilogy* (item 104)

68. *In Sleep, in Thunder*

    Completed 11 December 1981, Waccabuc, NY
    Six Poems of Robert Lowell
    for tenor and fourteen instrumentalists
    fl(picc, afl), ob(eh), cl(bcl), bn, hn, c tpt, tb, pno, perc(1), 2 vn, va, vc, db
    1. "Dolphin"
    2. "Across the Yard: La Ignota"
    3. "Harriet"
    4. "Dies Irae"
    5. "Careless Night"
    6. "In Genesis"
    ca. 21:00
    Hendon Music (Boosey & Hawkes) M051209798 (HPS 979), study score, 1984
    Commissioned by the London Sinfonietta
    Dedication: "In memory of the poet and friend"
    Premiere: 26 October 1982, St. John's Smith Square, London, England; Neil Mackie (tenor), London Sinfonietta, Oliver Knussen (cond)

Autograph materials: Paul Sacher Foundation
Bibliography: Items 580, 597, 642, 644, 656, 741, 767, 769 2nd ed., 785, 814, 850, 866

Insomnia

See *A Mirror on Which to Dwell* (item 72)

L'Arno a Rovezzano

See *Tempo e tempi* (item 99)

69. *Let's Be Gay*

1937
for women's chorus (SSA) and two pianos
ca. 3:10
Hendon Music (Boosey & Hawkes) M051470914 (OCTB 7091), 1998
Text by John Gay, *The Beggar's Opera*
Commissioned by Nicholas Nabokov for a production of John Gay's *The Beggar's Opera* at Wells College
Premiere: Spring 1938, Wells College, Aurora, NY; Wells College Glee Club, Nicholas Nabokov (cond)
Autograph materials: Paul Sacher Foundation
Bibliography: Items 597, 760, 769 1st ed., 769 2nd ed.

The Line Gang

See *Three Poems of Robert Frost* (item 101)

70. *Luimen*

1997
for trumpet, trombone, harp, mandolin, guitar, and vibraphone
ca. 10:00
Hendon Music (Boosey & Hawkes), in preparation
Commissioned by the Nieuw Ensemble
Premiere: 31 March 1998, Amsterdam Paradiso; Nieuw Ensemble, Ed Spanjaard (cond)
Autograph materials: Paul Sacher Foundation
Bibliography: Item 769 2nd ed.

March

See *Eight Pieces for Four Timpani* (item 54)

71. *The Minotaur*

1947
for orchestra
2(picc),2(eh),2(bcl),2 – 4,2,2,0 – timp – perc(2) – pno – str
a. Ballet in one act and two scenes
ca. 33:00
Commissioned by Lincoln Kirstein for Ballet Society (predecessor to the New York City Ballet)
Premiere: 26 March 1947, Central High School of Needle Trades, New York, NY; Ballet Society: Elise Reiman (Pasiphae, Queen of Crete), Edward Bigelow (Minos, King of Crete), Tanaquil LeClerq (Ariadne), Leon Barzin (cond), John Taras (choreographer and Theseus), Joan Junyer (scenery and costumes)
b. Suite from *The Minotaur*
ca. 23:00
AMP 95548, 1956; reprint, distributed by Hal Leonard, HL50248580
Dedication: "To Lincoln Kirstein whose Ballet Society commissioned this score"
Autograph materials: Library of Congress has most sketches and a holograph score of *a*; Paul Sacher Foundation has two pages of sketches and some holograph materials from *b*
Bibliography: Items 594, 597, 668, 714, 769 1st ed., 769 2nd ed., 789

72. *A Mirror on Which to Dwell*

Completed 31 December 1975, Waccabuc, NY
Six Poems of Elizabeth Bishop
for soprano and chamber orchestra
1(picc, afl),1(eh),1(e♭cl, bcl),0 – 0,0,0,0 – perc(1) – pno – 1,0,1,1,1
1. "Anaphora" (sop, afl, ob, cl, vib, pno, vn, va, vc, db)
2. "Argument" (sop, afl, bcl, 4 bongos, pno, vc, db)
3. "Sandpiper" (sop, ob, pno, vn, va, vc, db)

4. "Insomnia" (sop, picc, mar, vn, va)
5. "View of the Capitol from the Library of Congress" (sop, fl(picc), ob, cl(bcl), perc, pno, vn, va, vc, db)
6. "O Breath" (sop, afl, eh, bcl, perc, vn, va, vc, db)

ca. 19:30

AMP 7701, 1977; reprint, distributed by Hal Leonard, HL50238610

Texts by Elizabeth Bishop

Commissioned by Speculum Musicae in honor of the United States bicentennial, with grants from the New York State Council on the Arts, the Mellon Foundation, Milton M. Scofield, Murray R. Socolof, Fred Sherry, and Bernard E. Brandes

Dedication: "To the artists who gave this work its first performance: Susan Davenny Wyner and Speculum Musicae"

Premiere: 24 February 1976, Hunter College Playhouse, New York, NY; Susan Davenny Wyner (ms), Speculum Musicae, Richard Fitz (cond)

Autograph materials: Paul Sacher Foundation

Bibliography: Items 554, 583, 586, 597, 605, 644, 652, 674, 677, 735, 741, 763, 765, 769 1st ed., 769 2nd ed., 785, 787, 788, 822, 864, 876, 891

Moto Perpetuo

See *Eight Pieces for Four Timpani* (item 54)

73. *Musicians Wrestle Everywhere*

1945

for chorus (SSATB) a cappella or with string accompaniment

ca. 3:30

Music Press, MP 119, 1948; Mercury Music Corp (Theodore Presser)

Text by Emily Dickinson

Broadcast premiere: 20 December 1945, WNBC Radio "Story of Music"

Concert premiere: 12 February 1946, New York Times Hall, New York, NY; Randolph Singers, David Randolph (cond)

Autograph materials: Paul Sacher Foundation

Bibliography: Items 668, 769 1st ed., 769 2nd ed., 789, 801

74. *Night Fantasies*

Begun ca. November 1978; completed "Rome-Waccabuc. April 12, 1980"
for piano
ca. 20:00
AMP 7852-2, 1982; "1995 Edition," distributed by Hal Leonard, HL50236290, ISBN 0-7935-5255-9
Commissioned by Paul Jacobs, Gilbert Kalish, Ursula Oppens, and Charles Rosen, with a matching grant from the American Music Center of New York, funded by the New York State Council for the Arts, the Mary Duke Biddle Foundation, and the Kaplan Fund
"Dedicated to Paul Jacobs, Gilbert Kalish, Ursula Oppens and Charles Rosen"
Premiere: 2 June 1980, Bath Festival; Ursula Oppens
Autograph materials: Paul Sacher Foundation
Bibliography: Items 504, 592, 597, 645, 662, 682, 683, 701, 702, 711, 712, 728, 739, 769 1st ed., 769 2nd ed., 770, 807, 824, 830

O Breath

See *A Mirror on Which to Dwell* (item 72)

75. *Oboe Concerto*

Completed 10 October 1987, Waccabuc, NY
for oboe, concertino group, and orchestra
Concertino: four va, perc(1)
Orchestra: 1(afl, picc),0,1(bcl),0 – 1,0,1,0 – perc(1) – str (10,8,2,6,4 or 8,6,0,4,2)
ca. 25:00
Hendon Music (Boosey & Hawkes) M051094844 (FSB 484), full score, 1990; M051660612 (WOB 61), oboe part, 1990
Commissioned by Paul Sacher for Heinz Holliger
Dedication: "To Paul Sacher"
Premiere: 17 June 1988, Grosser Tonhallesaal, Zürich Festival, Zürich, Switzerland; Heinz Holliger (ob), Collegium Musicum Zürich, John Carewe (cond)
Autograph materials: Paul Sacher Foundation

Bibliography: Items 589, 597, 671, 769 2nd ed., 772, 773, 776, 816

Òboe sommerso

See *Tempo e tempi* (item 99)

76. *Of Challenge and of Love*
1994
Five Poems of John Hollander
for soprano and piano
1. "High on Our Tower"
2. "Under the Dome"
3. "Am Klavier (At the Piano)"
4. "Quatrains from Harp Lake"
5. "End of a Chapter"
ca. 25:00
Hendon Music (Boosey & Hawkes) M051933228, in preparation
Commissioned by the Aldeburgh Foundation for Lucy Shelton with funding provided by the Rex Foundation
Premiere: 23 June 1995, Aldeburgh Festival; Lucy Shelton (sop), John Constable (pno)
Autograph materials: Paul Sacher Foundation
Bibliography: Items 769 2nd ed., 798, 817

Partita

See *Symphonia—Sum Fluxae Pretiam Spei* (item 93)

77. *Pastoral*
   a. for piano and English horn
      1940
      Premiere: 12 November 1944, ISCM Forum Group, New York, NY; Joseph Marx (eh), Elliott Carter (pno)
   b. adapted for viola or clarinet and piano at the request of Henry Cowell for publication in *New Music* 18, no. 3 (April 1945)
      ca. 1942
      Premiere: 1942, New York, NY; Ralph Hersh (va), Elliott Carter (pno)

c. for English horn and piano (including arrangements for viola and clarinet in A)
Merion Music (Theodore Presser), 144-40005, 1982
d. for English horn or E♭ alto saxophone, marimba, and string orchestra 1987–88
Merion Music, Inc. (Theodore Presser), 1993
ca. 10:00
Autograph materials: Library of Congress has holograph score on transparencies of *b* or *c*, and a photocopy of *a* with attached transpositions for viola; Paul Sacher Foundation has a holograph score of *b* or *c*, and all materials relating to *d*
Bibliography: Items 580, 769 1st ed., 769 2nd ed.

78. *Penthode*

Completed 9 June 1985, Waccabuc, NY
for five groups of four instrumentalists
1(picc, afl),1(eh),1(e♭cl),bcl(cbcl),1 – 1,2,1,1 – perc(3) – pno – 1,1,1,1,1
Group 1: c tpt, tbtb, hp, vn
Group 2: fl (picc, afl), hn, perc(1), db
Group 3: ob (eh), tuba, vn, vc
Group 4: cl (e♭cl), bcl (cbcl), c tpt, perc(1)
Group 5: bn, pno, perc(1), va
ca. 18:00
Hendon Music (Boosey & Hawkes) M051094813 (FSB 481), full score, 1989
Commissioned by the Ensemble InterContemporain
Dedication: "To Pierre Boulez and l'Ensemble InterContemporain"
Premiere: 26 July 1985, Royal Albert Hall, London; Ensemble InterContemporain, Pierre Boulez (cond)
Autograph materials: Paul Sacher Foundation
Bibliography: Items 597, 603, 626, 743, 769 2nd ed., 772, 815, 817a, 860

79. *Piano Concerto*

Completed in Waccabuc, NY in 1965*
a. for piano, concertino group, and orchestra

Concertino: fl, eh, bcl, vn, va, vc, db
Orchestra: 2(2 picc),2,2,2,cbn – 4,3,3,1 – timp(2) – str (min. 7,6,5,4,3; max. 10,9,7,7,5)
ca. 26:00
AMP 6715, 1967; "1991 printing," distributed by Hal Leonard, HL50238090, ISBN 0-7935-1130-5
Commissioned by Jacob Lateiner through the Ford Foundation
Dedicated "To Igor Stravinsky on his 85th birthday, with great admiration and friendship"
Premiere: 6 January 1967, Boston, MA; Jacob Lateiner (pno), Boston Symphony Orchestra, Erich Leinsdorf (cond)
b. Reduction for two pianos by the composer, AMP 6715, 1967; "1991 printing," distributed by Hal Leonard, HL50224850, ISBN 0-7935-1131-3
Autograph materials: Library of Congress has ca. 7,500 pages of sketches; Paul Sacher Foundation has ca. 360 pages of sketches and several holograph scores, including the autograph full score
Bibliography: Items 485, 516, 584, 597, 600, 615, 617, 673, 711, 742, 758, 769 1st ed., 769 2nd ed., 795, 832, 844, 871

*According to a program note, the work was begun in 1964, but Carter's notebooks, now at the Paul Sacher Foundation, show that he was planning the concerto as early as October 1961.

80. *Piano Sonata*

1945–46; revised 1982
ca. 20:00
Music Press, 1948; Mercury Music Corporation (Theodore Presser), 1948; revised edition, 450-00234, 1982
Broadcast premiere: 16 February 1947, New York, NY; Webster Aitken, piano
Concert premiere: 5 March 1947, New York, NY; James Sykes, piano
Autograph materials: New York Public Library for the Performing Arts; Library of Congress; Paul Sacher Foundation
Bibliography: Items 420, 504, 614, 663, 668, 682, 702, 713, 728, 758, 769 1st ed., 769 2nd ed., 789, 799, 824, 830, 831, 845, 851, 859, 861, 877, 879

81. *Pocahontas*
   1936–39
   Ballet legend in one act
   Commissioned by Lincoln Kirstein for Ballet Caravan
   Dedication: Lincoln Kirstein
   a. for piano
      1936
      ca. 18:00
      Premiere: 17 August 1936, Keene State College, Keene, NH; Lew Christensen (choreography), Ruthanna Boris, Charles Laskey, Harold Christensen, Erick Hawkins (cast)
      Unpublished
   b. for orchestra
      1939
      3,2,2,2 – 4,3,3,1 – timp – perc(4) – harp – pno – str
      ca. 39:00
      Premiere: 24 May 1939, American Lyric Theatre, Martin Beck Theater, New York, NY; Ballet Caravan, Fritz Kitzinger (cond), Karl Free (scenery and costumes), Leda Anchutina, Erick Hawkins, Eugene Loring, and Harold Christensen (cast)
   c. Suite from the ballet
      1939; revised ca. 1960
      for orchestra (as above but with third flute doubling piccolo)
      ca. 20:00
      1. Overture
      2. John Smith and Rolfe Lost in the Virginia Forest
      3. Princess Pocahontas and Her Ladies
      4. Torture of John Smith
      5. Pavanne (Farewell of Pocahontas)
      Published for the Juilliard Foundation by Edwin Kalmus, 1941; revised version, AMP 7213, 1969; reprint, distributed by Hal Leonard, HL50238270
      Awarded: Juilliard Publication Award, 1940
      Autograph materials: Most materials in Paul Sacher Foundation; Library of Congress has holograph score of ?*b*
      Bibliography: Items 420, 584, 594, 597, 760, 764, 769 1st ed., 769 2nd ed., 789, 835

Quatrains from Harp Lake

See *Of Challenge and of Love* (item 76)

82. *Quintet for Piano and String Quartet*

 1997

 ca. 10:00

 Hendon Music (Boosey & Hawkes), in preparation

 Premiere: 18 November 1998, Coolidge Auditorium, Library of Congress, Washington, DC; Ursula Oppens (pno), the Arditti String Quartet

 Autograph materials: Paul Sacher Foundation

 Bibliography: Item 769 2nd ed.

83. *Quintet for Piano and Winds*

 "The work was composed in Southbury, Connecticut, during the summer of 1991."

 for oboe, B♭ clarinet (doubling E♭ clarinet), bassoon, horn, and piano

 ca. 24:00

 Hendon Music (Boosey & Hawkes) M051212330 (HPS 1233), study score, 1994; M051103706 (ENB 370), score and parts, 1994

 Commissioned by Heinz Holliger and KölnMusik

 Dedication: "for Heinz Holliger and KölnMusik"

 Premiere: 13 September 1992, Kölner Philharmonie, Cologne, Germany; Members of KölnMusik: Heinz Holliger (ob), Elman Schmid (cl), Klaus Thunemann (bn), Radovan Vlatković (hn), András Schiff (pno)

 Autograph materials: Paul Sacher Foundation

 Bibliography: Items 603, 769 2nd ed., 817

Recitative

See *Eight Pieces for Four Timpani* (item 54)

Recitative and Improvisation for Four Kettledrums

See *Eight Pieces for Four Timpani* (item 54)

Remembrance

See *Three Occasions for Orchestra* (item 100)

Riconoscenza per Goffredo Petrassi
See *Three Recollections* (item 102)

The Rose Family
See *Three Poems of Robert Frost* (item 101)

Saëta
See *Eight Pieces for Four Timpani* (item 54)

Sandpiper
See *A Mirror on Which to Dwell* (item 72)

84. *Scrivo in vento*
ca. 4 May–22 June 1991
for flute
ca. 5:00
Hendon Music (Boosey & Hawkes) M051591329 (WFB 132), 1991
Commissioned by Robert Aitken
Dedication: "for Robert Aitken"
Premiere: 20 July 1991, Centre Acanthes Festival, Avignon, France; Robert Aitken (fl)
Autograph materials: Paul Sacher Foundation
Bibliography: Items 585, 658, 659, 769 2nd ed.

Segreto del poeta
See *Tempo e tempi* (item 99)

85. *Shard*
1997
for guitar
ca. 3:00
Hendon Music (Boosey & Hawkes), in preparation
Dedication: David Starobin
Commissioned by David Starobin
Premiere: 11 June 1997, Humlebæk, Denmark; David Starobin
Autograph materials: Paul Sacher Foundation
Bibliography: Item 769 2nd ed.

86. *Sonata for Flute, Oboe, Cello, and Harpsichord*

   1952

   ca. 17:30

   AMP 9612-73, 1962; reprint, distributed by Hal Leonard, HL50224940, ISBN 0-7935-8633X (score and parts), HL50480574 (study score)

   Commissioned by Sylvia Marlowe for the Harpsichord Quartet of New York

   Dedication: On Carter's autograph fair copy the dedication reads "To: The Harpsichord Quartet." On the printed score the dedication is to Kurt Stone.

   First Performance: November 1953, Carnegie Recital Hall, New York, NY; Harpsichord Quartet of New York: Sylvia Marlowe (hps), Claude Monteux (fl), Henry Shulman (ob), Bernard Greenhouse (vc).

   Awarded: Walter W. Naumburg Musical Foundation Award, 1956

   Autograph materials: Library of Congress has sketches; Paul Sacher Foundation has holograph scores; New York Public Library for the Performing Arts has a photocopy of the holograph score

   Bibliography: Items 505, 597, 668, 769 1st ed., 769 2nd ed., 789, 870

   Sonata for Piano

   See *Piano Sonata* (item 80)

87. *Sonata for Violoncello and Piano*

   Completed 11 December 1948, Dorset, VT–New York, NY

   ca. 20:00

   Society for the Publication of American Music, 1953; "Corrected edition," AMP 6629-47, 1966; "1992 edition," distributed by Hal Leonard, HL50227330, ISBN 0-7935-1743-5

   Commissioned by Bernard Greenhouse

   Dedication: "To Bernard Greenhouse"

   Premiere: 27 February 1950, Town Hall, New York, NY; Bernard Greenhouse (vc), Anthony Makas (pno)

   Autograph materials: Library of Congress

Bibliography: Items 420, 485, 505, 558, 584, 597, 616, 663, 667, 668, 677, 732, 769 1st ed., 769 2nd ed., 789, 823, 827, 852

Statement—Remembering Aaron

See *Three Recollections* (item 102)

88. *String Quartet No. 1*

Begun ca. 1950, completed "Tucson-Dorset Sept. 1951"

ca. 40:00

AMP 95544-119, 1956; "1994 Edition," distributed by Hal Leonard, HL50237060, ISBN 0-7935-3734-7 (score), HL50227260, ISBN 0-7935-3785-1 (parts); Edition of String Quartets 1–5 published jointly by AMP and Hendon Music (Boosey & Hawkes) M051213412 (HPS 1341), 1998

Dedication: "To the Walden Quartet of the University of Illinois"

Premiere: 26 February 1953, McMillan Theater, Columbia University, New York, NY; Walden Quartet: Homer Schmitt (vn I), Bernard Goodman (vn II), John Garvey (va), Robert Swenson (vc)

Awarded: First prize, Concours international de quatours à cordes, Liège, Belgium, 1953. Carter had to renounce the prize because the premiere had already been given.

Autograph materials: Library of Congress has most materials; Paul Sacher Foundation has two pages of sketches and a photocopy of holograph score with corrections

Bibliography: Items 462, 485, 506, 521, 541, 558, 580, 584, 586, 597, 616, 619, 624, 629, 638, 641, 660, 663, 666, 668, 672, 686, 700, 704, 713, 715, 718, 749, 769 1st ed., 769 2nd ed., 783, 788, 789, 790, 795, 800, 802, 847, 848, 865, 874, 875

89. *String Quartet No. 2*

Completed 19 March 1959, Waccubuc, NY

ca. 20:00

AMP 9609-62, 1961; "Second, Corrected Edition," 1962; "Third, Corrected Edition," 1981; "Fourth, Corrected Edition," distributed by Hal Leonard, HL50480491, ISBN 0-7935-6772-6 (score), HL50488558, ISBN 0-6340-0252X (parts), 1989; Edition of String Quartets 1–5 published jointly by AMP and Hendon Music (Boosey & Hawkes) M051213412 (HPS 1341), 1998

Commissioned for $500 by the Stanley String Quartet. When the piece proved too difficult for them, Carter had to return the commission money in order to get the piece performed.

Premiere: 25 March 1960, the Juilliard School, New York, NY; the Juilliard String Quartet: Robert Mann (vn I), Isidore Cohen (vn II), Raphael Hillyer (va), Claus Adam (vc)

Awarded: Pulitzer Prize for Music, 1960; New York Music Critics' Circle Award, 1960; UNESCO First Prize, 1961

Autograph materials: Paul Sacher Foundation has most materials; Library of Congress has holograph score on transparencies

Bibliography: Items 485, 506, 550, 558, 586, 597, 600, 616, 619, 629, 638, 660, 666, 669, 672, 677, 687, 690, 710, 717, 718, 769 1st ed., 769 2nd ed., 779, 780, 781, 788, 791, 795, 824, 847, 865, 873, 875

90. *String Quartet No. 3*

1971

ca. 20:00

AMP 7303, 1973; reprint, distributed by Hal Leonard, HL50238300, ISBN 0-6340-0253-8 (score); Edition of String Quartets 1–5 published jointly by AMP and Hendon Music (Boosey & Hawkes) M051213412 (HPS 1341), 1998

Commissioned by the Juilliard School for the Juilliard String Quartet

Dedication: "for the Juilliard String Quartet"

Premiere: 23 January 1973, Alice Tully Hall, Lincoln Center, New York, NY; the Juilliard String Quartet: Earl Carlyss (vn I), Robert Mann (vn II), Samuel Rhodes (va), Claus Adam (vc)

Awarded: Pulitzer Prize for Music, 1973

Autograph materials: Library of Congress has most materials; Paul Sacher Foundation has one holograph draft score and

photocopies of a set of parts and seven other holograph scores with corrections
Bibliography: Items 507, 586, 597, 600, 615, 629, 665, 672, 685, 707, 710, 711, 717, 718, 731, 732, 758, 769 1st ed., 769 2nd ed., 808, 836, 847, 865, 872, 875

91. *String Quartet No. 4*

"Composed during part of 1985–86 in New York City, Waccabuc [NY], and at the American Academy in Rome." Completed "Waccabuc, June 1986"

ca. 24:00

Hendon Music (Boosey & Hawkes) M051211302 (HPS 1130), study score, 1989; M051102778 (ENB 277), score and parts, 1989; Edition of String Quartets 1–5 published jointly by AMP and Hendon Music (Boosey & Hawkes) M051213412 (HPS 1341), 1998

Commissioned by the Composers String Quartet, the Sequoia String Quartet, and the Thouvenel String Quartet; financed in part by the National Endowment for the Arts

Dedication: "To the Composers Quartet"

Premiere: 17 September 1986, Festival Miami, Miami, FL; The Composers String Quartet: Matthew Raimondi (vn I), Anahid Ajemian (vn II), Jean Dane (va), Mark Shuman (vc)

Autograph materials: Paul Sacher Foundation

Bibliography: Items 597, 629, 651, 655, 712, 744, 751, 769 2nd ed., 772, 773, 815

92. *String Quartet No. 5*

1995

ca. 20:00

Hendon Music (Boosey & Hawkes) M051212699 (ENB 454), study score, 1995; M051104543 (score and parts), 1995; Edition of String Quartets 1–5 published jointly by AMP and Hendon Music (Boosey & Hawkes) M051213412 (HPS 1341), 1998

Commissioned by the Arditti String Quartet

Dedication: "for the Arditti Quartet"

Premiere: 19 September 1995, Antwerp, Belgium; the Arditti String Quartet

Autograph materials: Paul Sacher Foundation
Bibliography: Items 769 2nd ed., 817

Suite for Timpani

See *Eight Pieces for Four Timpani* (item 54)

93. *Symphonia—Sum Fluxae Pretiam Spei*
    1. *Partita*
    2. *Adagio tenebroso*
    3. *Allegro scorrevole*

    1. *Partita*
       1993
       for orchestra
       picc,2(picc),2,eh,2(e♭cl),bcl,2,cbn – 4,3,3,1 – timp – perc(4) – pno – str
       ca. 15:00
       Hendon Music (Boosey & Hawkes) M051096244, full score, in preparation
       Premiere: 17 February 1994, Symphony Hall, Chicago, IL; the Chicago Symphony Orchestra, Daniel Barenboim (cond)
    2. *Adagio tenebroso*
       1994–95
       for orchestra
       3(2 picc),2,eh,2(e♭cl),bcl,2,cbn – 4,3,3,1 – timp – perc(4) – pno – str
       ca. 10:00
       Hendon Music (Boosey & Hawkes) M051096251 (full score), in preparation
       Commissioned by the BBC for the one hundredth anniversary of the Proms
       Premiere: 13 September 1995, BBC Proms, Royal Albert Hall, London; BBC Symphony, Andrew Davis (cond)
    3. *Allegro scorrevole*
       1996–97
       for orchestra
       3(2picc),2,eh,2(e♭cl),bcl,2,cbn – 4,3,3,1 – perc(4) – harp – pno – str
       ca. 15:00

Hendon Music (Boosey & Hawkes) M051096312 (full score), in preparation
Commissioned by the Cleveland Orchestra
Dedication: the Cleveland Orchestra, and Oliver Knussen
Premiere: 22 May 1997, Severance Hall, Cleveland, OH; Cleveland Orchestra, Christoph von Dohnányi (cond)
Awarded: Lauréat du Prix de Composition Musicale 1998, by a jury led by Henri Dutilleux
Autograph materials: Paul Sacher Foundation
Bibliography: Items 630, 769 2nd ed., 798 (2. only), 817, 825 (1. only)

94. *Symphony No. 1*

Completed 19 December 1942, Sante Fe, NM; revised 1954
for orchestra
2,2,2(e♭cl),2 – 2,2,1,0 – timp – str
ca. 25:00
AMP 96145-146, 1961; reprint, distributed by Hal Leonard, HL50237700
Dedication: "To my wife"
Premiere: 27 April 1944, Fourteenth Annual Festival of American Music, Rochester, NY; Eastman-Rochester Symphony Orchestra, Howard Hanson (cond)
Autograph materials: Library of Congress; Paul Sacher Foundation
Bibliography: Items 764, 769 1st ed., 769 2nd ed., 789, 809

95. *A Symphony of Three Orchestras*

June 1976–31 December 1976
Orchestra 1: 0,0,0,0 – 3,2,2,btb,1 – timp – 8,0,4,3,2
Orchestra 2: 0,0,2(bcl),e♭cl—0,0,0,0 – vib,xyl,chimes,mar – 2,0,0,3,1
Orchestra 3: picc,2,2,eh,0,2,cbn – 2,0,0,0 – perc – 8,0,4,0,2
ca. 17:00
AMP 7715, 1978; reprint, distributed by Hal Leonard, HL50238670
Commissioned by the New York Philharmonic under a commissioning grant to six orchestras (Boston, Chicago, Cleve-

land, Los Angeles, New York, and Philadelphia) from the National Endowment for the Arts, a federal agency, in celebration of the United States bicentennial
"Dedicated to the New York Philharmonic and Pierre Boulez, its music director"
Premiere: 17 February 1977, Avery Fisher Hall, New York, NY; New York Philharmonic, Pierre Boulez (cond)
Autograph materials: Paul Sacher Foundation
Bibliography: Items 554, 580, 597, 600, 674, 711, 736, 742, 765, 768, 769 1st ed., 769 2nd ed., 788, 824, 827

96. *Syringa*

Completed 1 September 1978
for mezzo-soprano, bass, guitar, and ten instrumentalists
afl, eh, bcl, tb, perc(1), pno, vn, va, vc, db
ca. 20:00
AMP 7782, 1980; reprint, distributed by Hal Leonard, HL50238740
English poem by John Ashbery; ancient Greek texts by Aeschylus, Archilochus, Hesiod, Homer, Ibycus, Mimnermus, Orpheus, Plato, Sappho, and unknown authors, chosen by the composer
"Ashbery himself approached Carter with the idea of a collaboration" (Schiff, item 769, 1st ed., p. 302). The collaboration was made possible by a composer-librettist grant from the National Endowment for the Arts.
Dedication: "To Sir William and Lady Glock"
Premiere: 10 December 1978, New York, NY; Jan DeGaetani (ms), Thomas Paul (b), Speculum Musicae, Harvey Sollberger (cond)
Autograph materials: Paul Sacher Foundation
Bibliography: Items 580, 583, 597, 623, 644, 694, 696, 738, 741, 763, 765, 769 1st ed., 769 2nd ed., 778, 785

97. *Tarantella* (Finale to *Mostellaria* [item 25])

ca. 6:00
a. for men's chorus (TTBB) and piano four hands
1936

AMP A 793, 1971; "1993 Printing," distributed by Hal Leonard, HL50226760, ISBN 0-7935-3023-7; *Words and Music: The Composer's View*, ed. Lawrence Berman. Cambridge, MA: Music Department of Harvard University, 1972
Texts by Ovid, *Fasti*, book V, lines 183–99 and 331–77
Commissioned by the Harvard Glee Club
Dedication: "To the Harvard Glee Club"
Premiere: 29 April 1937, Harvard University, Cambridge, MA; Harvard Glee Club, G. Wallace Wordsworth (cond)

b. for men's chorus (TTBB) and orchestra
1937; revised 1971
3(picc),2,3(bcl),3(cbn) – 4,3,3,1 – timp – perc – xyl – str
17 May 1937, Symphony Hall, Boston, MA; Harvard Glee Club, Boston Pops Orchestra, G. Wallace Woodworth (cond)
Autograph materials: Paul Sacher Foundation
Bibliography: Items 583, 597, 769 1st ed., 769 2nd ed.

98. *Tell Me Where Is Fancy Bred*

1938
for alto voice and guitar
ca. 3:00
AMP, 1972, guitar part edited by Stanley Silverman; reprint, distributed by Hal Leonard, HL50225820
Text by William Shakespeare, *The Merchant of Venice* III:2
Commissioned by Orson Welles and the Mercury Theater as incidental music for Shakespeare's *The Merchant of Venice*
Autograph materials: Library of Congress; Paul Sacher Foundation
Bibliography: Items 597, 769 1st ed., 769 2nd ed.

99. *Tempo e tempi*

1998–99
Song cycle on Italian poems by Eugenio Montale, Giuseppe Ungaretti, and Salvatore Quasimodo
for soprano, English horn, bass clarinet, violin, and cello

1. "Tempo e tempi" (Eugenio Montale) (for Raffaele Pozzi) (sop, vn, eh, bcl)
2. "Godimento" (Giuseppe Ungaretti) (sop, ob, cl, vn, vc)
3. "Una colomba" (Giuseppe Ungaretti) (for Charles Neidich) (sop, cl)
4. "Ed è subito sera" (Salvatore Quasimodo) (for Heinz Holliger) (sop, ob, cl, vn, vc)
5. "Òboe sommerso" (Salvatore Quasimodo) (for Heinz Holliger) (sop, ob)
6. "L'Arno a Rovezzano" (Eugenio Montale) (sop, ob, cl, vn, vc)
7. "Uno" (Giuseppe Ungaretti) (for Fred Sherry) (sop, vc)
8. "Segreto del poeta" (Giuseppe Ungaretti) (sop, ob, cl, vn, vc)

Hendon Music (Boosey & Hawkes), in preparation
Autograph materials: Paul Sacher Foundation

100. *Three Occasions for Orchestra*

   1. *A Celebration of Some 100 × 150 Notes*
   2. *Remembrance*
   3. *Anniversary*

   3(2 picc),2,eh,2,bcl,2,cbn – 4,3,3,1 – timp – perc(2) – 16,14,12,10,8

   1. *A Celebration of Some 100 × 150 Notes*
      1986
      ca. 3:00
      Commissioned by the Houston Symphony Orchstra to celebrate the 150th anniversary of the founding of the state of Texas
      Dedication: "For the Houston Symphony Orchestra"
      Premiere: 10 April 1987, Jones Hall, Houston, TX; the Houston Symphony Orchestra, Sergiu Commissiona (cond)

   2. *Remembrance*
      Completed 8 March 1988
      ca. 7:00
      Commissioned by the Fromm Foundation at Harvard University for the 1988 Tanglewood Festival of Contemporary Music
      Dedication: "In memory of Paul Fromm"

Premiere: 10 August 1988, Tanglewood Festival, Lenox, MA; Tanglewood Festival Orchestra, Oliver Knussen (cond)
3. *Anniversary*
Completed 25 May 1989
ca. 6:00
Dedication: "For Helen [Carter]"
Premiere (as the third movement of *Three Occasions for Orchestra*): 5 October 1989, Royal Festival Hall, London; BBC Symphony Orchestra, Oliver Knussen (cond)
Hendon Music (Boosey & Hawkes) M051094806 (FSB 480), full score, 1992
Autograph materials: Paul Sacher Foundation
Bibliography: Item 597 (2 only), 745 (1 only), 769 2nd ed., 772 (1 and 2 only)

101. *Three Poems of Robert Frost*
   1. "Dust of Snow" (ca. 1:30)
   2. "The Rose Family" (ca. 1:30)
   3. "The Line Gang" (ca. 2:00)

   a. for voice and piano
      1942
      AMP 194631-3, 1947 (1 only)
      AMP 194632-3, 1947 (2 only)
      AMP 7742, *American Art Songs,* compiled by Barry O'Neal, 1980, 16–18, 19–21. M1619.A49 (1 and 2 only)
      AMP 7454, 1975; reprint, distributed by Hal Leonard, HL50249350, ISBN 0-7935-1326-X (all three)
   b. for voice and chamber orchestra
      1974
      withdrawn
   c. for voice and chamber orchestra
      1980
      Autograph materials: Paul Sacher Foundation
      Bibliography: Items 769 1st ed., 769 2nd ed., 785

102. *Three Recollections*
   1. *Statement—Remembering Aaron*

2. *Riconoscenza per Goffredo Petrassi*
3. *Fantasy—Remembering Roger*

1. *Statement—Remembering Aaron*
   1999
   for violin
   ca. 3:00
   Hendon Music (Boosey & Hawkes), in preparation
   Dedication: Ole Böhn
2. *Riconoscenza per Goffredo Petrassi*
   Completed 30 April 1984, New York, NY
   for violin
   ca. 4:00
   Hendon Music (Boosey & Hawkes) M051351022 (SAB 102), 1984
   Dedication: "*Riconoscenza per Goffredo Petrassi* on the occasion of his 80th birthday with profound esteem and affectionate friendship" ("*Riconoscenza per Goffredo Petrassi* in occasione del suo ottantesimo compleanno, con profonda stima e affettuosa amicizia")
   Premiere: 15 June 1984, in the medieval refectory of the Abbey of Fossanova, Priverno, Italy; Georg Mönch (vn)
   Autograph materials: Paul Sacher Foundation
3. *Fantasy—Remembering Roger*
   1999
   for violin
   ca. 3:00
   Hendon Music (Boosey & Hawkes), in preparation
   Dedication: Rolfe Schulte
   Bibliography (2 only): Items 595, 596, 605, 710, 742, 769
   2nd ed. 772

103. *To Music*
   1937
   for mixed chorus (SATB) a cappella, with soprano solo
   ca. 7:00
   Robert Herrick: *To Music, to Becalm His Fever*
   Premiere: Spring 1938, New York; Lehman Engel Madrigal Singers, Lehman Engel (cond). According to Schiff (p. 79),

the piece was later performed by Edgard Varèse and his workers' chorus at the Greenwich House Music School in New York.
Winner: Choral Contest sponsored by the WPA (Works Progress Administration) Federal Music Project in conjunction with the Columbia Broadcasting System and Columbia Records
Peer International Corporation 337-17, 1955
Autograph materials: Paul Sacher Foundation
Originally part of *Madrigal Book* (item 6)
Bibliography: Items 597, 760, 769 1st ed., 769 2nd ed.

104. *Trilogy*
    1. *Bariolage*
    2. *Inner Song*
    3. *Immer neu*

    1. *Bariolage*
    Completed 3 January 1992, New York
    for harp
    ca. 7:00
    Dedication: "to Ursula Holliger"
    Premiere: 23 March 1992, Salle Patino, Geneva, Switzerland; Ursula Holliger
    Hendon Music (Boosey & Hawkes) M051380206 (SHB 20), 1993
    2. *Inner Song*
    Completed 18 January 1992, Santa Monica, CA
    ca. 5:00
    a. for oboe
    Dedication: "to Heinz Holliger [/] in memory of Stefan Wolpe"
    Premiere: 25 April 1992, Witten New Music Days, Witten, Germany; Heinz Holliger (ob)
    Hendon Music (Boosey & Hawkes) M051660605 (WOB 60), 1993
    b. for soprano saxophone (transcribed by Marcus Weiss)
    Hendon Music (Boosey & Hawkes) M051680665
    3. *Immer neu*
    Completed 25 February 1992, New York
    for oboe and harp

ca. 5:00
Dedication: "to Ursula and Heinz Holliger"
Premiere (as third movement of *Trilogy*): 30 June 1992, Pontino Festival, Sermoneta, Italy; Heinz Holliger (ob), Ursula Holliger (hp)

4. Complete work
Hendon Music (Boosey & Hawkes) M051103782 (ENB 378), 1994
Premiere: 30 June 1992, Pontino Festival, Sermoneta, Italy; Heinz Holliger (ob), Ursula Holliger (hp)
Commissioned by Heinz Holliger
Autograph materials: Paul Sacher Foundation
Bibliography: Items 769 2nd ed., 817

105. *Triple Duo*

Completed 7 February 1983, Waccabuc, NY—New York, NY
for fl(picc), B♭ cl(e♭cl, bcl), perc(1), pno, vn, vc
ca. 20:00
Hendon Music (Boosey & Hawkes) M051209828 (HPS 982), study score, 1985
"Commissioned by the British Broadcasting Corporation for the Fires of London and affectionately dedicated to that ensemble and its prime mover, Peter Maxwell Davies"
Premiere: 23 April 1983, Symphony Space, New York, NY; the Fires of London: Philippa Davies (fl/picc), David Campbell (cl/e♭cl/bcl), Stephen Pruslin (pno), Gregory Knowles (perc), Rosemary Furniss (vn), Jonathan Williams (vc)
Autograph materials: Paul Sacher Foundation
Bibliography: Items 597, 740, 741, 769 2nd ed., 772, 773, 814, 826

Una colomba

See *Tempo e tempi* (item 99)

Under the Dome

See *Of Challenge and of Love* (item 76)

Uno

See *Tempo e tempi* (item 99)

106. *Variations for Orchestra*

2(picc),2,2,2 – 4,3,3,1 – timp – perc – harp – str
Written "during 1955 from sketches made in 1953 and 1954 at the American Academy in Rome." Completed 14 November 1955, Dorset, VT
ca. 24:00
AMP 95818-150, 1957; Corrected edition, 1966 (on title page) or 1967 (on cover); "1993 Edition," AMP 8075, distributed by Hal Leonard, HL50237050. ISBN 0-7935-3121-7. "We at Associated Music Publishers are pleased to publish this newly engraved edition on the occasion of Elliott Carter's 85th birthday"
Commissioned by the Louisville Philharmonic Society, Inc., with the support of the Rockefeller Foundation
Dedication: "To the Louisville Orchestra and Robert Whitney, Conductor"
Premiere: 21 April 1956, Columbia Auditorium, Louisville, KY; Louisville Orchestra, Robert Whitney (cond)
Autograph materials: Library of Congress has most materials; Paul Sacher Foundation has two rejected pages from the holograph score and a photocopy of the holograph score with corrections
Bibliography: Items 420, 485, 558, 565, 597, 616, 668, 769 1st ed., 769 2nd ed., 790, 794, 833, 880

View of the Capitol from the Library of Congress
See *A Mirror on Which to Dwell* (item 72)

107. *Violin Concerto*

1990
for violin and orchestra
2(picc),picc,2,eh,2(e♭cl, bcl),bcl,2,cbn – 4,3,3,1 – perc(2) – 16,14,12,10,8 or 14,12,10,8,6
ca. 26:00
Hendon Music (Boosey & Hawkes) M051095162 (FSB 516), full score, 1991; M051351374 (SAB 137), violin part, 1991
Commissioned jointly by the San Francisco Symphony through the generosity of Mrs. Ralph I. Dorfman and by Ole Böhn

Dedication: Herbert Blomstedt and Ole Böhn
Premiere: 2 May 1990, San Francisco, CA; Ole Böhn (vn), the San Francisco Symphony, Herbert Blomstedt (cond)
Awarded: *Gramophone* Award for Best Contemporary Composition, 1993
Autograph materials: Paul Sacher Foundation
Bibliography: Items 580, 589, 603, 627, 630, 746, 769 2nd ed., 774, 777

108. *Voyage*

    1943
    ca. 6:00
    Text by Hart Crane, *Voyages,* III
    a. for medium voice and piano
        1942–43
        Valley Music Press, Smith College, Northampton, MA, 1945; AMP 7202, 1973; reprint, distributed by Hal Leonard, HL50225880
        Dedication: "To Hope and John Kirkpatrick"
        Premiere: 16 March 1947, the League of Composers, Museum of Modern Art, New York, NY; Helen Boatwright (sop), Helmut Baerwald (pno)
    b. for medium voice and orchestra
        1974–75, revised 1979
        New York Premiere: May 1975; Faith Esham (sop), Juilliard Ensemble, Richard Dufallo (cond)
    Autograph materials: Paul Sacher Foundation
    Bibliography: Items 417, 769 1st ed., 769 2nd ed.

109. *Warble for Lilac Time*

    1943; revised ca. 1954
    Text by Walt Whitman
    ca. 7:00
    a. for soprano or tenor and piano
        Premiere: 16 March 1947, the League of Composers, Museum of Modern Art, New York, NY; Helen Boatwright (sop), Helmut Baerwald (pno)
        Peer International Corporation 356-16, 1956
    b. for soprano and chamber orchestra
        flute, two clarinets, bassoon, harp, and strings

Premiere: 14 September 1946, Yaddo, Saratoga Springs, NY; Helen Boatwright (sop), Yaddo Orchestra, Frederick Fennell (cond)
Autograph materials: Paul Sacher Foundation has most materials; Library of Congress has photocopy of holograph score with corrections
Bibliography: Items 769 1st ed., 769 2nd ed.

110. *What Next?*

1998
comic chamber opera in one act
ca. 40:00
Hendon Music (Boosey & Hawkes), in preparation
Libretto by Paul Griffiths after Jacques Tati's film *Traffic*
Commissioned by the Deutsche Staatsoper Unter den Linden
Premiere: 16 September 1999, Deutsche Staatsoper Unter den Linden, Berlin, Germany; Simone Nold (Rose), Hanno Müller-Brachmann (Harry or Larry), Lynne Dawson (Mama), William Joyner (Zen), Hilary Summers (Stella), Daniel Barenboim (cond), Nicolas Brieger (director), Gisbert Jäkel (set design), Jorge Jara (costumes), Micaela von Marcard (dramaturgy)
Autograph materials: Paul Sacher Foundation

111. *Woodwind Quintet*

1948
for flute, oboe, clarinet, horn, and bassoon
ca. 8:00
AMP 95415-22, 1955; "1992 printing," distributed by Hal Leonard, HL50237000, ISBN 0-7935-1572-6
Dedication: "To Mademoiselle Nadia Boulanger"
Premiere: 27 February 1949, National Association for American Composers and Conductors, New York Times Hall, New York, NY; Martin Orenstein (fl), David Abosch (ob), Louis Paul (cl), Pinson Bobo (hn), Mark Popkin (bn)
Autograph materials: Library of Congress has most materials; Paul Sacher Foundation has four pages of sketches
Bibliography: Items 580, 769 1st ed., 769 2nd ed.

Discography of Commercial Recordings of Elliott Carter's Compositions

For those works that may be performed either alone or as part of a larger cycle *(Symphonia, Trilogy, Three Occasions for Orchestra,* and *Three Recollections)* the principal citation is of the complete cycle *(Partita,* for example, is listed under *Symphonia—Sum Fluxae Pretiam Spei).* Cross-references from the individual parts of each cycle are also provided. The recordings of each composition are listed in the order in which they were released, except for reissues, which are listed in chronological order immediately following the original release. When releases differ only in format or catalog number, these are listed on separate lines at the beginning of the entry. Titles of recordings are provided only if they are distinct from the names of the included compositions. The names of performers, the dates and locations of recording, timings, and credits for production, engineering, and program notes have been provided whenever possible. On recordings that include compositions by other composers, the "notes by" reference is only to those notes that specifically refer to works by Carter.

A 6 Letter Letter to Paul Sacher for His 90th Birthday

112. Editiones Roche 72118 (CD) (1996) (Private Release)

   Heinz Holliger (eh)
   Recorded 27 April 1996, Musiksaal des Stadt-Casinos, Basel, Switzerland

6:18
Producer: Rolf Grolimund
Engineer: Charles Suter
With spoken introduction by Heinz Holliger (1:36)
With Elliott Carter: *Oboe Concerto* (item 243); Pierre Boulez: *Sur incises;* Harrison Birtwistle: *Four Settings of Paul Celan;* Luciano Berio: *KOL OD (Chemins VI)*

90+

113. Bridge 9090 (CD) (1997)

    The Complete Music for Piano
    Charles Rosen (pno)
    Recorded December 1996, MasterSound, Astoria, NY
    6:13
    Producers: Klaas A. Posthuma, David Starobin
    Engineers: Klaas A. Posthuma, David Merrill
    Notes by Charles Rosen
    With Elliott Carter: *Night Fantasies* (item 233); *Piano Sonata* (item 265)

114. Auvidis Montaigne MO 782091 (CD) (1998)

    Ursula Oppens (pno)
    Recorded 15–19 July 1996, All Saints Church, London
    5:35
    Recording Supervisor: François Eckert
    Sound Engineer: Bob Harrison
    Notes by Bayan Northcott
    With Elliott Carter: *String Quartet No. 5* (item 325); *Sonata for Violoncello and Piano* (item 305); *Figment* (item 194); *Fragment* (item 195); *Duo for Violin and Piano* (item 149)

115. Pianovox PIA 501-2 (CD) (1998)

    Florence Millet (pno)
    Recorded July 1997, Espace de projection, IRCAM (Institut de Recherche et Coordination Acoustique/Musique), Centre Georges Pompidou, Paris
    5:46
    Recording Supervision: Franck Ollu

Recording and Editing Engineer: Franck Rossi
Notes by Max Noubel
With Elliott Carter: *Night Fantasies* (item 239)

Across the Yard: La Ignota

See *In Sleep, in Thunder*

Adagio

See *Eight Pieces for Four Timpani*

Adagio tenebroso

See *Symphonia—Sum Fluxae Pretiam Spei*

Allegro scorrevole

See *Symphonia—Sum Fluxae Pretiam Spei*

Am Klavier (at the Piano)

See *Of Challenge and of Love*

Anaphora

See *A Mirror on Which to Dwell*

Anniversary

See *Three Occasions for Orchestra*

Argument

See *A Mirror on Which to Dwell*

Brass Quintet

116. Columbia Odyssey Y 34137 (Stereo lp) (1976)

The American Brass Quintet: Raymond Mase (tpt), Louis Ranger (tpt), Edward Birdwell (hn), Herbert Rankin (tb), Robert Biddlecome (btb)

Recorded 31 March–1 April 1975, Columbia Recording Studios, New York, NY
16:39
Producer: Thomas Frost
Engineers: Bud Graham, Ray Moore
Notes by Elliott Carter
With Elliott Carter: *Eight Pieces for Four Timpani* (item 162); *A Fantasy about Purcell's* Fantasia upon One Note (item 191)

117. Collins Classics 12292 (CD) (1991)

   The Wallace Collection, John Wallace
   no personnel listed except Simon Wright (director)
   Recorded October 1990, Abbey Road Studios
   17:06
   Producer: John H. West
   Engineer: David Flower
   Notes by John Humphries
   With Benjamin Britten: *Fanfare for St. Edmundsbury, Russian Funeral, Simple Symphony* (arr); Michael Tippett: *Fanfare for the Four Corners, Sonata for Four Horns, Festal Brass with Blues;* Witold Lutosławski: *Mini Overture*

Canaries

See *Eight Pieces for Four Timpani*

Canon for 3: In Memoriam Igor Stravinsky

118. Desto DC 7133 (Stereo lp) (1973)

   New Music for Trumpet, Played by Gerard Schwarz
   Two performances: (a) Gerard Schwarz (tpt), Louis Ranger (tpt), Stanley Rosenzweig (tpt); (b) Gerard Schwarz (flugelhorn), Louis Ranger (cornet), Stanley Rosenzweig (tpt)
   (a) 1:40; (b) 1:38
   Engineer: Jerry Bruck
   Notes by Gerard Schwarz
   With Richard Moryl: *Salvos;* Charles Whittenberg: *Polyphony for Trumpet Solo;* Stefan Wolpe: *Solo Piece for Trumpet;* Henry Brant: *Concerto for Trumpet and Nine Instruments*

   Reissued as item 119

Discography of Commercial Recordings 69

119. Phoenix PHCD 115 (CD) (1990)

120. Crystal S 361 (Stereo lp) (1976)

    Music for Trumpet
    Thomas Stevens (tpt), Mario Guarneri (tpt), Roy Poper (tpt)
    1:03
    Notes by Thomas Stevens
    With Igor Stravinsky: *Fanfare for a New Theatre;* Paul Hindemith: *Sonata for Trumpet and Piano;* Chou Wen-Chung: *Soliloquy of a Bhiksuni;* Robert Hall Lewis: *Monophony VII;* Harold Budd: *New York, No. 5*

121. Capriccio 10 439 (CD) (1992)

    Modern Trumpet
    Reinhold Friedrich (tpt), Wolfgang Bauer (tpt), Markus Mester (tpt)
    Recorded 22–26 June 1992, Heilig Geist Kirche, Bad Vilbel, Germany
    1:15
    Recording supervision (Tonmeister): Hans Bernhard Bätzing
    Recording engineer: Wolfgang Decker
    Notes by Dr. Anette Unger; English translation by Lionel Salter
    With Igor Stravinsky: *Fanfare for a New Theatre;* Arthur Honegger: *Intrada für Trompete und Klavier;* Hans Werner Henze: *Sonatina für Solo-Trompete;* Paul Hindemith: *Sonate für Trompete und Klavier;* Stefan Wolpe: *Solo Piece for Trumpet;* Nikos Skalkottas: *Concertino für Trompete und Klavier;* Hans Erich Apostel: *Sonatine in 3 Sätzen für Trompete solo,* op. 42a; Wilhelm Killmayer: *Tre pezzi;* Sofia Gubaidulina: *Zwei Balladen für 2 Trompeten und Klavier; Trio für drei Trompeten; Lied ohne Worte*

Canon for 4

122. New Albion NA019 CD (CD) (1989)

    California EAR Unit: Dorothy Stone (fl), James Rohrig (bcl), Robin Lorentz (vn), Erika Duke (vc)

Recorded at the California Institute of the Arts
4:01
Producers: Rand Steiger, Peter Otto
Engineer: Mark Waldrep
Notes by Ruth Dreier
With Elliott Carter: *Enchanted Preludes* (item 179); *Esprit rude/Esprit doux* (item 184); Arthur Jarvinen: *Egyptian Two Step*; Rand Steiger: *Quintessence*; Michael Torke: *The Yellow Pages*; Karlheinz Stockhausen: *Dr. K-Sextet*; Louis Andriessen: *Hoketus*

123. GM Recordings GM2020CD (CD) (1990)

Perle/Carter
Da Capo Chamber Players: Patricia Spencer (fl), Laura Flax (bcl), Joel Lester (vn), André Emelianoff (vc)
Recorded 5 February 1988, Merkin Concert Hall, New York, NY
4:04
Producers: Gunther Schuller, Judith Sherman
Engineer: Judith Sherman
Notes by Elliott Carter
With Elliott Carter: *Enchanted Preludes* (item 180); *Pastorale* (item 249); *Esprit rude/Esprit doux* (item 186); George Perle: *Sonata for Cello and Piano*; *Lyric Piece*; *Sonata a quattro*

Canonic Suite

124. Vanguard Classics 99163 (CD) (1998)

Aurelia Saxophone Quartet: Johan van der Linden (ssax), André Arends (asax), Arno Bornkamp (tsax), Willem van Merwijk (bsax)
Blow!
Recorded in concert, 29 June 1997, De Rode Hoed, Amsterdam
5:29
Recording producer: Ted Diehl
Engineer: Bert vander Wolf

Discography of Commercial Recordings   71

Canto
See *Eight Pieces for Four Timpani*

Careless Night
See *In Sleep, in Thunder*

A Celebration of Some 100 × 150 Notes
See *Three Occasions for Orchestra*

Changes

125. Bridge BDG 2004 (Stereo lp) (1984)

>   David Starobin (guitar)
>   *New Music with Guitar, Volume 2*
>   Recorded March–April 1984, Holy Trinity Episcopal Church, New York, NY
>   6:57
>   Producer: David Starobin
>   Engineer: David Hancock
>   Notes by William K. Bland
>   With Toru Takemitsu: *Toward the Sea;* John Anthony Lennon: *Another's Fandango;* David Del Tredici: *Acrostic Song;* Barbara Kolb: *Songs before an Adieu*

>   Reissued as item 126

126. Bridge BCD 9009 (CD) (1988)

>   *New Music with Guitar: Selected Works from Volumes 1, 2, & 3*
>   With Stephen Sondheim: *Sunday Song Set;* Milton Babbitt: *Composition for Guitar;* Toru Takemitsu: *Toward the Sea;* John Anthony Lennon: *Another's Fandango;* Barbara Kolb: *Three Lullabies;* William Bland: *A Fantasy-Homage to Victoria;* Hans Werner Henze: *Carillon, récitatif, masque*

127. Bridge BCD 9044 (CD) (1994)

    Elliott Carter: Eight Compositions (1943–1993)
The Group for Contemporary Music: David Starobin (guitar)
Recorded 10 February 1994, MasterSound, Astoria, NY
7:46
Producers: David Starobin, Michael Calvert
Engineer: Ben Rizzi
Notes by David Schiff
With Elliott Carter: *Gra* (item 196); *Enchanted Preludes* (item 182); *Duo for Violin and Piano* (item 147); *Scrivo in vento* (item 278); *Con leggerezza pensosa* (item 128); *Riconoscenza per Goffredo Petrassi* (item 359); *Sonata for Violoncello and Piano* (item 301)

Con leggerezza pensosa

128. Bridge BCD 9044 (CD) (1994)

    Elliott Carter: Eight Compositions (1943–1993)
The Group for Contemporary Music: Charles Neidich (cl), Rolf Schulte (vn), Fred Sherry (vc)
Recorded 16 March 1993, MasterSound, Astoria, NY
5:17
Producers: David Starobin, Michael Calvert
Engineer: Ben Rizzi
Notes by David Schiff
With Elliott Carter: *Gra* (item 196); *Enchanted Preludes* (item 182); *Duo for Violin and Piano* (item 147); *Scrivo in vento* (item 278); *Changes* (item 127); *Riconoscenza per Goffredo Petrassi* (item 359); *Sonata for Violoncello and Piano* (item 301)

Concerto for Oboe

See *Oboe Concerto*

Concerto for Orchestra

129. Columbia M 30112 (Stereo lp) (1970)

    New York Philharmonic, Leonard Bernstein (cond)

Discography of Commercial Recordings 73

     Recorded 11 February 1970, New York, NY
     23:47
     Producer: Richard Killough
     Engineers: Fred Plaut, John Guerriere, Ray Moore
     Notes by Elliott Carter
     With William Schuman: *In Praise of Shahn*

     Issued in the United Kingdom as item 130

130. CBS S 73198 (1973)

     With Aaron Copland: *Connotations; Inscape*

     Reissued as item 131

131. CRI SD 469 (Stereo lp) (1982)

     Music of Elliott Carter
     Notes by Elliott Carter, David Schiff
     With Elliott Carter: *Syringa* (item 333)

     Also reissued as item 132

132. Sony Classical SMK 60203 (1998)

     Reissue Producer: Louise de la Fuente
     Reissue Engineers: Ellen Fitton, Andreas Meyer
     Notes by Leonard Bernstein, Tim Page
     With Charles Ives: *The Unanswered Question; Holidays (Symphony); Central Park in the Dark*

133. Virgin Classics VC 7 91503-2 (CD) (1992)

     London Sinfonietta, Oliver Knussen (cond)
     Recorded 15–16 February 1991, Henry Wood Hall, London
     20:54
     Producers: Oliver Knussen with Colin Matthews
     Balance Engineer: Tryggvi Tryggvason
     Notes by Elliott Carter, Oliver Knussen, Bayan Northcott
     With Elliott Carter: *Three Occasions for Orchestra* (item 344); *Violin Concerto* (item 377)

134. Arte Nova Classics 74321 2773 2 (CD) (1995)

SWF Symphony Orchestra, Michael Gielen (cond)
Recorded 23 April 1992, SWF Hans Rosbaud Studio, Baden-Baden, Germany
22:23
Producing Engineer: Wolfgang Wtorczyk
Sound Engineer: Norbert Vossen
Notes by Stefan Lipka
With Elliott Carter: *Piano Concerto* (item 254); *Three Occasions for Orchestra* (item 345)

Concerto for Piano
See *Piano Concerto*

Concerto for Violin
See *Violin Concerto*

The Defense of Corinth

135. Harvard Glee Club F-HGC 64 (1964)

Thomas G. Gutheil (narrator), Harvard Glee Club, Elliot Forbes (cond)
Recorded 24 April 1964, Cambridge, MA
ca. 12:00
With Heinrich Schutz: *Deutsches Magnificat;* Guillaume Dufay: *Magnificat;* Johannes Brahms: *Fünf Gesange,* op. 104; Hans Leo Hassler: *Chromatic Motet;* Samuel Barber: *Reincarnations*

136. Vox SVBX 5353 (Stereo lp) (1977)

America Sings (1920–1950)
Jan Opalach (narrator), Edward Green, Mark Suttonsmith (pno), Columbia University Men's Glee Club, Gregg Smith (cond)
Recorded Spring 1975, the American Academy and Institute of Arts and Letters, New York, NY

14:12
Notes by Gregg Smith
With Elliott Carter: *Musicians Wrestle Everywhere* (item 226); Samuel Barber: *A Stopwatch and an Ordnance Map;* Leonard Bernstein: Choruses from *The Lark;* Aaron Copland: *Two Pieces for Treble Choir;* Henry Cowell: *Luther's Chorale to His Son;* Irving Fine: *The Choral New Yorker;* Lukas Foss: *Behold I Build a House;* George Gershwin: *Two Madrigals;* Charles Ives: *Two Election Songs;* Walter Piston: *Psalm and Prayer of David;* Wallingford Riegger: *Who Can Revoke;* William Schuman: *Prelude;* Charles Seeger: *Chant;* Roger Sessions: *Turn, O Liberstad;* Louise Talma: *Let's Touch the Sky;* Virgil Thomson: *Four Southern Hymns; Alleluia*

Reissued as item 137

137. GSS Recordings GSS 103 (Stereo lp) (1984)

Producer: Raymond Marunas
Engineer: David Hancock
With Elliott Carter: *Tarantella* (item 338); *Emblems* (item 175); *The Harmony of Morning* (item 198); *Heart Not So Heavy As Mine* (item 205); *Musicians Wrestle Everywhere* (item 227); *To Music* (item 364)

Also reissued as item 138

138. CRI CD 648 (CD) (1993)

Producer: Gregg Smith
Notes by Gregg Smith and Joseph R. Dalton, Elliott Carter
With Elliott Carter: *Warble for Lilac Time* (item 383); *Voyage* (item 379); *Three Poems of Robert Frost* (item 355); *Tarantella* (item 339); *Emblems* (item 176); *The Harmony of Morning* (item 199); *Heart Not So Heavy As Mine* (item 206); *Musicians Wrestle Everywhere* (item 228); *To Music* (item 365)

139. Koch International Classics 3-7415-2H1 (CD) (1998)

John Oliver Chorale, Alan Brody (speaker), Henry Lussier, Robert Allard, Brett Johnson, Warren P. Ziegler (soloists),

Martin Amlin (pno), Frank Corliss (pno), John Oliver (music director)
Recorded May 1997, Emmanuel Church, Boston, MA
13:28
Producer: Susan Napodano DelGiorno
Engineer: Silas Brown
Notes by Elliott Carter, Steven Ledbetter
With Elliott Carter: *To Music* (item 366); *Tarantella* (item 340); *Harvest Home* (item 202); *Emblems* (item 178); *Let's Be Gay* (item 216); *Heart Not So Heavy As Mine* (item 208); *The Harmony of Morning* (item 201); *Musicians Wrestle Everywhere* (item 230)

Dies Irae

See *In Sleep, in Thunder*

Dolphin

See *In Sleep, in Thunder*

Double Concerto

for harpsichord and piano with two chamber orchestras

140. Epic LC 3830 (Mono lp) (1962)

Epic BC 1157 (stereo lp) (1962)
Ralph Kirkpatrick (hps), Charles Rosen (pno), English Chamber Orchestra, Gustav Meier (cond)
Recorded 7–8 September 1961
22:46
Producer: Jane Friedmann
Notes by Elliott Carter
With Leon Kirchner: *Concerto for Violin, Cello, Ten Winds and Percussion*

Issued in the United Kingdom as item 141

141. EMI ALP 2052 (Mono lp) (Reviewed April 1965)

EMI ASD 601 (stereo lp) (reviewed April 1965)
With Elliott Carter: *Piano Sonata* (item 258)

Discography of Commercial Recordings   77

142. Columbia MS 7191 (Stereo lp) (1968)

   C.B.S. 72717 (reviewed July 1969) (United Kingdom)
   C.B.S. S 34 61093 (reviewed June 1970) (France)
   Paul Jacobs (hps), Charles Rosen (pno), English Chamber Orchestra, Frederik Prausnitz (cond)
   Recorded 4 January 1968
   24:02
   Producer: Andrew Kazdin
   Engineers: Edward Kramer, Murray Zimney
   Notes by Elliott Carter
   With Elliott Carter: *Variations for Orchestra* (item 374)

143. Nonesuch H 71314 (Stereo lp) (1975)

   Paul Jacobs (hps), Gilbert Kalish (pno), the Contemporary Chamber Ensemble, Arthur Weisberg (cond)
   Recorded September 1973
   22:36
   Recording Directors: Helmuth Kolbe, Joanna Nickrenz
   Engineers: Helmuth Kolbe, Robert Lattman
   Notes by Elliott Carter
   With Elliott Carter: *Duo for Violin and Piano* (item 145)

   Reissued as item 144

144. Elektra Nonesuch 79183-2 (CD) (1992)

   Notes by Elliott Carter
   With Elliott Carter: *Sonata for Flute, Oboe, Cello, and Harpsichord* (item 288); *Sonata for Violoncello and Piano* (item 296)

Duo for Violin and Piano

145. Nonesuch H 71314 (Stereo lp) (1975)

   Paul Zukofsky (vn), Gilbert Kalish (pno)
   Recorded ca. March 1975, RCA Recording Studios, New York, NY
   17:24
   Recording Director: Joanna Nickrenz
   Engineer: Paul Goodman

Notes by Elliott Carter
With Elliott Carter: *Double Concerto* (item 143)

146. Sony Classical S2K 47229 (2 CD) (1991)

    Robert Mann (vn), Christopher Oldfather (pno)
    Recorded 28 May–15 June 1991, American Academy and Institute of Arts and Letters, New York, NY
    21:03
    Producer: Gary Schultz
    Engineer: Charles Harbutt
    Notes by Elliott Carter, Robert P. Morgan, and Leonard Stein and Peter Zaferes
    With Elliott Carter: *String Quartet No. 1* (item 311); *String Quartet No. 2* (item 316); *String Quartet No. 3* (item 321); *String Quartet No. 4* (item 324)

147. Bridge BCD 9044 (CD) (1994)

    Elliott Carter: Eight Compositions (1943–1993)
    The Group for Contemporary Music: Rolf Schulte (vn), Martin Goldray (pno)
    Recorded 8 April 1993, MasterSound, Astoria, NY
    21:27
    Producers: David Starobin, Michael Calvert
    Engineer: Ben Rizzi
    Notes by David Schiff
    With Elliott Carter: *Gra* (item 196); *Enchanted Preludes* (item 182); *Scrivo in vento* (item 278); *Changes* (item 127); *Con leggerezza pensosa* (item 128); *Riconoscenza per Goffredo Petrassi* (item 359); *Sonata for Violoncello and Piano* (item 301)

148. Victoria VCD 19094 (CD) (1996)

    Contemporary Music from America
    Ole Böhn (vn), Noël Lee (pno)
    Recorded December 1995, Jar Church
    22:20
    Recording Producer: Arne-Peter Rognan
    Recording Engineers: Anita Jenstad, Robert Smits

With Elliott Carter: *Riconoscenza per Goffredo Petrassi* (item 361); Walter Piston: *Sonata*; Ruth Crawford: *Sonata*; Noël Lee: *Trièdre*.

149. Auvidis Montaigne MO 782091 (CD) (1998)

    Irvine Arditti (vn), Ursula Oppens (pno)
    Recorded 15–19 July 1996, All Saints Church, London
    19:09
    Recording Supervisor: François Eckert
    Sound Engineer: Bob Harrison
    Notes by Bayan Northcott
    With Elliott Carter: *String Quartet No. 5* (item 325); *90+* (item 114); *Sonata for Violoncello and Piano* (item 305); *Figment* (item 194); *Fragment* (item 195)

Dust of Snow

See *Three Poems of Robert Frost*

Eight Etudes and a Fantasy

150. CRI 118 (Mono lp) (1958)

    CRI SD 118 (stereo lp) (1958)
    Members of the New York Woodwind Quintet: Murray Panitz (fl), Jerome Roth (ob), David Glazer (cl), Bernard Garfield (bn)
    20:43
    Notes by Peggy Glanville-Hicks
    With Quincy Porter: *String Quartet No. 8*

151. Concert-Disc CM 1229 (Mono lp) (1963)

    Concert-Disc CS 229 (stereo lp) (1963)
    Members of the New York Woodwind Quintet: Samuel Baron (fl), Jerome Roth or Ronald Roseman (ob), David Glazer (cl), Arthur Weisberg (bn)
    Recorded 1961
    18:34
    Producer: Leonard Sorkin

Engineer: Malcolm Chisholm or Bert Whyte
Notes by Samuel Baron
With Gunther Schuller: *Woodwind Quintet;* Irving Fine: *Partita for Wind Quintet*

Reissued as item 152

152. Boston Skyline BSD 137 (CD) (1996)

    From the Vault: The Best of the New York Woodwind Quintet v. 1
    Producer: Wayne Wadhams
    Engineers: Wayne Wadhams, John Servies
    With Samuel Barber: *Summer Music;* John Barrows: *March;* Carl Nielsen: *Woodwind Quintet;* Paul Piern: *Pastorale;* Anton Reicha: *Woodwind Quintet;* Jan Sweelinck: *Variations*

153. Candide CE 31016 (Stereo lp) (1969)

    C.B.S. S 34 61145 (reviewed December 1970) (France)
    Vox STGBY 644 (reviewed September 1971) (United Kingdom)
    Members of the Dorian Woodwind Quintet: Karl Kraber (fl), Charles Kuskin (ob), William Lewis (cl), Jane Taylor (bn)
    Recorded 1966, Capitol Records Studio B
    18:20
    Notes by William B. Ober
    With Elliott Carter: *Woodwind Quintet* (item 388); Hans Werner Henze: *Quintett*

    Reissued as item 154

154. *Chamber Music*

    Musical Heritage Society MHS 4876 (stereo lp) (1983)
    Notes by David Schiff
    With Elliott Carter: *String Quartet No. 3* (item 318)

155. *Eight Etudes* Only

    Classics Record Library SQM 80-5731 (stereo 4 lp) (1975)
    *Classics Record Library SQM 5707-02 (stereo lp) (n.d.)

The Chamber Music Society of Lincoln Center
Members of the Chamber Music Society of Lincoln Center:
Paula Robison (fl), Leonard Arner (ob), Gervase de Peyer (cl), Loren Glickman (bn)
12:23
Notes by Harris Goldsmith
With *Ludwig van Beethoven: *String Trio*, op. 9, no. 1; *Robert Schumann: *Fantasy Pieces*, op. 73; W. A. Mozart: *Piano Quartet*, K. 493; J. S. Bach: *Concerto for Oboe, Violin, Strings, and Continuo*, S. 1060; Gabriel Fauré: *Two Pieces for Flute and Piano: Sicilienne*, op. 78; *Fantasy*, op. 79; *Dolly: Suite*, op. 56; Moritz Moszkowski: *Suite*, op. 71; Robert Schumann: *Andante and Variations;* Joseph Haydn: *String Trio*, op. 53, no. 1; Johannes Brahms: *Two Songs*, op. 91; Camille Saint–Saëns: *Caprice on Danish and Russian Airs*, op. 79

Complete work reissued as item 156

156. Musical Heritage Society MHS 824704X (MHS 4704–4705) (2 Stereo lp) (1983)

    Three Centuries of Chamber Music
    12:23
    Notes by Michael Keeley
    With J. S. Bach: *Concerto for Oboe, Violin, Strings, and Continuo*, S. 1060; Jospeh Haydn: *String Trio*, op. 53, no. 1; Moritz Moszkowski: *Suite*, op. 71; Gabriel Fauré: *Two Pieces for Flute and Piano; Dolly: Suite*, op. 56; Camille Saint–Saëns: *Caprice on Danish and Russian Airs*, op. 79

157. River City Studios 44711 (Stereo lp) (1985)

    20th Century Chamber Music
    La Sonore Wind Quintet
    Recorded at First Presbyterian Church, Mt. Pleasant, MI
    Notes by Paolo Petazzi
      With Jean Françaix: *Quintette*

158. Stradivarius STR 33304 (CD) (1991)

    Musica per quartetto e quintetto a fiati

Quintetto Arnold: Renato Rivolta (fl), Francesco Pomarico (ob), Maurizio Longoni (cl), Leonardo Dosso (bn)
Recorded 22–23 October and 19–20 November 1990, Chiesa della Misericordia, Turin, Italy
18:13
Notes by Paolo Petazzi
With Elliott Carter: *Woodwind Quintet* (item 394); Franco Donatoni: *Blow*; György Kurtág: *Quintetto per Fiati*, op. 2; György Ligeti: *Zehn Stücke für Bläserquintett*

159. Cambria CD 1091 (CD) (1992)

    Another View: American Classics for Winds
    Sierra Wind Quintet: Richard Soule (fl), Stephen Caplan (ob), Felix Viscuglia (cl), Kristin Wolfe (bn)
    Recorded at St. Andrews Catholic Church, Boulder City, NV
    Producer: Stephen Caplan
    Recorded by Curt Miller
    18:16
    Notes by David Wright
    With David Diamond: *Partita*; Walter Piston: *Quintet for Winds*; Gunther Schuller: *Suite for Wind Quintet*

160. KOCH Schwann 3-1153-2 (CD) (1992)

    The Aulos Wind Quintet Plays Music by American Composers v. 1
    Aulos Woodwind Quintet: Peter Rijks (fl), Diethelm Jonas (ob), Karl-Theo Adler (cl), Dietmar Ullrich (hn), Ralph Sabow (bn)
    Recorded 1989–1990, Jesus-Christus-Kirche, Berlin, Germany
    17:23
    Producer: Jean Cullerier
    Engineer: W. Gottschalk, Helge Jörns
    With Elliott Carter: *Woodwind Quintet* (item 395); Samuel Barber: *Summer Music*; John Cage: *Music for Wind Instruments*; Gunther Schuller: *Suite for Woodwind Ensemble*

161. cpo 999 453-2 (CD) (1998)

> Ensemble Contrasts: Michael Faust (fl), Christian Hommel (ob), David Smeyers (cl), Dag Jensen (bn)
> Recorded October 1995, Hürth-Knapsack, Feierabendhaus der Hoechst AG; November 1995 and March 1996, Funkhaus Köln
> 19:28
> Recording Supervisor: Wolfgang Müller
> Recording Engineers: Franz-Peter Esser, Mark Hohn, Christian Meurer
> With Elliott Carter: *Woodwind Quintet* (item 398); *Esprit rude/Esprit doux* (item 189); *Enchanted Preludes* (item 183); *Sonata for Flute, Oboe, Cello, and Harpsichord* (item 292)

Eight Pieces for Four Timpani

1. Saëta
2. Moto Perpetuo
3. Adagio
4. Recitative
5. Improvisation
6. Canto
7. Canaries
8. March

162. Columbia Odyssey Y 34137 (Stereo lp) (1976)

> Morris Lang (timp)
> Recorded 28 May and 23–24 June 1975, Columbia Recording Studios, New York, NY
> 24:41
> Producer: Thomas Frost
> Engineers: Bud Graham, Ray Moore
> Notes by Elliott Carter
> With Elliott Carter: *Brass Quintet* (item 116); *A Fantasy about Purcell's* Fantasia upon One Note (item 191)

163. 4, 2, 1, and 5 only

> Erato STU 71106 (stereo lp) (1978)

Percussion v. 2
Sylvio Gualda (timp)
Recorded April 1977, L'Eglise du Liban, Paris
12:56
Notes by Gerard Mannoni
With Iannis Xenakis: *Psappha*; Nguyen Thien Dao: *May*

164. 4, 6, 1, and 8 only

BIS LP-256 (stereo lp) (1984)
Neue Musik für Schlagzeug
Gert Mortenson (timp)
Recorded in performance 14 January 1982, Studio 2 Danmarks Radio
3:22; 2:52; 4:01; 2:30
With Per Nørgård *I Ching*; Iannis Xenakis: *Psappha*

Reissued as item 165

165. *The Contemporary American "C"*

BIS CD-52 (CD) (1995)
With Aaron Copland: *Piano Sonata*; Paul Creston: *Sonata for Alto Saxophone and Piano*, op. 19; George Crumb: *Five Pieces for Piano*; John Cage: *Second Construction*

Elegy (Version for String Quartet)

166. New England Conservatory NEC-115 (Distributed by Golden Crest Records) (Quadrophonic lp) (1977)

The Composers String Quartet Plays Literature of American Contemporary Composers.
The Composers String Quartet: Matthew Raimondi (vn I), Anahid Ajemian (vn II), Jean Dane (va), Michael Rudiakov (vc)
Notes by Elliott Carter
With Gunther Schuller: *String Quartet No. 1;* Richard Swift: *String Quartet IV;* Igor Stravinsky: *Double Canon;* Henry Cowell: *Quartet Euphometric*

Discography of Commercial Recordings 85

167. Etcetera KTC 1066 (CD) (1988)

Elliott Carter: *The Works for String Quartet Vol. II: Quartets 2 & 3, Elegy*
The Arditti String Quartet: Irvine Arditti (vn I), David Alberman (vn II), Levine Andrade (va), Rohan de Saram (vc)
Recorded June 1988, St. Silas Church, Kentish Town, London
4:15
Producer: Roy Emerson
Engineer: Martin Haskell
Notes by David Harvey
With Elliott Carter: *String Quartet No. 2* (item 315); *String Quartet No. 3* (item 320)

168. Auvidis Montaigne MO 782010 (CD) (1994)

The Arditti String Quartet: Irvine Arditti (vn I), David Alberman (vn II), Garth Knox (va), Rohan de Saram (vc)
Recorded June 1991 and December 1992, WDR (Westdeutscher Rundfunk) Köln
3:39
Recording supervision: Stefan Hahn
Engineer: Manfred Hill
Notes by Franck Mallet (French), Kyle Gann (English), Gisela Gronemeyer (German)
With Conlon Nancarrow: *String Quartet No. 1*; Charles Ives: *Scherzo*; Jay Alan Yim: *Autumn Rhythm*; Morton Feldman: *Structures*; Alvin A. Lucier: *Fragments*; La Monte Young: *On Remembering a Naiad*; John Cage: *Four*

Also issued as item 168a

168a. *1974 Arditti Quartet 1994*

Auvidis Montaigne MO 782070 (CD) (1994)
With Arnold Schoenberg: *String Quartet No. 2* (excerpt); *Weihnachtsmusik*; György Kurtág: *Officium breve in memoriam A. Szervánsky* (excerpt); Mauricio Kagel: *String Quartet No. 2* (excerpt); Helmut Lachenmann: *Tanzsuite mit Deutschlandied* (excerpt); Pascal Dusapin: *Time Zones* (excerpt); Anton Webern: *Fünf Sätze*, op. 5 (excerpt); Brian

Ferneyhough: *Adagissimo*; Luigi Nono: *Fragmente–Stille, an Diotima* (excerpt); Iannis Xenakis: *Tetras* (excerpt); François-Bernard Mâche: *Eridan* (excerpt); Wolfgang Rihm: *Im Innersten* (excerpt); Harrison Birtwistle: *Movement*

169. Musikszene Schweitz MGB CD 6144 (1996)

    Amati Quartett
    Recorded 25–28 June 1996, Radiostudio Zürich
    4:32
    With Leonard Bernstein: *Sonata for Clarinet and Piano*; Walter Piston: *String Quartet No. 1*; Irving Fine: *Sonata for Violin and Piano*; Aaron Copland: *Sextet for Clarinet, String Quartet, and Piano*.

Elegy (version for viola and piano)

170. ECM 1316 (25043-1) (Stereo lp; CD) (1986)

    ECM 1316 (827 744-1) (stereo lp; CD) (1986)
    ECM 78118-21316-2 (CD) (1986)
    Elegies
    Kim Kashkashian (va), Robert Levin (pno)
    Recorded in New York, NY
    4:02
    Producer: Manfred Eicher
    Engineers: Marc Aubort, Joanna Nickrenz
    With Benjamin Britten: *Lachrymae*; op. 48; Ralph Vaughan Williams: *Romanze*; Alexander Glasunov: *Elegie*, op. 44; Franz Liszt: *Romance oubliée*; Zoltán Kodály: *Adagio*; Henri Vieuxtemps: *Elegie*, op. 30

171. Crystal CD 636 (CD) (1991)

    Paul Cortese (va), Jon Klibonoff (pno)
    Recorded 10–12 June 1991, Concordia College, Bronxville, NY
    3:57
    With William Bergsma: *Fantastic Variations on a Theme from Tristan*; Alan Hovaness: *Chahagir for Viola Solo*, op. 56,

no. 1; George Rochberg: *Sonata for Viola and Piano*; Vincent Persichetti: *Parable XVI for Solo Viola,* op. 130

172. Albany TROY 141-2 (CD) (1994)

    Lawrence Wheeler (va), Ruth Tomfohrde (pno)
    Recorded 1994, Dudley Recital Hall, University of Houston
    3:55
    With Paul Creston: *Suite for Viola;* Bernhard Heiden: *Sonata for Viola;* George Rochberg: *Sonata for Viola*

Elegy (version for string orchestra)

173. Nonesuch D 79002 (Stereo lp) (1980)

    Nonesuch 79002-2 (CD) (1980)
    American Music for Strings
    Los Angeles Chamber Orchestra, Gerard Schwarz (cond)
    Recorded 2 April 1980, Ambassador Auditorium, Pasadena, CA
    4:59
    Producers: Marc J. Aubort, Joanna Nickrenz
    Engineers: Elite Recordings, Inc., and Roger Mayer, Elektra Sound Recorders
    Notes by: Elliott Carter, Eric Salzman
    With Samuel Barber: *Serenade For Strings;* David Diamond: *Rounds for String Orchestra;* Irving Fine: *Serious Song*

174. Albany TROY 194 (CD) (1996)

    Metamorphosen Chamber Orchestra, Scott Yoo (cond)
    Recorded April 1994, Campion Center, Weston, MA
    4:29
    With Dan Coleman: *Long ago, this radiant day;* John Corigliano: *Voyage for Strings;* Irving Fine: *Serious Song;* Elena Ruehr: *Shimmer;* Ellen Taaffe Zwilich: *Prologue and Variations*

Emblems

175. GSS Recordings GSS 103 (Stereo lp) (1984)

> Men's choruses of the Gregg Smith Singers and the Long Island Symphonic Choral Association, Paul Suits (pno), Gregg Smith (cond)
> Recorded May 1982, Central Islip High School Auditorium, Islip, NY
> 14:50
> Producer: Raymond Marunas
> Engineer: David Hancock
> With Elliott Carter: *Tarantella* (item 338); *The Harmony of Morning* (item 198); *Heart Not So Heavy As Mine* (item 205); *Musicians Wrestle Everywhere* (item 227); *To Music* (item 364); *The Defense of Corinth* (item 137)
>
> Reissued as item 176

176. CRI CD 648 (CD) (1993)

> Producer: Gregg Smith
> Notes by Gregg Smith and Joseph R. Dalton, Elliott Carter
> With Elliott Carter: *Warble for Lilac Time* (item 383); *Voyage* (item 379); *Three Poems of Robert Frost* (item 355); *Tarantella* (item 339); *The Harmony of Morning* (item 199); *Heart Not So Heavy As Mine* (item 206); *Musicians Wrestle Everywhere* (item 228); *To Music* (item 365); *The Defense of Corinth* (item 138)

177. Koch 3-7178-2H1 (CD) (1994)

> John Oliver Chorale, John Oliver (music director)
> Recorded October 1992, Emmanuel Church, Boston, MA
> 14:07
> Producer and Engineer: Michael Fine
> Notes by Steven Ledbetter
> With Elliott Carter: *The Harmony of Morning* (item 200); *Heart Not So Heavy As Mine* (item 207); *Musicians Wrestle Everywhere* (item 230); Bright Sheng: *Two Folk Songs from Chinhai*; Martin Amlin: *Time's Caravan*; William Thomas McKinley: *4 Text Settings*
>
> Reissued as item 178

Discography of Commercial Recordings 89

178. Koch International Classics 3-7415-2H1 (CD) (1998)

   Notes by Elliott Carter, Steven Ledbetter
   With Elliott Carter: *To Music* (item 366); *Tarantella* (item 340); *Harvest Home* (item 202); *Let's Be Gay* (item 216); *Heart Not So Heavy As Mine* (item 208); *The Defense of Corinth* (item 139); *The Harmony of Morning* (item 201); *Musicians Wrestle Everywhere* (item 231)

Enchanted Preludes

179. New Albion NA019 CD (CD) (1990)

   California EAR Unit: Dorothy Stone (fl), Erika Duke (vc)
   Recorded at the California Institute of the Arts
   5:30
   Producers: Rand Steiger, Peter Otto
   Engineer: Mark Waldrep
   Notes by Ruth Dreier
   With Elliott Carter: *Canon for 4* (item 122); *Esprit rude/Esprit doux* (item 184); Arthur Jarvinen: *Egyptian Two Step;* Rand Steiger: *Quintessence;* Michael Torke: *The Yellow Pages;* Karlheinz Stockhausen: *Dr. K-Sextet;* Louis Andriessen: *Hoketus*

180. GM Recordings GM2020CD (CD) (1990)

   Perle/Carter
   Da Capo Chamber Players: Patricia Spencer (fl), André Emelianoff (vc)
   Recorded 15–16 September 1988, State University of New York at Purchase
   6:07
   Producers: Gunther Schuller, Judith Sherman
   Engineer: Judith Sherman
   Notes by [author not listed] quoting Elliott Carter
   With Elliott Carter: *Canon for 4* (item 123); *Pastorale* (item 249); *Esprit rude/Esprit doux* (item 186); George Perle: *Sonata for Cello and Piano; Lyric Piece; Sonata a quattro*

181. ECM New Series 1391 (ECM New Series 839 617-2) (CD) (1990)

    Philippe Racine (fl), Thomas Demenga (vc)
    Recorded April 1989, Radio DRS, Studio Zürich
    6:21
    Producer: Manfred Eicher
    Recording Engineer: Peter Laenger
    Notes by Heinz Holliger, Wolfgang Sandner
    With Elliott Carter: *Esprit rude/Esprit doux* (item 187); *Riconoscenza per Goffredo Petrassi* (item 357); *Triple Duo* (item 371); J. S. Bach: *Suite No. 3 for Violoncello Solo*

182. Bridge BCD 9044 (CD) (1994)

    Elliott Carter: Eight Compositions (1943–1993)
    The Group for Contemporary Music: Harvey Sollberger (fl), Fred Sherry (vc)
    Recorded 20 May 1993, MasterSound, Astoria, NY
    6:30
    Producers: David Starobin, Michael Calvert
    Engineer: Ben Rizzi
    Notes by David Schiff
    With Elliott Carter: *Gra* (item 196); *Duo for Violin and Piano* (item 147); *Scrivo in vento* (item 278); *Changes* (item 127); *Con leggerezza pensosa* (item 128); *Riconoscenza per Goffredo Petrassi* (item 359); *Sonata for Violoncello and Piano* (item 301)

183. cpo 999 453-2 (CD) (1998)

    Ensemble Contrasts: Michael Faust (fl), Georg Faust (vc)
    Recorded October 1995, Hürth-Knapsack, Feierabendhaus der Hoechst AG; November 1995 and March 1996, Funkhaus Köln
    5:47
    Recording Supervisor: Wolfgang Müller
    Recording Engineers: Franz-Peter Esser, Mark Hohn, Christian Meurer
    With Elliott Carter: *Woodwind Quintet* (item 398); *Esprit rude/Esprit doux* (item 189); *Eight Etudes and a Fantasy*

(item 161); *Sonata for Flute, Oboe, Cello, and Harpsichord* (item 292)

End of a Chapter

See *Of Challenge and of Love*

Esprit rude/Esprit doux

184. New Albion NA019 CD (CD) (1989)

California EAR Unit: Dorothy Stone (fl), Theresa Tunnicliff (cl)
Recorded at the California Institute of the Arts
4:38
Producers: Rand Steiger, Peter Otto
Engineer: Mark Waldrep
Notes by Ruth Dreier
With Elliott Carter: *Enchanted Preludes* (item 179); *Canon for 4* (item 122); Arthur Jarvinen: *Egyptian Two Step*; Rand Steiger: *Quintessence*; Michael Torke: *The Yellow Pages*; Karlheinz Stockhausen: *Dr. K-Sextet*; Louis Andriessen: *Hoketus*

185. Erato ECD 75553 (CD) (1990)

Erato 2292-45364-2 (CD) (1990)
Ensemble InterContemporain: Sophie Cherrier (fl), André Trouttet (cl)
Recorded December 1987, Espace de Projection, Institut de Recherche et Coordination Acoustique/Musique (IRCAM), Centre Georges Pompidou, Paris
4:45
Producer: Michel Garcin
Engineers: Didier Arditi, Alain Jacquinot
Notes by Elliott Carter, Pierre Boulez
With Elliott Carter: *Oboe Concerto* (item 240); *A Mirror on Which to Dwell* (item 224); *Penthode* (item 251)

186. GM Recordings GM2020CD (CD) (1990)

   Perle/Carter
   Da Capo Chamber Players: Patricia Spencer (fl), Laura Flax (cl)
   Recorded 5 February 1988, Merkin Concert Hall, New York, NY
   4:27
   Producers: Gunther Schuller, Judith Sherman
   Engineer: Judith Sherman
   Notes by [author not listed] quoting Elliott Carter
   With Elliott Carter: *Enchanted Preludes* (item 180); *Canon for 4* (item 123); *Pastorale* (item 249); George Perle: *Sonata for Cello and Piano; Lyric Piece; Sonata a quattro*

187. ECM New Series 1391 (839 617-2) (CD) (1990)

   Philippe Racine (fl), Ernesto Molinari (cl)
   Recorded April 1989, Radio DRS, Studio Zürich
   4:46
   Producer: Manfred Eicher
   Recording Engineer: Peter Laenger
   Notes by Heinz Holliger, Wolfgang Sandner
   With Elliott Carter: *Enchanted Preludes* (item 181); *Riconoscenza per Goffredo Petrassi* (item 357); *Triple Duo* (item 371); J. S. Bach: *Suite No. 3 for Violoncello Solo*

188. Centaur CRC 2274 (CD) (1996)

   Earplay: Janet Kutulas (fl), Peter Josheff (cl)
   Recorded 25 November 1994, 20 February 1995, 9 April 1995, Knuth Hall, San Francisco State University
   4:52
   Producer: Lolly Lewis
   Engineer: Paul Stubblebine
   With Ursula Mamlock: *Rhapsody;* Richard Festinger: *Septet;* Wayne Peterson: *Labyrinth;* Andrew Frank: *Points of Departure;* David Vayo: *Poem;* Gustavo Moretto: *Silenciosamente*

189. cpo 999 453-2 (CD) (1998)

   Ensemble Contrasts: Michael Faust (fl), David Smeyers (cl)

Recorded October 1995, Hürth-Knapsack, Feierabendhaus der Hoechst AG; November 1995 and March 1996, Funkhaus Köln
5:23
Recording Supervisor: Wolfgang Müller
Recording Engineers: Franz-Peter Esser, Mark Hohn, Christian Meurer
With Elliott Carter: *Woodwind Quintet* (item 398); *Eight Etudes and a Fantasy* (item 161); *Enchanted Preludes* (item 183); *Sonata for Flute, Oboe, Cello, and Harpsichord* (item 292)

Esprit rude/Esprit doux II

190. Auvidis Montaigne MO 782089 (CD) (forthcoming)

Nieuw Ensemble: Harrie Starreveld (fl), Harmen De Boer (cl), Herman Halewijn (mar)
With *Luimen* (item 217) and other works

A *Fantasy about Purcell's* Fantasia upon One Note

191. Columbia Odyssey Y 34137 (Stereo lp) (1976)

The American Brass Quintet: Raymond Mase (tpt), Louis Ranger (tpt), Edward Birdwell (hn), Herbert Rankin (tb), Robert Biddlecome (btb)
Recorded 31 March–1 April 1975, Columbia Recording Studios, New York, NY
3:04
Producer: Thomas Frost
Engineers: Bud Graham, Ray Moore
Notes by Elliott Carter
With Elliott Carter: *Brass Quintet* (item 116); *Eight Pieces for Four Timpani* (item 162)

192. Capriccio 10361 (CD) (1992)

Frankfurt Radio Orchestra Brass Ensemble, Lutz Köhler (cond)
Recorded 20–23 June 1990, Justinuskirche Hochst

With J. S. Bach (arr. Mowat): *Brandenburg Concerto No. 3*; Henry Purcell: *Fantasies*; Aaron Copland: *Fanfare for the Common Man*; Samuel Barber: *Mutation from Bach*; G. F. Handel (arr. Howarth): *Music for the Royal Fireworks*

193. Hyperion CDA 66517 (CD) (1992)

> *From the Steeples and the Mountains: American Brass Music*
> London Gabrieli Brass Ensemble, Christopher Larkin (cond)
> Recorded 14–15 July 1991, All Hallows, Gospel Oak, London
> 3:08
> Notes by Peter Dickinson
> With Charles Ives: *From the Steeples and the Mountains*; *Processional: Let There Be Light*; Samuel Barber: *Mutations from Bach*; Roy Harris: *Chorale for Organ and Brass*; Virgil Thomson: *Family Portrait*; Henry Cowell: *Grinnell Fanfare*; *Tall Tale*; *Hymn and Fuguing Tune No. 12*; *Rondo*; Philip Glass: *Brass Sextet*; Carl Ruggles: *Angels*

Figment

194. Auvidis Montaigne MO 782091 (CD) (1998)

> Rohan de Saram (vc)
> Recorded 15–19 July 1996, All Saints Church, London
> 5:04
> Recording Supervisor: François Eckert
> Sound Engineer: Bob Harrison
> Notes by Bayan Northcott
> With Elliott Carter: *String Quartet No. 5* (item 325); *90+* (item 114); *Sonata for Violoncello and Piano* (item 305); *Fragment* (item 195); *Duo for Violin and Piano* (item 149)

Fragment

195. Auvidis Montaigne MO 782091 (CD) (1998)

> Arditti String Quartet: Irvine Arditti (vn I), Graeme Jennings (vn II), Garth Knox (va), Rohan de Saram (vc)
> Recorded 15–19 July 1996, All Saints Church, London
> 4:02

Recording Supervisor: François Eckert
Sound Engineer: Bob Harrison
Notes by Bayan Northcott
With Elliott Carter: *String Quartet No. 5* (item 325); *90+* (item 114); *Sonata for Violoncello and Piano* (item 305); *Figment* (item 194); *Duo for Violin and Piano* (item 149)

Gra

196. Bridge BCD 9044 (CD) (1994)

    Elliott Carter: Eight Compositions (1943–1993)
    The Group for Contemporary Music: Charles Neidich (cl)
    Recorded 12 July 1993, MasterSound, Astoria, NY
    4:35
    Producers: David Starobin, Michael Calvert
    Engineer: Ben Rizzi
    Notes by David Schiff
    With Elliott Carter: *Enchanted Preludes* (182); *Duo for Violin and Piano* (item 147); *Scrivo in vento* (item 278); *Changes* (item 127); *Con leggerezza pensosa* (item 128); *Riconoscenza per Goffredo Petrassi* (item 359); *Sonata for Violoncello and Piano* (item 301)

The Harmony of Morning

197. Vox Box SVBX 5354 (Stereo 3 lp) (1979)

    America Sings: American Choral Music
    Women's Choir of the Gregg Smith Singers and Chamber Orchestra, Gregg Smith (cond)
    Recorded April 1976, Walt Whitman Auditorium, Brooklyn College, Brooklyn, NY
    9:24
    Notes by Gregg Smith
    With William Bergsma: *Riddle Me This;* Giuseppe Chihara: *Lie Lightly, Gentle Earth;* Jacob Druckman: *Madrigale;* Lou Harrison: *Mass (to St. Anthony);* Michael Hennagin: *The House on the Hill;* Andrew Imbrie: *On the Beach at Night;* Carolyn Madison: *Two Pieces;* William Mayer: *The*

Eve of St. Agnes; Edmund Najera: *In dulci jubilo;* Ned Rorem: *Missa brevis;* Ronald Roxbury: *Four Motets;* William Schuman: *Mail Order Madrigals;* Gregg Smith: *Legend;* Donald Waxman: *Thomas Hardy Songs*

Reissued as item 198

198. GSS Recordings GSS 103 (stereo lp) (1984)

Producer: Raymond Marunas
Engineer: David Hancock
With Elliott Carter: *Tarantella* (item 338); *Emblems* (item 175); *Heart Not So Heavy As Mine* (item 205); *Musicians Wrestle Everywhere* (item 227); *To Music* (item 364); *The Defense of Corinth* (item 137)

Also reissued as item 199

199. CRI CD 648 (CD) (1993)

Producer: Gregg Smith
Recording Engineer: David Hancock
Notes by Gregg Smith and Joseph R. Dalton, Elliott Carter
With Elliott Carter: *Warble for Lilac Time* (item 383); *Voyage* (item 379); *Three Poems of Robert Frost* (item 355); *Tarantella* (item 339); *Emblems* (item 176); *Heart Not So Heavy As Mine* (item 206); *Musicians Wrestle Everywhere* (item 228); *To Music* (item 365); *The Defense of Corinth* (item 138)

200. Koch 3-7178-2H1 (CD) (1994)

John Oliver Chorale, John Oliver (music director)
Recorded October 1992, Emmanuel Church, Boston, MA
9:35
Producer and Engineer: Michael Fine
With Elliott Carter: *Emblems* (item 178); *Heart Not So Heavy As Mine* (item 207); *Musicians Wrestle Everywhere* (item 230); Bright Sheng: *Two Folk Songs from Chinhai;* Martin Amlin: *Time's Caravan;* William Thomas McKinley: *4 Text Settings*

Reissued as item 200

Discography of Commercial Recordings 97

201. Koch International Classics 3-7415-2H1 (CD) (1998)

Notes by Elliott Carter, Steven Ledbetter
With Elliott Carter: *To Music* (item 366); *Tarantella* (item 340); *Harvest Home* (item 202); *Emblems* (item 178); *Let's Be Gay* (item 216); *Heart Not So Heavy As Mine* (item 208); *The Defense of Corinth* (item 139); *Musicians Wrestle Everywhere* (item 231)

Harriet

See *In Sleep, in Thunder*

Harvest Home

202. Koch International Classics 3-7415-2H1 (CD) (1998)

John Oliver Chorale, John Oliver (music director)
Recorded May 1997, Emmanuel Church, Boston, MA
4:15
Producer: Susan Napodano DelGiorno
Engineer: Silas Brown
Notes by Elliott Carter, Steven Ledbetter
With Elliott Carter: *To Music* (item 366); *Tarantella* (item 340); *Emblems* (item 178); *Let's Be Gay* (item 216); *Heart Not So Heavy As Mine* (item 208); *The Defense of Corinth* (item 139); *The Harmony of Morning* (item 201); *Musicians Wrestle Everywhere* (item 231)

Heart Not So Heavy As Mine

203. Society for the Preservation of the American Musical Heritage MIA 116 (Stereo lp) (1961)

Choral Music in 20th-Century America
Hamline A Cappella Choir, Robert Holliday (cond)
4:23
With Charles Ives: *A Christmas Carol; Turn Ye, Turn Ye*; Russell Harris: *It Was Beginning Winter; The Moon Is Hiding*; Relly Raffman: *Triptych*; Glenn Glasow: *Two Egrets*; Paul

Fetler: *April*; Kenneth Gaburo: *Three Dedications*; George Antheil: *Fragments from Shelley*

204. Nonesuch H 1115 (Mono lp) (1966)

   Nonesuch H 71115 (stereo lp) (1966)
   The Dove Descending
   Canby Singers, Edward Tatnall Canby (cond)
   4:20
   Production supervised by Teresa Sterne
   Notes by Edward Tatnall Canby
   With Elliott Carter: *Musicians Wrestle Everywhere* (item 225); Johannes Brahms: *Songs,* op. 110, nos. 1 and 2; op 93a, nos. 2 and 3; Don Carlo Gesualdo: *O Vos Omnes*; Hans Leo Hassler: *Cantata Domino; O Aufenhalt meins Leben*; Paul Hindemith: *6 Chansons; Frauenklage*; Claudio Monteverdi: *Ohimése Tanto Amatel; Zeffiro torna*; Claude Sermisy: *Au joly boys*; Igor Stravinsky: *The Dove Descending Breaks the Air*; Peter Warlock: *Corpus Christi*

205. GSS Recordings GSS 103 (stereo lp) (1984)

   The Gregg Smith Singers, Gregg Smith (cond)
   Recorded 1983, Holy Trinity Episcopal Church, New York, NY
   4:28
   Producer: Raymond Marunas
   Engineer: David Hancock
   With Elliott Carter: *Tarantella* (item 338); *Emblems* (item 175); *The Harmony of Morning* (item 198); *Musicians Wrestle Everywhere* (item 227); *To Music* (item 364); *The Defense of Corinth* (item 137)

   Reissued as item 206

206. CRI CD 648 (CD) (1993)

   Producer: Gregg Smith
   Notes by Gregg Smith and Joseph R. Dalton, Elliott Carter
   With Elliott Carter: *Warble for Lilac Time* (item 383); *Voyage* (item 379); *Three Poems of Robert Frost* (item 355); *Tarantella* (item 339); *Emblems* (item 176); *Heart Not So Heavy*

As Mine (item 206); *Musicians Wrestle Everywhere* (item 228); *To Music* (item 365); *The Defense of Corinth* (item 138)

207. Koch 3-7178-2H1 (CD) (1994)

    John Oliver Chorale, John Oliver (music director)
    Recorded October 1992, Emmanuel Church, Boston, MA
    4:25
    Producer and Engineer: Michael Fine
    With Elliott Carter: *Emblems* (item 178); *The Harmony of Morning* (item 200); *Musicians Wrestle Everywhere* (item 230); Bright Sheng: *Two Folk Songs from Chinhai*; Martin Amlin: *Time's Caravan*; William Thomas McKinley: *4 Text Settings*

    Reissued as item 208

208. Koch International Classics 3-7415-2H1 (CD) (1998)

    Notes by Elliott Carter, Steven Ledbetter
    With Elliott Carter: *To Music* (item 366); *Tarantella* (item 340); *Harvest Home* (item 202); *Emblems* (item 178); *Let's Be Gay* (item 216); *The Defense of Corinth* (item 139); *The Harmony of Morning* (item 201); *Musicians Wrestle Everywhere* (item 231)

209. AmCam Recordings ACR 10307 (CD) (1995)

    Darest Thou, O Soul: Twentieth Century American Choral Music
    Alexandria Choral Society, Kerry Krebill (artistic director)
    Recorded 26–28 June and 1 July 1995, Bradley Hills Presbyterian Church, Bethesda, MD
    4:48
    Producer: AmCam Recordings
    Recording Engineer: Mark Huffman
    With Hale Smith: *Toussaint L'Overture*; William Schuman: *Carols of Death*; Ned Rorem: *In Time of Pestilence*; Robert Evett: *The Mask of Cain*; Robert Shafer: *miracles—five poems of e. e. cummings*; Garrison Hull: *A Profound Whisper*; Russell Woolen: *Ave Maria*; *Ingrediente domino*; Daniel Gawthrop: *Close Now Thine Eyes*

High on Our Tower

See *Of Challenge and of Love*

Holiday Overture

210. CRI SD 475 (Stereo lp) (1982)

    Elliott Carter: The Early Music
    American Composers Orchestra, Paul Dunkel (cond)
    Recorded February 1982, Walt Whitman Auditorium, Brooklyn College, Brooklyn, NY
    9:11
    Producer: Carter Harman
    Recorded by David Hancock
    Notes by David Schiff
    With Elliott Carter: *Symphony No. 1* (item 328); *Pocahontas* (suite from the ballet) (item 274)

    Reissued as item 211

211. CRI ACS 6003 (Cassette) (1985)

    Music of Elliott Carter
    With Elliott Carter: *Syringa* (item 334); *Symphony No. 1* (item 329)

    Also reissued as item 212

212. CRI CD 610 (CD) (1991)

    With Elliott Carter: *Pocahontas* (suite from the ballet) (item 275); *Syringa* (item 335)

Improvisation

See *Eight Pieces for Four Timpani*

In Genesis

See *In Sleep, in Thunder*

Inner Song

See *Trilogy*

In Sleep, in Thunder

1. "Dolphin"
2. "Across the Yard: La Ignota"
3. "Harriet"
4. "Dies Irae"
5. "Careless Night"
6. "In Genesis"

213. Wergo WER 60124 (Stereo lp) (1986)

    Nonesuch 79110-1 (stereo lp; CD) (1986)
    Martyn Hill (ten), London Sinfonietta, Oliver Knussen (cond)
    Recorded 29 February 1984, Rosslyn Hill Chapel, London
    18:59
    Producer: Oliver Knussen
    Engineer: John Whiting
    Notes by David Schiff
    With Elliott Carter: *Triple Duo* (item 369)

    Reissued as item 214

214. Wergo 6278-2 (286-278-2) (CD) (1995)

215. Bridge BCD 9014 (CD) (1989)

    Elliott Carter: The Vocal Works (1975–1981)
    Jon Garrison (ten), Speculum Musicae, Robert Black (cond)
    Recorded 20–21 October 1987, RCA Studio A, New York, NY
    20:31
    Producer: David Starobin
    Engineer: Joe Lopes
    Notes by Lloyd Schwartz
    With Elliott Carter: *Three Poems of Robert Frost* (item 354); *Syringa* (item 336); *A Mirror on Which to Dwell* (item 223)

Insomnia

See *A Mirror on Which to Dwell*

Let's Be Gay

216. Koch International Classics 3-7415-2H1 (CD) (1998)

   John Oliver Chorale, Martin Amlin (pno), Frank Corliss (pno), John Oliver (music director)
   Recorded May 1997, Emmanuel Church, Boston, MA
   3:14
   Producer: Susan Napodano DelGiorno
   Engineer: Silas Brown
   Notes by Elliott Carter, Steven Ledbetter
   With Elliott Carter: *To Music* (item 366); *Tarantella* (item 340); *Harvest Home* (item 202); *Emblems* (item 178); *Heart Not So Heavy As Mine* (item 208); *The Defense of Corinth* (item 139); *The Harmony of Morning* (item 201); *Musicians Wrestle Everywhere* (item 231)

The Line Gang

See *Three Poems of Robert Frost*

Luimen

217. Auvidis Montaigne MO 782089 (CD) (Forthcoming)

   Nieuw Ensemble
   With *Esprit rude/Esprit doux II* (item 190) and other works

March

See *Eight Pieces for Four Timpani*

The Minotaur

218. Elektra Nonesuch 79248-2 (CD) (1990)

   New York Chamber Symphony, Gerard Schwarz (cond)

Recorded 6 December 1988, the Manhattan Center, New York, NY
32:49
Producer/Engineer: Max Wilcox
Notes by Lloyd Schwartz
With Elliott Carter: "Dust of Snow" and "The Rose Family" from *Three Poems of Robert Frost* (item 350); *Piano Sonata* (item 263)

The Minotaur (suite from the ballet)

219. Mercury MG50103 (Mono lp) (1956)

    Mercury MRL 2515 (mono lp) (1956) (United Kingdom)
    Eastman-Rochester Symphony Orchestra, Howard Hanson (cond)
    Recorded ca. January 1956
    26:30
    Notes by David Hall
    With Colin McPhee: *Tabuh-Tabuhan*

    Reissued as item 220

220. Mercury Golden Imports SRI 75111 (Nono lp, Electronically Altered to Simulate Stereo) (1978)

    With Henry Cowell: *Symphony No. 4;* Wallingford Riegger: *New Dance*

A Mirror on Which to Dwell

1. "Anaphora"
2. "Argument"
3. "Sandpiper"
4. "Insomnia"
5. "View of the Capitol from the Library of Congress"
6. "O Breath"

221. 2 and 3 only

    Le temps musical 3
    Radio France/IRCAM (4 stereo cassettes) (1980)

Deborah Cook (sop), Ensemble InterContemporain, Pierre Boulez (cond)
Recorded 17–23 February 1978, Centre Georges Pompidou and the Théâtre de la Ville, Paris
5:38; 4:20
Producer: Jean-Pierre Derrien
With Pierre Boulez: *Éclat;* György Ligeti: *Concerto de chambre;* Olivier Messiaen: *Mode de valeurs et d'intensités;* Pierre Boulez: "Introduction à une histoire du temps musical de G. de Machaut à nos jours"

222. Columbia M 35171 (Stereo lp) (1980)

    CBS Masterworks 76812
    Susan Davenny Wyner (sop), Speculum Musicae, Richard Fitz (cond)
    Recorded at CBS Recording Studios, New York, NY
    19:39
    Producer: Andrew Kazdin
    Engineers: Bud Graham, Milt Cherin, Larry Keyes
    Notes by Elliott Carter
    With Elliott Carter: *A Symphony of Three Orchestras* (item 331)

223. Bridge BCD 9014 (CD) (1989)

    Elliott Carter: The Vocal Works (1975–1981)
    Christine Schadeberg (sop), Speculum Musicae, Donald Palma (cond)
    Recorded 2–3 December 1988, RCA Studio A, New York, NY
    17:09
    Producer: David Starobin
    Engineer: Paul Zinman
    Notes by Lloyd Schwartz
    With Elliott Carter: *Three Poems of Robert Frost* (item 354); *Syringa* (item 336); *In Sleep, in Thunder* (item 215)

224. Erato ECD 75553 (CD) (1990)

    Erato 2292-45364-2 (CD) (1990)

Phyllis Bryn-Julson (sop), Ensemble InterContemporain, Pierre Boulez (cond)
Recorded December 1987, Espace de Projection, IRCAM (Institut de Recherche et Coordination Acoustique/ Musique), Centre Georges Pompidou, Paris
18:36
Producer: Michel Garcin
Engineers: Didier Arditi, Alain Jacquinot
Notes by Elliott Carter, Pierre Boulez
With Elliott Carter: *Oboe Concerto* (item 240); *Esprit rude/Esprit doux* (item 185); *Penthode* (item 251)

Moto Perpetuo

See *Eight Pieces for Four Timpani*

Musicians Wrestle Everywhere

225. Nonesuch H 1115 (Mono lp) (1966)

    Nonesuch H 71115 (stereo lp) (1966)
    The Dove Descending
    Canby Singers, Edward Tatnall Canby (cond)
    3:44
    Production supervised by Teresa Sterne
    Notes by Edward Tatnall Canby
      With Elliott Carter: *Heart Not So Heavy As Mine* (item 204); Johannes Brahms: *Songs,* op. 110, nos. 1 and 2; op 93a, nos. 2 and 3; Don Carlo Gesualdo: *O Vos Omnes;* Hans Hassler: *Cantata Domino; O Aufenhalt meins Leben;* Paul Hindemith: *6 Chansons; Frauenklage;* Claudio Monteverdi: *Ohimése Tanto Amatel; Zeffiro Torna;* Claude Sermisy: *Au joly boys;* Igor Stravinsky: *The Dove Descending Breaks the Air;* Peter Warlock: *Corpus Christi*

226. Vox SVBX 5353 (Stereo lp) (1977)

    America Sings (1920–1950)
    Gregg Smith Singers, Gregg Smith (cond)
    Recorded 1983, Holy Trinity Episcopal Church, New York, NY

3:13
Notes by Gregg Smith
With Elliott Carter: *The Defense of Corinth* (item 136); Samuel Barber: *A Stopwatch and an Ordnance Map;* Leonard Bernstein: Choruses from *The Lark;* Aaron Copland: *Two Pieces for Treble Choir;* Henry Cowell: *Luther's Chorale to His Son;* Irving Fine: *The Choral New Yorker;* Lukas Foss: *Behold I Build a House;* George Gershwin: *Two Madrigals;* Charles Ives: *Two Election Songs;* Walter Piston: *Psalm and Prayer of David;* Wallingford Riegger: *Who Can Revoke;* William Schuman: *Prelude;* Charles Seeger: *Chant;* Roger Sessions: *Turn, O Liberstad;* Louise Talma: *Let's Touch the Sky;* Virgil Thomson: *Four Southern Hymns; Alleluia*

?Reissued as item 227

227. GSS Recordings GSS 103 (Stereo lp) (1984)

Producer: Raymond Marunas
Engineer: David Hancock
With Elliott Carter: *Tarantella* (item 338); *Emblems* (item 175); *The Harmony of Morning* (item 198); *Heart Not So Heavy As Mine* (item 205); *To Music* (item 364); *The Defense of Corinth* (item 137)

Also reissued as item 228

228. CRI CD 648 (CD) (1993)

Producer: Gregg Smith
Recording Engineer: David Hancock
Notes by Gregg Smith and Joseph R. Dalton, Elliott Carter
With Elliott Carter: *Warble for Lilac Time* (item 383); *Voyage* (item 379); *Three Poems of Robert Frost* (item 355); *Tarantella* (item 339); *Emblems* (item 176); *The Harmony of Morning* (item 199); *Heart Not So Heavy As Mine* (item 206); *To Music* (item 365); *The Defense of Corinth* (item 138)

229. Deutsche Grammophon 2530 912 (Stereo lp) (1978)

American Choral Music of the 20th Century

Tanglewood Festival Chorus, John Oliver (cond)
3:05
Notes by Michael Steinberg
With Charles Ives: Psalms 24, 67, and 90; Jacob Druckman: *Antiphonies;* Aaron Copland: *In the Beginning*

230. Koch 3-7178-2H1 (CD) (1994)

John Oliver Chorale, John Oliver (music director)
Recorded October 1992, Emmanuel Church, Boston, MA
3:11
Producer and Engineer: Michael Fine
With Elliott Carter: *Emblems* (item 178); *The Harmony of Morning* (item 200); *Heart Not So Heavy As Mine* (item 207); Bright Sheng: *Two Folk Songs from Chinhai;* Martin Amlin: *Time's Caravan;* William Thomas McKinley: *4 Text Settings*

Reissued as item 231

231. Koch International Classics 3-7415-2H1 (CD) (1998)

Notes by Elliott Carter, Steven Ledbetter
With Elliott Carter: *To Music* (item 366); *Tarantella* (item 340); *Harvest Home* (item 202); *Emblems* (item 178); *Let's Be Gay* (item 216); *Heart Not So Heavy As Mine* (item 208); *The Defense of Corinth* (item 139); *The Harmony of Morning* (item 201)

Night Fantasies

232. Etcetera ETC 1008 (Stereo lp) (1983)

Etcetera KTC 1008 (CD) (1988)
Charles Rosen (pno)
Recorded 1982 in Holland
22:12
Producer and Engineer: Klaas A. Posthuma
Notes by Charles Rosen
With Elliott Carter: *Piano Sonata* (item 264)

Reissued as item 233

233. Bridge 9090 (CD) (1997)

   The Complete Music for Piano
   With Elliott Carter: *Piano Sonata* (item 265); *90+* (item 113)

234. Nonesuch 79047-1 (Stereo lp) (1983)

   Paul Jacobs (pno)
   Recorded August 1982, RCA Studio A, New York, NY
   22:18
   Producer and Engineer: Max Wilcox
   Notes by Elliott Carter (item 504), Paul Jacobs (item 682)
   With Elliott Carter: *Piano Sonata* (item 262)

235. Bridge BCD 9001 (CD) (1986)

   Aleck Karis (pno)
   Recorded 6–8 February 1984, Holy Trinity Episcopal Church, New York, NY
   22:12
   Producer: William Daghlian
   Engineer: David B. Hancock
   Notes by Aleck Karis
   With Frederic Chopin: *Fantaisie*, op. 49; Robert Schumann: *Carnaval*, op. 9

236. Music & Arts CD 604 (CD) (1989)

   Ursula Oppens (pno)
   Recorded 1989, State University of New York at Purchase
   21:32
   Producer/Engineer: Judith Sherman
   Notes by Susan Feder
   With Conlon Nancarrow: *Tango?*; William Bolcom: *The Dead Moth Tango*; Michael Sahl: *Tango from the Exiles*; Julius Hemphill: *Parchment*; John Adams: *Phrygian Gates*; Lukas Foss: *The Curriculum Vitae Tango*; David Jaggard: *Tango*

   Reissued as item 237

237. Music & Arts MUA 862 (2 CD) (1995)

With Conlon Nancarrow: *Tango?*; William Bolcom: *The Dead Moth Tango*; Michael Sahl: *Tango from the Exiles*; Julius Hemphill: *Parchment*; John Adams: *Phrygian Gates*; Lukas Foss: *The Curriculum Vitae Tango*; David Jaggard: *Tango*; Conlon Nancarrow: *Two Canons for Ursula*; Frederic Rzewski: *Mayn Yingele*; Charles Wuorinen: *Blue Bamboula*; Tobias Picker: *Old and Lost Rivers*; John Harbison: *Sonata for Piano No. 1 "Roger Sessions in Memoriam"*; Anthony Davis: *Middle Passage*

238. Neuma 450-76 (CD) (1991)

Stephen Drury (pno)
Recorded July 1990, Jordan Hall, New England Conservatory, Boston, MA
21:15
Producers: Joel Gordon, Stephen Drury
Engineer: Joel Gordon
Notes by Stephen Drury
With John Cage: *Études australes* (Book I)

239. Pianovox PIA 501-2 (CD) (1998)

Florence Millet (pno)
Recorded July 1997, Espace de projection, IRCAM (Institut de Recherche et Coordination Acoustique/Musique), Centre Georges Pompidou, Paris
21:58
Recording Supervision: Franck Ollu
Recording and Editing Engineer: Franck Rossi
Notes by Max Noubel
With Elliott Carter: *90+* (item 115)

O Breath

See *A Mirror on Which to Dwell*

Oboe Concerto

240. Erato ECD 75553 (CD) (1990)

    Erato 2292-45364-2 (CD) (1990)
    Concertino: Heinz Holliger (ob), Vincent Bauer, Michel Cerutty (perc), Jean Sulem, Garth Knox, Louis Fima, Nathalie Baudoin (va); Ensemble InterContemporain, Pierre Boulez (cond)
    Recorded December 1987, Espace de Projection, IRCAM (Institut de Recherche et Coordination Acoustique/ Musique), Centre Georges Pompidou, Paris
    19:48
    Producer: Michel Garcin
    Engineers: Didier Arditi, Alain Jacquinot
    Notes by Elliott Carter, Pierre Boulez
    With Elliott Carter: *Esprit rude/Esprit doux* (item 185); *A Mirror on Which to Dwell* (item 224); *Penthode* (item 251)

241. Reissued as:

    Erato 4509-98496-2 (5 CD) (ca. 1995)

242. Col Legno AU 31800 (4 CD) (1991)

    40 Jahre Donaueschinger Musiktage 1950–1990
    Heinz Holliger (ob), SWF Symphony Orchestra Baden-Baden; Michael Gielen (cond)
    Recorded in Donaueschingen, Germany
    18:43
    Notes by Josef Häusler
    With Karl Amadeus Hartmann: *2. Sinfonie;* Pierre Boulez: *Polyphonie X* (excerpt); *Poésie pour pouvoir; Structures II;* Luigi Nono: *Due espressioni;* Iannis Xenakis: *Metastaseis;* Krzysztof Penderecki: *Anaklasis;* György Ligeti: *Atmosphères;* Karlheinz Stockhausen: *Punkte;* Igor Stravinsky: *In memoriam Dylan Thomas;* Bernd Alois Zimmermann: *Sonate für Bratsche solo;* Heinz Holliger: *Pneuma;* Helmut Lachenmann: *Schwankungen am Rand;* Andreas Raseghi: *Kammerquartett;* Olivier Messiaen: *Réveil des oiseaux;* Wolfgang Rihm: *Frau/Stimme;* Johannes Kalitzke: *Nachtschleife*

Discography of Commercial Recordings   111

243. Editiones Roche 72118 (CD) (1996) (Private Release)

    Concertino: Heinz Holliger (ob), [others not listed]; Ensemble InterContemporain, Pierre Boulez (cond)
    Recorded 27 April 1996, Musiksaal des Stadt-Casinos, Basel, Switzerland
    19:22
    Producer: Rolf Grolimund
    Engineer: Charles Suter
    With Elliott Carter: *A 6 Letter Letter* (item 112); Pierre Boulez: *Sur Incises;* Harrison Birtwistle: *Four Settings of Paul Celan;* Luciano Berio: *KOL OD (Chemins VI)*

Of Challenge and of Love

1. "High on Our Tower"
2. "Under the Dome"
3. "Am Klavier (At the Piano)"
4. "Quatrains from Harp Lake"
5. "End of a Chapter"

244. Koch International Classics 3-7425-2-H1 (CD) (1997)

    Lucy Shelton (sop), John Constable (pno)
    Recorded 18–20 May 1996, All Saints Church, Peterham, England
    22:18
    Producer and Engineer: Tryggvi Tryggvason
    Notes by Richard Wilson
    With Elliott Carter: *Three Poems of Robert Frost* (item 353); *Warble for Lilac Time* (item 385); *Voyage* (item 382); Igor Stravinsky: *Storm–Cloud; Two Songs on Poems of Gorodetsky,* op. 6; *Pastorale; Two Poems of Konstantin Balmont; Three Little Songs: Recollections of Childhood; Berceuse; Three Tales for Children; Four Russian Songs; Russian Maiden's Song; The Owl and the Pussy-Cat*

Partita

See *Symphonia—Sum Fluxae Pretiam Spei*

Pastorale (version for clarinet and piano)

245. Orion ORS 77275 (Stereo lp) (1977)

   Pastorale
   John Russo (cl), Lydia Walton Ignacio (pno)
   8:47
   Notes by C. Jacqueline Hogue
   With John Russo: *Sonata No. 4 for Clarinet and Piano*; François Devienne: *Sonata No. 1 for Clarinet and Piano*; John Davidson: *Introduction and Dance*

   Reissued as item 246

246. CRS Master Recordings CD 9255 (CD) (1992)

   Contemporary/Classic Masters
   With John Russo: *Sonata No. 4 for Clarinet and Piano; Larghetto for Clarinet, Viola, and Piano*; François Devienne: *Sonata No. 1 for Clarinet and Piano*; Robert Dusek: *Gray Dawn*; John Davidson: *Introduction and Dance*; David Hush: *Partita No. 1 for Violoncello Solo*; Carl Harrison: *Songs from a Child's Garden*

247. Grenadilla GS 1018 (Stereo lp) (1978)

   Pastorale
   Else Ludewig-Verdehr (cl), David Liptak (pno)
   8:54
   Notes by Rosario Mazzeo
   With Mario Castelnuovo-Tedesco: *Sonata for Clarinet and Piano*, op. 128; Vincent Frohne: *Study for Clarinet Solo*, op. 17

248. Golden Crest Records RE 7075 (Stereo lp) (1982)

   Music for Clarinet
   Keith Wilson (cl), Donald Currier (pno)
   9:56
   With Paul Hindemith: *Sonata for Clarinet and Piano*; Quincy Porter: *Quintet for Clarinet and Strings*

Discography of Commercial Recordings 113

249. GM Recordings GM2020CD (CD) (1990)

    Perle/Carter
    Da Capo Chamber Players: Laura Flax (cl), Sarah Rothenberg (pno)
    Recorded 15–16 September 1988, State University of New York at Purchase
    9:10
    Producers: Gunther Schuller, Judith Sherman
    Engineer: Judith Sherman
    Notes by Elliott Carter
    With Elliott Carter: *Enchanted Preludes* (item 180); *Canon for 4* (item 123); *Esprit rude/Esprit doux* (item 186); George Perle: *Sonata for Cello and Piano; Lyric Piece; Sonata a quattro*

Pastorale (version for english horn and piano)

250. Crystal CD 328 (CD) (1996)

    Carolyn Hove (eh), Gloria Cheng (pno)
    Recorded: December 1994 and January 1996, Little Bridges Auditorium, Pomona College, Claremont, CA
    9:18
    With Paul Hindemith: *Sonata for English Horn and Piano;* Esa-Pekka Salonen: *Second Meeting;* John Marvin: *Five Pieces for English Horn and Piano;* Vincent Persichetti: *Parable XV for English Horn Solo,* op. 128; Thomas Stevens: *Triangles IV*

Penthode

251. Erato ECD 75553 (CD) (1990)

    Erato 2292-45364-2 (CD) (1990)
    Ensemble InterContemporain, Pierre Boulez (cond)
    Recorded December 1987, Espace de Projection, IRCAM (Institut de Recherche et Coordination Acoustique/ Musique), Centre Georges Pompidou, Paris
    19:21

Producer: Michel Garcin
Engineers: Didier Arditi, Alain Jacquinot
Notes by Elliott Carter, Pierre Boulez
With Elliott Carter: *A Mirror on Which to Dwell* (item 224); *Oboe Concerto* (item 240); *Esprit rude/Esprit doux* (item 185)

Piano Concerto

252. RCA Victor LM 3001 (Mono lp) (1968)

   RCA Victor LSC 3001 (stereo lp) (1968)
   R.C.A. RB 6756 (mono lp) (reviewed November 1968) (United Kingdom)
   R.C.A. SB 6756 (stereo lp) (reviewed November 1968) (United Kingdom)
   Jacob Lateiner (pno), Boston Symphony Orchestra, Erich Leinsdorf (cond)
   Recorded in performance 7–8 January 1967, Symphony Hall, Boston, MA
   26:07
   Producer: Howard Scott
   Recording Engineer: Bernard Keville
   Notes by Michael Steinberg
   With Michael Colgrass: *As Quiet As*

253. New World Records NW 347 (Stereo lp) (1986)

   New World Records NW 347-2 (80347) (CD) (1986)
   Ursula Oppens (pno), Cincinnati Symphony Orchestra, Michael Gielen (cond)
   Recorded in performance 5–6 October 1984, Music Hall, Cincinnati, OH
   22:30
   Recording Engineer: Brent Reider
   Notes by David Schiff
   With Elliott Carter: *Variations for Orchestra* (item 375)

254. Arte Nova Classics 74321 2773 2 (CD) (1995)

   Ursula Oppens (pno), SWF Symphony Orchestra, Michael Gielen (cond)

Recorded 27 April 1992, SWF Hans Rosbaud Studio, Baden-Baden, Germany
22:31
Producing Engineer: Helmut Hanusch
Sound Engineer: Norbert Vossen
Notes by Stefan Lipka
With Elliott Carter: *Three Occasions for Orchestra* (item 345); *Concerto for Orchestra* (item 134)

Piano Sonata

255. American Recording Society ARS 25 (Mono lp) (1952)

    Beveridge Webster (pno)
    Recorded in New York, NY
    With Elliott Carter: *Sonata for Violoncello and Piano* (item 293)

    Reissued as item 256

256. Desto D 419 (Mono lp) (1965)

    Desto DST 6419 (mono lp, electronically altered to simulate stereo) (1965)

257. Epic LC 3850 (Mono lp) (1962)

    Epic BC 1250 (stereo lp) (1962)
    Charles Rosen (pno)
    Recorded 25 April 1961
    21:22
    Notes by Charles Rosen
    With Elliott Carter: *Pocahontas* (suite from the ballet) (item 273)

258. Issued in the United Kingdom As:

    EMI ALP 2052 (mono lp) (reviewed April 1965)
    EMI ASD 601 (stereo lp) (reviewed April 1965)
    With Elliott Carter: *Double Concerto* (item 141)

259. Dover HCR 5265 (Mono lp) (1966)

    Dover HCR-ST 7014 (stereo lp) (1966)

Dover HCR-ST 7265 (stereo lp) (1966)
Modern American Piano Music
Beveridge Webster (pno)
22:16
Notes by Roger Kamien
With Aaron Copland: *Piano Variations;* Roger Sessions: *Second Sonata for Piano*

260. Valois MB 755 (Stereo lp) (1966) (France and Germany)

    Noël Lee (pno)
    Notes by Noël Lee
    With Aaron Copland: *Piano Variations;* Roger Sessions: *Second Sonata for Piano*

261. Orion ORS 79342 (Stereo lp) (1979)

    Evelinde Trenkner (pno)
    Recorded at the Pleshakov-Kaneko Music Institute, Palo Alto, CA
    26:07
    Notes by Evelinde Trenkner
    With Franz Liszt: *Praludium und Fuge uber den Names Bach;* Alfredo Casella: *Due ricercari sul nome BACH;* Arthur Honegger: *Preludio arioso et fughette sur le nom de BACH*

262. Nonesuch 79047-1 (Stereo lp) (1983)

    Paul Jacobs (pno)
    Recorded August 1982, RCA Studio A, New York, NY
    26:28
    Producer and Engineer: Max Wilcox
    Notes by Elliott Carter (item 504), Paul Jacobs (item 682)
    With Elliott Carter: *Night Fantasies* (item 234)

    Reissued as item 263

263. Elektra Nonesuch 79248-2 (CD) (1990)

    Notes by Lloyd Schwartz
    With Elliott Carter: "Dust of Snow" and "The Rose Family" from *Three Poems of Robert Frost* (item 350); *The Minotaur* (item 218)

Discography of Commercial Recordings 117

264. Etcetera ETC 1008 (Stereo lp) (1983)

   Etcetera KTC 1008 (CD) (1988)
   Charles Rosen (pno)
   Recorded 1982, in Holland
   22:12
   Producer: Klaas A. Posthuma
   Notes by Charles Rosen
   With Elliott Carter: *Night Fantasies* (item 232)

   Reissued as item 265

265. Bridge 9090 (CD) (1997)

   The Complete Music for Piano
   With Elliott Carter: *Night Fantasies* (item 233); *90+* (item 113)

266. Factory FACD 256 (CD) (1989)

   Rolf Hind (pno)
   Recorded at Bishop's Gate Hall, London
   23:59
   Notes by Peter Urpeth
   With György Ligeti: *Études, Book I*; Steve Martland: *Kgakala*; Olivier Messiaen: *Le Courlis cendre*

267. Virgin Classics VC 7 91163-2 (CD) (1991)

   American Piano Sonatas Vol. One
   Peter Lawson (pno)
   Recorded November–December 1989, Abbey Road Studio No. 1, London
   25:00
   Notes by Wilfrid Mellers
   With Aaron Copland: *Piano Sonata*; Charles Ives: *Three Page Sonata*; Samuel Barber: *Piano Sonata*, op. 26

268. Continuum CCD 1028–1029 (2 CD) (1991)

   Transatlantic Piano
   John McCabe (pno)
   Recorded 3–11 September 1990, Rosslyn Hill Chapel, London

26:09
Notes by Calum MacDonald, John McCabe
With John Adams: *Phrygian Gates;* André Previn: *The Invisible Drummer;* George Rochberg: *Carnival Music;* Richard Rodney Bennett: *Noctuary;* Aaron Copland: *Piano Sonata*

269. Chant du monde LDC 278 1067 (CD) (1991)

Musique américaine pour piano
Noël Lee (pno)
Recorded 9–11 September 1991, Eglise Luthérienne Saint-Pierre, Paris
23:00
Notes by Noël Lee
With Louis Moreau Gottschalk: *Souvenir de Porto-Rico,* op. 31; *The Dying Poet (Le Poète mourant); Grand Scherzo,* op. 57; Edward MacDowell: *Sea Pieces (Marines),* op. 55; Aaron Copland: *Piano Variations;* John Cage: *In a Landscape*

270. Program Promotions PP-2 (CD) (1992)

Inspired 20th Century Piano Music
Michael Kieran Harvey (pno)
Recorded in Mittagong, NSW, Australia
21:45
With Igor Stravinsky: *Trois mouvements de Petrouchka;* Graham Hair: *Under Aldebaran;* Carl Vine: *Piano Sonata*

271. Melodiya MEL CD 10 00529 (CD) (1997)

Veda Zuponcic (pno)
Recorded 1992, studios of Russian State Radio
21:14
Engineers: V. Ivanov, E. Shakhnazaryan
Notes by Dr. Hoyle Carpenter
With Vivian Fine: *Toccatas and Arias;* Aaron Copland: *Passacaglia;* Norman Dello Joio: *Sonata No. 3;* George Gershwin: *Preludes for Piano*

272. Koch 3-7622-2H1 (CD) (1999)

John Owings (pno)
Recorded November 1997, Ed Landreth Auditorium, Texas Christian University, Fort Worth, TX
22:58
Produced and Engineered by José Feghali
With Samuel Barber: *Sonata for Piano;* Aaron Copland: *Piano Sonata*

Pocahontas (suite from the ballet)

273. Epic LC 3850 (Mono lp) (1962)

Epic BC 1250 (stereo lp) (1962)
Zürich Radio Orchestra, Jacques Monod (cond)
21:24
Notes by Charles Rosen
With Elliott Carter: *Piano Sonata* (item 257)

274. CRI SD 475 (Stereo lp) (1982)

American Composers Orchestra, Paul Dunkel (cond)
Recorded February 1982, Walt Whitman Auditorium, Brooklyn College, Brooklyn, NY
19:54
Producer: Carter Harman
Recorded by David Hancock
Notes by David Schiff
With Elliott Carter: *Symphony No. 1* (item 328); *Holiday Overture* (item 210)

Reissued as item 275

275. CRI CD 610 (CD) (1991)

With Elliott Carter: *Holiday Overture* (item 212); *Syringa* (item 335)

Quatrains from Harp Lake

See *Of Challenge and of Love*

Quintet for Piano and Winds

276. Philips 445 095-2 (CD) (1997)
> *Inner Song*
> Elmar Schmid (cl), Heinz Holliger (ob), Klaus Thunemann (bn), Radovan Vlatković (hn), András Schiff (pno)
> Recorded December 1993, La Musica Théatre, La Chaux-de-Fonds, Switzerland
> 23:07
> Recording Producer: Volker Straus
> Recording Engineer: Evert Menting
> Notes by Paul Griffiths, Uta Ruscher, Alain Poirier
> With Elliott Carter: *Trilogy* (item 368); Sándor Veress: *Sonatine for Oboe, Clarinet, and Bassoon; Diptych;* Heinz Holliger: *Quintet for Piano and Four Wind Players*

Recitative

See *Eight Pieces for Four Timpani*

Remembrance

See *Three Occasions for Orchestra*

Riconoscenza per Goffredo Petrassi

See *Three Recollections*

The Rose Family

See *Three Poems of Robert Frost*

Saëta

See *Eight Pieces for Four Timpani*

Sandpiper

See *A Mirror on Which to Dwell*

Scrivo in vento

277. La Flute Traversière 93 04-6 (CD) (1993)

   Made in the U.S.A.
   Kathleen Chastain (fl)
   5:35
   With Walter Piston: *Sonata*; Edgard Varèse: *Density 21.5*; Noël Lee: *Variations antiques*; Samuel Barber: *Canzone*; Aaron Copland: *Duo for Flute and Piano*

278. Bridge BCD 9044 (CD) (1994)

   Elliott Carter: Eight Compositions (1943–1993)
   The Group for Contemporary Music: Harvey Sollberger (fl)
   Recorded 20 May 1993, MasterSound, Astoria, NY
   5:55
   Producers: David Starobin, Michael Calvert
   Engineer: Ben Rizzi
   Notes by David Schiff
   With Elliott Carter: *Gra* (item 196); *Enchanted Preludes* (item 182); *Duo for Violin and Piano* (item 147); *Changes* (item 127); *Con leggerezza pensosa* (item 128); *Riconoscenza per Goffredo Petrassi* (item 359); *Sonata for Violoncello and Piano* (item 301)

279. Neuma 450-88 (CD) (1994)

   The Now and Present Flute
   Patricia Spencer (fl)
   Recorded 3–5 and 10 June 1993, State University of New York at Purchase
   5:47
   Notes by Patricia Spencer
   With George Perle: *Monody I*; Louise Talma: *Conversations*; Arthur Krieger: *Intimate Exchanges*; Pierre Boulez: *Sonatine for Flute and Piano*; Shirish Korde: *Tenderness of Cranes*; Stephen Jaffe: *Three Figures and a Ground*; Salvatore Martirano: *Phleu*

280. Skarbo D SK 4966

Kathleen Chastain (fl)

Shard

281. Bridge 9084 (CD) (1998)

David Starobin (guitar)
Recorded from June 1997 to February 1998
2:37
Producer: Becky Starobin
Engineer: David Merrill
Notes by David Starobin
With Stephen Jaffe: *Spinoff;* Jorge Morel: *Reflexiones Latinas;* Mario Lavista: *Natarayah;* William Bland: *Rag Nouveau;* Bent Sørensen: *Angelus Waltz;* John Anthony Lennon: *Gigolo;* Steve Mackey: *San Francisco Shuffle;* Richard Wernick: *Da'ase;* Apostolos Paraskevas: *Chase Dance;* John Duarte: *Valse en Rondeau;* Milton Babbitt: *Danci;* Michael Starobin; *The Snoid Trucks Up Broadway;* Jonathan Harvey: *Sufi Dance;* Per Nørgård: *Serenita;* Poul Ruders: *Chaconne;* Paul Lansky: *Crooked Courante;* Bryan Johanson: *Open Up Your Ears.*

Sonata for Flute, Oboe, Cello, and Harpsichord

282. Columbia ML 5576 (Mono lp) (1960)

Columbia MS 6176 (stereo lp) (1960)
Anabel Brieff (fl), Josef Marx (ob), Lorin Bernsohn (vc), Robert Conant (hps)
Recorded 16 May 1957
17:23
Notes by Michael Steinberg
With Harold Shapero: *String Quartet No. 1*

Reissued as item 283

283. Columbia CML 5576 (Mono lp) (1968)

Columbia CMS 6176 (stereo lp) (1968)

Also reissued as item 284

284. AMS 6176 (Stereo lp) (1974)

285. Decca DL 10108 (Mono lp) (1965)

   Decca DL 710108 (stereo lp) (1965)
   Samuel Baron (fl), Ronald Roseman (ob), Alexander Kouguell (vc), Sylvia Marlowe (hps)
   15:53
   Producer: Israel Horowitz
   Notes by Sylvia Marlowe
   With Manuel de Falla: *Concerto for Harpsichord, Flute, Oboe, Clarinet, Violin, and Cello;* Ned Rorem: *Lovers, a Narrative for Harpsichord, Oboe, 'Cello, and Percussion;* Henri Sauguet: *Suite royale*

   Reissued as item 286

286. Serenus SRS 12056 (Stereo lp) (1974)

   Sylvia Marlowe Plays Harpsichord Music of the 20th Century

287. Nonesuch H 71234 (Stereo lp) (1969)

   Harvey Sollberger (fl), Charles Kuskin (ob), Fred Sherry (vc), Paul Jacobs (hps)
   Recorded August 1968, Rutgers Presbyterian Church, New York
   15:30
   Recording Engineer: Marc J. Aubort
   Notes by Elliott Carter (item 505)
   With Elliott Carter: *Sonata for Violoncello and Piano* (item 295)

   Reissued as item 288

288. Elektra Nonesuch 79183-2 (CD) (1992)

   With Elliott Carter: *Sonata for Violoncello and Piano* (item 296); *Double Concerto* (item 144)

289. Deutsche Grammophon 2530 104 (Stereo lp) (1971)

   American Chamber Music

Boston Symphony Chamber Players: Doriot Anthony Dwyer (fl), Ralph Gomberg (ob), Jules Eskin (vc), Robert Levin (hps)
15:29
Producers: Karl Faust, Tom Mowrey
Engineer: Günter Hermanns
Notes by Sheila Keats
With Charles Ives: *Largo for Violin, Clarinet, and Piano;* Quincy Porter: *Quintet for Oboe and String Quartet*

290. New England Conservatory NEC 109 (Distributed by Golden Crest Records) (Stereo lp) (1975)

Contemporary American Music
New England Conservatory of Music Chamber Players: Jolie Troob (fl), Cheryl Priebe (ob), Gloria Johns (vc), Christopher Kies (hps), John Heiss (cond)
16:57
Notes by John Heiss
With Milton Babbitt: *Composition for 4 Instruments;* Igor Stravinsky: *Fanfare for Two Trumpets;* Henry Brant: *Angels and Devils*

291. Cedille CDR 90000 011 (CD) (1992)

20th Century Baroque
Rembrandt Chamber Players: Sandra Morgan (fl), Robert Morgan (ob), Barbara Haffner (vc), David Schrader (hps)
Recorded 19–23 December 1991, First United Methodist Church, Evanston, IL
15:54
Producer: James Ginsburg
Engineer: Bill Maylone
Notes by Anne Shreffler
With Dominick Argento: *Elizabethan Songs;* Manuel de Falla: *Concerto for Harpsichord, Flute, Oboe, Clarinet, Violin, and Cello;* Ilja Hurnik: *Sonata da camera*

291a. XCP 5016 (CD) 1993)

Musiques du XXe siècle

Quatuor Jean-Marie Leclair: Michael Raynié (fl), Daniel Thiery (ob), Yves Potrel (vc), Marie-Paule Nounou (hps)
Recorded December 1992, Salle Beracasa, Opéra Berlioz Le Corum, Montpellier
16:05
Producer: Laurent Cuniot
Engineer: Frédéric Muñoz
Notes by Jean-Pierre Bellan (French), Tessa Thiery-Ballard (English)
With Ilja Hurnik: *Sonata da Camera;* Jean Doué: *Séquences;* David Gow: *Harpsichord Quartet, op. 28;* Tristan Clais: *Le Clavecin libéré*

292. cpo 999 453-2 (CD) (1998)

Ensemble Contrasts: Michael Faust (fl), Christian Hommel (ob), Johannes Wohlmacher (vc), Ilton Wjuniski (hps)
Recorded October 1995, Hürth-Knapsack, Feierabendhaus der Hoechst AG; November 1995 and March 1996, Funkhaus Köln
16:00
Recording Supervisor: Stephan Hahn
Recording Engineers: Franz-Peter Esser, Mark Hohn, Christian Meurer
With Elliott Carter: *Woodwind Quintet* (item 398); *Esprit rude/Esprit doux* (item 189); *Eight Etudes and a Fantasy* (item 161); *Enchanted Preludes* (item 183)

Sonata for Violoncello and Piano

293. American Recording Society ARS 25 (Mono lp) (1952)

Bernard Greenhouse (vc), Anthony Makas (pno)
20:59
With Elliott Carter: *Piano Sonata* (item 255)

Reissued as item 294

294. Desto D 419 (Mono lp) (1965)

Desto DST 419 (mono lp, electronically altered to simulate stereo) (1965)

295. Nonesuch H 71234 (Stereo lp) (1969)

  Joel Krosnick (vc), Paul Jacobs (pno)
  Recorded August 1968, Rutgers Presbyterian Church, New York
  21:27
  Coordinated by Teresa Sterne
  Recording Engineer: Marc J. Aubort
  Notes by Elliott Carter (item 505)
  With Elliott Carter: *Sonata for Flute, Oboe, Cello, and Harpsichord* (item 287)

  Reissued as item 296

296. Elektra Nonesuch 79183-2 (CD) (1992)

  With Elliott Carter: *Sonata for Flute, Oboe, Cello, and Harpsichord* (item 288); *Double Concerto* (item 144)

297. Golden Crest RE 7081 (Stereo lp) (1979)

  The Art of Michael Rudiakov
  Michael Rudiakov (vc), Ursula Oppens (pno)
  20:48
  With J. S. Bach: *Suite No. 1*, S. 1007

298. Finlandia FACD 362 (CD) (1988)

  Contemporary Music for Cello and Piano
  Anssi Karttunen (vc), Tuija Hakkila (pno)
  Recorded September–December 1987, Järvenpää Hall, Järvenpää, Finland
  21:15
  Notes by Anssi Karttunen
  With Jouni Kaipainen: *Trois morceaux de l'aube*, op. 15; Edison Denisov: *Cello Sonata;* Paavo Heininen: *Serenade*, op. 31, no. 1; Erik Bergman: *Quo vadis*, op. 102

299. Musikproduktion Dabringhaus und Grimm MD+G L 3397 (CD) (1992)

  Cellosonaten von 1948
  Tilmann Wick (vc), Heasook Rhee (pno)

Recorded March 1992, Fürstliche Reitbahn, Arolsen
21:27
With Nikolai Miaskovsky: *Sonata for Violoncello and Piano No. 2*, op. 81; Francis Poulenc: *Sonata for Violoncello and Piano*

300. Boston Records BR1006 (CD) (1994)

    Anthony Ross (vc), Evelyne Brancart (pno)
    Recorded 2 September 1992, Indiana University
    23:33
    Notes by Steven Ledbetter
    With Sergei Rachmaninoff: *Sonata in G Minor*, op. 19

301. Bridge BCD 9044 (CD) (1994)

    Elliott Carter: Eight Compositions (1943–1993)
    The Group for Contemporary Music: Fred Sherry (vc), Charles Wuorinen (pno)
    Recorded 10 November 1992, MasterSound, Astoria, NY
    19:55
    Producers: David Starobin, Michael Calvert
    Engineer: Ben Rizzi
    Notes by David Schiff
    With Elliott Carter: *Gra* (item 196); *Enchanted Preludes* (item 182); *Duo for Violin and Piano* (item 147); *Scrivo in vento* (item 278); *Changes* (item 127); *Con leggerezza pensosa* (item 128); *Riconoscenza per Goffredo Petrassi* (item 359)

302. Tall Poppies TP032 (CD) (1994)

    Prokofiev & Carter
    David Pereira (vc), Lisa Moore (pno)
    Recorded January 1993
    21:31
    With Sergei Prokofiev: *Sonata in C major for cello and piano*, op. 119

303. Centaur CRC 2267 (CD) (1996)

    Rhonda Rider (vc), Lois Shapiro (pno)
    Recorded 3–4 August 1993, Campion Center, Weston, MA

22:01
Notes by Allen Anderson
With Samuel Barber: *Sonata for Violoncello and Piano*, op. 6; Seymour Shifrin: *Sonata for Violoncello and Piano*

304. Arabesque Z 6682 (CD) (1996)

> *In the Shadow of World War II*
> Joel Krosnick (vc), Gilbert Kalish (pno)
> Recorded 19–21 December 1995, Purchase Conservatory of Music Recital Hall
> 22:00
> With Sergei Prokofiev: *Sonata for Violoncello and Piano in C major*, op. 119; Francis Poulenc: *Sonata for Violoncello and Piano*

305. Auvidis Montaigne MO 782091 (CD) (1998)

> Rohan de Saram (vc), Ursula Oppens (pno)
> Recorded 15–19 July 1996, All Saints Church, London
> 21:18
> Recording Supervisor: François Eckert
> Sound Engineer: Bob Harrison
> Notes by Bayan Northcott
> With Elliott Carter: *String Quartet No. 5* (item 325); *90+* (item 114); *Figment* (item 194); *Fragment* (item 195); *Duo for Violin and Piano* (item 149)

Sonata for Piano

See *Piano Sonata*

String Quartet No. 1

306. Columbia ML 5104 (Mono lp) (1956)

> Walden Quartet of the University of Illinois: Homer Schmitt (vn I), Bernard Goodman (vn II), John Garvey (va), Robert Swenson (vc)
> Recorded 2 February 1955
> 39:41

Notes by Elliott Carter, William Glock
With [no other works]
Reissued as item 307

307. Columbia CML 5104 (Mono lp) (1968)

Also reissued as item 308

308. Columbia AML 5104 (Mono lp) (1974)

309. Nonesuch H 71249 (Stereo lp) (1970)

Nonesuch NON 32803 (stereo lp) (reviewed August 1975) (France)
Elektra Nonesuch 71249-2 (CD) [after 1983]
The Composers String Quartet: Matthew Raimondi (vn I), Anahid Ajemian (vn II), Jean Dupouy (va), Michael Rudiakov (vc)
Recorded 21–23 April 1970
37:41
Coordinated by Teresa Sterne
Engineering: Marc J. Aubort, Joanna Nickrenz
Notes by Elliott Carter (item 506)
With Elliott Carter: *String Quartet No. 2* (item 313)

310. Etcetera KTC 1065 (CD) (1988)

Elliott Carter: The Works for String Quartet Vol. I: String Quartets 1 + 4
The Arditti String Quartet: Irvine Arditti (vn I), David Alberman (vn II), Levine Andrade (va), Rohan de Saram (vc)
Recorded June 1988, St. Silas Church, Kentish Town, London
38:03
Producer: Roy Emerson
Engineer: Martin Haskell
Notes by David Harvey
With Elliott Carter: *String Quartet No. 4* (item 322)

311. Sony Classical S2K 47229 (2 CD) (1991)

> The Juilliard String Quartet: Robert Mann (vn I), Joel Smirnoff (vn II), Samuel Rhodes (va), Joel Krosnick (vc)
> Recorded 8–10 December 1990, American Academy and Institute of Arts and Letters, New York, NY
> 41:45
> Producer: Gary Schultz
> Engineer: Charles Harbutt
> Notes by Elliott Carter, Robert P. Morgan, and Leonard Stein and Peter Zaferes
> With Elliott Carter: *String Quartet No. 2* (item 316); *String Quartet No. 3* (item 321); *String Quartet No. 4* (item 324); *Duo for Violin and Piano* (item 146)

String Quartet No. 2

312. RCA Victor LM 2481 (Mono lp) (1961)

> RCA Victor LSC 2481 (stereo lp) (1961)
> The Juilliard String Quartet: Robert Mann (vn I), Isidore Cohen (vn II), Raphael Hillyer (va), Claus Adam (vc)
> 21:20
> Producer: Peter Dellheim
> Recording Engineer: Allan Ballentine
> Notes by Michael Steinberg
> With William Schuman: *String Quartet No. 3*

313. Nonesuch H 71249 (Stereo lp) (1970)

> Nonesuch NON 32803 (stereo lp) (reviewed August 1975) (France)
> Elektra Nonesuch 71249-2 (CD)
> The Composers String Quartet: Matthew Raimondi (vn I), Anahid Ajemian (vn II), Jean Dupouy (va), Michael Rudiakov (vc)
> Recorded 21–23 April 1970
> 19:55
> Coordinator: Teresa Sterne
> Engineering: Marc J. Aubort, Joanna Nickrenz
> Notes by Elliott Carter (item 506)
> With Elliott Carter: *String Quartet No. 1* (item 309)

Discography of Commercial Recordings

314. Columbia M 32738 (Stereo lp) (1974)

    Columbia MQ 32738 (quadraphonic lp) (1974)
    The Juilliard String Quartet: Robert Mann (vn I), Earl Carlyss (vn II), Raphael Hillyer (va), Claus Adam (vc)
    Recorded 19–20 February 1969
    21:25
    Producer: Richard Killough
    Engineers: Fred Plaut, Edward T. Graham, Raymond Moore
    Notes by Robert Hurwitz with quotations from Elliott Carter
    With Elliott Carter: *String Quartet No. 3* (item 317)

315. Etcetera KTC 1066 (CD) (1988)

    Elliott Carter: The Works for String Quartet Vol. II: Quartets 2 & 3, Elegy
    The Arditti String Quartet: Irvine Arditti (vn I), David Alberman (vn II), Levine Andrade (va), Rohan de Saram (vc)
    Recorded June 1988, St. Silas Church, Kentish Town, London
    20:08
    Producer: Roy Emerson
    Engineer: Martin Haskell
    Notes by David Harvey
    With Elliott Carter: *String Quartet No. 3* (item 320); *Elegy* (item 167)

316. Sony Classical S2K 47229 (2 CD) (1991)

    The Juilliard String Quartet: Robert Mann (vn I), Joel Smirnoff (vn II), Samuel Rhodes (va), Joel Krosnick (vc)
    Recorded 28 May–15 June 1991, American Academy and Institute of Arts and Letters, New York, NY
    23:17
    Producer: Gary Schultz
    Engineer: Charles Harbutt
    Notes by Elliott Carter, Robert P. Morgan, and Leonard Stein and Peter Zaferes
    With Elliott Carter: *String Quartet No. 1* (item 311); *String Quartet No. 3* (item 321); *String Quartet No. 4* (item 324); *Duo for Violin and Piano* (item 146)

String Quartet No. 3

317. Columbia M 32738 (Stereo lp) (1974)

    Columbia MQ 32738 (quadraphonic lp) (1974)
    The Juilliard String Quartet: Robert Mann (vn I), Earl Carlyss (vn II), Samuel Rhodes (va), Claus Adam (vc)
    Recorded 19–21 November 1973
    21:32
    Producer: Jay David Saks
    Engineers: Fred Plaut, Edward T. Graham, Raymond Moore
    Notes by Robert Hurwitz with quotations from Elliott Carter
    With Elliott Carter: *String Quartet No. 2* (item 314)

318. Musical Heritage Society MHS 4876 (Stereo lp) (1983)

    The Composers String Quartet: Matthew Raimondi (vn I), Anahid Ajemian (vn II), Jean Dane (va), Mark Shuman (vc)
    Recorded at Vanguard Sound Studio, New York, NY
    19:19
    Notes by David Schiff
    With Elliott Carter: *Eight Etudes and a Fantasy* (item 154)

319. RCA Red Seal RS 9006 (Stereo lp) (1983)

    Arditti String Quartet
    Recorded February 1982, Henry Wood Hall, London
    Notes by David Schiff
    With Brian Ferneyhough: *Quartet No. 2;* Jonathan Harvey: *Quartet No. 2*

320. Etcetera KTC 1066 (CD) (1988)

    Elliott Carter: The Works for String Quartet Vol. II: Quartets 2 & 3, Elegy
    The Arditti String Quartet: Irvine Arditti (vn I), David Alberman (vn II), Levine Andrade (va), Rohan de Saram (vc)
    Recorded June 1988, St. Silas Church, Kentish Town, London
    20:12
    Producer: Roy Emerson
    Engineer: Martin Haskell
    Notes by David Harvey

With Elliott Carter: *String Quartet No. 2* (item 315); *Elegy* (item 167)

321. Sony Classical S2K 47229 (2 CD) (1991)

    The Juilliard String Quartet: Robert Mann (vn I), Joel Smirnoff (vn II), Samuel Rhodes (va), Joel Krosnick (vc)
    Recorded 28 May–15 June 1991, American Academy and Institute of Arts and Letters, New York, NY
    21:15
    Producer: Gary Schultz
    Engineer: Charles Harbutt
    Notes by Elliott Carter, Robert P. Morgan, and Leonard Stein and Peter Zaferes
    With Elliott Carter: *String Quartet No. 1* (item 311); *String Quartet No. 2* (item 316); *String Quartet No. 4* (item 324); *Duo for Violin and Piano* (item 146)

String Quartet No. 4

322. Etcetera KTC 1065 (CD) (1988)

    Elliott Carter: The Works for String Quartet Vol. I: String Quartets 1 + 4
    The Arditti String Quartet: Irvine Arditti (vn I), David Alberman (vn II), Levine Andrade (va), Rohan de Saram (vc)
    Recorded June 1988, St. Silas Church, Kentish Town, London
    20:47
    Producer: Roy Emerson
    Engineer: Martin Haskell
    Notes by David Harvey
    With Elliott Carter: *String Quartet No. 1* (item 310)

323. Music & Arts CD 606 (CD) (1990)

    The Composers String Quartet: Matthew Raimondi (vn I), Anahid Ajemian (vn II), Maureen Gallagher (va), Mark Shuman (vc)
    Recorded 1988, State University of New York at Purchase
    24:34
    Producer/Engineer: Judith Sherman

Notes by Aaron Copland, Elliott Carter
With Milton Babbitt: *Fifth String Quartet;* Mel Powell: *String Quartet 1982*

324. Sony Classical S2K 47229 (2 CD) (1991)

   The Juilliard String Quartet: Robert Mann (vn I), Joel Smirnoff (vn II), Samuel Rhodes (va), Joel Krosnick (vc)
   Recorded 28 May–15 June 1991, American Academy and Institute of Arts and Letters, New York, NY
   28:53
   Producer: Gary Schultz
   Engineer: Charles Harbutt
   Notes by Elliott Carter, Robert P. Morgan, and Leonard Stein and Peter Zaferes
   With Elliott Carter: *String Quartet No. 1* (item 311); *String Quartet No. 2* (item 316); *String Quartet No. 3* (item 321); *Duo for Violin and Piano* (item 146)

String Quartet No. 5

325. Auvidis Montaigne MO 782091 (CD) (1998)

   Arditti String Quartet: Irvine Arditti (vn I), Graeme Jennings (vn II), Garth Knox (vla), Rohan de Saram (vc)
   Recorded 15–19 July 1996, All Saints Church, London
   20:26
   Recording Supervisor: François Eckert
   Sound Engineer: Bob Harrison
   Notes by Bayan Northcott
   With Elliott Carter: *Sonata for Violoncello and Piano* (item 305); *90+* (item 114); *Figment* (item 194); *Fragment* (item 195); *Duo for Violin and Piano* (item 149)

Symphonia—Sum Fluxae Pretiam Spei

1. *Partita*
2. *Adagio tenebroso*
3. *Allegro scorrevole*

326. 1. Only

Teldec 4509-99596-2 (CD) (1995)
Chicago Symphony Orchestra, Daniel Barenboim (cond)
Recorded 1 June 1994, WDR (Westdeutscher Rundfunk) Köln
16:43
Recording Producer: Otto Nielen
Engineer: Christoph Gronarz
Notes by Elliott Carter, Phillip Huscher
With Luciano Berio: *Continuo;* Toru Takemitsu: *Visions*

Symphony No. 1

327. The Louisville Orchestra First Edition Records LOU 611 (Mono lp) (1961)

   The Louisville Orchestra, Robert Whitney (cond)
   26:30
   Notes by Elliott Carter
   With Alexei Haieff: *Divertimento*

328. CRI SD 475 (Stereo lp) (1982)

   Elliott Carter: The Early Music
   American Composers Orchestra, Paul Dunkel (cond)
   Recorded February 1982, Walt Whitman Auditorium, Brooklyn College, Brooklyn, NY
   25:12
   Producer: Carter Harman
   Recorded by David Hancock
   Notes by David Schiff
   With Elliott Carter: *Holiday Overture* (item 210); *Pocahontas* (suite from the ballet) (item 274)

   Reissued as:

329. CRI ACS 6003 (Stereo Cassette) (1985)

   Music of Elliott Carter
   Notes by David Schiff

With Elliott Carter: *Syringa* (item 334); *Holiday Overture* (item 211)

Also reissued as:

330. CRI CD 552 (CD) (1988)

Notes by Susan Feder
With Francis Thorne: *Symphony No. 5;* Nicolas Roussakis: *Fire and Earth and Water and Air*

A Symphony of Three Orchestras

331. Columbia M 35171 (Stereo lp) (1980)

CBS Masterworks 76812
New York Philharmonic, Pierre Boulez (cond)
Recorded 22 February 1977, Avery Fisher Hall, New York, NY
15:42
Producer: Andrew Kazdin
Engineers: Bud Graham, Milt Cherin, Larry Keyes
Notes by Elliott Carter
With Elliott Carter: *A Mirror on Which to Dwell* (item 222)

Reissued as item 332

332. Sony Classical SMK 68 334 (CD) (1995)

Producer/Engineer: Bejun Mehta
Notes by Robert Adelson
With Edgard Varèse: *Déserts; Ecuatorial; Hyperprism*

Syringa

333. CRI SD 469 (Stereo lp) (1982)

Music of Elliott Carter
Jan DeGaetani (ms), Thomas Paul (bar), Speculum Musicae, the Group for Contemporary Music, Harvey Sollberger (cond)

Recorded 11–13 May 1981, Holy Trinity Episcopal Church, New York, NY
20:00
Producer: Carter Harman
Recorded by David Hancock
Notes by Elliott Carter; David Schiff
With Elliott Carter: *Concerto for Orchestra* (item 131)

Reissued as item 334

334. CRI ACS 6003 (Stereo Cassette) (1985)

Music of Elliott Carter
Notes by David Schiff
With Elliott Carter: *Holiday Overture* (item 211); *Symphony No. 1* (item 329)

Also reissued as item 335

335. CRI CD 610 (CD) (1991)

Notes by David Schiff, Elliott Carter
With Elliott Carter: *Holiday Overture* (item 212); *Pocahontas* (suite from the ballet) (item 275)

336. Bridge BCD 9014 (CD) (1989)

Elliott Carter: The Vocal Works (1975–1981)
Katherine Ciesinski (ms), Jan Opalach (bbar), Speculum Musicae, William Purvis (cond)
Recorded 5–6 December 1988, MasterSound, Astoria, NY
18:53
Producer: Judith Sherman
Engineer: Paul Zinman
Notes by Lloyd Schwartz
With Elliott Carter: *Three Poems of Robert Frost* (item 354); *A Mirror on Which to Dwell* (item 223); *In Sleep, in Thunder* (item 215)

Tarantella

337. Carillon 118 (Mono lp) (1961)

> *Harvard in Song*
> Harvard Glee Club, Elliot Forbes (cond)

338. GSS Recordings GSS 103 (Stereo lp) (1984)

> The Gregg Smith Singers, Paul Suits (pno), Jerald Stone (pno)
> Recorded May 1982, Central Islip High School Auditorium, Islip, NY
> 5:19
> Producer: Raymond Marunas
> Engineer: David Hancock
> With Elliott Carter: *Emblems* (item 175); *The Harmony of Morning* (item 198); *Heart Not So Heavy As Mine* (item 205); *Musicians Wrestle Everywhere* (item 227); *To Music* (item 364); *The Defense of Corinth* (item 137)
>
> Reissued as item 339

339. CRI CD 648 (CD) (1993)

> Producer: Gregg Smith
> Notes by Gregg Smith and Joseph R. Dalton, Elliott Carter
> With Elliott Carter: *Warble for Lilac Time* (item 383); *Voyage* (item 379); *Three Poems of Robert Frost* (item 355); *Emblems* (item 176); *The Harmony of Morning* (item 199); *Heart Not So Heavy As Mine* (item 206); *Musicians Wrestle Everywhere* (item 228); *To Music* (item 365); *The Defense of Corinth* (item 138)

340. Koch International Classics 3-7415-2H1 (CD) (1998)

> John Oliver Chorale, Martin Amlin (pno), Frank Corliss (pno), John Oliver (music director)
> Recorded May 1997, Emmanuel Church, Boston, MA
> 5:41
> Producer: Susan Napodano DelGiorno
> Engineer: Silas Brown
> Notes by Elliott Carter, Steven Ledbetter

Discography of Commercial Recordings 139

With Elliott Carter: *To Music* (item 366); *Harvest Home* (item 202); *Emblems* (item 178); *Let's Be Gay* (item 216); *Heart Not So Heavy As Mine* (item 208); *The Defense of Corinth* (item 139); *The Harmony of Morning* (item 201); *Musicians Wrestle Everywhere* (item 231)

Tell Me Where Is Fancy Bred?

341. Columbia MC 6 (12 Mono 12" 78 rpm) (1938)

    [unidentified] (alto), [unidentified] (gui)
    From the Orson Welles Mercury Theatre production of William Shakespeare's *The Merchant of Venice*

342. Turnabout TV 34727 (Stereo lp) (1978)

    20th Century Music for Voice and Guitar
    Rosalind Rees (sop), David Starobin (gui)
    Recorded 1976, American Academy of Arts and Letters
    3:24
    Notes by William Bland
    With William Schuman: *Orpheus with His Lute*; Andrew Imbrie: *Tell Me, Where Is Fancy Bred?*; Harold Blumenfeld: *Rilke*; Lou Harrison: *Serenade*; Igor Stravinsky: *Four Songs*; William Bland: *Song for David*; Barbara Kolb: *The Sentences*; John Cage: *The Wonderful Widow of Eighteen Springs*; Gregg Smith: *Steps*

    Reissued as item 343

343. Vox Box CDX 5145 (2 CD) (1995)

    20th Century Voices in America
    With George Rochberg: *Tableaux; Quartet No. 2 for Soprano and Strings*; John Cage: *The Wonderful Widow of Eighteen Springs*; William Schuman: *Orpheus and His Lute*; Andrew Imbrie: *Tell Me Where Is Fancy Bred*; Harold Blumenfeld: *Rilke*; Gregg Smith: *Steps*; Barbara Kolb: *The Sentences*; Shulamit Ran: *O the Chimneys*

Three Occasions for Orchestra

1. A Celebration of Some 100 × 150 Notes
2. Remembrance
3. Anniversary

344. Virgin Classics VC 7 91503-2 (CD) (1992)

London Sinfonietta, Oliver Knussen (cond)
Recorded 3 June 1991, Blackheath Concert Hall
3:13 (1); 5:49 (2); 6:57 (3)
Producers: Oliver Knussen with Colin Matthews
Balance Engineer: Tryggvi Tryggvason
Notes by Elliott Carter, Oliver Knussen, Bayan Northcott
With Elliott Carter: *Concerto for Orchestra* (item 133); *Violin Concerto* (item 377)

345. Arte Nova Classics 74321 2773 2 (CD) (1995)

SWF Symphony Orchestra, Michael Gielen (cond)
Recorded 4 May 1992, Grande Auditório Gulbekian, Lisbon, Portugal
3:32 (1); 6:31 (2); 6:57 (3)
Producing Engineer: Helmut Hanusch
Sound Engineer: Madeira Neves (Radio Portugal)
Notes by Stefan Lipka
With Elliott Carter: *Piano Concerto* (item 254); *Concerto for Orchestra* (item 134)

346. 1. Only

EMI CDM 566 1372
Leaving Home, Vol. 2
City of Birmingham Symphony Orchestra, Simon Rattle (cond)
Recorded 1995

Three Poems of Robert Frost
(version for voice and piano)

1. "Dust of Snow"
2. "The Rose Family"
3. "The Line Gang"

Discography of Commercial Recordings 141

347. 1. and 2. Only

Hargail HN 708 (mono 10" 78 rpm) (1947)
American Songs
William Hess (ten), Robert Fizdale (pno)
With Theodore Chanler: *The Doves; Three Epitaphs*

348. Unicorn RHS 253 (Stereo lp) (1978)

Unicorn UN1-72017 (stereo lp) (1978)
An American Anthology
Meriel Dickinson (ms), Peter Dickinson (pno)
Recorded 28 March 1977, All Saints Church, Petersham, Surrey, England
4:40
With Elliott Carter: *Voyage* (item 378); George Gershwin: *I Got Rhythm; A Foggy Day in London Town; They All Laughed;* Aaron Copland: *In Evening Air; Night Thoughts; Poet's Song;* Virgil Thomson: *Two by Marianne Moore; Portrait of F. B. (Francis Blood);* John Cage: *Five Songs*

349. 1. and 2. Only

Elektra Nonesuch 79178-2 (CD) (1988)
Songs of America: On Home, Love, Nature, and Death
Jan DeGaetani (ms), Gilbert Kalish (pno)
Recorded 21–23 December 1987, American Academy and Institute of Arts and Letters, New York, NY
2:12
With Stephen Foster: *Beautiful Child of Song;* Charles Wakefield Cadman: *The Moon Drops Low* (from *Four American Indian Songs);* Ruth Crawford: *Home Thoughts; White Moon; Joy;* Milton Babbitt: *The Widow's Lament in Springtime;* Warren Benson: *American Primitive* (from *Three Solitary Songs*); George Crumb: *The Sleeper;* Irving Fine: *My Father* (from *Mutability*); Carrie Jacobs-Bond: *Nothin' but Love; I Love You Truly; Her Greatest Charm;* Sergius Kagen: *The Junk Man;* Mario Davidovsky: *Lost;* John Cage: *Little Four Paws;* William Schuman: *Dozing on the Lawn* (from *Time to the Old);* Charles Ives: *She Is Not Fair; The All-Enduring; Sunrise;* Rebecca Clarke: *Lethe;*

Ned Rorem: *Interlude* (from *Poems of Love and the Rain*); Samuel Adler: *Time, You Old Gypsy Man*; Stanley Walden: *Grandma (Millie)* (from *Suite, Three Ladies*); Aaron Jay Kernis: *Stein × Seven*, no. 6; William Bolcom: *Waitin'* (from *Cabaret Songs*); Aaron Copland: *There Came a Wind Like a Bugle* (from *Twelve Poems of Emily Dickinson*)

Reissued as item 350

350. Elektra Nonesuch 79248-2 (CD) (1990)

Producer: Teresa Sterne
Engineer/Musical Production: Max Wilcox
Notes by Lloyd Schwartz
With Elliott Carter: *The Minotaur* (item 218); *Piano Sonata* (item 263)

351. 1. and 2. Only

Albany TROY 081 (CD) (1993)
Paul Sperry Sings an American Sampler from Billings to Bolcom
Paul Sperry (ten), Irma Vallecillo (pno)
Notes by Paul Sperry
With Louise Talma: *Pied Beauty; Leap before You Look; Rain Song*; William Schuman: *Orpheus with His Lute*; Hugo Weisgall: *My Sweet Old Etcetera*; Morton Lauridsen: *When Frost Moves Fast; And What of Love?*; Kurt Weill: *Dirge for Two Veterans*; Celius Dougherty: *Love in the Dictionary; The Bird and the Beast*; Ben Weber: *Mourn, Mourn*; William Bolcom: *George; Waitin'*; John Duke: *Bells in the Rain*; William Flanagan: *Horror Movie*; Henry Cowell: *Who Wrote This Fiendish "Rite of Spring"?*; John Musto: *Shadow of the Blues*; Robert Beaser: *Quicksilver*; Ned Rorem: *For Poulenc; Spring*; Samuel Barber: *Solitary Hotel*; Charles Griffes: *The Lament of Ian the Proud*; William Billings: *David's Lamentation* (arr. Elie Siegmeister); Stephen Foster: *No One to Love* (arr. Warren Swenson); Warren Swenson: *The Lepidoptera Waltz*; Maury Yeston: *I Don't Wanna Rock and Roll*.

Discography of Commercial Recordings 143

352. Music & Arts CD900 (CD) (1995)

Three Modern American Song Cycles
Phyllis Bryn-Julson (sop), Mark Markham (pno)
Recorded 7–9 June 1994, State University of New York at Purchase
1:06 (1); 0:58 (2); 1:35 (3)
Notes by Louis Karchin
With Elliott Carter: *Voyage* (item 381); *Warble for Lilac Time* (item 384); Charles Wuorinen: *A Winter's Tale*; Gunther Schuller: *Six Early Songs*

353. Koch International Classics 3-7425-2-H1 (CD) (1997)

Lucy Shelton (sop), John Constable (pno)
Recorded 18–20 May 1996, All Saints Church, Petersham, England
1:22 (1); 1:14 (2); 2:12 (3)
Producer and Engineer: Tryggvi Tryggvason
Notes by Richard Wilson
With Elliott Carter: *Warble for Lilac Time* (item 385); *Voyage* (item 382); *Of Challenge and of Love* (item 244); Igor Stravinsky: *Storm–Cloud; Two Songs on Poems of Gorodetsky*, op. 6; *Pastorale; Two Poems of Konstantin Balmont; Three Little Songs: Recollections of Childhood; Berceuse; Three Tales for Children; Four Russian Songs; Russian Maiden's Song; The Owl and the Pussy-Cat*

Three Poems of Robert Frost
(version for voice and chamber orchestra)

1. "Dust of Snow"
2. "The Rose Family"
3. "The Line Gang"

354. Bridge BCD 9014 (CD) (1989)

Elliott Carter: The Vocal Works (1975–1981)
Patrick Mason (bar), Speculum Musicae, David Starobin (cond)
Recorded 21 October 1987, RCA Studio A, New York, NY

1:22 (1); 1:20 (2); 2:00 (3)
Producer: Judith Sherman
Engineer: Joe Lopes
Notes by Lloyd Schwartz
With Elliott Carter: *A Mirror on Which to Dwell* (item 223); *Syringa* (item 336); *In Sleep, in Thunder* (item 215)

355. CRI CD 648 (CD) (1993)

Rosalind Rees (sop), Adirondack Chamber Orchestra, Gregg Smith (cond)
Recorded 3–4 August 1982, St. Agnes Catholic Church, Lake Placid, NY
4:40
Producer: Gregg Smith
Recording Engineer: David Hancock
Notes by Gregg Smith and Joseph R. Dalton, Elliott Carter
With Elliott Carter: *Warble for Lilac Time* (item 383); *Voyage* (item 379); *Tarantella* (item 339); *Emblems* (item 176); *The Harmony of Morning* (item 199); *Heart Not So Heavy As Mine* (item 206); *Musicians Wrestle Everywhere* (item 228); *To Music* (item 365); *The Defense of Corinth* (item 138)

Three Recollections

1. *Statement—Remembering Aaron*
2. *Riconoscenza per Goffredo Petrassi*
3. *Fantasy—Remembering Roger*

356. 2. Only

New World Records NW 333 (stereo lp) (1986)
New World Records 80333-2 (CD) (1997)
Hidden Sparks
Maryvonne Le Dizes-Richard (vn)
Recorded January 1985, IRCAM (Institut de Recherche et Coordination Acoustique/Musique) Centre Georges Pompidou, Paris
4:28
Producer: Elizabeth Ostrow

Recording Engineer: Didier Arditi
Notes by Tim Page
With Tod Machover: *Hidden Sparks;* Ralph Shapey: *Fantasy for Violin and Piano;* John Melby: *Concerto for Violin and Computer-Synthesized Tape*

357. 2. Only

ECM New Series 1391 (839 617-2) (CD) (1990)
Hansheinz Schneeberger (vn)
Recorded April 1989, Radio DRS, Studio Zürich
4:25
Producer: Manfred Eicher
Recording Engineer: Peter Laenger
Notes by Heinz Holliger, Wolfgang Sandner
With Elliott Carter: *Esprit rude/Esprit doux* (item 187); *Enchanted Preludes* (item 181); *Triple Duo* (item 371); J. S. Bach: *Suite No. 3 for Violoncello Solo*

358. 2. Only

Neuma 450-81 (CD) (1993)
New Music Series Vol. 3
Carol Lieberman (vn)
6:07
Producer: Shirish Korde
With Harvey Sollberger: *Riding the Wind II, III, IV;* Pozzi Escot: *Visione;* Andrew Imbrie: *Short Story;* Robert Carl: *Time/Memory/Shadow;* Thomas Delio: *Contrecoup . . .*

359. 2. Only

Bridge BCD 9044 (CD) (1994)
Elliott Carter: Eight Compositions (1943–1993)
The Group for Contemporary Music: Rolf Schulte (vn)
Recorded 10 November 1992, MasterSound, Astoria, NY
6:30
Producers: David Starobin, Michael Calvert
Engineer: Ben Rizzi
Notes by David Schiff
With Elliott Carter: *Gra* (item 196); *Enchanted Preludes* (item 182); *Duo for Violin and Piano* (item 147); *Scrivo in vento*

(item 278); *Changes* (item 127); *Con leggerezza pensosa* (item 128); *Sonata for Violoncello and Piano* (item 301)

360. 2. Only

Auvidis Montaigne MO 789003 (CD) (1995)
Solo Violin
Irvine Arditti (vn)
Recorded 28–29 January 1989, Conservatoire de Musique, Liège, Belgium
4:10
Notes by Philippe Albera
With Franco Donatoni: *Argot;* Julio Estrada: *Canto oculto;* Brian Ferneyhough: *Intermedio alla ciaccona;* James Dillon: *Del cuarto elemento;* Luis de Pablo: *Il violino spagnolo*

361. 2. Only

Victoria VCD 19094 (CD) (1996)
Contemporary Music from America
Ole Böhn (vn)
Recorded December 1995, Jar Church
5:56
Recording Producer: Arne-Peter Rognan
Recording Engineers: Anita Jenstad, Robert Smits
With Elliott Carter: *Duo for Violin and Piano* (item 148); Walter Piston: *Sonata;* Ruth Crawford: *Sonata;* Noël Lee: *Trièdre.*

362. 2. Only

CRI CD 706 (CD) (1996)
Songs of Solitude
Curtis Macomber (vn)
Recorded 10 May 1991, 5 February 1993, and 19–22 February 1995, Recital Hall, Music Division, State University of New York at Purchase
4:36
Producer and Engineer: Judith Sherman
Notes by Eric Salzman
With Shulamit Ran: *Inscriptions;* Mario Davidovsky: *Synchronisms No. 9;* John Harbison: *Four Songs of Solitude;*

Steven R. Gerber: *Fantasy; Three Songs without Words;*
Robert Parris: *Sonata for Violin Solo*

To Music

363. New World NW 219 (Stereo lp) (1977)

   New World 80219 (CD) (1996)
   Americana
   University of Michigan Chamber Choir, Thomas Hilbish (cond)
   Recorded at Hill Auditorium, University of Michigan, Ann Arbor, MI
   9:01
   Producer: Andrew Raeburn
   Engineer: Stan Tonkel
   Notes by Robert Morgan
   With Randall Thompson: *Americana;* Seymour Shifrin: *The Odes of Shang*

364. GSS Recordings GSS 103 (Stereo lp) (1984)

   The Gregg Smith Singers, Rosalind Rees (sop), Gregg Smith (cond)
   Recorded 1983, Holy Trinity Episcopal Church, New York, NY
   7:17
   Producer: Raymond Marunas
   Engineer: David Hancock
   With Elliott Carter: *Tarantella* (item 338); *Emblems* (item 175); *The Harmony of Morning* (item 198); *Heart Not So Heavy As Mine* (item 205); *Musicians Wrestle Everywhere* (item 227); *The Defense of Corinth* (item 137)

   Reissued as item 365

365. CRI CD 648 (CD) (1993)

   Producer: Gregg Smith
   Notes by Gregg Smith and Joseph R. Dalton, Elliott Carter
   With Elliott Carter: *Warble for Lilac Time* (item 383); *Voyage* (item 379); *Three Poems of Robert Frost* (item 355); *Taran-*

tella (item 339); *Emblems* (item 176); *The Harmony of Morning* (item 199); *Heart Not So Heavy As Mine* (item 206); *Musicians Wrestle Everywhere* (item 228); *The Defense of Corinth* (item 138)

366. Koch International Classics 3-7415-2H1 (CD) (1998)

    John Oliver Chorale, Annette Anfinrud (sop), John Oliver (music director)
    Recorded May 1997, Emmanuel Church, Boston, MA
    8:28
    Producer: Susan Napodano DelGiorno
    Engineer: Silas Brown
    Notes by Elliott Carter, Steven Ledbetter
    With Elliott Carter: *Tarantella* (item 340); *Harvest Home* (item 202); *Emblems* (item 178); *Let's Be Gay* (item 216); *Heart Not So Heavy As Mine* (item 208); *The Defense of Corinth* (item 139); *The Harmony of Morning* (item 201); *Musicians Wrestle Everywhere* (item 231)

Trilogy

1. Bariolage
2. Inner Song
3. Immer neu

367. 2. Only

    Auvidis Montaigne MO 782048 (CD) (1996)
    For Stefan Wolpe
    Ensemble Recherche: Peter Veale (ob)
    Recorded January–September 1992 and January 1993, WDR (Westdeutscher Rundfunk) Köln
    5:58
    With Stefan Wolpe: *Piece for Two Instrumental Units; Form for Piano; Form IV: Broken Sequences for Piano; Drei kleinere Canons*, op. 24a; *Three Canons for String Trio; Seven Pieces for Three Pianos*; Morton Feldman: *Extensions 4 for Three Pianos*; John Cage: *Five[4]—In Memory of Stefan Wolpe* (two realizations); Johannes Schöllhorn: *About the Seventh*

368. Philips 445 095-2 (CD) (1997)

> *Inner Song*
> Heinz Holliger (ob), Ursula Holliger (hp)
> Recorded December 1993, La Musica Théâtre, La Chaux-de-Fonds, Switzerland
> 7:41 (1); 6:37 (2); 4:58 (3)
> Recording Producer: Volker Straus
> Recording Engineer: Evert Menting
> Notes by Paul Griffiths, Uta Ruscher, Alain Poirier
> With Elliott Carter: *Quintet for Piano and Winds* (item 276); Sándor Veress: *Sonatine for Oboe, Clarinet, and Bassoon; Diptych;* Heinz Holliger: *Quintet for Piano and Four Wind Players*

Triple Duo

369. Wergo WER 60124 (Stereo lp) (1985)

> Nonesuch 79110 (stereo lp; CD) (1986)
> The Fires of London: Philippa Davies (fl), David Campbell (cl), Stephen Pruslin (pno); Gregory Knowles (perc), Rosemary Furniss (vn), Jonathan Williams (vc)
> Recorded 5 November 1984, St. Luke's Church, Hampstead, London
> 19:32
> Producer: Oliver Knussen
> Engineer: John Whiting
> Notes by David Schiff
> With Elliott Carter: *In Sleep, in Thunder* (item 213)
>
> Reissued as item 370

370. Wergo 6278-2 (286-278-2) (CD) (1995)

371. ECM New Series 1391 (839 617-2) (CD) (1990)

> Philippe Racine (fl), Ernesto Molinari (cl), Paul Cleemann (pno), Gerhard Huber (perc), Hansheinz Schneeberger (vn), Thomas Demenga (vc)
> Recorded October 1988, Radio DRS, Studio Basel

19:40
Producer: Christiane Nicolet
Recording Engineer: Erwin Bindzus
Notes by Heinz Holliger, Wolfgang Sandner
With Elliott Carter: *Esprit rude/Esprit doux* (item 187); *Enchanted Preludes* (item 181); *Riconoscenza per Goffredo Petrassi* (item 357); J. S. Bach: *Suite No. 3 for Violoncello Solo*

372. GM Recordings GM 2047CD (CD) (1997)

   The New York New Music Ensemble: Jayn Rosenfeld (fl), Jean Kopperud (cl), James Winn (pno), Daniel Druckman (perc), Linda Quan (vn), Chris Finckel (vc), Robert Black (cond)
   Recorded 17 November 1991, State University of New York at Purchase
   18:44
   Notes by Perry Goldstein
   With Jacob Druckman: *Come Round;* Peter Maxwell Davies: *Ave Maris Stella*

Under the Dome

See *Of Challenge and of Love*

Variations for Orchestra

373. LOU-58-3 (Mono lp) (1958)

   The Louisville Orchestra, Robert Whitney (cond)
   23:45
   Notes by Elliott Carter
   With Everett Helm: *Second Piano Concerto*

374. Columbia MS 7191 (Stereo lp) (1968)

   C.B.S. 72717 (stereo lp) (reviewed July 1969) (United Kingdom)
   C.B.S. S 34 61093 (stereo lp) (reviewed June 1970) (France)
   The New Philharmonia Orchestra, Frederik Prausnitz (cond)

Recorded: March 1967
25:38
Producer: Andrew Kazdin
Engineers: Edward Kramer, Murray Zimney
Notes by Elliott Carter
With Elliott Carter: *Double Concerto* (item 142)

375. New World Records NW 347-2 (Stereo lp; CD) (1986)

    Cincinnati Symphony Orchestra, Michael Gielen (cond)
    Recorded in performance 22 October 1985, Music Hall, Cincinnati, OH
    22:17
    Recording Engineer: Brent Reider
    Notes by David Schiff
    With Elliott Carter: *Piano Concerto* (item 253)

376. Deutsche Grammophon 2GH 431 698-2 (CD) (1994)

    Chicago Symphony Orchestra, James Levine (cond)
    Recorded July 1990, Orchestra Hall, Chicago, IL
    23:07
    Recording Producer: Christopher Alder
    Balance Engineer: Gregor Zielinsky
    Notes by David Hamilton
    With Gunther Schuller: *Spectra;* Milton Babbitt: *Correspondences;* John Cage: *Atlas eclipticalis*

View of the Capitol from the Library of Congress

See *A Mirror on Which to Dwell*

Violin Concerto

377. Virgin Classics VC 7 91503-2 (CD) (1992)

    Ole Böhn (vn), London Sinfonietta, Oliver Knussen (cond)
    Recorded 18 February 1991, Henry Wood Hall, London
    25:45
    Producers: Oliver Knussen with Colin Matthews
    Balance Engineer: Tryggvi Tryggvason

Notes by Elliott Carter, Oliver Knussen, Bayan Northcott
With Elliott Carter: *Three Occasions for Orchestra* (item 344); *Concerto for Orchestra* (item 133)

Voyage

378. Unicorn RHS 353 (Stereo lp) (1978)

    Unicorn UN1-72017 (stereo lp) (1978)
    An American Anthology
    Meriel Dickinson (ms), Peter Dickinson (pno)
    Recorded 28 March 1977, All Saints Church, Petersham, Surrey, England
    5:15
    With Elliott Carter: *Three Poems of Robert Frost* (item 348); George Gershwin: *I Got Rhythm; A Foggy Day in London Town; They All Laughed*; Aaron Copland: *In Evening Air; Night Thoughts; Poet's Song*; Virgil Thomson: *Two by Marianne Moore; Portrait of F. B. (Francis Blood)*; John Cage: *Five Songs*

379. CRI CD 648 (CD) (1993)

    Rosalind Rees (sop), Adirondack Chamber Orchestra, Gregg Smith (cond)
    Recorded 18 July 1982, St. Agnes Catholic Church, Lake Placid, NY
    5:49
    Producer: Gregg Smith
    Recording Engineer: David Hancock
    Notes by Gregg Smith and Joseph R. Dalton, Elliott Carter
    With Elliott Carter: *Warble for Lilac Time* (item 383); *Three Poems of Robert Frost* (item 355); *Tarantella* (item 339); *Emblems* (item 176); *The Harmony of Morning* (item 199); *Heart Not So Heavy As Mine* (item 206); *Musicians Wrestle Everywhere* (item 228); *To Music* (item 365); *The Defense of Corinth* (item 138)

380. Albany TROY 118 (CD) (1994)

    Permit Me Voyage

Mary Ann Hart (ms), Dennis Helmrich (pno)
5:46
Recorded 1–4 September 1992
Notes by Leslie Kandell
With Dominick Argento: *From the Diary of Virginia Woolf;* Henry Cowell: *How Old Is Song?; St. Agnes Morning;* William Flanagan: *Horror Movie; A Valentine to Sherwood Anderson;* Richard Hundley: *Arise my love; Moonlight's Watermelon; Straightway beauty on me waits; Some sheep are loving;* Ricky Ian Gordon: *Once I Was; Afternoon on a Hill;* Gary Schocker: *Mama Called*

381. Music & Arts CD900 (CD) (1995)

    Three Modern American Song Cycles
    Phyllis Bryn-Julson (sop), Mark Markham (pno)
    5:32
    With Elliott Carter: *Three Poems of Robert Frost* (item 352); *Warble for Lilac Time* (item 384); Charles Wuorinen: *A Winter's Tale;* Gunther Schuller: *Six Early Songs*

382. Koch International Classics 3-7425-2-H1 (CD) (1997)

    Lucy Shelton (sop), John Constable (pno)
    Recorded 18–20 May 1996, All Saints Church, Petersham, England
    5:47
    Producer and Engineer: Tryggvi Tryggvason
    Notes by Richard Wilson
    With Elliott Carter: *Three Poems of Robert Frost* (item 353); *Warble for Lilac Time* (item 385); *Of Challenge and of Love* (item 244); Igor Stravinsky: *Storm–Cloud; Two Songs on Poems of Gorodetsky,* op. 6; *Pastorale; Two Poems of Konstantin Balmont; Three Little Songs: Recollections of Childhood; Berceuse; Three Tales for Children; Four Russian Songs; Russian Maiden's Song; The Owl and the Pussy-Cat*

Warble for Lilac Time

383. CRI CD 648 (CD) (1993)

> Rosalind Rees (sop), Adirondack Chamber Orchestra, Gregg Smith (cond)
> Recorded 20 July 1982, St. Agnes Catholic Church, Lake Placid, NY
> 6:55
> Producer: Gregg Smith
> Recording Engineer: David Hancock
> Notes by Gregg Smith and Joseph R. Dalton, Elliott Carter
> With Elliott Carter: *Voyage* (item 379); *Three Poems of Robert Frost* (item 355); *Tarantella* (item 339); *Emblems* (item 176); *The Harmony of Morning* (item 199); *Heart Not So Heavy As Mine* (item 206); *Musicians Wrestle Everywhere* (item 228); *To Music* (item 365); *The Defense of Corinth* (item 138)

384. Music & Arts CD900 (CD) (1995)

> *Three Modern American Song Cycles*
> Phyllis Bryn-Julson (sop), Mark Markham (pno)
> 6:20
> With Elliott Carter: *Three Poems of Robert Frost* (item 352); *Voyage* (item 381); Charles Wuorinen: *A Winter's Tale;* Gunther Schuller: *Six Early Songs*

385. Koch International Classics 3-7425-2-H1 (CD) (1997)

> Lucy Shelton (sop), John Constable (pno)
> Recorded 18–20 May 1996, All Saints Church, Petersham, England
> 7:17
> Producer and Engineer: Tryggvi Tryggvason
> Notes by Richard Wilson
> With Elliott Carter: *Three Poems of Robert Frost* (item 353); *Voyage* (item 382); *Of Challenge and of Love* (item 244); Igor Stravinsky: *Storm–Cloud; Two Songs on Poems of Gorodetsky*, op. 6; *Pastorale; Two Poems of Konstantin Balmont; Three Little Songs: Recollections of Childhood;*

Berceuse; Three Tales for Children; Four Russian Songs; Russian Maiden's Song; The Owl and the Pussy-Cat

Woodwind Quintet

386. Classic Editions CE 2003 (1953) (lp)

    An American Woodwind Symposium
    New Art Wind Quintet: Andrew Lolya (fl), Melvin Kaplan (ob), Irving Neidich (cl), Elizabeth Bobo (hn), Tina di Dario (bn)
    8:35
    Notes by Elliott Carter
    With Ingolf Dahl: *Allegro and Arioso;* Henry Cowell: *Suite for Wind Quintet;* Roger Goeb: *Quintet for Woodwinds;* Vincent Persichetti: *Pastoral for Winds;* Walter Piston: *Three Pieces for Flute, Clarinet and Bassoon;* Wallingford Riegger: *Woodwind Quintet,* op. 51.

387. RCA Victor LM 6167 (3 Mono lps) (1966)

    RCA Victor LSC 6167 (3 stereo lps) (1966)
    R.C.A. RB 6692 (mono lp) (reviewed February 1967) (United Kingdom)
    R.C.A. SB 6692 (stereo lp) (reviewed February 1967) (United Kingdom)
    Boston Symphony Chamber Players: Doriot Anthony Dwyer (fl), Ralph Gomberg (ob), Gino Cioffi (cl), James Stagliano (hn), Sherman Walt (bn)
    8:11
    Producer: Richard Mohr
    Notes by Peter Ustinov
    With W. A. Mozart: *Quartet for Flute and Strings,* K. 285; *Quartet for Oboe and Strings,* K. 370; Johannes Brahms: *Quartet for Piano and Strings,* op. 60; Ludwig van Beethoven: *Serenade for Flute, Violin, and Viola,* op. 25; Irving Fine: *Fantasia for String Trio;* Aaron Copland: *Vitebsk, Study on Jewish Themes;* Walter Piston: *Divertimento for Nine Instruments*

388. Candide CE 31016 (Stereo lp) (1969)

> C.B.S. S 34 61145 (reviewed December 1970) (France)
> Vox STGBY 644 (reviewed September 1971) (United Kingdom)
> Dorian Wind Quintet: Karl Kraber (fl), Charles Kuskin (ob), William Lewis (cl), Barry Benjamin (hn), Jane Taylor (bn)
> 7:50
> Notes by William B. Ober
> With Elliott Carter: *Eight Etudes and a Fantasy* (item 153); Hans Werner Henze: *Quintett*

389. Vox SVBX 5307 (3 Stereo lp) (1977)

> *The Avant Garde Woodwind Quintet in the U.S.A.*
> Karl Kraber (fl), Charles Kuskin (ob), Jerry Kirkbride (cl), Barry Benjamin (hn), Jane Taylor (bn)
> Recorded 1976
> 7:50
> With Samuel Barber: *Summer Music;* Arthur Berger: *Quartet in C Major;* Luciano Berio: *Children's Play;* Irving Fine: *Partita;* Lukas Foss: *The Cave of the Winds;* Mario Davidovsky: *Synchronisms No. 8;* Jacob Druckman: *Delizie contente che l'alme beate;* Gunther Schuller: *Quintet for Woodwinds & Horn;* Karel Husa: *Preludes for Flute, Clarinet, and Bassoon*

390. Melbourne Records SMLP 4040 (Stereo lp) (1980)

> *The York Winds Play Music*
> The York Winds: Douglas Stewart (fl), Lawrence Cherney (ob), Paul Grice (cl), Harcus Hennigar (hn), Gerald Robinson (bn)
> Recorded 16–18 March 1980, Club Harmonie, Toronto
> 8:44
> With Brian Cherney: *Notturno;* Bernard Heiden: *Sinfonia for Woodwind Quintet;* John Rea: *Reception and Offering Music*

391. Musical Heritage Society 4782 (Stereo lp) (1983)

> *20th Century Works for Wind Ensemble*

Soni Ventorum Wind Quintet
8:00
With Samuel Barber: *Summer Music,* op. 31; Irving Fine: *Partita;* Joseph Goodman: *Scherzo for Wind Quintet*

392. KM Records KM 15131 (Stereo lp) (198-?)

    Travis Chamber Players (U.S. Air Force Band of Golden Gate)
    Recorded in the Community Center, Davis, CA
    8:39
    With Ludwig van Beethoven (arr. Kinningham): *Zapfenstreich; March in C for Military Band;* Richard Strauss: *Serenade,* op. 7; Ferenc Farkas: *Antiche Danze Ungheres I;* Harry Breuer (arr. Woelfel): *Bit O Rhythm;* Wilke Renwick: *Dance;* Jean Joseph Mouret: *Rondeau;* Jean Baptiste Lully: *Overture* to *Cadmus et Hermione;* John Philip Sousa: *Washington Post March*

393. Premiere PRCD 1006 (CD) (1990)

    American Winds, volume one
    Boehm Quintette: Sheryl Henze (fl), Phyllis Lanini (ob), Steven Hartman (cl), Joseph Anderer (hn), Robert Wagner (bn)
    7:49
    Producer: Gregory K. Squires
    Notes by Michael Leavitt
    With Walter Piston: *Quintet for Wind Instruments; Three Pieces for Flute, Clarinet and Bassoon;* Irving Fine: *Partita for Wind Quintet;* Elie Siegmeister: *Ten Minutes for Four Players;* Vincent Persichetti: *Pastoral for Wind Quintet*

394. Stradivarius STR 33304 (CD) (1991)

    Musica per Quartetto e Quintetto a Fiati
    Quintetto Arnold: Renato Rivolta (fl), Francesco Pomarico (ob), Maurizio Longoni (cl), Sebastiano Panebianco (hn), Leonardo Dosso (bn)
    Recorded 22–23 October and 19–20 November 1990, Chiesa della Misericordia, Turin, Italy
    7:39
    Notes by Paolo Petazzi

With Elliott Carter: *Eight Etudes and a Fantasy* (item 158); Franco Donatoni: *Blow*; György Kurtág: *Quintetto per fiati*, op. 2; György Ligeti: *Zehn Stücke für Bläserquintett*

395. KOCH Schwann 3-1153-2 (CD) (1992)

    The Aulos Wind Quintet Plays Music by American Composers v. 1
    The Aulos Woodwind Quintet: Peter Rijks (fl), Diethelm Jonas (ob), Karl-Theo Adler (cl), Dietmar Ullrich (hn), Ralph Sabow (bn)
    Recorded 1989–1990, Jesus-Christus-Kirche, Berlin, Germany
    8:12
    Producer: Jean Cullerier
    Engineers: W. Gottschalk, Helge Jörns
    With Elliott Carter: *Eight Etudes and a Fantasy* (item 160); Samuel Barber: *Summer Music;* John Cage: *Music for Wind Instruments;* Gunther Schuller: *Suite for Woodwind Ensemble*

396. Crystal CD 752 (CD) (1993)

    Westwood Woodwind Quintet: John Barcellona (fl), Peter Christ (ob), David Atkins (cl), Joseph Meyer (hn), David Muller (bn)
    Recorded May 1992 and January 1993, Lincoln Theatre, Mount Vernon, WA
    8:00
    Notes by David Muller
    With William Bergsma: *Concerto for Wind Quintet;* George Rochberg: *Into the Dark Wood;* John Biggs: *Scherzo for Wind Quintet;* Anthony Plog: *Animal Ditties for Speaker and Wind Quintet;* Gunther Schuller: *Suite for Wind Quintet;* William Schuman: *Dances for Woodwind Quintet and Percussion*

397. Summit DCD 149 (CD) (1995)

    Lieurance Woodwind Quintet: Frances Shelly (fl), Willa Henigman (ob), W. James Jones (cl), Nicholas E. Smith (hn), Nancy E. Lutes (bn)

Discography of Commercial Recordings 159

With Irving Fine: *Partita for Wind Quintet;* Arthur Berger: *Quintet for Winds in C;* Vincent Persichetti: *Pastorale for Wind Quintet;* John Barrows: *March;* Samuel Barber: *Summer Music,* op. 31

398. cpo 999 453-2 (CD) (1998)

Ensemble Contrasts: Michael Faust (fl), Christian Hommel (ob), David Smeyers (cl), Volker Grewel (hn), Dag Jensen (bn)
Recorded October 1995, Hürth-Knapsack, Feierabendhaus der Hoechst AG; November 1995 and March 1996, Funkhaus Köln
8:04
Recording Supervisor: Wolfgang Müller
Recording Engineers: Franz-Peter Esser, Mark Hohn, Christian Meurer
With Elliott Carter: *Esprit rude/Esprit doux* (item 189); *Eight Etudes and a Fantasy* (item 161); *Enchanted Preludes* (item 183); *Sonata for Flute, Oboe, Cello, and Harpsichord* (item 292)

Annotated Bibliography of Carter Studies

I. Sources Written by Elliott Carter

Many of Carter's writings have appeared in two or more different forms and in different publications. Some have been reprinted unaltered, others under a different title or with minor additions or cuts, and some have been substantially revised. In what follows I have listed the original publication followed by all later versions in chronological order.

Collections

399. *WEC* *The Writings of Elliott Carter.* Ed. Else Stone and Kurt Stone. Bloomington and London: Indiana University Press, 1977. ISBN 0-253-36720-4. ML60.C22.

An essential resource for Carter studies, this volume collects in chronological order the majority of Carter's writings from 1937 to 1977, including book, dance, and music reviews, reports about musicians and special events, and articles about his own music. The sources are well documented and the index is excellent. Also provided is a list of Carter's writings not included in the collection. For reviews see items 634, 635, 639, 723, and 812.

400. *CARTER* *Carter* (in Italian). Ed. Enzo Restagno. Torino: E.D.T. (Edizioni di Torino), 1989. ISBN 887063051X. ML197.C332516 1989.

This volume consists of an extended interview with Enzo Restagno (see item 597), Italian translations of more than thirty of Carter's essays, a catalog of works, a short bibliography, and a short discography (alphabetical by record label). It was published on the occasion of the 1989 Settembre Musica festival in Torino, which featured Carter's music.

401. EC   Schiff, David. *Elliott Carter: edizione italiana aggiornata dall'autore.* Napoli: Edizioni Scientifiche Italiane, 1990. ISBN 88-7104-175-5.

Italian translation of the first edition of *The Music of Elliott Carter* (item 769) together with Italian translations of an article and an interview by Charles Rosen (items 600 and 758), excerpts from Carter's interview with Allen Edwards (item 584), and a selection of Carter's own writings (items 427, 433, 442, 459, 460, 477, and 485). The list of works, discography, and bibliography have been updated to include materials that postdate the English publication of the first edition of Schiff's book. There is an index of Carter's works and an index of names; both are integrated for the entire volume.

402. CEL   *Collected Essays and Lectures, 1937–1995.* Ed. Jonathan W. Bernard. Rochester, NY: University of Rochester Press, 1997. ISBN 1-878822-70-5. ML197.C3425 1996.

Essentially a revision and update of *WEC* (item 399) this volume collects a wide variety of reviews, essays, talks, and program notes in six chapters arranged by topic. Although roughly two-thirds of the fifty-nine essays are also found in the earlier *Writings*, the remaining essays, written between 1953 and 1995, are of considerable interest and represent a substantial expansion of the primary source material on Carter availible to the general public. Also valuable are the several sources previously available only in significantly abridged form, here restored to full length. For a review see item 818.

Other Sources

403. "The Agony of Modern Music in America." In *CEL,* 53–57.

According to Bernard (*CEL,* p. 344), this article was written in early 1955 and "probably intended for delivery to the meeting of [the ISCM] in Baden-Baden that year." It combines a review of *The Agony of Modern Music* by Henry Pleasants (New York: Simon and Schuster, 1955)—which Carter calls "stupid but rhetorically very effective"—with an account of the factionalism surrounding the merger of the League of Composers with the U.S. section of the ISCM. Carter is concerned that the League's more conservative outlook may come to dominate the new organiztaion and lead to the neglect of the more progressive aesthetic championed by the ISCM.

404. "Un altro passo avanti (1958)." See "A Further Step" (item 453).

405. "An American Destiny." *Listen: The Guide to Good Music* 9, no. 1 (November 1946): 4–7. Reprinted in *WEC*, 143–50, and in *CEL*, 93–98.

    Italian translation ("Un destino americano [Charles Edward Ives]"), trans. Elena Racca Bruno, in *CARTER*, 145–50.

In this laudatory essay Carter admires Ives's success in two completely different fields (insurance and music composition) and sketches a biographical portrait of Ives that emphasizes his artistic and philosophical beliefs. The critical tone found occasionally in Carter's earlier essays on Ives (items 411 and 474) is absent here.

406. "American Figure, with Landscape." *Modern Music* 20, no. 4 (May–June 1943): 219–25. Excerpts reprinted with comment in Minna Lederman, *The Life and Death of a Small Magazine (Modern Music, 1924–1946)*, 43–46. (Brooklyn, NY: Institute for Studies in American Music, 1983. ISAM monographs, no. 18. ISBN 0-914678-20-5. ML200.5.L4 1983.) Complete article reprinted in *WEC*, 87–93, and in *CEL*, 134–38.

Carter presents Henry Franklin Belknap Gilbert (1868–1928) as an American composer of some merit forgotten by the generation that followed him. The article includes an interesting section about the formulation in Gilbert's day of a "sequence of periods . . . to cover our national musical evolution" and some consideration of Gilbert's anti-European aesthetic, but Carter is less interested in resurrecting Gilbert's music than in presenting a cautionary tale to his peers. "After the first fine frenzy of the modern music movement had died down and Gilbert was forgotten, a whole group of composers started rediscovering the virtues of simplicity, of ascetic Americanism, and of many other qualities which he had prefigured. They claimed these as their own invention, as if Gilbert and his fellow nationalists had never existed." Carter ends with a warning: "It would be unfortunate for our culture if the present generation were as easily swept aside as all previous ones have been, yet this is the lesson which our history seems to indicate."

407. "American Music in the New York Scene, 1940." *Modern Music* 17, no. 2 (January–February 1940): 93–101. Reprinted in *WEC*, 87–93, and in *CEL*, 48–53.

Italian translation ("La musica americana sulla scena newyorchese, 1940"), trans. Elena Racca Bruno, in *CARTER*, 104–8.

A brief consideration of the development of American music prefaces reviews of numerous works by American composers. Most striking is Carter's rave review of Roy Harris's *Third Symphony*, which Carter had greeted with little enthusiasm only a year earlier (see item 538). Carter also praises the music of Roger Sessions in his review of an all-Sessions concert given by the Composers' Forum Laboratory and briefly mentions works by Walter Piston *(Concertino for Piano and Orchestra)*, William Schuman *(American Festival Overture)*, John Alden Carpenter *(Skyscrapers)*, Howard Hanson *(Third Symphony)*, Edward Burlingame Hill *(Violin Concerto)*, Randall Thompson *(Second Symphony)*, David Diamond *(Cello Sonata; Quintet for Flute, String Trio, and Piano;* and *Elegy in Memory of Maurice Ravel)*, and Lazare Saminsky *(Two Chorales* and *Violin Pieces)*. Also mentioned are works by Otto Luening, Florent Schmitt, Robert McBride, and Ernst Lévy, commissioned by harpsichordist Ralph Kirkpatrick, and performances by the New York Philharmonic of Arthur Bliss's *Suite from "Checkmate"* and Jaromir Weinberger's *Christmas*. Finally, consideration of some pieces "intended for the masses" by Henry Brant, Morton Gould, George Kleinsinger, and Earl Robinson leads Carter to conclude, "I wouldn't be at all surprised if works like the Sessions *Quartet* or the Harris *Symphony* were to become more popular than these self-conscious and restricted compositions ever will be."

408. "La base rhythmique de la musique américaine." See "The Rhythmic Basis of American Music" (item 530).

409. "Le basi ritmiche della musica americana." See "The Rhythmic Basis of American Music" (item 530).

410. "Brass Quintet." In *WEC*, 322–25. Reprinted in *CEL*, 256–58.
    Italian translation ("Quintetto per ottoni"), trans. Elena Racca Bruno, in *CARTER*, 281–83.

Carter wrote this brief talk to preface the world premiere of his *Brass Quintet*, (item 42) which was given over BBC radio on 20 October 1974. In it, he expresses his pleasure that the premiere is taking place on Charles Ives's one hundredth birthday "because it helps to repay the great debt I owe him personally and musically." This leads to an interesting section in which Carter compares his own musical personality to that of Ives and to a description of the dramatic (and quite anthropomorphic) plan of the quintet.

Carter. Listed above as item 400.

411. "The Case of Mr. Ives." *Modern Music* 16, no. 3 (March 1939): 172–76. Published together with "Further Notes on the Winter Season 1938/9." Both reprinted in *WEC*, 48–51. "The Case of Mr. Ives" only reprinted in *Perspectives of New Music* 2, no. 2 (Spring–Summer 1964): 27–29, and in *CEL*, 87–90.
    Italian translation of both ("Il caso Ives" and "Altre note sulla stagione d'inverno 1938–39"), trans. Elena Racca Bruno, in *CARTER*, 93–96 and 96–99.

A review of the first two performances of Ives's *Concord Sonata* at Town Hall in New York on 20 January and 24 February 1939. Carter combines a warm and affectionate portrait of his early friendship with Ives with a quite harsh and unrestrained critique of the *Sonata*. About Ives: "a gleam would come into his eyes as fiery excitement seized him, and he would smash out a fragment of *Emerson*, singing loudly and exclaiming with burning enthusiasm. . . . It was a dynamic, staggering experience, which is hard even now to think of clearly. . . . [W]e always came away from Ives full of life's glad new wine and a thousand projects for the future." About the sonata: "In form and esthetic it is basically conventional . . . full of the paraphernalia of the overdressy sonata school, cyclical themes, contrapuntal development sections that lead nowhere, constant harmonic movement which does not clarify the form, and dramatic rather than rhythmical effects." The review is a fascinating record of the power of Ives's influence on Carter and the degree to which Carter struggled with it. The review caused a breach in their relationship that was mended only after many years. It remains one of the most significant turning points in Carter's career. (Also see items 405, 411, 414, 433, and 474.)

Carter's harsh review of the *Concord Sonata* was partly a response to the "present canonization" of Ives on the eve of World War II, and in part a reflection of his own changing tastes, which were shifting away from the avant-garde and toward a neoclassic aesthetic exemplified by Nadia Boulanger, with whom Carter had studied during the previous years. It is thus quite telling that Carter begins the second part of the present article, "Further Notes on the Winter Season 1938/9," by observing, "Nothing could be a greater jump than from Ives to Nadia Boulanger, who during the winter conducted the Philharmonic in performances of great precision, clarity, and understanding." Though Carter praises Boulanger, he quickly dismisses the pieces by Antoni Szalowski and Jean Françaix that she conducted, mentioning only the Françaix *Piano Concerto*. The article continues with moderate praise for Bartók's *Rhapsody for Clarinet and Violin* played by Joseph Szigeti and Benny Goodman, high praise for Stravinsky's *Concerto for Two Pianos*, played by Edward Steuermann and Bronislaw Gimpel at a New School concert, and brief reviews of Copland's *Sextet,* Hindemith's *Symphonic Dances,* Vladimir Dukelsky's *Dédicaces,* Hunter Johnson's *Andante,* Henry Brant's *Viola Sonata,* Norman Cazden's *Three Sonatas,* David van Vactor's *Symphony in D,* Robert Sanders's *Little Symphony,* Harold Brown's *Experiments,* Hunter Johnson's *Serenade for Flute and Clarinet,* and unnamed works by Herman Chaloff and Margaret Purcell. A short section at the end of the article summarizes Hendrik Willem van Loon's *Deliberate Reflections* on the state of the American musician, published in *Greenwich* [CT] *Time.*

412. "The Challenge of the New." See "Reel vs. Real" (item 526).

413. "The Changing Scene, New York." *Modern Music* 17, no. 4 (May–June 1940): 237–41. Reprinted in *WEC*, 81–85.

"War abroad is having its predicted effect, and our musical attention turns increasingly to home-made composition." Pride of place goes to Walter Piston, whose *Violin Concerto* is favorably reviewed and whose *Carnival Song* is mentioned in passing. A review of John Kirkpatrick's all-American concert at Town Hall affords Carter the opportunity of praising Aaron Copland's *Piano Variations*: "one of the finest pieces in contemporary piano literature." From the same concert are reviews of works by Hunter Johnson *(Sonata)* and Robert Palmer *(Sonata* [No. 1 (1938)] and *String Quartet* [No. 1 (1939)]) and mention of Roger Sessions's "by now familiar" *Piano Sonata* [No. 1 (1930)]. An all-American evening by John Charles Thomas is mentioned but not reviewed (Carter did not attend).

The second part of the article includes a review of the League of Composers' program of North and South American music. Mentioned or reviewed are Roger Sessions's *Quartet* [No. 1 (1936)]; Roy Harris's *Soliloquy* for viola and piano and *Dance*; Bernard Wagenaar's *Third String Quartet*; Rudolf Révil's *Parisian Night-Club Songs*; Harold Shapero's *Three Pieces for Three Pieces*; an early unpublished *Sonata for Violin and Piano* by Bernhard Heiden; and Donald Fuller's *Trio for Clarinet, Cello, and Piano*. There are more extended reviews of performances by the New York Philharmonic of Benjamin Britten's *Violin Concerto* and Bernard Herrmann's cantata *Moby Dick* and a dismissal in passing of Sergey Prokofiev's *Cello Concerto* played by the Boston Symphony ("pretty ineffective, so let's forget it").

414. "Charles Ives Remembered." In *Charles Ives Remembered: An Oral History*, ed. Vivian Perlis, 131–45. New Haven: Yale University Press, 1974. Reprinted in *WEC*, 258–69, and in *CEL*, 98–107.

Italian translation ("Ricordo di Charles Ives"), trans. Sonia Bergamasco, in *CARTER*, 214–23.

According to Else Stone and Kurt Stone's note in *WEC*, Carter wrote this article "*after* his interview with Vivian Perlis" (italics in original), probably revising and editing a transcript. The result, conversational in tone, is a reminiscence that touches on many subjects, including Ives's life and character, his revisions of his scores, and his influence on other composers. Most valuable for Carter scholars are the substantial sections of the article dealing with Carter's changing relationship with Ives and Ives's music. These sections illustrate the long and emotional process through which Carter came to terms with one of his most important musical influences.

415. "La chiusura della stagione 1937 a New York." See "Season's End in New York, 1937" (item 539).

416. "La chiusura della stagione. New York primavera 1938." See "Season's End in New York, 1938" (item 540).

Collected Essays and Lectures, 1937–1995. Listed above as item 402.

417. "A Commentary on the Poem by the Composer." In *Voyage*, by Elliott Carter, 1. South Hadley, MA, and Northhampton, MA: The Valley Music Press, 1945. Reprinted in David Schiff, *The Music of Elliott Carter*, 326–27. (London: Eulenburg Books; New York: Da Capo Press, 1983. ISBN 0-903873-06-0. ML410.C3293 S34 1983.) Also reprinted in David Schiff, *The Music of Elliott Carter*, 328–29. (London: Faber; Ithaca, NY: Cornell University Press, 1998. ISBN 0-8014-3612-5.)

For his composition *Voyage* (item 108), Carter set part III of Hart Crane's poem "Voyages." That section of the poem is reprinted in the Valley Music Press edition of the score, together with Carter's note, which he begins: "To help the singer (and possibly the listener) in forming an interpretation of the text of this song . . . it would perhaps be pertinent to describe something of what it has meant to the composer." Carter's commentary, an excellent example of his thinking and writing style at this stage in his life, is a close reading of the poem in terms of its "three protagonists: the Sea (which is the medium through which everything in the poem moves and changes and to which every idea is referred), Love (to whom the poem is addressed) and the Poet."

418. "'The Composer Is a University Commodity.'" *College Music Symposium* 10 (Fall 1970): 68–70. Reprinted in *WEC*, 279–82, and in *CEL*, 83–85.

This article is Carter's response to a questionnaire: "The Composer in Academia—Reflections on a Theme of Stravinsky." Carter takes up Stravinsky's theme (that "a composer is or isn't; he cannot learn the gift that makes him one," and that university teaching may "not be the right contrast for a composer's noncomposing time") by listing the "BAD" and "GOOD" aspects of university composition teaching. Although he notes that ten years separate Stravinsky's comment from his article, Carter still finds that the bad considerably outweighs the good.

419. "Composers by the Alphabet." *Modern Music* 19, no. 1 (November–December 1941): 70–71.

A brief and quite harsh review of the encyclopedia *Great Modern Composers*, edited by Oscar Thompson: "As an introduction to contemporary composers and their music for readers who are not familiar with the subject [the book] is not of much value. Still less is it of value to those who already know something of the subject and want to know more."

420. "The Composer's Choices." In *WEC*, 192–97. Reprinted in *CEL*, 210–14.
    Italian translation ("Le scelte del compositore"), trans. by Angelo Bozzo, in *CARTER*, 180–84.

This article is a transcript of a radio lecture commissioned by the Fromm Foundation sometime around 1960. In it Carter describes and plays recorded excerpts from his *Pocahontas Suite* (item 81c), *Piano Sonata* (item 80), *Sonata for Violoncello and Piano* (item 87), *Eight Etudes and a Fantasy* (item 53), and *Variations for Orchestra* (item 106), prefaced by some disparaging remarks about the state of American interest in serious music. The broadcast ended with a complete performance of the *Variations*.

421. "The Composer's Viewpoint." *National Music Council Bulletin* 7, no. 1 (September 1946): 10–11. Reprinted in *WEC*, 140–43, and in *CEL*, 3–5.

Beneath Carter's casual and mildly comic tone is a plea to composers, performers, audiences, and publishers to encourage the production of "interesting and durable" music rather than "real novelty merchandise, that is intended to sell for a short time and be forgotten for good." Both the good humor and the seriousness of purpose are typical of Carter's writings. Perhaps for this reason Carter and Jonathan Bernard chose this essay to lead off *CEL* (item 402), published in 1997.

422. "*Concerto for Orchestra.*" In Edward Downes, *The New York Philharmonic Guide to the Symphony*, 246–48. New York: Walker & Co., 1976. ISBN 0-8027-0540-5. Reprinted in *WEC*, 308–10.

Program note for the world premiere of the *Concerto for Orchestra* (item 49), given by the New York Philharmonic, conducted by Leonard Bernstein, on 5 February 1970.

423. "Coolidge Crusade; WPA; New York Season, 1938." *Modern Music* 16, no. 1 (November–December 1938): 33–38. Reprinted in *WEC*, 39–43.

In the first part of this article Carter reviews works commissioned by Elizabeth Sprague Coolidge and performed at the New York Public Library: Ernst Toch's *Quintet for Piano and Strings*, op. 64; Louis Gruenberg's *Quartet;* Frederick Jacobi's quintet for piano and strings, *Hagiographia;* and Webern's *String Quartet*, op. 28. Carter praises the Toch and the Gruenberg, is cooler toward the Jacobi, and calls the Webern "absorbing if puzzling listening." He also mentions (but did not hear) Frank Bridge's *String Quartet No. 4.*

The second part of the article is devoted to reviews of Paul Hindemith's *St. Francis;* Copland's *Music for the Theater;* Stravinsky's *Symphonie des psaumes* and *Les Noces;* David Diamond's *Overture;* works by Roger Sessions, Aaron Copland, Roy Harris, Walter Piston, and Quincy Porter performed at the Westminster Choir School Festival; and William Schuman's *Second Symphony,* performed by the Greenwich Orchestra under Edgar Schenkman at a WPA (Works Progress Administration) concert. Unimpressed by Schuman's "three long orchestral crescendi over three long pedals," Carter observes, "The day for discovering a new kind of plasticity and free-moving harmonies and lines seems to be here." The discussion of Schuman leads to a disappointed appraisal of the work of the WPA Composers' Forum Laboratory in New York. After three years of concerts, "The famous remain famous and the obscure remain obscure. These concerts appear to have done nothing more than to give a small group of friends and others a chance to hear their works."

424. "Cronache d'attualità: Italia." See "Current Chronicle: Italy" (item 427).

425. "Cronache d'attualità: New York 1959." See "Current Chronicle: New York, 1959" (item 429).

426. "Current Chronicle: Germany, 1960." *Musical Quarterly* 46, no. 3 (July 1960): 367–71. Reprinted with the added subtitle "[Reviews of *Rasputin's End* by Nicolas Nabokov and *Lady Macbeth of Mzensk* by Dmitri Shostakovitch]" in *WEC*, 212–16, and as "*Rasputin's End* and *Lady Macbeth of Mtsensk*" in *CEL*, 28–31.

Carter, while pleasantly surprised by the lavishness of the productions of these operas (*Macbeth* in Düsseldorf, *Rasputin* in Cologne), is dismayed by the "total disregard for musical unity, taste, and coherence" he perceives in Shostakovitch's opera, although he also says the composer's "gusto and very real musical talent" make the opera worth hearing. The Nabokov is praised for its "warm, human lyricism," both dramatically apt and musically interesting.

427. "Current Chronicle: Italy." *Musical Quarterly* 45, no. 4 (October 1959): 530–41. Reprinted with the added subtitle "[Review of the ISCM Festival, Rome, 1959]" in *WEC*, 173–84, and, with one musical example omitted, as "ISCM Festival, Rome" in *CEL*, 18–28.
Italian translation ("Cronache d'attualità: Italia"), trans. Angelo Bozzo, in *CARTER*, 163–73.
Italian translation ("Cronaca dall'Italia"), in *EC*, 571–86.

Carter's twofold purpose in this article is to describe the kinds of bureaucratic difficulties encountered by the orgainizers of the ISCM festival and to report on the most promising music heard there. He identifies two main approaches used by composers at the festival. In the first ("design"), more traditional ideas about themes, motifs, chords, and so forth predominate. In the second ("sound"), these elements are secondary to those of tone color and texture. Singled out for praise are Goffredo Petrassi's *Serenata,* Boulez's *Improvisations sur Mallarmé II,* and Bo Nilsson's *Ein irrender Sohn.*

428. "Current Chronicle: New York." *Musical Quarterly* 52, no. 1 (January 1966): 93–101. Reprinted in *WEC,* 248–55; as "Edward Steuermann" in *The Not Quite Innocent Bystander: Writings of Edward Steuermann,* ed. Clara Steuermann, David Porter, and Gunther Schuller (Lincoln, NE: University of Nebraska Press, 1989. ISBN 0-8032-4191-7. ML60.S84513 1989.); and as "Edward Steuermann" in *CEL,* 151–58.

This eulogy for the composer and pianist Edward Steuermann includes a brief analysis of his *Suite for Chamber Orchestra,* a fond recollection of a performance he gave of the Chopin *Preludes* at the Juilliard School, and a short sketch of his biography.

429. "Current Chronicle: New York, 1959." *Musical Quarterly* 45, no. 3 (July 1959): 375–81. Reprinted with the added subtitle "[Review of the *Violin Concerto* by Roger Sessions]" in *WEC,* 166–73, and as "Roger Sessions: Violin Concerto" in *CEL,* 175–80.

Italian translation ("Cronache d'attualità: New York, 1959"), trans. Elena Racca Bruno, in *CARTER,* 157–62.

This tribute to Sessions and his *Violin Concerto* traces the development of two motives first heard in the piece's opening measures. Carter praises Sessions for his imaginative approach to musical form and laments the fact that his concerto is not as well known as its European peers.

430. "Dankesworte von Elliott Carter." In *Ernst-von-Siemens Musikpreis 1981,* 19–22. Zug, Switzerland: Ernst von Siemens Stiftung, 1981.

In these remarks made on receipt of the Ernst-von-Siemens Musikpreis, Carter attributes much of his success to the skill of his performers and the patience and interest of his audiences.

431. "Un destino americano (Charles Edward Ives)." See "An American Destiny" (item 405).

432. "Documenti di un'amicizia con Ives." See "Documents of a Friendship with Ives" (item 433).

433. "Documents of a Friendship with Ives." *Parnassus* 3, no. 2 (Summer 1975): 300–15. Reprinted in *Tempo* 117 (June 1976): 2–10. Also reprinted in *WEC*, 331–43, and in *CEL*, 107–18.
    Italian translation ("Documenti di un'amicizia con Ives"), trans. Elena Racca Bruno, in *CARTER*, 224–34.
    Italian translation ("Documenti di un'amicizia con Ives") in *EC*, 631–48.

This article contains excerpts of a dozen or so letters between Carter and Charles Ives and/or his wife, Harmony, written between approximately 1926 and 1954, connected by Carter's 1975 commentary. The first is Ives's letter of recommendation for Carter's application to Harvard, and the last is a response from Mrs. Ives to Carter's letter of condolence after Ives's death.

434. "*Double Concerto for Harpsichord and Piano with Two Chamber Orchestras* (1961); *Duo for Violin and Piano* (1974)." See notes for sound recording of Elliott Carter, *Double Concerto* and *Duo*, Nonesuch H 71314 (item 503).

435. "Edward Steuermann." See "Current Chronicle: New York" (item 428).

436. "'Elle est la musique en personne': A Reminiscence of Nadia Boulanger." In *CEL*, 281–92.

This essay is Carter's most detailed and eloquent tribute to his most important teacher. He expresses great admiration for the combination of ceaseless curiosity, strict discipline, and pedagogical flexibility that characterized Boulanger's teaching and describes in some detail various memories of her classes and of his student days in Paris. These include the exercises he wrote in harmony and counterpoint, the study of the Bach cantatas and a good deal of Renaissance and early Baroque music, and the upheaval in Paris that accompanied Hitler's rise to power in Germany. Carter concludes, "The ideals of workmanship, of care, of detail, and of large conception she instilled very deeply, and they have remained ever living in a way that I do not think any other teacher could ever have made them for me."

437. "Elliott Carter Objects." Letter to the Editor, *New York Times*, 20 October 1968, sec. 2 (Arts and Leisure).

A response to an article by Harold Schonberg (item 782) regarding the future of the symphony. Carter first notes that the source of his remarks quoted in Schonberg's article was an informal panel discussion that was recorded and published without his knowledge or consent (see item 579). He then defends his claim that "contemporary music of each new period gives that period a new point of view about the musical past" by citing changing approaches to the music of J. S. Bach in the nineteenth and twentieth centuries. He also cites Adam Carse's book *The Orchestra from Beethoven to Berlioz* as his source for the claim that orchestras in the nineteenth century played a preponderance of contemporary music. He concludes with a thinly veiled rebuke: "Mr. Schonberg might remember, too, that neither Béla Bartók, Arnold Schoenberg nor Charles Ives enjoyed much respect during their lifetimes here on the part of his colleagues, and it certainly was not he who is responsible for their present recognition."

438. "Elliott Cook Carter." In *25th Anniversary Report of the Harvard Class of 1930*, 165–69. Cambridge, MA: Harvard University Press, 1955.

439. "Elliott Cook Carter." In *50th Anniversary Report of the Harvard Class of 1930*, 836–38. Cambridge, MA: Harvard University Press, 1980.

440. "Espressionismo e musica americana." See "Expressionism and American Music" (item 442).

441. "The European Roots of American Musical Culture." In *CEL*, 62–72.
Originally published in a significantly abridged version as "The Milieu of the American Composer," *Perspectives of New Music* 1, no. 1 (Fall 1962): 149–51. Reprinted in *High Fidelity* 27, no. 9 (September 1977): MA-16, MA-27, and in *WEC*, 216–18. Also published as "Composing: Art or Anarchy" in the *Chicago Daily News*, circa 1963.
French translation of excerpts from the abridged version ("La musique américaine: une plante dépaysée"), trans. Thierry Beauvert, *Le monde de la musique* 117 (December 1988): 92.

According to Bernard (*CEL*, p. 344), this article "was originally written as a radio address, under commission by the North German (Hamburg) Radio in September 1961." An interesting comment on the internationalization and professionalization of Western art music prefaces Carter's survey of the interaction between European and American musical culture. Carter touches on such issues as the historical continuity and commercial pressures on musical traditions and institutions, the educational role of music, the training of musicians, French and German influences on American music, jazz, the role of the university, and the postwar European avant-garde. The original publication, "The Milieu of the American Composer" (item 482), is a dramatically abridged version incorporating only Carter's critique of the European avant-garde and his concluding paragraph.

442. "Expressionism and American Music." *Perspectives of New Music* 4, no. 1 (Fall–Winter 1965): 1–13. Revised version in *Perspectives on American Composers*, ed. Benjamin Boretz and Edward T. Cone, 217–29 (New York: W. W. Norton, 1971). ISBN 0393021556. ML200.1.B67. Revised version reprinted in *WEC*, 230–43, and (with further revised notes) in *CEL*, 72–83.
German translation of the revised version ("Expressionismus und amerikanische Musik"), trans. Felix Meyer, in *Amerikanische Musik seit Charles Ives* (Laaber: Laaber Verlag, 1987), 275–87, ISBN 3-89007-117-1. ML200.5.A6 1987.

Italian translation ("Espressionismo e musica americana") in *EC*, 603–20.

According to Bernard, "This text originated as a paper given at the Convegno Internazionale di Studi sull'Espressionismo at the Maggio Fiorentino in 1964" (*CEL*, p. 344). In this article Carter compares European and American avant-garde traditions in the twentieth century. He laments the passing of a golden age in the first decades of the century, when the works of Ives, Varèse, Ruggles, Rudhyar, Cowell, Crawford, and others were frequently performed in America, then speculates on the reciprocal influence between American composers and their European counterparts, including Schoenberg and his followers, during this period. Carter posits two complementary preoccupations of expressionism—the intensification of expression, and constructivism—and gives examples of each, including an interesting discussion of Ives's aesthetic in relation to his European contemporaries.

443. "Fallacy of the Mechanistic Approach." *Modern Music* 23, no. 3 (Summer 1946): 228–30. Reprinted in *WEC*, 118–21, and in *CEL*, 15–16.

In this review of Joseph Schillinger's *System of Musical Composition*, Carter disdains the book's "violent invective, dogmatic assertion, repetition of ideas and phrases, and a certain megalomania," which come "straight out of middle Europe in the early twenties, when the application of a mechanistically conceived scientific method to the arts was all the rage." On the other hand, he admires the book for being "the most comprehensive tabulation of musical elements, devices, and procedures that probably has ever been made." Combining a genuine interest in Schillinger's materials with a harsh critique of their mechanical application to music, this review provides a fascinating picture of Carter's thinking at the beginning of an important transitional phase in his career.

444. "Films and Theatre." *Modern Music* 20, no. 3 (March–April 1943): 205–7. Excerpts reprinted in *WEC*, 86–87.

Carter reviews Louis Gruenberg's music for the film *Commandos Strike at Dawn* ("very expert") and comments on the music in René Clair's *I Married a Witch* and Alfred Hitchcock's *Shadow of a*

Doubt ("both conventional and without character"). There are also reviews of two plays: Sidney Kingsley's *The Patriots* and Thornton Wilder's "polyhistoric human circus" *The Skin of Our Teeth*. Unfortunately, Carter's biting reviews of the film *The Siege of Leningrad* and of the George M. Cohan musical *Yankee Doodle Dandy* (starring James Cagney) are missing from the *WEC* reprint.

445. "Fine inverno, New York 1937." See "Late Winter, New York, 1937" (item 475).

446. "For Pierre Boulez on His Sixtieth." See "For Pierre on His Sixtieth" (item 447).

447. "For Pierre on His Sixtieth." In *Pierre Boulez: Eine Festschrift zum 60. Geburtstag am 26. März 1985*, ed. Josef Häusler, 12–13. Vienna: Universal Edition, 1985. ISBN 3-7024-0177-6. ML410.B773 P55 1985. Reprinted as "For Pierre Boulez on His Sixtieth" in *CEL*, 199–200.
    German translation ("Für Pierre zum Sechzigsten"), trans. Josef Häusler, in the original publication, 14–15.
    Italian translation ("Per Pierre, in occasione dei suoi sessant'anni"), trans. Paola Garelli Pugliaro, in *CARTER*, 261–62.

Noting that the music profession and its public are "almost frozen in the rigid patterns of older musical thought," Carter praises Boulez for his "determination to break this hard crust of institutional ice and to allow the new to take its artistic flight." Carter is also quick to point out that Boulez "did not call into question musical composition itself nor a number of very fundamental concepts on which it is based, as did some others at the time."

448. Foreword to *Selected Essays and Reviews 1948–1968*, by Richard Franko Goldman, ed. Dorothy Klotzman, vii–ix. Brooklyn: Institute for Studies in American Music, 1980. ISAM Monographs no. 13. ISBN 0-914678-13-2. ML60.G592. Also printed as "In Memory of Richard Franko Goldman," *American Music Center Newsletter* 22, no. 4 (Fall 1980): 13.

A brief tribute to Goldman's activities as bandleader, writer, editor, and critic.

449. "France Amérique Ltd." In *Paris—New York,* 7–11. Paris: Centre Georges Pompidou, 1977. ISBN 2-85850-040-1. Reprinted in *Paris—New York,* 21–26. (Paris: Editions du Centre Pompidou [ISBN 2-85850-615-9]/Editions Gallimard [ISBN 2-07-011224-1], 1991.)

This substantial historical essay is an important source for Carter's view of history during the period in which his own musical training took place. Both the introduction and conclusion are addressed to the great differences between European and American musical culture. In the absence of a respected elite in the United States, Americans continue to rely on European authorities to lead the formation of public taste. This puts composers in America in a difficult position. The body of the essay deals with a variety of French influences on American life, from Rosseau and de Tocqueville to Pierre Boulez. Carter discusses the large numbers of composers and intellectuals who went to Paris in the 1920s, with particular emphasis on the powerful influence of Nadia Boulanger. He also touches on European and American national styles of composition, the interaction between folk and concert musics, and the role of immigrants in American musical life.

450. "The Function of the Composer." *Bulletin of the Society for Music in the Liberal Arts College* 3, no. 1, suppl. 3 (1952): 1–7. Reprinted with the subtitle "[in teaching the general college student]" in *WEC,* 150–58.

In this address, originally presented at the Annual Meeting of the Society for Music in the Liberal Arts College, Rochester, New York, 29 December 1951, Carter's subject is the value of having composers teach music to general college students (i.e., nonmusic majors). He describes the curricular experiments that took place at St. John's College (where Carter taught in the early 1940s) and reports mixed results. He suggests that composers are more likely than other members of the music department "to make the past have a meaning for the general student in terms of his own life," but his tone is mainly skeptical. He is especially concerned about the detrimental effects of asking composers "to serve on committees, to appear on quiz programs, to administer various projects, to write articles, and the rest. . . . These extraneous activities take a terrible toll of time and energy and thought away from his own work."

451. "Für Pierre zum Sechzigsten." See "For Pierre on His Sixtieth" (item 447).

452. "Further Notes on the Winter Season 1938/9." See "The Case of Mr. Ives" (item 411).

453. "A Further Step." In *The American Composer Speaks 1770–1965*, ed. Gilbert Chase, 245–54. Baton Rouge: Louisiana State University Press, 1966. Reprinted in *WEC*, 185–91, and in *CEL*, 5–11.

  Spanish translation ("Un paso adelante"), *Buenos Aires Musical* 14, numero speciale (December 1959): 63–67.

  Italian translation ("Un altro passo avanti [1958]"), trans. Elena Racca Bruno, in *CARTER*, 174–79.

This survey of the musical landscape in 1958 finds Carter grappling with many of the issues that most preoccupied composers after World War II. Among the topics Carter addresses are form in the music of Debussy and Stravinsky, improvisation, the influence of the musical past in the form of recordings and musicological research, the danger of alienating the musical public, and European total serialism. Carter views all of these subjects as parts of an international "re-examination of musical discourse" that seeks "a new direction away from pre-established techniques."

454. "Gabriel Fauré." *Listen: The Guide to Good Music* 6, no. 1 (May 1945): 8–9, 12. Reprinted in *WEC*, 107–10, and in *CEL*, 119–22.

  Italian translation ("Gabriel Fauré"), trans. Angelo Bozzo, in *CARTER*, 123–26.

  Both reprints and the Italian translation omit the brief discography "Fauré's Music on Records," which appeared with the original article.

In this tribute to the French composer Carter draws attention to Fauré's subtlety and economy of means. "Adherents of this music find in its understated romanticism a world of deep feeling that often puts to shame those who carry on with empty grandiloquence." For Carter, "Fauré stands out as one of the great figures of French music."

455. "The Genial Sage." In *Paul Rosenfeld, Voyager in the Arts*, ed. Jerome Mellquist and Lucie Wiese, 163–65. New York: Creative Age Press, 1948. Reprinted with a new introductory note by Carter in *CEL*, 306–7.

A brief eulogy for Paul Rosenfeld, who wrote an early article about Carter's music (item 760) and with whom Carter planned to collaborate on a never-realized book about Charles Ives. In his introductory note to the reprint, Carter provides an interesting list of his influences in the years 1925 and 1926, when he first encountered Rosenfeld's book of critical essays on modern composers, *Musical Portraits* (item 892).

456. "The *Gesamtkunstwerk*." In *CEL*, 319–31.

In this wide-ranging essay, Carter discusses a variety of attempts to combine music with one or more of the other arts. Topics include Wagner's music dramas, the theatricality of performers, improvisation, synaesthesia and color organs, Wassily Kandinsky's play *Der gelbe Klang*, Schoenberg's *Die glückliche Hand*, Berg's operas, Eisenstein's films, Antonin Artaud's theater of cruelty, and Bertolt Brecht's Epic Theater. According to Bernard (*CEL*, pp. 348–49), "This text originated as a lecture given during Carter's semester as Visiting Professor at the Massachusetts Institute of Technology (Fall 1966)" and may have been revised for other occasions.

457. "Homage to Ravel, 1875–1937/Vacation Novelties, New York." *Modern Music* 15, no. 2 (January–February 1938): 96–103. Excerpts reprinted in *WEC*, 21–22.

A brief, eloquent tribute to Ravel, who had recently died, followed by scathing reviews of Charles Wakefield Cadman's *Dark Dancers of the Mardi Gras* ("I considered hissing the work but found that the dated stupidity of the style amused me") and Daniel Gregory Mason's *A Lincoln Symphony* ("small music about a great subject").

Missing from the reprint are Carter's reviews of a piano concerto by Isidor Achron; a setting of the Gettysburg Address ("On this speech Jacob Weinberg unleashed a turgid Wagnerian storm of passion that might well have embarrassed Lincoln as much as it did me"); William Grant Still's *Symphony in G minor—Song of a New Race*; Robert McBride's ballet *Showpiece;* Virgil Thomson's *Scenes from the Holy Infancy;* Poulenc's *Concerto for Two Pianos and Orchestra* and *Sept Chansons;* and arrangements of Greek Church chants by Nicolas Nabokov. Of particular interest are Carter's comments about Arnold Bax's *Third Symphony* and Eugene Goossens's *Intermezzo from Don Juan:* "When we have excellent modern pieces like Sessions's *Black Maskers* and *Symphony* or Aaron Copland's *First Symphony* and *Ode*, to mention but a few lying around waiting to be played again and again, why do we have to put up with foreign trash?" Carter also makes some provocative comments about opera: "[Verdi's] *Otello* is particularly important to us now for it may lead the public out of the Wagnerian miasma and get it to see how much more serious, yes even more profound, the spare, melodic works of the best of the Italians can be." He also praises the London Intimate Opera Company for their performances of seventeenth- and eighteenth-century operas, including Purcell's *Don Quixote* ("The evening was worth while just for the chance of hearing this first-rate music") and works by Arne, Dibdin, and Carey with three singers, string quartet, and piano.

458. "IGNM-Jury vor neuen Problemen." See "Sixty Staves to Read: This Was One of the Problems Faced by ISCM Jury in Cologne" (item 542).

459. "Igor Stravinsky 1882–1971." *Perspectives of New Music* 9, no. 2, and 10, no. 1 (double issue, 1971): 1–6. Reprinted in *WEC*, 301–6, and as part I of "Igor Stravinsky 1882–1971: Two Tributes" in *CEL*, 141–45. (Part II is item 460.) Italian translation, trans. Raffaele Pozzi, in *EC*, 621–27.

Carter's eulogy leads off a special memorial issue of *Perspectives of New Music* published not long after Stravinsky's death in 1971. Carter tells the story of hearing Stravinsky's *Le sacre du printemps* conducted by Pierre Monteux in New York in the mid-1920s and immediately deciding to become a composer. Carter also remarks on the "very telling quality of attack" of Stravinsky's piano playing and begins a consideration of the "'unified fragmentation'" he hears in Stravinsky's music by telling a revealing anecdote about a party at which Stravinsky showed him his sketchbooks.

460. "Igor Stravinsky 1882–1971." *Proceedings of the American Academy of Arts and Letters and the National Institute of Arts and Letters,* second series, no. 22 (1972), 84–86. Reprinted in *WEC,* 306–8, and as part II of "Igor Stravinsky 1882–1971: Two Tributes" in *CEL,* 145–46. (Part I is item 459.)
    Italian translation, trans. Raffaele Pozzi, in *EC,* 628–30.

A brief eulogy stressing Stravinsky's originality, his wit, and his ability to excel at each of the the various musical styles and genres he took up throughout his life.

461. "Igor Stravinsky 1882–1971: Two Tributes." See "Igor Stravinsky 1882–1971" (items 459 and 460).

462. "Illinois Festival—Enormous and Active." *Bulletin of the Society for Music in the Liberal Arts College* 3, no. 1 (1952), Supplement 3. Reprinted in *Bulletin of the American Composers Alliance* 3, no. 2 (1953): 17. Also reprinted in the *New York Herald Tribune,* 5 April 1953, and in *WEC,* 150–58.

Carter begins with a New Yorker's surprise at the "vast prairie perspectives" of Illinois and notes that the "broadness of surroundings is reflected in the broadness of taste that informs the annual Festival of Contemporary Arts." There follows a brief review of the musical events of the festival, including an "unexceptionable" performance of his *String Quartet No. 1* (item 88), played by the Walden String Quartet.

463. "In memoria di Stefan Wolpe." See "In Memoriam: Stefan Wolpe 1902–1972" (item 466).

464. "In Memoriam: Paul Fromm." *Ovation* 8, no. 11 (December 1987): 18. Reprinted in *A Life for New Music: Selected Papers of Paul Fromm,* ed. David Gable and Cristoph Wolff,

8–9. (Cambridge, MA: Department of Music, Harvard University, 1988. ISBN 0-674-53088-8. ML60.F86 1988.)

Brief remarks on the state of contemporary music institutions and on Fromm's extraordinary contribution to the cause of contemporary music, made at a memorial service at the University of Chicago on 4 October 1988.

465. "In Memoriam: Roger Sessions, 1896–1985." In *CEL*, 180–85.

According to Bernard's note (*CEL*, p. 346), "The author [Carter] and editor [Bernard] collaborated in conflating two previously published . . . essays for this edition." These are items 533 and 534.

466. "In Memoriam: Stefan Wolpe 1902–1972." *Perspectives of New Music* 11, no. 1 (Fall–Winter 1972): 3–5. Reprinted in *WEC*, 318–20, and in *CEL*, 185–87. Reprinted as "Stefan Wolpe (1902–1972): In Memoriam," *Tempo* 102 (1972): 17–18. Revised version reprinted as "Stefan Wolpe 1902–1972," *Proceedings of the American Academy of Arts and Letters and the National Institute of Arts and Letters*, second series, no. 23 (1973): 115–17.

Italian translation ("In memoria di Stefan Wolpe"), trans. Angelo Bozzo, in *CARTER*, 212–13.

This brief but ardent tribute is particularly notable for an anecdote about Wolpe, as guest lecturer, sitting down at the piano and exploring the compositional possibilities of each interval for a class Carter was teaching. "As he led us from the smallest one, a minor second, to the largest, a major seventh—which took all afternoon—music was reborn, new light dawned, we all knew we would never again listen to music as we had." Stefan Bauer-Mengelberg responded to Carter's tribute with a letter to the editor pointing out several inaccuracies (see item 613).

467. "In Memory of Richard Franko Goldman." See Foreword to *Selected Essays and Reviews 1948–1968*, by Richard Franko Goldman (item 448).

468. "In the Theatre." *Modern Music* 15, no. 1 (November–December 1937): 51–53. Reprinted in *WEC*, 17–19.

A generally enthusiastic review of the Salzburg Opera Guild's productions of Milhaud's *Le Pauvre Matelot,* Monteverdi's *Coronation of Poppea,* Mozart's *Così fan Tutte,* Ibert's *Angélique,* and Rossini's *Matrimonial Market.* Also reviewed are Virgil Thomson's music for Shakespeare's *Antony and Cleopatra,* Marc Blitzstein's music for *Julius Caesar,* Samuel Barlow's music for *Amphitryon 38,* and Thomson's music for the film *The River,* which is singled out for special praise.

469. "Introduction to a Poetry Reading Session by W. H. Auden." In *WEC,* 256–57. Reprinted as "Introduction to a Poetry Reading by W. H. Auden" in *CEL,* 307–9.

Originally delivered at the Hunter College Playhouse, January 1969. Carter's introduction consists primarily of quotations and comments documenting Auden's relationship to music, particularly those that intersect Carter's own aesthetic beliefs. The tone is suitably light, in spite of one or two pointed remarks such as the description of Auden as "someone to pay attention to even if you don't agree with him."

470. Introduction to *Mademoiselle: Conversations with Nadia Boulanger,* by Bruno Monsaingeon, 12–13. Manchester: Carcanet Press, 1985.

A loving tribute by Carter to one of his most important musical influences. Though quite short, Carter's deep feeling for Nadia Boulanger and "the extraordinary human and moral radiance resulting from her intense dedication to music" is present in every sentence. Also see item 436.

471. "ISCM Festival, Amsterdam." In *CEL,* 40–43.

In this article Carter describes his experiences as a member of the ISCM Festival international jury in 1962–63. "Here we were faced with the complicated challenge of representing as many different countries as possible, and as many different styles as we could, and at the same time trying to find interesting pieces that would provide effective contrasts among themselves on programs." In practice this aim is often compromised by practical matters (such as the difficulty of dealing with nontraditional notation and the expense of equipment rental) and a good deal of promising music must be rejected.

472. "ISCM Festival, Rome." See "Current Chronicle: Italy" (item 427).

473. "Ives oggi: il suo mondo e la sua sfida esistenziale." See "Ives Today: His Vision and Challenge" (item 474).

474. "Ives Today: His Vision and Challenge." *Modern Music* 21, no. 4 (May–June 1944): 199–202. Reprinted in *WEC*, 98–102, and in *CEL*, 90–93.
     Italian translation ("Ives oggi: il suo mondo e la sua sfida esistenziale"), trans. Elena Racca Bruno, in *CARTER*, 115–18.

Written just prior to Ives's seventieth birthday on 20 October 1944, this brief article combines a tribute to Ives's *Essays before a Sonata*, a capsule survey of his work, and a call for more performances of his music in the future.

475. "Late Winter, New York, 1937." *Modern Music* 14, no. 3 (March–April 1937): 147–54. Reprinted in *WEC*, 5–10.
     Italian translation ("Fine inverno, New York 1937"), trans. Elena Racca Bruno, in *CARTER*, 81–85.

Reviews of three New York Philharmonic concerts featuring composer-conductors conducting Mozart. Georges Enesco conducted the *Symphony in G Minor*, K. 550, Carlos Chávez conducted the *Symphony in C Major*, K. 551, and Igor Stravinsky conducted the *Piano Concerto in G Major*, K. 453, with Beveridge Webster as soloist. There is also commentary on Enesco's *Symphony in E-flat*, *Octet for Strings*, *Suite for Orchestra No. 2*, *Rumanian Rhapsody No. 2*, and *Cello Sonata*; and Chávez's *Caballos de vapor (H.P.)*, *Sinfonia India*, *Antigona*, *Tierra mojada*, *Spirals*, and *Sonatina* for violin and piano.
   Also reviewed are performances of Alban Berg's *Violin Concerto* played by Louis Krasner with Serge Koussevitzky and the Boston Symphony; Gian Francesco Malipiero's *Julius Caesar*; Bernard Wagenaar's *Third Symphony*, at the Juilliard School;

Schoenberg's *Fourth String Quartet*, played by the Kolisch String Quartet at the New York Public Library; Hindemith's *Sonata in E*, played by Szigeti; Paul Nordoff's *Prelude and Three Small Fugues*, Lazare Saminsky's *Songs for Three Queens*, and Otto Luening's *Prelude to a Hymn Tune by William Billings*, all played by the Philharmonic Chamber Orchestra in the Bennington Series; a concert by Wesley Sontag and the Mozart String Sinfonietta featuring Quincy Porter's *Ukranian Suite*, Samuel Barber's *Dover Beach*, and Goddard Lieberson's *Homage to Handel*, as well as works by several lesser-known composers; and a performance of Tikhon Khrennikov's *Symphony* [No. 1] by the Philadelphia Orchestra and Eugene Ormandy.

476. "Lettera dall'Europa." See "Letter from Europe" (item 477).

477. "Letter from Europe." *Perspectives of New Music* 1, no. 2 (Spring 1963): 195–205. Reprinted in *WEC*, 219–30, and in *CEL*, 31–40.
    Italian translation ("Lettera dall'Europa") in *EC*, 587–601.

A lively and thoughtful contemporary critique of the European postwar avant-garde. After commenting on the increasing popular success of European festivals of modern music (most following the "artistic orientation" of the Darmstadt school), Carter addresses the aesthetic issues raised by "'post-Webernism,'" aleatoric composition, total serialization, new approaches to texture, and "musical happenings." Recalling the avant-garde of the 1910s and 1920s, Carter is critical of postwar composers who are preoccupied with the "physical materials of music" without regard to how they are perceived by an audience. This lack of interest in listener psychology, he says, is precisely what led to the decline of the avant-garde in the earlier period. In the works of the postwar "neo-avant-garde," Carter finds that "there is usually a stultifying intellectual poverty that no amount of arithmetic patterning will overcome." The article concludes with a lengthy report from the 1962 Warsaw Festival and a eulogy for the conductor Hans Rosbaud.

478. Letter to the Editor, *Journal of Music Theory* 7, no. 2 (Winter 1963): 270–73.

Presumably written in response to Gardner Read's review of *The Modern Composer and His World,* ed. John Beckwith and Udo Kasmets (Toronto: University of Toronto Press, 1961), and *American Composers on American Music,* ed. Henry Cowell (New York: Frederick Ungar Publishing Co., 1962). The review appears in *Journal of Music Theory* 6, no. 2 (fall 1962): 304–8, with a passing reference to notation: "The sham of much avant-garde notation is sharply attacked by Schuller, who rightly insists that no composer is justified in notating literally unplayable music." In his letter Carter summarizes different methods of notating "'artificial divisions'" (quintuplets, septuplets, etc.) and asks if *JMT* readers know of any other systems. He concludes with a plea for notational consistency among composers.

479. Letter to the Editor, *Musical America* 84, no. 7 (September 1964): 4.

Carter's reply to an interview with Sir John Barbirolli (item 881) "in which the conductor fired a number of salvos at contemporary music." Writing from Berlin, Carter responds by attacking Barbirolli's "appalling sentimentalization" of pieces from the Fitzwilliam Virginal Book "which reveal his lack of understanding even for old music. This old ham is beyond curing." The Barbirolli interview also drew responses from Roger Sessions, Henry Cowell, and Walter Piston, among others.

480. Letter to the Editor, *Notes* 41, no. 1 (1984): 195.

An angry response to Andrew Mead's review (item 708) of the first edition of David Schiff's book *The Music of Elliott Carter* (item 769). Carter takes Mead to task for making his review "a rostrum for a polemic in favor of 'set-theory' analysis, despite its irrelevance to the book" and ascribes the perceived weaknessess in the book to himself, saying "the music is described in the composer's own terms, with all of what Mead considers their looseness, indefiniteness, and weak intellectual content." Also see Mead's reply (item 709).

481. "La mia ammirazione per Roger Sessions." See "Roger Sessions Admired" (item 534).

482. "The Milieu of the American Composer." See "The European Roots of American Musical Culture" (item 441).

483. "More about Balanchine." *Modern Music* 14, no. 4 (May–June 1937): 237–39. Reprinted in *WEC*, 14–15, and in *CEL*, 295–96.

Reviews of three ballets by Balanchine to music of Stravinsky: *Baiser de la fée, Jeu de cartes,* and *Apollon musagète.* "No one has ever worked out flow in dancing as well as Balanchine."

484. "Mozart's Human Touch." *Musical Times* 132 (November 1991): 549.

In spite of its brevity (ca. 500 words) this article is one of Carter's most candid and informative descriptions of his changing musical aesthetic during the 1950s and early 1960s. He credits discussions with Charles Rosen prior to the publication of Rosen's *The Classical Style* and his increasing dissatisfaction with the "textural formula" of "the figured-bass period" with his growing interest in the music of Haydn, early Beethoven, and Mozart. In the second paragraph Carter warns against "mechanical repetition and its frequently disastrous results," which he contrasts with Mozart's "impression of constant human awareness."

485. "Music and the Time Screen." In *Current Thought in Musicology,* ed. John W. Grubbs, 63–88. Symposia in the Arts and the Humanities, no. 4. Austin and London: University of Texas Press, 1976. ISBN 0-292-71017-8. ML3797.1.C87. Reprinted in *WEC*, 343–65, and in *CEL*, 262–80.
    French translation ("La musique et l'écran du temps"), trans. Stéphane Goldet, *Entre temps* 4 (June 1987): 55–67.
    Italian translation ("La musica e lo schermo del tempo"), trans. Elena Racca Bruno, in *CARTER,* 235–54.
    Italian translation ("La musica e lo schermo-tempo") in *EC,* 649–75.

Carter's lengthiest and most detailed account of his compositional methods, framed by a survey of philosophical opinions about time. Citing Martin Heidegger, Edmund Hüsserl, Charles Koechlin (item 888), Suzanne Langer, Pierre Suvchinsky (item 896), and others,

Carter examines various philosophical classifications of time (mathematically measured, psychological, etc.) and says that thinking about them led him to "a thoroughgoing reassessment of musical materials" around 1945. He then takes up his own works in roughly chronological order, from the *Sonata for Violoncello and Piano* (item 87) through the *Concerto for Orchestra* (item 49) to illustrate his musical responses to thinking about time. Both the technical details and the language with which Carter connects them to his philosophical interests make this article essential reading for those wishing to understand Carter's musical personality. According to Stone and Stone, this article is a "[r]evised version of a lecture given at the University of Texas at Austin in 1965."

486. "Music As a Liberal Art." *Modern Music* 22, no. 1 (November 1944): 12–16. Reprinted in *WEC*, 102–6, and, with documentation of sources added, in *CEL*, 309–13.
    Italian translation ("La musica come arte liberale"), trans. Elena Racca Bruno, in *CARTER*, 119–22.

In the first part of this article Carter argues that the study of music should include consideration of its moral, ethical, and philosophical aspects and not simply be technical training. For Carter, "the purely practical approach is largely responsible for the low estate to which music . . . has fallen." Citing Plato, Aristotle, Galileo Galilei, and Thomas Morley, Carter contrasts music's present status as a "poor relation of the arts and sciences" with its past glories as one of the "'seven liberal arts.'" In the second part of the article, as "an illustration of how music can be brought back into the general life of a university," Carter describes his experiences at St. John's College, where music played a central role in the curriculum of all students.

487. "Music Criticism." In *WEC*, 310–18. Reprinted in *CEL*, 335–42.

According to Stone and Stone (*WEC*, 310) this article was originally "[r]ead over the BBC as part of a series on 'Composers and Criticism,' edited by Elaine Padmore (Aug. 1972)." Exploring the nebulous relationship between "words about musical compositions and compositions themselves," Carter compares several verbal descriptions of Schoenberg's *Pierrot Lunaire*, concluding that they tell us more about their respective authors and the time periods in which they wrote than about the composition itself. Carter also considers the power of earlier works to influence later ones (Mozart's discovery of the works of J. S. Bach and his sons) and of later works to influence our perception of earlier ones (as Stravinsky's "neo-Classic" music forces us to hear Baroque music anew). The role of critics like Adorno, and of "journalist critics" in America, is briefly considered, and Carter concludes with the assertion that a composer's self-criticism is the most important criticism of all.

488. "Music of the Twentieth Century." In *Encyclopaedia Britannica*, vol. 16, 16–18. Chicago: Encyclopaedia Britannica, 1953.

489. "La musica americana sulla scena newyorchese, 1940." See "American Music in the New York Scene, 1940" (item 407).

490. "La musica come arte liberale." See "Music As a Liberal Art" (item 486).

491. "La musica e lo schermo del tempo." See "Music and the Time Screen" (item 485).

492. "La musica e lo schermo-tempo." See "Music and the Time Screen" (item 485).

493. "Musical Reactions—Bold and Otherwise." *Modern Music* 15, no. 3 (March–April 1938): 199. Reprinted in *WEC*, 27.

A brief review of Deems Taylor's book *Of Men and Music*. "Though interestingly written, and with considerable love for his art, one could wish that Mr. Taylor's taste were a little less dated, a little less well geared to the demands of the radio audience."

494. "La Musique américaine: une plante dépaysée." See "The European Roots of American Musical Culture" (item 441).

495. "La Musique aux États-Unis." *Synthèses* 9, no. 96 (May 1954): 206–11.

Annotated Bibliography of Carter Studies 191

A survey of various American styles of composition. Carter estimates the number of "composers of quality" (compositeurs de qualité) at around 1,500 and remarks on the enormous diversity of compositional styles among them. America was roused from its provincial lethergy by the arrival of Bartók, Schoenberg, and Stravinsky prior to World War I and by the jazz of the same time. These influences inspired "a remarkable freedom with respect to tradition revealed by these iconoclasts" (une remarquable liberté vis-à-vis de la tradition, révélée par ces iconoclastes).

496. "La Musique et l'écran du temps." See "Music and the Time Screen" (item 485).

497. "La Musique sérielle aujourd'hui" (in English). In *CEL,* 17–18.
French translation, *Preuves* 177 (November 1965): 32–33.

According to Bernard (*CEL,* p. 343), this article, written in English in 1965 and slightly revised in 1994, was "first published, in French, as part of a symposium of brief articles by several authors." It is a brief critique of total serialism (the "musique sérielle" of the title), which Carter views as a reaction to "the hidebound conservatism of the music profession after World War II. In Europe, where this traditionalism has seemed even more oppressive and deadening than in America, the reaction to it . . . has been especially intense." Arguing that the total serialists have restricted themselves to "one limited angle" of the work of Schoenberg, Berg, and Webern, Carter concludes that they "have dealt with tiny musical microstructures, the basic material of music, but very little with the potential of their interconnection for musical thought and expression."

498. "My Neoclassicism." In *Die klassizistische Moderne in der Musik des 20. Jahrhunderts,* ed. Hermann Danuser, 309–10. Publications of the Paul Sacher Foundation, vol. 5. Winterthur: Amadeus, 1997. ISBN 3-905049-73-2.

According to a note in the Elliott Carter clippings file at the New York Public Library for the Performing Arts, this brief essay was originally written as a preconcert talk given on 25 February 1995. Here Carter gives a fascinating nutshell summary of his early musical training and developing aesthetic and also provides something of a history lesson, speculating on the influence of Stravinsky and Hindemith, the philosophies of Irving Babbitt and Alfred North Whitehead, and the impact of two world wars on twentieth-century musical thought and development.

499. "The New Compositions: The Trend Is to the Clear and Intelligible." *Saturday Review* 27, no. 4 (22 January 1944): 32–33.

This article paints a revealing portrait of American musical life during World War II and of Carter's tastes during that time. In it he notes that the publication of serious music in the United States has changed dramatically with the arrival in America of composers such as Stravinsky, Hindemith, Milhaud, and Schoenberg, who fled Europe to escape the war. As a consequence, "American publishers are beginning to broaden their scope," providing music by a much wider range of composers than previously. As for contemporary compositional trends, Carter notes the passing of an era (ca. 1910–1930) when composers used "all kinds of novel devices with apparent disregard for what audiences thought." Now older composers are "engaged in a systematization of their personal musical languages with a view to making them more widely understood," while younger composers "no longer make their way by odd and unusual sound effects but by using the musical material of our time in a personal and meaningful way." Carter then points to a number of recently published examples, such as Barber's *Violin Concerto*, Copland's *A Lincoln Portrait*, Hindemith's *Ludus Tonalis*, and works by Paul Bowles, Gail Kubik, Robert Palmer, William Schuman, Virgil Thomson, Douglas Moore, Henry Cowell, and Carl Ruggles. Unfortunately, neither this article, nor its companion, "What's New in Music" (item 572), was reprinted in either *WEC* or *CEL*.

500. "New Publications of Music." *Saturday Review* 29, no. 4 (26 January 1946): 34–38. Reprinted in *WEC*, 111–16.

Carter surveys the compositional scene prior to reviewing new scores, including Benjamin Britten's *A Ceremony of Carols* and *Peter Grimes*, Bernard Rogers's *The Passion*, Lukas Foss's *The Prairie*, Arnold Schoenberg's *Ode to Napoleon*, Burrill Phillips's *Declaratives*, Marcelle de Manziarly's *Three Fables of La Fontaine*,

Paul Bowles's *David* and *In the Woods*, Igor Stravinsky's *Sonata for Two Pianos* and *Scènes de ballet*, Paul Hindemith's *Symphonic Metamorphoses of Themes by Carl Maria von Weber*, Aaron Copland's *Appalachian Spring*, Walter Piston's *Symphony No. 1*, Sergey Prokofiev's *Suites* from *Romeo and Juliet* and *Alexander Nevsky*, Samuel Barber's *Capricorn Concerto*, David Diamond's *Rounds*, and his own *Voyage* and *Holiday Overture*.

501. "The New York Season—(Continued) 1937." *Modern Music* 14, no. 2 (January–February 1937): 90–92. Reprinted as "The New York Season, 1937" in *WEC*, 3–5.

Reviews of Philip James's orchestral work *Bret Harte*, Webern's *German Dances*, and Anis Fuleihan's *Symphony*, conducted by Barbirolli; Jaromir Weinberger's *Schwanda*; Jean-Jules Roger-Ducasse's *Sarabande* and Muzio Clementi's *Symphony in C Major*, completed by Alfredo Casella and conducted by Paul Stassevitch; Clementi's *D Major Symphony* (also completed by Casella), Arthur Foote's *Suite in E Major* for string orchestra, and Edward MacDowell's *Second Piano Concerto*, conducted by Koussevitzky; and Milhaud's *Deuxième* and *Troisième symphonies* from his *Cinq symphonies* for small orchestra and Honegger's *Pastorale d'été*, conducted by Hans Lange in the Philharmonic Chamber Orchestra series.

502. "The New York Season Opens." *Modern Music* 17, no. 1 (October–November 1939): 34–38. Reprinted in *WEC*, 64–68.

Carter opens with a scathing review of Sibelius ("since audiences well trained in nineteenth-century heroics will stand for a lot of tedium, his music has what it takes to be popular at this time") and follows that with a scathing review of the ASCAP Festival of American Music ("another perfect illustration of my text—the magniloquent and grandiose symphonic style is the popular, prestige style of today"). Included in the ASCAP Festival review are comments about Frederick Jacobi's *Violin Concerto* ("It is neat, beautifully written for the solo instrument, and well worked out formally"), Henry Hadley's *In Bohemia*, John Herbert MacDowell's *Indian Suite*, Ernest Bloch's *Winter-Spring*, and Roy Harris's *Johnny Comes Marching Home*. In the last part of the article Carter summarizes the state of the Composers' Forum Laboratory and briefly mentions works by Jaromir Weinberger *(Under the Spreading Chestnut Tree)* and Mario Castelnuovo-Tedesco *(Concerto for Piano and Orchestra No. 2* and *Overture to Twelfth Night).*

503. Notes for sound recording of Elliott Carter, *Double Concerto* and *Duo for Violin and Piano,* Nonesuch H 71314. Reprinted with some additional material as "*Double Concerto for Harpsichord and Piano with Two Chamber Orchestras* (1961); *Duo for Violin and Piano* (1974)" in *WEC,* 326–30, and as "*Double Concerto,* 1961, and *Duo,* 1974" in *CEL,* 258–62.

   Italian translation *("Doppio concerto per clavicembalo, pianoforte e 2 orchestre da camera* (1961); *Duo per violino e pianoforte"),* trans. Elena Racca Bruno, in *CARTER,* 284–87.

The inclusion of these two works (items 51 and 52) on a single recording leads Carter to compare them. Both were written on commission, had relatively long periods of gestation, treat two contrasting sound sources "as opposing members of a pair," which imitate each other little, and both give the impression of "being continuous, of evolving constantly from beginning to end." The material added in the reprints consists of two quotations from Alexander Pope's *Dunciad,* which, according to Stone and Stone (*WEC,* p. 329), were "inserted from an earlier program note."

504. Notes for sound recording of Elliott Carter, *Night Fantasies* (item 74) and *Piano Sonata* (item 80), Nonesuch 79047-1.

This brief but forceful and eloquent note contains valuable information about the close connections between the composer and the four pianists who commissioned *Night Fantasies,* the connections between that work and the earlier *Piano Sonata,* and Carter's aesthetic in the early 1980s. Also see Paul Jacobs's note for the same recording (item 682).

505. Notes for sound recording of Elliott Carter, *Sonata for Violoncello and Piano* (item 87) and *Sonata for Flute, Oboe, Cello, and Harpsichord* (item 86), Nonesuch H 71234. Reprinted in *WEC,* 269–73, and as "Two Sonatas, 1948 and 1952" in *CEL,* 228–31.

Italian translation ("*Sonata per violoncello e pianoforte* [1948]; *Sonata per flauto, oboe, violoncello, e clavicembalo* [1953]"), trans. Sonia Bergamasco, in *CARTER*, 269–72.

Citing a range of influences from Wallace Stevens to Balinese gamelans, Carter describes the process of musical exploration that transformed his compositional style in the late 1940s and early 1950s.

506. Notes for sound recording of Elliott Carter, *String Quartet No. 1* (item 88) and *String Quartet No. 2* (item 89), Nonesuch H 71249. Reprinted in *WEC*, 274–79, and as "String Quartets Nos. 1, 1951, and 2, 1959" in *CEL*, 231–35.
   Italian translation ("*Quartetti per archi n. 1* [1951] e *n. 2* [1959]"), trans. Sonia Bergamasco, in *CARTER*, 273–76.

These notes, written for a 1970 recording, are Carter's retrospective view of compositions written ten and twenty years earlier. "Hearing these two quartets now, I get the impression of their living in different time worlds, the first in an expanded one, the second in a condensed and concentrated one." In addition to an informative comparison of the two pieces, the notes contain a reminiscence of Carter's famous sojourn in the Arizona desert in 1950–51, during which time he wrote his *String Quartet No. 1*.

507. Notes for sound recording of Elliott Carter, *String Quartet No. 3* (item 90), Columbia M 32738. Reprinted as "String Quartet No. 3 (1971)" in *WEC*, 320–22.
   Italian translation ("*Quartetto per archi n. 3* [1971]"), trans. Sonia Bergamasco, in *CARTER*, 279–80.

Carter's program note focuses on the work's large-scale form and contains a diagram of the combinations of movements played by the quartet's two duos.

508. Notes for sound recording of Elliott Carter, *A Symphony of Three Orchestras*, Columbia M 35171. See "*A Symphony of Three Orchestras* (1976)" (item 554).

509. "O Fair World of Music!" *Modern Music* 16, no. 4 (May–June 1939): 238–43. Reprinted in *WEC*, 55–59.

Italian translation ("O meraviglioso mondo della musica!"), trans. Elena Racca Bruno, in *CARTER*, 100–103.

A lighthearted and charming review of the musical goings-on at the New York World's Fair. Walking among the exhibition buildings, Carter is disdainful of the "ubiquitous loudspeakers," and the most poignant moment in his report is an account of a group of largely ignored musicians playing a Haydn symphony on a platform. "A few feet from the heart of the orchestra not a note they played could be heard." There are brief comments about Kurt Weill's score for *Railroads on Parade* and Aaron Copland's for Ralph Steiner's film *The City;* an account of Ferde Grofé with a group playing folk songs on the Hammond organ and Hammond Novachord; and a rather snide review of Robert Russell Bennett's music to accompany the fountains at the Lagoon of Nations ("Perhaps it was the problem of making music loud enough to be heard above the rush of waters that determined the choice of this clever orchestrator"). Carter also mentions Hanns Eisler's music for the Petroleum exhibit, William Grant Still's for the Perisphere, and Vittorio Giannini's for IBM ("a kind of *Heldenleben* that worked in national anthems from every nation"), as well as several notable performers, including the Coldstream Guards' Band at the British pavilion and Juanita Hall's Negro Melody Singers. Of the works presented in the Hall of Music Carter is most enthusiastic about *Chôros No. 8* and *Chôros No. 10* by Heitor Villa-Lobos and also mentions Karol Szymanowski's *Symphonie concertante,* op. 60, Stanislaw Wiechowich's *Polish Wedding Dance* from *Chmiel,* and Jonel Perlea's *Variations on an Original Theme.*

510. "O meraviglioso mondo della musica!" See "O Fair World of Music!" (item 509).

511. "Once Again Swing; Also 'American Music.'" *Modern Music* 16, no. 2 (January 1939): 99–103. Reprinted in *WEC,* 43–47, and in *CEL,* 45–48. Excerpts reprinted in Minna Lederman, *The Life and Death of a Small Magazine (Modern Music, 1924–1946),* 172–73. (Brooklyn: Institute for Studies in American Music, 1983. ISAM monographs, no. 18. ISBN 0-914678-20-5.)

The first section of this article is a review of a Carnegie Hall concert documenting the history of jazz. Carter focuses less on the music than on the differences between jazz and "serious music": "Certainly the main factor is the hall itself. A concert hall performance of the usual kind takes place as a ritual in which public and performer are ultimately subservient to the ideas of a composer who has put his notes on paper. Swing, on the other hand, is the glorification of the performer." In the article's second section Carter reviews serveral works performed by the Musical Art Quartet: Daniel Gregory Mason's *Intermezzo,* Quincy Porter's *Sixth Quartet,* and quartets by Rudolph Forst and Mark Wessel. Also reviewed are two premieres by Aaron Copland: *El Salón México* ("clearly a milestone in the composer's development") and *An Outdoor Overture.* Carter praises Copland as "one of the most important, original, and inspiring figures in contemporary music either here or in Europe." Finally, Carter makes brief mention of two pieces "trotted forth" by Barbirolli—Arnold Bax's "tedious" *Fourth Symphony* and Charles Haubiel's "pedantic-fancy" *Passacaglia*—and praises *The Lives of St. Cyril and St. Methodius* by Bŏzidar Širola performed by Hugh Ross and Schola Cantorum.

512. "On Edgard Varèse." In *The New Worlds of Edgard Varèse: A Symposium,* ed. Sherman Van Solkema, 1–7. ISAM Monographs, no. 11. Brooklyn: Institute for Studies in American Music, Brooklyn College, 1979. ISBN 0-914678-11-6. ML410.V27N5. Reprinted in *CEL,* 146–51.
    Italian translation (Su Edgard Varèse), trans. Paola Garelli Pugliaro, in *CARTER,* 255–60.

According to Stone and Stone (*WEC,* p. 369), this brief laudatory essay was "written in French and read over transatlantic telephone, Oct. 29, 1975, for broadcast over Radio-France (ORTF)" on a program about Varèse. Carter describes Varèse as the most striking of the experimental composers of the 1920s, and his comments center on Varèse's novel use of rhythm and the prominent role of percussion in his works. Not surprisingly, Carter often praises the elements of Varèse's music that remind him of his own. For example: "What has interested recent composers, also, is that Varèse's music does not depend on thematic motifs for its continuity, but rather the relationship between vertical, harmonic structures, instrumental sonorities, spacings, and of course, the play of rhythmic motifs." Carter also takes an active part in the "Discussion" that followed the reading of this paper at the Varèse symposium (see item 577).

513. "One Touch of Venus" (in German). See "Theatre and Films, 1943" (item 555).

514. "On Saint-John Perse and the *Concerto for Orchestra*." In *CEL,* 250–56.

This text originated as notes for a lecture-demonstration held on 5 February 1974 as part of an "Informal Evenings" concert given by Pierre Boulez and the New York Philharmonic. According to Bernard (*CEL,* p. 347), "[t]he manuscript . . . exists largely as a collection of fragments, which for this edition have been assembled into a coherent essay." The result is quite seamless, moving from a concise summary of the musical ideas Carter wanted to bring together in the *Concerto for Orchestra* (item 49) to an overview of his reading of the four sections of Perse's poem, *Vents,* which, he says "[gave] a kind of shape and character to the multiple-layered music I wished to write."

515. "Opening Notes, New York, 1937." *Modern Music* 15, no. 1 (November–December 1937): 36–37. Reprinted in *WEC,* 16–17.

Review of Bartók's *Music for Strings, Percussion, and Celesta* and Gardner Read's *Symphony in A minor,* played at the first concert of the New York Philharmonic's season. "Bartók's work is the finest of his compositions to be heard in these parts for a long time. It has much greater clarity than his more recent quartets and is less choppy, with greater broadness than the *Dance Suite.*" Read's piece, which won the Philharmonic's prize contest the previous year, does not fare so well: "If he had stuck more tenaciously to a unifying expressive conception, instead of to an intellectual one, his work might have had greater coherence."

516. "The Orchestral Composer's Point of View." In *The Orchestral Composer's Point of View: Essays on Twentieth-Century Music by Those Who Wrote It,* ed. Robert Stephan Hines, 39–61. Norman, OK: University of Oklahoma Press, 1970. Reprinted in *WEC,* 282–300, and in *CEL,* 235–50.

Italian translation ("Il punto di vista del compositore di musica per orchestra"), trans. Sonia Bergamasco, in *CARTER*, 196–211.

This article divides neatly into two parts. The first half is a despairing look at the conditions surrounding the production of new orchestral music in America in the late 1960s. The second half is an unusually detailed discussion of Carter's compositional methods in his orchestral music through the *Piano Concerto* (item 79). Of particular interest are the descriptions of the harmonic and rhythmic designs of the *Double Concerto* (item 51) and the *Piano Concerto*. This material is invaluable for analysts of Carter's music.

517. "Orchestras and Audiences; Winter, 1938." *Modern Music* 15, no. 3 (March–April 1938): 167–71. Reprinted in *WEC*, 28–31.

Carter makes passing reference to the Ravel memorial concerts played in Boston by Koussevitzky and the Boston Symphony, then reviews the same conductor and orchestra playing Hindemith's *Kammermusik No. 5* and *Concert Music for Strings and Brass*, the former with the composer as soloist. Also reviewed is the first concert performance of the *Suite* from Stravinsky's *Jeu de cartes*, played by Eugene Ormandy and the Philadelphia Orchestra, as well as "six well-stereotyped, contemporary impressionistic Roumanian composers of no interest," Edward MacDowell's *Launcelot and Elaine*, Walter Piston's *Suite*, and Germaine Tailleferre's *Violin Concerto*, all played by the New York Philharmonic, conducted by Georges Enesco (the Tailleferre was "delightful, gay and unpretentious, with a very fine slow movement"); and a concert by Hugh Ross and the Schola Cantorum featuring Frederick Delius's *Mass of Life* and Vladimir Dukelsky's *The End of St. Petersburg*. Also mentioned are the High-Low Concerts founded by Dukelsky (also known as Vernon Duke), which presented music by Aaron Copland, Marc Blitzstein, and Paul Bowles, as well as Duke Ellington and Count Basie.

518. "Parla un compositore americano." See "Shop Talk by an American Composer" (item 541).

519. "Un paso adelante." See "A Further Step" (item 453).

520. "Per Pierre, in occasione dei suoi sessant'anni." See "For Pierre on His Sixtieth" (item 447).

521. Program note to *String Quartet No. 1* (item 88). 1994 edition. New York: Associated Music Publishers, 1994.

This important comment reveals that Carter had to renounce the first prize in the Concours international de quatuors à cordes in Liège, Belgium (awarded in 1953), because his quartet had already been performed. Carter also notes the influence of Scriabin, Ives, and Nancarrow evident in certain aspects of the quartet.

522. "Il punto di vista del compositore di musica per orchestra." See "The Orchestral Composer's Point of View" (item 516).

523. "*Rasputin's End* and *Lady Macbeth of Mtsensk*." See "Current Chronicle: Germany, 1960" (item 426).

524. "Recent Festival in Rochester, 1938." *Modern Music* 15, no. 4 (May–June 1938): 241–43. Reprinted in *WEC*, 31–33.

Report about the eighth annual Eastman School Festival of American Music "almost entirely under the untiring baton of Howard Hanson." Carter reviews David Diamond's *Elegy in Memory of Maurice Ravel*, Vladimir Ussachevsky's *Cantata*, Charles Vardell's *Symphony No. 1*, Aaron Copland's *Saga for the Prairie (Music for Radio)*, and two dance scores: Bernard Rogers's *Five Fairy Tales* and Burrill Phillips's *Play Ball!* The latter is favorably compared with Kay Swift's *Alma Mater*.

525. "The Recent Works of Goffredo Petrassi (1960)." See "Two Essays on Goffredo Petrassi" (item 563).

526. "Reel vs. Real." *Newsletter of the American Symphony League* 11, no. 5–6 (July 1960): 8–10. Revised version reprinted as "The Challenge of the New" in *CEL*, 11–15.

A transcript (probably revised for publication) of talks given by Carter and Vladimir Ussachevsky, who were the guest speakers at the annual Composers' Luncheon held on 17 June 1960 during the American Symphony Orchestra League national convention in St.

Louis. According to Bernard (*CEL*, p. 343), Carter's talk was originally entitled "The Challenge of Electronic Music." It was later intended for publication in *Hi-Fi/Stereo Review* but was abandoned in 1962 because of editorial differences between Carter and his editor. The article contrasts composing for electronics and composing for the symphony orchestra. The advantages of the electronic medium are tempered by its comparatively early state of development. On the other hand, the decline of "the durable orchestral repertory" in the twentieth century may "reduce the orchestras first to being museums for a narrow band of musical history and finally to closing shop altogether for lack of anything new to display." The differences between the original article and the revised reprint are slight.

527. "Remembering Balanchine." In *I Remember Balanchine: Recollections of the Ballet Master by Those Who Knew Him*, ed. Francis Mason, 163–69. New York: Doubleday, 1991. Revised version in *CEL*, 299–304.

A collection of reminiscences about the choreographer. Recalling the ballets he saw at the Théâtre des Champs-Elysées in 1933 (when he was a student), Carter says, "In my opinion, Balanchine never did anything quite as interesting as that again." Carter also discusses Lincoln Kirstein's efforts to bring Balanchine to the United States and to found the School of American Ballet, Ballet Caravan, and the New York City Ballet, and Balanchine's sense of obligation to "insure the success of the new company" by doing ballets that were "guaranteed to be successful." There are also recollections of Balanchine's personality, his rehearsal techniques, his relationship with Stravinsky, and a number of his ballets from *Cotillon* (which Carter saw in 1932) to *Robert Schumann's "Davidsbündlertänze"* (1980). The original publication may have been transcribed from an interview. The reprint has many minor revisions that adapt the text to better suit the article format.

528. "Reminiscence of Italy." In *CEL*, 292–94.
   Italian translation ("Ricordo dell'Italia") in *EC*, 567–70.

A very brief memoir of Carter's many trips to Italy, from a childhood visit with his mother in the early 1920s to festivals of his music held in the 1980s.

529. "Reminiscences on Music." *Musical Newsletter* 1, no. 2 (January 1972): 3–6.

This brief excerpt from the then forthcoming *Flawed Words and Stubborn Sounds* (item 584) includes Carter's recollections of his studies with Nadia Boulanger and the influences of Ives, Varèse, Copland, Sessions, and (in passing) Ruggles.

530. "The Rhythmic Basis of American Music." *The Score and I.M.A. Magazine* 12 (June 1955): 27–32. Reprinted in *WEC*, 160–66, and in *CEL*, 57–62.

French translation ("La base rhythmique de la musique américaine"), trans. Jacques Demierre, *Contrechamps* 6 (April 1986): 105–11.

Italian translation ("Le basi ritmiche della musica americana"), trans. Angelo Bozzo, in *CARTER*, 151–56.

This article is an important source of information about Carter's evolving thoughts on rhythm in the mid-1950s. A perceptive analysis of the differences between rhythmic practice in jazz and in jazz-inspired concert music leads to a discussion of rhythm in the music of Roy Harris, Aaron Copland, Roger Sessions, Charles Ives, and Conlon Nancarrow. Noting that performances of rhythmically difficult works by these composers are rare, and that Copland, Harris, and Sessions have "lately become much more conservative in this respect," Carter concludes that "only a few American composers are seriously concerned with rhythmic problems."

531. "Ricordo dell'Italia." In *EC*, 567–70. See "Reminiscence of Italy" (item 528).

532. "Riflessioni su *Tre per sette*." See "Two Essays on Goffredo Petrassi" (item 563).

533. "Roger Sessions, 1896–1985." *Proceedings of the American Academy of Arts and Letters and the National Institute of Arts and Letters,* second series, no. 36 (1985): 57–62. Also see item 465.

A brief biographical sketch and commentary on Sessions's music.

534. "Roger Sessions Admired." *Perspectives of New Music* 23, no. 2 (Spring–Summer 1985): 120–22. Also see item 465. Italian translation ("La mia ammirazione per Roger Sessions"), trans. Paola Garelli Pugliaro, in *CARTER*, 263–65.

Carter praises Sessions's artistic integrity, emphasizes his interest in the practical side of music composition (sometimes at the expense of "theoretical correctness"), and considers at some length the relative sparseness of Sessions's dynamic and articulation markings, which Carter says have made performance and comprehension of Sessions's works more difficult.

535. "Roger Sessions: *Violin Concerto.*" See "Current Chronicle: New York, 1959" (item 429).

536. "Le scelte del compositore." See "The Composer's Choices" (item 420).

537. "Scores for Graham; Festival at Columbia." *Modern Music* 23, no. 1 (Winter 1946): 53–55. Reprinted in *WEC*, 116–18.

Carter reviews ballet scores written for Martha Graham by Aaron Copland *(Appalachian Spring)*, Paul Hindemith *(Hérodiade)*, and Carlos Chávez *(Dark Meadow)*, as well as dances by Merce Cunningham *(Mysterious Adventure,* to music for prepared piano by John Cage) and Erick Hawkins *(John Brown,* to music by Charles Mills). Carter praises the "ingenious fancy" of Cage's music: "This score, a maze of shivery strange and delicate noises, is a play of sound with neutral content and mood which allowed the dancer great latitude." Also reviewed are two concerts by the Walden String Quartet and an orchestral concert conducted by Howard Hanson, all part of a festival of American music at Columbia University. Carter is unimpressed by Henry Brant's *Saxophone Concerto* but praises Wallingford Riegger's *String Quartet No. 1,* op. 30 and Robert Palmer's *First String Quartet.* His opinion of William Bergsma's *Second Quartet* is mixed, and works by Frederick Jacobi *(Second Quartet),* Robert Russell Bennett *(Water Music),* Robert McBride *(Quintet),* and Alvin Etler *(Six from Ohio)* rate only a passing mention.

538. "Season of Hindemith and Americans, 1939." *Modern Music* 16, no. 4 (May–June 1939): 249–54. Reprinted in *WEC*, 60–63.

In addition to a brief overview of Hindemith's recent compositions and a review of "the most interesting" of them—the *Quartet for Clarinet, Violin, Cello, and Piano*, Carter chronicles many recent performances of contemporary works. There is a lukewarm review of Roy Harris's *Third Symphony* ("if only the whole were as good as some of the parts"), which contrasts sharply with Carter's later opinion (expressed in "American Music in the New York Scene, 1940," item 407), as well as comments on the recent U.S. premiere of Shostakovitch's *Fifth Symphony* and a performance of Schoenberg's *Das Buch der hängenden Gärten* ("the Schoenberg songs give us a taste of impressionism; though of the tortured, German variety they are just as beautiful"). Carter also notes performances of works by Aaron Copland *(An Outdoor Overture)*, Walter Piston *(Concertino for Piano and Orchestra)*, Paul Nordoff *(Concerto for Two Pianos)*, William Schuman *(Prologue* for chorus and orchestra), Roger Sessions *(Quartet)*, Frederick Jacobi *(Ave Rota)*, Irving Feigen (songs), Paul Bowles *(Pieces for a Farce)*, Lukas Foss (unnamed "very Hindemith-like pieces"), and Robert Palmer (whose *String Quartet* [No. 1] Carter calls "the most hopeful piece of the whole series"). Also mentioned is a concert of "leftist songs" by Hanns Eisler, Marc Blitzstein, Alex North, and Goddard Lieberson.

539. "Season's End in New York, 1937." *Modern Music* 14, no. 4 (May–June 1937): 215–17. Reprinted in *WEC*, 11–13.
Italian translation ("La chiusura della stagione 1937 a New York"), trans. Elena Racca Bruno, in *CARTER*, 86–88.

Carter reviews Hindemith's *Fourth String Quartet*, played at a League of Composers' concert; his viola concerto *Der Schwanendreher*, performed by the New York Philharmonic with the composer as soloist; and briefly comments on the revised versions of his *Five Songs on Old Texts* for mixed voices. Also reviewed are Stravinsky's *Jeu de cartes;* Roger Sessions's *String Quartet No. 1* (a Chamber Music Society of America recital); Aaron Copland's *Symphony* [No. 1], Honegger's *King David*, and Strauss's *Elektra* (a League of Composers' Philharmonic concert); Honegger's *Second*

String Quartet (a Pro-Arte Quartet recital); Szymanowski's *Harnasie;* Kodály's *Dances of Galanta* (a Philadelphia Orchestra concert); Goddard Lieberson's *Tango* for piano and orchestra; and Israel Citkowitz's *The Lamb* for women's voices.

540. "Season's End in New York, 1938." *Modern Music* 15, no. 4 (May–June 1938): 228–33. Reprinted in *WEC,* 34–38.
Italian translation ("La chiusura della stagione. New York primavera 1938"), trans. Elena Racca Bruno, in *CARTER,* 89–92.

Carter prefaces his reviews of an assortment of pieces with a bleak commentary on the state of contemporary music criticism. He argues that large sums of money depend on the judgment of critics of the visual and literary arts, and that the high stakes encourage critical responsibility. In music, however, the only money to be made is in performance, and thus there are no such economic pressures on critics of contemporary compositions. The result is contemporary music critics who "need make no effort to understand, or even to be literate in [their] condemnation." In his reviews Carter is most impressed by Malipiero's *Symphony,* Bernard Wagenaar's *Triple Concerto for Flute, Cello, and Harp,* David Diamond's *Quintet* for flute, piano, and string trio, and Dante Fiorillo's *Concerto for Piano, Oboe, and Horn.* He is hardest on Harl McDonald's *Fourth Symphony:* "the ineptitude of the form and harmony of this symphony was surprising, considering that he had such a good model as Tchaikovsky to go by."

541. "Shop Talk by an American Composer." *The Musical Quarterly* 46, no. 2 (April 1960): 189–201. Reprinted in *Problems of Modern Music,* ed. Paul Henry Lang, 51–63 (New York: W. W. Norton, 1960. ISBN 393 00115 6), and in *Contemporary Composers on Contemporary Music,* ed. Elliott Schwartz and Barney Childs, 261–73. (New York: Holt, Rinehart and Winston, 1967.) Also reprinted in *WEC,* 199–211, and in *CEL,* 214–24.
Italian translation ("Parla un compositore americano"), trans. Paola Garelli Pugliaro, in *CARTER,* 185–95.

An article in the form of an interview. According to Stone and Stone (*WEC,* p. 199), "Carter wrote the following after a symposium at

Princeton University, in an attempt to present a concentrated version of his ideas and the students' reactions and questions." Thus, Carter's responses to the questions (and perhaps the questions themselves) were carefully revised before publication. Carter begins with a lengthy preface in which he expresses his opposition to the use of compositional systems as a shortcut to achieving artistic quality. In the question-and-answer section Carter is occasionally defensive when he perceives a question as a slight to his music, but he offers some interesting examples from his *String Quartet No. 1* (item 88) in addition to commenting on various subjects including the vagueries of program notes, metric modulation (an unusually opaque explanation), twelve-tone techniques, performance difficulties, and electronic music. He concludes with an important and extended commentary on Charles Ives.

542. "Sixty Staves to Read: This Was One of the Problems Faced by ISCM Jury in Cologne." In *WEC*, 197–99. First published in the *New York Times*, 24 January 1960.

   German translation ("IGNM-Jury vor neuen Problemen"), trans. Gertrud Marbach, *Melos* 27, no. 6 (June 1960): 165–66.

A brief article describing the deliberations of the jury responsible for programming the 1960 ISCM Festival concerts in Cologne. Carter comments on the large number of nontraditional scores and describes the difficulties of dealing with complex seating plans for the ensembles and the abundance of nontraditional instruments and nonstandard notation. In spite of these difficulties, he reports there was considerable agreement among the members of the jury.

543. "The Sleeping Beauty." *Modern Music* 14, no. 3 (March–April 1937): 175–76. Reprinted in *WEC*, 10–11.

Review of the first American performance with orchestra of the complete *Sleeping Beauty* by Tchaikovsky, choreographed by Catherine Littlefield, which took place in Philadelphia. "Had her troupe been better she might have rivaled Radio City Music Hall in sumptuousness and absurdity."

544. "Some Reflections on *Tre per sette* (1986)." See "Two Essays on Goffredo Petrassi" (item 563).

545. "Soviet Music." In *CEL*, 331–35.

Carter here presents a historical summary of the activities of a variety of twentieth-century Russian and Soviet composers, writers, and artists and discusses their influence on the arts in Europe and America. Acording to Bernard, the essay was written "for a symposium at Sarah Lawrence College on the modern Soviet Union and delivered there on 24 May 1967." The published version is a composite of a partially redubbed tape recording of Carter's lecture and a typescript that "correponds only loosely to the recording."

546. "Stefan Wolpe 1902–1972." See "In Memoriam: Stefan Wolpe 1902–1972" (item 466).

547. "Stravinsky and Other Moderns in 1940." *Modern Music* 17, no. 3 (March–April 1940): 167–70. Reprinted in *WEC*, 74–81. Excerpts reprinted as "Stravinsky in 1940" in *CEL*, 138–40.
    Italian translation ("Stravinsky e altri moderni nel 1940"), trans. Elena Racca Bruno, in *CARTER*, 109–14.

Part I is a thoughtful summary of Stravinsky's career and music up to 1940, in the context of the American concert hall. Carter notes that after more than thirty years of worldwide fame, Stravinsky is primarily known for only two early works—*The Firebird* and *Petrouchka*, and that he has had to introduce the public to his more recent music "assiduously, and by painfully slow steps." On the music, however, Carter is enthusiastic: "From [the *Octet*] on, Stravinsky in his non-theatrical music has been bringing to a condensation point the various atmospheres of his stage works."

Part II is most notable for reviews of Charles Ives's *Sonata No. 4 for Violin and Piano* ("It is not nearly so well made as the first *Violin Sonata*, and it is less interesting"), works by Quincy Porter, Walter Piston, and William Schuman, and a Contemporary Concerts program organized by Mark Brunswick, Roger Sessions, and Edward Steuermann including music by Webern *(Five Pieces for String Quartet)*, Alban Berg *(Four Pieces for Clarinet and Piano)*, Béla Bartók *(Second Violin Sonata)*, and Ernest Bloch (*Quartet* [No. 1 (1916)]). Also reviewed are a performance by the Ballet Theatre with music by Darius Milhaud *(Création du monde)*, Kurt Weill *(Dreigroschenoper)*, Alexandr Mosolov (*Zavod* [Iron

Foundry]), Arthur Honegger ("early piano pieces"), Sergey Prokofiev *(Peter and the Wolf)*, Henry Brant (for Saroyan's *Great American Goof)*; a Czecho-Slovak benefit concert featuring Germaine Leroux performing Bohuslav Martinů's *Second Piano Concerto* and Prokofiev's *Second Violin Concerto;* a Composers' Forum Laboratory concert featuring music by Douglas Moore *(Ballad of William Sycamore),* Henry Cowell ("several works"), and Paul Creston (*Sonata* ["Suite?" according to Stone and Stone] *for Violin* and *Sonata for Alto Saxophone)*; and a League of Composers' concert featuring songs by Alexander von Zemlinsky, a string quartet by Karol Rathaus, Nikolai Lopatnikov's *Cello Sonata,* Paul Dessau's *Psalm III,* and Stefan Wolpe's *March and Variations,* which Carter says "was in my opinion the only work on the program with signs of real originality."

548. "Stravinsky e altri moderni nel 1940." See "Stravinsky and Other Moderns in 1940" (item 547).

549. "Stravinsky in 1940." See "Stravinsky and Other Moderns in 1940" (item 547).

550. "*String Quartet No. 2.*" In WEC, 273–74.

Reprint of Carter's program note for a performance of the *String Quartet No. 2* (item 89) by the Composers String Quartet on 15 April 1970 at Alice Tully Hall in New York.

551. "*String Quartet No. 3.*" See notes for sound recording of Elliott Carter, *String Quartet No. 3* (item 507).

552. "*String Quartets No. 1* (1951) *and No. 2* (1959)." See notes for sound recording of Elliott Carter, *String Quartet No. 1* and *String Quartet No. 2* (item 506).

553. "Su Edgard Varèse." See "On Edgard Varèse" (item 512).

554. "*A Symphony of Three Orchestras* (1976)." In WEC, 366–67. Reprinted, with additional material, as notes for

sound recording of Elliott Carter, *A Symphony of Three Orchestras* and *A Mirror on Which to Dwell,* Columbia M 35171.
  Italian translation *("Una sinfonia di 3 orchestre"),* trans. Elena Racca Bruno, in CARTER, 288–89.

According to Stone and Stone, this is Carter's program note for the world premiere, given by the New York Philharmonic, conducted by Pierre Boulez, in February 1977. The additional material in the reprint consists of a program note for the other work on the recording (the song cycle *A Mirror on Which to Dwell* [item 72]) and a paragraph comparing the registral descents of *A Symphony of Three Orchestras* (item 95) to "a similar fall from poetic heights" in the first song, "Anaphora," of that cycle.

555. "Theatre and Films, 1943." *Modern Music* 20, no. 4 (May–June 1943): 282–84. Reprinted in WEC, 93–95.

Reviews of *A Tree on the Plains* (libretto by Paul Horgan, music by Ernst Bacon), performed at Columbia University; *The Wind Remains,* by Paul Bowles (a setting of the masque from the last act of García-Lorca's *Asi que pasen cinco años*), with musical direction by Leonard Bernstein, at the Museum of Modern Art; and film scores by Roy Webb (for *The Human Comedy*) and Max Steiner (for *Mission to Moscow*).

556. "Theatre and Films, 1943." *Modern Music* 21, no. 1 (November–December 1943): 50–53. Excerpts in WEC, 95–98, and in CEL, 304–5.
  German translation ("One Touch of Venus"), in *Über Kurt Weill,* trans. Josef Heinzelmann, ed. David Drew, 137–38 (Frankfurt am Main: Suhrkamp Verlag, 1975).

Reviews of Kurt Weill's *One Touch of Venus* and film scores by Copland *(North Star)* and Alexandre Tansman *(Flesh and Fantasy).* The article includes remarks cut from the reprints about a Broadway revival of *The Merry Widow,* the Soviet film *We Will Come Back* ("one wonders why we dignify our enemies [the Nazis] as super-gangsters while the Russians treat them as inhuman fools beneath contempt"), the American film *Constant Nymph* (with a score by Eric Korngold), and the British film *The Great Mr. Handel.* Carter praises the last for "the genuine sympathy and understanding shown a great composer and his life of work in this film." The selective editing in the *WEC* version (reprinted in *CEL*) somewhat skews the presentation of Carter's original review. The German translation contains only the review of Weill's *One Touch of Venus*.

557. "The Three Late Sonatas of Debussy." In *CEL*, 122–33.

According to Bernard (*CEL*, p. 345), this text "originated as a lecture, delivered at Princeton University in 1959." It was revised for publication from "one continuous draft accompanied by a great deal of more fragmentary . . . material, much of which . . . has been incorporated where possible." The result covers a great deal of ground, including Debussy's music criticism; the reception history of his music; his relation, in terms of both technique and aesthetic outlook, to his contemporaries in music and the other arts; and his handling of phrasing and form in his mature works, with emphasis on the three late sonatas.

558. "The Time Dimension in Music." *Music Journal* 23, no. 8 (November 1965): 29–30. Reprinted in *WEC*, 243–47, and in *CEL*, 224–28.

According to Bernard (*CEL*, p. 347), this article was "originally a lecture presented at Bowdoin College, 21 August 1965." In it, Carter describes several passages from his own works that illustrate his interest in the manipulation of musical time. This discussion is prefaced by a comment acknowledging the influence of the generation of Schoenberg and Stravinsky, not for their "retreat from reason and emphasis on 'emotion,'" but for the way they "had completely re-examined the traditional postulates about music and the hearing of music."

559. "Time Lecture." In *CEL*, 313–18.

In the first part of this essay Carter discusses the Platonic conception of time, the Pythagorean derivation of musical intervals, and philosophies of time by modern writers, including Pierre Suvchinsky (see item 896), Igor Stravinsky, and Gisèle Brelet. The second part is a fascinating three-page summary of Carter's view of how musical time was approached in the baroque, classical, romantic, and twentieth-century eras, by composers such as Handel, Mozart,

Chopin, Wagner, and Schoenberg. According to Bernard (*CEL*, p. 348), this lecture was "Given at Harvard University in 1965."

560. "To Be a Composer in America." In *CEL*, 201–10.

According to Bernard (*CEL*, p. 346), the text was "Delivered (under an unknown title) on 27 March 1953, at the University of Illinois" and revised for publication in 1994. It contains one of Carter's most eloquent and informative assessments of his experience as a composer in America and his perspective on the pieces, composers, and events that helped shape the course of American music in the early twentieth century. The article also documents Carter's thinking about aesthetic and technical matters during an important period of transition in his career.

561. "To Think of Milton Babbitt." *Perspectives of New Music* 14, no. 2, and 15, no. 1 (double issue, 1976): 29–31. Reprinted in *CEL*, 197–99.

Carter's brief contribution leads off the essay section of a special issue in honor of Babbitt's sixtieth birthday. Leaving an explication of Babbitt's "Rameau-like" contribution to twelve-tone theory to others, Carter concentrates on praising Babbitt's compositions, lamenting the often poor performances they receive, and expressing optimism that as the quality of performances improves, Babbitt's music will be more widely appreciated.

562. "Tribute to Paul Jacobs." Eulogy given during funeral services for Paul Jacobs on 27 September 1983, reprinted in the program book from "A Concert in Memory of Paul Jacobs," 24 February 1984, Symphony Space, New York, NY.

In his eulogy, Carter recalls his friendship and many creative collaborations with Paul Jacobs, dating back to the mid-1950s.

563. "Two Essays on Goffredo Petrassi." In *CEL*, 187–97.
    Italian translation of the second essay ("Riflessioni su *Tre per sette*"), without the musical examples included in the English version, in *Petrassi*, ed. Enzo Restagno, 310–12 (Torino: E.D.T. [Edizioni di Torino], 1986), ISBN 88-7063-044-7.

According to Bernard (*CEL*, p. 346), the first essay, "The Recent Works of Goffredo Petrassi," was written "at Luciano Berio's request for a projected new periodical that never came into being." It is a capsule survey of Petrassi's music and aesthetic approach, to 1958, with emphasis on the *Serenata* (1958) and the *Invenzione concertata* (1956–57).

The second essay, "Some Reflections on *Tre per sette*," was first published in Italian without the musical examples added for the English version. It is a brief appreciation of Petrassi's composition, in which Carter points out a few of the passages he admires. "In describing such small details I have tried to show microscopically some of the pleasures the work contains for me."

564. "Two Sonatas, 1948 and 1952." See notes for sound recording of Elliott Carter, *Sonata for Violoncello and Piano* and *Sonata for Flute, Oboe, Cello, and Harpsichord* (item 505).

565. "*Variations for Orchestra.*" In Edward Downes, *The New York Philharmonic Guide to the Symphony*, 250–51. New York: Walker & Co., 1976. ISBN 0-8027-0540-5. Reprinted in *WEC*, 308–10.
    Italian translation ("Variazioni per orchestra"), trans. Angelo Bozzo, in *CARTER*, 277–78.

According to Stone and Stone (*WEC*, p. 308), this brief program note was "originally written in 1955 and revised for the performance by the New York Philharmonic, April 1972, Lorin Maazel, conductor."

566. "Variazioni per orchestra." See "*Variations for Orchestra*" (item 565).

567. "Vassar Choir Concert Features Belgian Music." *New York Herald Tribune*, 15 March 1945, p. 17.

This review, which was not printed in all editions of the paper, covers a concert of early Belgian music given by the Vassar Choir under the direction of E. Harold Geer, with organist Kathleen Funk Pearson and harpsichordist Ralph Kirkpatrick. "By and large it was an ambitious program for amateur singers and there seemed to be too little variety of vocal color and shading to sustain interest to the end, despite the obvious charm of the voices."

568. "Wallingford Riegger." *American Composers Alliance Bulletin* 2, no. 1 (February 1952): 3. Reprinted in *WEC*, 158–59.

In this brief commentary, which seems to have been intended, at least in part, to publicize an upcoming performance of Riegger's *Third Symphony* by Dimitri Mitropoulos and the New York Philharmonic, Carter praises Riegger for having "followed the dictates of his own personality and musical instinct . . . without caring whether he was or was not in step with the fashions of the time." He also notes that time has made Riegger's music less forbidding to the general public: "what was once so puzzling now seems fascinating and strongly expressive."

569. "Walter Piston." *Musical Quarterly* 32, no. 3 (July 1946): 354–75. Reprinted, without the list of works found in the original article, in *WEC*, 121–40, and in *CEL*, 158–75. Abbreviated version reprinted in *The Book of Modern Composers*, 2nd ed., revised and enlarged. (New York: Alfred A. Knopf, 1950.)
    Italian translation, also without the list of works, trans. Angelo Bozzo, in *CARTER*, 127–44.

One of Carter's longer essays, this homage to Walter Piston combines a substantial biographical sketch with a survey of Piston's compositions, illustrated with numerous musical examples. Carter divides Piston's works into two periods, before and after 1938: "If in the first period he is occupied with integrating and assimilating modern techniques, in the second there is an urge toward directness and simplicity." Carter's praise is unequivocal: "[Piston's] works have a uniform excellence that seems destined to give them an important position in the musical repertory."

570. "Was ist amerikanische Musik?" See "What Is American Music?" (item 571).

571. "What Is American Music?" *Österreichische Musikzeitschrift* 31, no. 10 (October 1976, special English issue): 4–6.
    German translation ("Was ist amerikanische Musik?") in the regular German version of the same issue: 468–70.

In searching for a definition of "American music" Carter identifies several differences between American and European cultural life. In the United States composers work in comparative isolation without much contact with one another or a sophisticated musical public. Whereas European composers "carefully [coordinate] musical means and ends at every level," it is "the very absence of this sharpness of focus . . . that gives the good works of American music their special freshness." Finally, "European artists have to fit into certain cultural standards and canons that their country demands. We in America are free because our culture doesn't make this kind of demand on us. We are left as individuals to float in a kind of cultural limbo."

572. "What's New in Music." *Saturday Review* 28, no. 3 (20 January 1945): 13–14, 34.

A survey of recent American publications of music. The first section includes seventeenth- and eighteenth-century music by Bach, Buxtehude, and others and music by more recent composers such as Fauré and Mahler (who is praised for his orchestrations). The second part of the article takes up music by Carter's contemporaries such as Schoenberg, Hindemith, Stravinsky, Walter Piston, William Schuman, Virgil Thomson, and others.

573. "With the Dancers." *Modern Music* 15, no. 1 (November–December 1937): 55–56. Reprinted in *WEC*, 19–20.

Review of ballets performed by the Littlefield Ballet: Poulenc's *Aubade*, *Poème* (to Ravel's *Pavane*), and *Choreartium* (to music by Bach); and the Russian Ballet: *Gods Go A-Begging* (to music by Handel), *Francesca da Rimini*, and *Coq d'Or*.

574. "With the Dancers." *Modern Music* 15, no. 2 (January–February 1938): 118–22. Reprinted in *WEC*, 23–26, and in *CEL*, 296–99.

Review of ballets performed in connection with the month-long Dance International festival that took place in New York in December 1937. Carter reviews the Littlefield Ballet's *Barn Dance* ("based on fiddler tunes in conventional arrangements") and the Ballet Caravan's *Showpiece* (to a commissioned score by Robert McBride). After a polite review of performances by Ruth St. Denis, Carter launches a lengthy attack on modern dance as practiced by several of St. Denis's pupils including Martha Graham, Doris Humphrey, Charles Weidman, and Tamiris. Only Hanya Holm's *Trend* receives guarded praise. Also praised are two ballets performed by the Ballet Caravan at the Avery Memorial in Hartford, Connecticut: Virgil Thomson's *Filling Station* and Paul Bowles's *Yankee Clipper*.

The Writings of Elliott Carter. Listed above as item 399.

II. Interviews and Panel Discussions with Elliott Carter as a Participant

Collections

575. *EEC   Entretiens avec Elliott Carter*. Geneva: Contrechamps Editions, 1992. ML410.C3293 A5 1992.

A collection of French translations of excerpts from three interviews: Allen Edwards, "Une conversation avec Elliott Carter" (see item 584); Charles Rosen, "Entretien avec Elliott Carter" (see item 600); and Heinz Holliger, "Entretien avec Elliott Carter" (see item 589).

Panel Discussions

576. "Ben Weber and Virgil Thomson Questioned by Eight Composers." *Possibilities* 1 (Winter 1947/1948): 18–24.

Carter's question to Weber is more a credo about the usefulness of the twelve-tone method, to which "What do you think?" has been added at the end. Nevertheless, Carter states his position clearly: "The strict and free use of 12-tone rows in composition seems to me to have no other value than as a discipline for the composer and a method of enhancing the coherence of music much like canons and fugues. Like them, this procedure only has a remote connection with the expression and style of the music." Weber responds that he thinks it unlikely he could achieve the same results with another method. To Thomson, Carter poses a question about "automatic musical writing," wondering, if a piece has arisen from a "semi-euphoric state of automatism" (Thomson), how it can hold the attention of a listener. Thomson's reply begins, "Don't confuse a disciplined spontaneity with the laziness of a loose tongue."

Carter, Elliott. "Shop Talk by an American Composer." Listed above as item 541.

577. "Discussion." In *The New Worlds of Edgard Varèse: A Symposium*, ed. Sherman Van Solkema, 75–90. ISAM Monographs, no. 11. Brooklyn: Institute for Studies in American Music, Brooklyn College, 1979. ISBN 0-914678-11-6. ML410.V27N5.

A conversation among four participants in a symposium on Edgard Varèse held at the City University of New York in April 1977: Elliott Carter, Chou Wen-Chung, Robert P. Morgan, and Sherman Van Solkema, with later questions from audience members Dika Newlin, Ruth Julius, Claire Brook, and Bruce Macintyre. Mostly there is polite discussion of each of the papers. (Also see item 512.)

578. "International Music Congress Forum." *Music and Artists* 2, no. 1 (February–March 1969): 23–29.

A panel discussion, moderated by Aaron Copland, involving Pauline Olivieros, Murray Schaefer, Earle Brown, Paul Williams, Ben Johnston, Laszlo Somfai, Morton Subotnick, Morton Feldman, Peter Maxwell Davies, Roger Sessions, John Eaton, Gilles Lefebvre, and Carter. Each says their piece in turn. Carter comments near the end: "So far this whole discussion has been assuming that a 'music public' exists today the way it has in the past: a public which somehow commissioned works and determined their particular style." He goes on to say that the current situation lacks this "public directive," and so "the composer must choose—whether to lead the public, or to lead his own private life and not bother about the public."

579. "The Symphony: Is It Alive? Or Just Embalmed?" *New York Times*, 22 September 1968, sec. 2 (Arts and Leisure).

Quotations from a panel discussion moderated by Paul Hume with Carter, Lukas Foss, and Leon Kirchner. Carter's comments begin, "I think that unless the situation changes very drastically, not only will there be no future for new music in the symphony orchestra world, but the symphony orchestra world itself will die."

Interviews

580. Bernard, Jonathan W. "An Interview with Elliott Carter." *Perspectives of New Music* 28, no. 2 (Summer 1990): 180–214.

This interview is one of the longest and most substantial in print. Subjects include Carter's compositional development; his recent works, concerts, and recordings; his literary influences; the improving quality of performances of his music; his return to vocal music in the mid-1970s; the poem *Vents* and his *Concerto for Orchestra* (item 49); American music; the influence of the Darmstadt school; and the teaching of composition. The last part of the interview is a particularly interesting discussion of more technical issues surrounding Carter's compositional methods, including his *Harmony Book*.

581. Boretz, Benjamin. "Conversation with Elliott Carter." *Contemporary Music Newsletter* 2, no. 8 (November–December 1968), 1–4. Reprinted in revised form in *Perspectives of New Music* 8, no. 2 (Spring–Summer 1970), 1–22.

Carter's *Double Concerto* (item 51) is the launching pad for a highly abstract and philosophical discussion about what is meant by "surface," "idea," "structure," "resolution," and so on. Initially published as a lightly edited transcript, this "conversation" was completely rewritten and substantially enlarged by the participants before publication in *Perspectives of New Music*. (Carter's first response, for example, is transformed from a straightforward description of the concerto's instrumentation to a disquisition on Noam Chomsky.) Such editorial revisions are common in the secondary literature on Carter, as Carlton Gamer points out in his review of *Flawed Words and Stubborn Sounds* (item 657). In spite of their often self-conscious verbosity, these articles are a valuable source of information about Carter's thinking in the late 1960s.

582. Dreier, Ruth. "Elliott Carter." *Musical America* 108, no. 5 (November 1988): 6–10.

This fairly brief but interesting interview was published to honor Carter's eightieth birthday. In it Carter speaks about concert acoustics, his compositional methods, and the responses of performers to his works.

583. Dufallo, Richard. "Elliott Carter." In *Trackings*, 269–85. Oxford and New York: Oxford University Press, 1989. ISBN 019505816X. ML390.D815 1989.

This wide-ranging interview, conducted on 29 May 1986, is particularly good on Carter's early career, including his relationship with Ives and the influence of the early modernist composers, and his experiences as a student in Boston (where he often heard Koussevitzky conduct the Boston Symphony Orchestra), Cambridge (where he studied at Harvard with Walter Piston and Gustav Holst), and Paris (where he studied with Nadia Boulanger). Other topics include musical life in post–World War II America; a summary of Carter's visits to Aspen in 1973, 1974, and 1979; Goffredo Petrassi; Igor Stravinsky; Edgard Varèse; and Carter's own compositional process, including brief discussions of *Tarantella* (item 97), *Syringa* (item 96), and *A Mirror on Which to Dwell* (item 72).

584. Edwards, Allen. *Flawed Words and Stubborn Sounds*. New York: Norton, 1971. ISBN 0393021599. ML410.C3293 E3. Excerpts printed as "Reminiscences on Music," *Musical Newsletter* 1, no. 2 (January 1972): 3–6.

Italian translation of excerpts ("Una conversazione con Elliott Carter"), trans. Raffaele Pozzi, in *EC*, 551–63.

French translation of excerpts ("Une Conversation avec Elliott Carter"), trans. Suzanne Rollier, in *EEC*, 9–85.

This book-length "conversation," modeled on the Igor Stravinsky and Robert Craft dialogues, consists of a "condensed, reordered, and partly rewritten transcript of a series of tape-recorded interviews between Elliott Carter and [Allen Edwards] that took place at intervals over the period from 1968 to 1970." According to Edwards, the material discussed grew out of notes Carter made for a series of lectures given at Carleton College in 1966. The book is divided into three chapters, the first on musical culture in Europe and America in the twentieth century, the second on Carter's life and development as a composer, and the third on his music and developing musical language. More than twenty-five years after its original publication this remains one of the most comprehensive and often-cited sources on Carter and his music. For reviews see itesm 633, 640, 657, and 752.

Entretiens avec Elliott Carter. Listed above as item 575.

585. Ford, Andrew. "Gentility and Apocalypse; Elliott Carter." In *Composer to Composer: Conversations about Contemporary Music,* 2–9. St. Leonards, Australia: Allen & Unwin, 1993. ISBN 1-86373-443-0. London: Quartet, 1993. ISBN: 0-7043-7061-1.

This interview, conducted in June 1991, contains some interesting comments by Carter on the composition of *Scrivo in vento* (item 84), then in progress, and on his compositional process in general.

586. Gagne, Cole, and Tracy Caras. "Elliott Carter." In *Soundpieces: Interviews with American Composers,* 87–99. Metuchen, NJ: Scarecrow Press, 1982. ISBN 0-8108-1474-9. ML390.S668.

A very brief biographical introduction and a catalog of works from 1933 to 1980 frame this interview conducted on 10 August 1975. The conversation touches on Carter's neoclassical period, metric modulation, electronic music, Carter's education and background, twelve-tone and aleatoric techniques, the first three string quartets, the *Concerto for Orchestra* (item 49), and vocal music. (Although he was then engaged in the composition of *A Mirror on Which to Dwell* (item 72), Carter says only "I'm thinking of writing some more songs.") The tone is relaxed and conversational, and there seems to be little in the way of editorial revision.

587. Gauthier, André. "Elliott Carter: 'A la manière de Rameau.'" *Les nouvelles littéraires* 55, no. 2569 (27 January–3 February 1977): 13.

A brief monologue in which Carter comments that during the years that separate his first string quartet from his second he "evolved towards the serial language, and used it, but very freely" (j'ai évolué vers le langage sériel et je l'ai employé, mais très librement). He also expresses interest in electronic music, although he says he doesn't have time to study it in sufficient depth.

588. Gelles, George. "An Interview with Elliott Carter." *Amacadmy: The Newsletter of the American Academy in Rome* 2, no. 1 (July 1979): 3–5.

Carter here comments that his experiences teaching at St. John's College in the early 1940s were a strong influence on his developing mature style. The interview also includes some dispirited remarks about serious music in America in the twentieth century and the younger generation of composers.

589. Holliger, Heinz. "Abseits des Mainstreams: Ein Gespräch mit dem amerikanischen Komponisten Elliott Carter." Trans. Sigfried Schibli. *Neue Zeitschrift für Musik* 152, no. 3 (March 1991): 4–9.

French translation ("Elliott Carter: écrire par couches superposées"), trans. Daniel Haefliger, with German abstract ("Elliott Carter: Komponieren mit sich überlagernden Schichten"), *Dissonanz • Disonance* 31 (February 1992): 10–13. Also printed as "Entretien avec Elliott Carter" in *EEC*, 101–9.

Significantly abridged English translation of the French translation ("Conversation with Elliott Carter"), trans. John Bunge, *Sonus* 14, no. 2 (Spring 1994): 5–12.

A very interesting and candid conversation that explores in some detail Carter's aesthetic of combining layers of differently constituted music. Similar procedures in the music of Ives, Mozart, Verdi, and others are discussed, and Carter talks about the influence of Stravinsky and Schoenberg on his mature style. Other topics (mostly omitted from the English translation) include Carter's *Violin Concerto* (item 107) and its relation to the one by Alban Berg; Carter's *Oboe Concerto* (item 75) (which was written for Holliger); and musical notation, phrasing, and performance difficulties. The interview was originally conducted in English in 1991. The English version listed above was translated from the French translation of the German translation of the English original.

590. Hurwitz, Robert. "Elliott Carter: The Communication of Time." *Changes in the Arts* 78 (November 1972): 10–11.

A brief interview in which Carter discusses his ideas about musical time, music education, orchestral performances of new music, and its accessibility to contemporary audiences.

591. Johnston, Robert. "Elliott Carter's Imagery Drawn from Modern Life." *Music Magazine* 8, no. 5 (November–December 1985): 12–14, 33.

A particularly lively discussion of the role of contemporary music in twentieth-century society, the difficulty of teaching music composition, Carter's dislike of electronic music, musical life in Europe, and Carter's extramusical sources of inspiration. The interview was conducted at the Banff Center in Canada and revised by Carter for publication.

592. Kerner, Leighton. "Creators on Creating: Elliott Carter." *Saturday Review*, December 1980, 38–42.

In his brief answers to Kerner's brief, sometimes testy questions, Carter touches on his working methods, the performance of complex music and the reactions of general audiences, and his then recently completed solo piano piece, *Night Fantasies* (item 74).

593. Knussen, Sue. "Elliott Carter in Interview." *Tempo* 197 (July 1996): 2–5.

This brief interview contains an interesting anecdote about Stravinsky teaching Carter to drive on the left side of the road when they were both teaching at Dartington Hall. Carter also touches on his background, his relationship with Ives, his influences, and his belief in the unity of musical works.

594. Messinis, Mario. "Elliott Carter: sulla musica moderna." *Musica/Realtà* 5, no. 15 (December 1984): 24–27.

In this interview, conducted at the Pontino Festival in June 1983, Carter's primary topic is his own compositional development. He discusses his early dislike of expressionism, his ballets *Pocahontas* (item 81) and *The Minotaur* (item 71), the music of Charles Ives and its influence on his own music, and his feelings about serialism.

595. Pozzi, Raffaele. "Elliott Carter: Talking to Raffaele Pozzi." See Pozzi, Raffaele, "Elliott Carter" (item 596).

596. ———. "Elliott Carter" (in Italian). *Piano Time* 24 (March 1985): 31–33.

English translation ("Elliott Carter: Talking to Raffaele

Pozzi"), trans. Louise Forster, *Tempo* 167 (December 1988): 14–17.

In this brief interview Carter discusses his early musical training, the differences between European and American musical culture, his music for piano, his lack of interest in electronic music, and his then most recent work, *Riconoscenza per Goffredo Petrassi* (item 102.2), which was premiered at the 1984 Pontino Festival, during which the interview took place.

597. Restagno, Enzo. "Un'autobiografia dell'autore raccontata da Enzo Restagno." In *CARTER*, 3–77.

English translation ("Elliott Carter: In Conversation with Enzo Restagno for Settembre Musica 1989"), trans. Katherine Silberblatt. ISAM Monographs, no. 32 (Brooklyn: Institute for Studies in American Music, 1989). ISBN 0-914678-35-3. ML410.C3293 A3 1991.

This is a transcript of a lengthy series of interviews conducted in French and Italian in 1989 and first published in Italian in connection with the 1989 Settembre Musica festival in Turin, Italy. Carter made "a number of small changes" in the English translation. The first half of the book is of particular interest. Its subject matter includes Carter's experiences as a boy growing up in New York City, his studies with Nadia Boulanger in the 1930s, and his feelings about Charles Ives, Igor Stravinsky, Edgard Varèse, Arnold Schoenberg, and many other composers, writers, and visual artists. The second half is mainly a discussion of Carter's career and each of his compositions in chronological order, from his earliest works to *Remembrance* (item 100.2), with many short digressions. For a review see item 721.

598. ———. *Elliott Carter: In Conversation with Enzo Restagno for Settembre Musica 1989*. See Restagno, Enzo, "Un'autobiografia dell'autore raccontata da Enzo Restagno" (item 597).

599. Rosen, Charles. "Intervista ad Elliott Carter." See Rosen, Charles, "An Interview with Elliott Carter" (item 600).

600. ———. "An Interview with Elliott Carter." In *The Musical Languages of Elliott Carter*, 33–43. Washington, DC: Library

of Congress, 1984. ISBN 0-8444-0449-7. ML410.C3293R7 1984. French translation ("Entretien avec Elliott Carter"), trans. Carlo Russi, *Contrechamps* 6 (April 1986): 112–22. Revised version in *EEC*, 87–109. Italian translation ("Intervista ad Elliott Carter") in *EC*, 529–49.

This lengthy interview contains some of Carter's most candid and informative comments about his compositions. Here he often describes his own feelings that led to the familiar scenarios associated with many of his works, from the *Piano Sonata* (item 80) to *Night Fantasies* (item 74). The interview, which was originally produced for the BBC in April 1983, was revised for publication.

601. ———. "Entretien avec Elliott Carter." See Rosen, Charles, "An Interview with Elliott Carter" (item 600).

602. Smith, Patrick J. "Elliott Carter: Musician of the Month." *High Fidelity,* August 1973, MA-4–MA-5.

A brief and lively monologue in which Carter inveighs against young publicity-seeking composers and comments on a variety of topics including writing for the musical theater, preparing for the exhibit of his manuscripts at the New York Public Library for the Performing Arts (see item 610), and the high cost of publishing his orchestral scores.

603. Szersnovicz, Patrick. "Le Temps restitué." *Le monde de la musique* 117 (December 1988): 90–94.

A long and candid interview, given in Badenweiler on 6 November 1988. Carter touches on his ideas about musical time, his admiration for the music of Alban Berg, and his feelings about a number of other musicians including Nadia Boulanger, Schoenberg and Stravinsky, Bartók, Ligeti, Messiaen, Britten, Boulez, Berio, and Stockhausen. He also describes his lifelong interest in Mozart and in the Bach cantatas and comments briefly on metric modulation, and on his recent compositions, including *Penthode* (item 78), the *Violin Concerto* (item 107), and the *Quintet for Piano and Winds* (item 83). Objecting to the suggestion that his music is most developed in the areas of rhythm and form, Carter says: "My music is based above all on harmony. The fundamental element is my harmonic choices" (Ma musique est avant tout fondée sur l'harmonie. L'élément fondamental, ce sont mes choix harmoniques).

604. "Le Tournant des années cinquante." In *Acanthes, An XV: Composer, enseigner, jouer la musique d'aujourd'hui*, ed. Cécile Gilly and Claude Samuel, 136–43. Paris: Van De Velde, 1991. ISBN 2-85868-173-2.

A short, candid interview on the occasion of the fifteenth anniversary of the Centre Acanthes. Topics include American music, Carter's musical development, rhythm, the education of young composers, and the role of the university in American musical life. All are covered quite briefly.

605. Vlad, Roman. "Goffredo Petrassi, Elliott Carter: cronaca di un'amicizia." Interview with Elliott Carter and Goffredo Petrassi. Ed. Raffaele Pozzi. *Piano Time* 30 (September 1985): 32–37.

In this friendly conversation Carter and Petrassi discuss the importance of the ISCM in the 1930s and its diminished importance since that time; the powerful influence of dodecaphony in European music after the war and their own feelings about serial techniques and serial music; several of their own compositions (Carter mentions *Riconoscenza per Goffredo Petrassi* [item 102.2.] and *A Mirror on Which to Dwell* [item 72]); and the relationship between music and poetry.

606. Wilson, Patrick. "Elliott Carter: *Eight Pieces for Four Timpani*." *Percussive Notes* 23, no. 1 (October 1984): 63–65.

In this interview, conducted on 15 April 1983 during a four-day Elliott Carter festival at the University of Southern California, Carter discusses his *Eight Pieces for Four Timpani* (item 54). The focus is primarily on performance practice (harmonics, drum heads, sticks, etc.), but Carter also talks about programming all eight pieces on one program, about the different editions of the pieces, and about the use of percussion in his other works.

607. Wolfthal, Marvin A. "Elliott Carter" (in Italian). *Musica* 3, no. 14 (1979): 232–33.

The main topic of this interview is the differences between musical culture in Europe and the United States. Carter laments the lack of public support for music in the United States and notes that it is particularly difficult for composers to learn to write for the orchestra because they have so few opportunities to do so, and because the works that are written are rarely played after their premieres. There are also brief discussions of composers Carter admires (Boulez, Nono, Lutosławski), of virtuosity and Vladimir Horowitz, and of music theater. Wolfthal suggests that the element of theatricality in Carter's chamber music, together with his return to vocal music in the 1970s, makes the time ripe for Carter to consider writing an opera. Carter replies that doing so would be "too problematic" (troppo problematica) both esthetically and practically (but see item 110).

III. Sources on Elliott Carter and His Music by Other Authors

Bibliographies and Discographies

Short, selected bibliographies and discographies appear frequently in articles about Carter and his music. Only those of exceptional length or interest are listed here.

608. Cundiff, Morgan. "A Guide to Elliott Carter Research Materials at the Library of Congress Music Division." In *The Musical Languages of Elliott Carter,* 45–85. Washington: Library of Congress, 1984.

Includes a chronological list of works to 1983, a lengthy bibliography (organized by topic), a list of performances of Carter's music given at the Library of Congress from 1952 to 1979 (arranged alphabetically by composition), and a catalog of Carter manuscripts and sketches held by the library. A great deal of this primary source material was on loan until 1988, when it was sold by Carter to the Paul Sacher Foundation in Basel, Switzerland. The remainder of the material, which was originally donated to the Library of Congress, remains there (see Appendix 2).

609. Doering, William T. *Elliott Carter: A Bio-Bibliography.* Bio-bibliographies in Music, no. 51. Westport, CT: Greenwood, 1993. ISBN 0-313-26864-9. ML134.C19D6.

The twenty-eight-page biography (including a two-page curriculum vitae) consists primarily of quotations from various secondary sources. More useful is the bibliography, which is divided into four sections: works and performances, discography, bibliography of material by Carter, and bibliography of material about Carter. "Works and Performances" is arranged by genre and supplemented by three appendices: an alphabetical listing of compositions, a chronological listing of compositions, and the names and addresses of Carter's publishers. The approximately forty-page discography, though prone to factual and proofreading errors, is quite comprehensive and contains cross-references to record reviews. The bibliographies contain a wealth of helpful information, though the author's annotations vary greatly in both quantity and quality. There is also a fourteen-page index and a helpful appendix of archival sources that lacks only a sufficient description of the holdings of the Paul Sacher Foundation (where the bulk of Carter's papers reside).

610. *Elliott Carter: Sketches and Scores in Manuscript.* New York: The New York Public Library and Readex Books, 1973. ISBN 0-87104-247-9. ML141.N4C4.

Catalog from an exhibition of Carter manuscripts on display in the Vincent Astor Gallery, Library and Museum of the Performing Arts, the New York Public Library at Lincoln Center, December 1973–February 1974. Both the exhibition and the catalog were prepared by Richard Jackson with assistance from Pamela S. Berlin and John Shepard. In addition there is a short introduction by Michael Steinberg, a list of works, a selective bibliography, a discography, and numerous photographs and illustrations of autograph sketches and scores.

611. Weber, Jerome F. *Carter and Schuman.* Discography Series, vol. 19. Utica, NY: J. F. Weber, 1978. ML156.5.C27W4.

This typewritten and stapled discography of music by Carter and William Schuman is a very valuable reference. The section on Carter comprises ten pages, with Carter's compositions listed in chronological order. Dates of composition and first performance are given. Many dates of recording are given, as are timings, dates of first appearance and deletion from the Schwann catalog, and dates of review in *Gramophone* magazine.

612. Whipple, Harold. "An Elliott Carter Discography." *Perspectives of New Music* 20, no. 1–2 (Fall–Winter 1981/Spring–Summer 1982): 169–81.

This discography, current to about 1982–83, is based on the one in the New York Public Library catalog *Elliott Carter: Sketches and Scores in Manuscript* (item 610), with independent confirmation of some recordings.

Books and Articles

613. Bauer-Mengelberg, Stefan. Letter to the Editor, *Tempo* 103 (1972): 63–64.

This letter corrects several inaccuracies in Carter's tribute to Stefan Wolpe (item 466). Carter had suggested that the symptoms of Wolpe's Parkinson's disease may have manifested themselves as a result of the strain of preparing revisions of his *Symphony* for performance by the New York Philharmonic. Bauer-Mengelberg points out that Wolpe made the revisions before the piece was accepted for performance by the Philharmonic and that Wolpe's illness was independent of these events.

614. Below, Robert. "Elliott Carter's *Piano Sonata*: An Important Contribution to Piano Literature." *Music Review* 34, nos. 3–4 (August–November 1973): 282–93.

A detailed analysis of the *Piano Sonata* (item 80) focusing primarily on a family of half-step motives found throughout the composition.

615. Bernard, Jonathan W. "Spatial Sets in Recent Music of Elliott Carter." *Music Analysis* 2, no. 1 (1983): 5–34.

Bernard's analyses of excerpts from the *Piano Concerto* (item 79), *Brass Quintet* (item 42), *Concerto for Orchestra* (item 49), and *String Quartet No. 3* (item 90) demonstrate various approaches to the organization of registral space in Carter's music. The distinction between interval and interval class, the use of chord voicings based on a specific interval repertory, the location of small collections in registrally fixed larger ones, and the symmetrical arrangement of pitches around an axis are all cited as evidence of Carter's spatial interests.

616. ———. "The Evolution of Elliott Carter's Rhythmic Practice." *Perspectives of New Music* 26, no. 2 (1988): 164–203.

Bernard describes the composition of Carter's works from the *Sonata for Violoncello and Piano* (item 87) through the *Double Concerto* (item 51) in terms of a series of progressively more refined rhythmic innovations. Particularly noteworthy is the idea that Carter's early interest in the "successive" presentation of rhythmic patterns gave way to one in which they are presented "simultaneously." Although the teleological organization of the article tends to slight the earlier works (they are necessarily cast in the subordinate role of precursors to the later works), Bernard's analyses throughout are thoughtful and enlightening. In a subsequent interview with Bernard (item 580) Carter called the article "excellent."

617. ———. "Premises and Applications of Spatial Analysis." In *Musikometrika* 2, ed. M. G. Boroda, 241–77. Quantitative Linguistics 43 (Bochum: Universitätsverlag Dr. N. Brockmeyer, 1990).

Bernard here discusses ways in which the vertical spacing of pitch-class sets operates in selected works of Varèse, Bartók, Carter, and Messiaen. In the section on Carter, two examples (one from the *Piano Concerto* [item 79], one from the sketches for that work) illustrate the integration of registrally fixed pitch collections and the trichord set classes on which the harmony of the piece is based.

618. ———. Review of *The Later Music of Elliott Carter: A Study in Music Theory and Analysis*, by David I. H. Harvey. *Music Analysis* 9, no. 3 (1990): 344–55.

Review of item 677. A detailed and balanced response to Harvey's book. Bernard praises Harvey's summary of the influences on "the eventually emergent Carterian aesthetic and musical point of view" but finds his terminology and analytical methodology problematic.

Bernard's most significant criticism involves the criteria by which Harvey partitions Carter's textures into hierarchical levels.

619. ———. "Problems of Pitch Structure in Elliott Carter's First and Second String Quartets." *Journal of Music Theory* 37, no. 2 (Fall 1993): 231–66.

Bernard here presents a series of very detailed and technical set-class and contour analyses of excerpts from Carter's first two string quartets (items 88 and 89). His aim is to illustrate the difficulty of verifying, in a rigorous way, the claims Carter and others have made that the two all-interval tetrachords are the principal formative elements in these works.

620. ———. "Elliott Carter and the Modern Meaning of Time." *Musical Quarterly* 79, no. 4 (Winter 1995): 644–82.

In this wide-ranging summary and analysis of the principal influences on Carter's thinking about musical time, Bernard considers literature, philosophy, dance, and film, including works by Charles Koechlin (item 888), Pierre Suvchinsky (item 896), Gisèle Brelet, Alfred North Whitehead, Marcel Proust, James Joyce, George Balanchine, and Sergei Eisenstein.

621. ———. "Poem as Non-Verbal Text: Elliott Carter's *Concerto for Orchestra* and Saint-John Perse's *Winds*. In *Analytical Strategies and Musical Interpretation*, ed. Craig Ayrey and Mark Everist, 169–204. Cambridge: Cambridge University Press, 1996. ISBN 0-521-46249-5. MT75.A62 1996.

Carter has long acknowledged Saint-John Perse's epic poem *Vents* (Winds) as an important source of inspiration for his *Concerto for Orchestra* (item 49). In this article Bernard explores the nature of that inspiration in great detail, providing a close reading of both the poem and its connections with Carter's composition.

622. ———. "Elliott Carter: *Concerto for Orchestra* (1965–69)." In the catalog of the exhibition *Settling New Scores: Music Manuscripts from the Paul Sacher Foundation*, at the Pierpont Morgan Library, 13 May–30 August 1998, ed. Felix Meyer, 121–26. Mainz: Schott, 1998. ISBN 3-7957-0347-6.

A detailed commentary on three of Carter's sketches for his *Concerto for Orchestra* (item 49) which are beautifully reproduced in color plates. Together, the plates and commentary provide a valuable source of information about Carter's working methods.

623. Black, Robert. "Boulez's Third Piano Sonata: Surface and Sensibility." *Perspectives of New Music* 20, nos. 1–2 (Fall–Winter 1981/Spring–Summer 1982): 182–98.

Part II of this essay begins with a brief commentary on *Syringa* (item 96), including an account of an interview with John Ashbery in which Ashbery says his poem "Litany" from the collection *As We Know* "had been suggested by a related idea of Carter's, expressed in his *Duo for Violin and Piano* (1973–74), of two separate argumentative forces."

624. Boykan, Martin. "Elliott Carter and the Postwar Composers." *Perspectives of New Music* 2, no. 2 (Spring–Summer, 1964): 125–28. Reprinted in *Perspectives on American Composers*, ed. Benjamin Boretz and Edward T. Cone, 213–16. (New York: Norton, 1971.)

Boykan holds up Carter, and his *String Quartet No. 1* (item 88) in particular, as a model for younger composers of the postwar generation. Carter's work "provides a moral lesson" that a composer's task is to "*choose* [his or her] language freshly for each work, and to choose from the whole range of musical possibilities" (italics in original).

625. Brandt, William E. "The Music of Elliott Carter: Simultaneity and Complexity." *Music Educators Journal* 60, no. 9 (May 1974): 24–32. Reprinted as "The Music of Elliott Carter" in *Breaking the Sound Barrier: A Critical Anthology of the New Music*, ed. Gregory Battcock, 221–34. (New York: E. P. Dutton, 1981. ISBN 0-525-47598-2.)

This summary of Carter's musical aesthetics and career includes a brief quotation from a previously unpublished letter, written in 1958, in which Carter says, "No part of my music is ever 'freely composed' but at the same time no part of my music is ever completely dictated by a rigid, mechanical preestablished routine or technique followed without regard for its musical effect."

Annotated Bibliography of Carter Studies

626. Brooks, Richard. Review of *Penthode* (item 78), by Elliott Carter. *Notes* 48, no. 2 (December 1991): 683–86.

An overview of the composition, together with a pitch and pitch-class analysis of the opening measures. "The uncompromising complexity of this music demands much from the listener, but great rewards in listening pleasure await those who make the effort." Brooks is skeptical about Carter's "long, continuous line," which is marked with brackets in the score: "Carter's line is much too complex to be able to memorize and gets completely lost in the thick ensemble texture."

627. Bye, Antony. "A Note on Elliott Carter's *Violin Concerto*." *Musical Times* 132, no. 1776 (1991): 75–76.

As the title suggests, this is a brief description of the concerto (item 107)—serving mainly to advertise the upcoming U.K. premiere—in light of Carter's earlier compositions.

628. ———. "Carter's 'Classic' Modernism." *Tempo* 189 (June 1994): 2–5.

Following David Schiff's lead (see item 773), Bye takes up the issue of "classicism" versus "modernism" in Carter's music. His premise is that "in modernist art the rupture between the moment-to-moment Dionysiac flux we perceive in the foreground and any subliminal coherence existing at a background level is complete." For Bye this "rupture" is exemplified by the opening of *Gra* (item 63), in which "pc-set recurrences are not reinforced by foreground restatements distinguished by shape." For a thoughtful response, see the letter to the editor by Guy Capuzzo (item 631).

629. ———. "Democratic Process." *Strad* 102, no. 1214 (1991): 528–29.

An overview of Carter's first three string quartets (items 88, 89, and 90) and their place in his evolving aesthetic is followed by a chronological descriptive overview of the *String Quartet No. 4* (item 91), accompanied by several musical examples.

630. Caltabiano, Ronald. "Elliott Carter: Towards the Tenth Decade." *Tempo* 207 (December 1998): 2–8.

Caltabiano surveys Carter's compositions from 1990 to 1998, emphasizing the *Violin Concerto* (item 107) and *Symphonia—Sum Fluxae Pretiam Spei* (item 93).

631. Capuzzo, Guy. Letter to the Editor, *Tempo* 204 (April 1998): 53.

A thoughtful response to the issues raised by Antony Bye in his article "Carter's 'Classic' Modernism" (item 628).

632. "Catálogo cronológico clasificado de la obra del compositor estadounidense Elliott Carter." *Boletin interamericano de música* 17 (May 1960): 23–27.

A list of Carter's published works arranged chronologically within each genre, from the *Incidental Music for Sophocles' "Philoctetes"* (1933) through the *String Quartet No. 2* (1959).

633. Chase, Gilbert. Review of *Flawed Words and Stubborn Sounds*, by Allen Edwards (interview with Elliott Carter). *Notes* 29, no. 2 (December 1972): 249–51.

Review of item 584. While noting that "if there was ever any spontaneity in these conversations, it has been carefully expunged," Chase nonetheless acknowledges "this is undoubtedly a book of permanent historical value."

634. Childs, Barney. Review of WEC. *Notes* 35, no. 1 (September 1978): 69–70.

Review of item 399. Childs praises Carter's "extensive humane learning" as revealed by his writings. He also notes "An important difference . . . from many other current composers is that Carter's development moves from American, not European models," including Henry Cowell, Henry Brant, and Conlon Nancarrow. Childs reproves those who prefer "the more recent European 'discoveries' of the same ideas."

635. Clements, Andrew. "Elliott Carter Views American Music." Review of WEC. *Music and Musicians* 26, no. 7 (March 1978): 32–34.

Review of item 399. Clements first presents a very concise and informative summary of Carter's career and aesthetic preoccupations. In the review that follows, he is most interested in Carter's early writings for *Modern Music* and about Charles Ives. "It stands as an enormously useful book on an era of American music dominated to a great extent by its author."

636. Cogan, Robert. "Elliott Carter: *Eight Etudes and a Fantasy*, Etude III." In *New Images of Musical Sound*, 66–72. Cambridge, MA, and London: Harvard University Press, 1984. ISBN 0-674-61585-9. MT6.C63N5 1984.

Cogan presents an analysis of Etude III of Carter's *Eight Etudes and a Fantasy* (item 53) in terms of its spectral variation as revealed in a series of eighteen photographs of a computer-generated spectrum graph, taken at different moments of a performance of the piece by the New England Conservatory Scholarship Woodwind Quartet.

637. ———. "The Art-Science of Music after Two Millennia." In *Concert Music, Rock, and Jazz Since 1945: Essays and Analytic Studies*, ed. Elizabeth West Marvin and Richard Hermann, 34–52. Rochester, NY: University of Rochester Press, 1995. ISBN 1-878822-42-x. ML 160.C737 1995.

Cogan mentions Carter's first two string quartets (items 88 and 89) and *Sonata for Violoncello and Piano* (item 87) in passing; more interesting is his polyrhythmic analysis of the theme of the *Canon for 3* (item 43).

638. Cogan, Robert, and Pozzi Escot. *Sonic Design: The Nature of Sound and Music*, 59–71, 204–7, 284–89. Englewood Cliffs, NJ: Prentice-Hall, 1976.

The introduction of Carter's *String Quartet No. 2* (item 89) is examined from three different perspectives in these three excerpts. In the first, "three distinct space fields" are established and traversed by the instruments. In the second, a "basic cell"—E-F-A♭-B♭—is manifest in various ways in the pitch and pitch-class domains. In the third, several pulsed lines are related by means of "beat [or metric] modulation." There is also a brief analysis of the cello solo that begins Carter's *String Quartet No. 1* (item 88).

639. Coker, Wilson. Review of *WEC. The Journal of Aesthetics and Art Criticism* 37, no. 3 (Spring 1979): 381.

Review of item 399. A short but insightful critique of Carter's collected writings. Although mildly critical of "Carter's chit-chat of encapsulated praise or dismissal" and the "somewhat piqued tone" of his reportage, Coker concludes "The book provides an on-the-spot survey of the age in which . . . American music came into its own."

640. Connolly, Justin. Review of *Flawed Words and Stubborn Sounds*, by Allen Edwards (interview with Elliott Carter). *Tempo* 99 (1972): 22–24.

Review of item 584. Connolly only briefly mentions the book he is reviewing in the course of this broad historical description of American musical culture and its place on the world stage. He nonetheless praises Carter lavishly: "It may well be that in Elliott Carter we have the most complete and rounded composer to have emerged from and transcended the difficulties of musical life in America."

641. Copland, Aaron. "America's Young Men of Music." *Music and Musicians* 9, no. 4 (December 1960): 11, 33.

This survey of younger American composers, transcribed from a talk Copland gave in London, contains a few paragraphs about Carter, together with an early photo. Copland's remarks are mostly about the *String Quartet No. 1* (item 88), in which "each separate instrument seemed to be playing a separate sonata for himself, and somehow, it all did add up into a string quartet." Carter's interest in "seeking out rather independent voice-writing" sometimes "creates rather strong clashes—rather difficult to take—but at any rate it gives the music a sound that no other composer's string quartet has, which is already something."

642. Coroniti, Joseph A. *Poetry As Text in Twentieth-Century Vocal Music: From Stravinsky to Reich*. Lewiston, NY: Edwin Mellen Press, 1992. ISBN 0-7734-9774-9.

A dismissive critique of Carter's setting of the last two lines of Robert Lowell's poem "In Genesis" from the song cycle *In Sleep, in*

Thunder (item 68). "This work brings to mind, again, the idea that music is not as semantically supple as poetry."

643. Danner, Gregory Guy. "The Use of Acoustic Measures of Dissonance to Characterize Pitch-Class Sets." *Music Perception* 3, no. 1 (Fall 1985): 103–22.

Carter's *Canon for 3* (item 43) is analysed in terms of the author's formula for calculating the "acoustic dissonance" of pitch (not pitch class) sets of various sizes.

644. Danuser, Hermann. "Spätwerk als Lyrik: Über Elliott Carters Gesänge nach Dichtungen von Elizabeth Bishop, John Ashbery und Robert Lowell" (Late work as lyric poetry: On Elliott Carter's songs on poems by Elizabeth Bishop, John Ashbery and Robert Lowell). In *Bericht über das internationale Symposion "Charles Ives und die amerikanische Musiktradition bis zur Gegenwart," Köln, 1988,* ed. Klaus Wolfgang Niemöller, 195–222. Regensburg: Gustav Bosse Verlag, 1990. ISBN 3-7649-2406-3. Reprinted as "Elliott Carter, Late Work as Lyric Poetry," trans. Matthias Truniger, in *Sonus* 19, no. 1 (Fall 1998): 53–66.

Danuser argues that Carter's career must be understood both as a contribution to the dominant trends of American compositional history and as a reaction against them. He divides Carter's music since 1950 into three groups: string quartets, concertos, and orchestral songs. The "dramatization of instrumental music" in the quartets of the 1950s and the opposition of individual to ensemble in the concertos of the 1960s both lead to the song cycles of the 1970s. The last are discussed primarily in terms of Carter's compositional methods, as documented in his sketches.

645. Darbellay, Étienne. "Continuité, coherence et formes de temps: A propos des *Night Fantasies* d'Elliott Carter" (Continuity, coherence, and time forms: On Elliott Carter's *Night Fantasies*). *Il saggiatore musicale: Rivista semestrale di musicologia* 2, no. 2 (1995): 297–327. Includes an abstract of the article in Italian.

The first part of this article is an analysis of the rhythmic structure of Carter's *Night Fantasies* (item 74), emphasizing the relationships between the work's underlying polyrhythm and its rhythmic surface. The second part is a discussion of neural networks and the philosophy of Alfred North Whitehead, which are applied, in broad strokes, to Carter's composition.

646. DeLio, Thomas. "Spatial Design in Elliott Carter's *Canon for 3*." *Winds Quarterly* 1 (Fall 1980): 9–15. Also in *Indiana Theory Review* 4, no. 1 (Fall 1980): 1–12.

An overview of the canonic structure of Carter's *Canon for 3* (item 43) introduces some observations about the registral distribution of pitches in the composition.

647. DeLone, Richard P. "Timbre and Texture in Twentieth-Century Music." In *Aspects of Twentieth-Century Music*, ed. Gary E. Wittlich, 66–207. Englewood Cliffs, NJ: Prentice Hall, 1975. ISBN 0-13-049346-5. ML197.A8.

DeLone's chapter includes brief analyses of the coda of Carter's *Double Concerto* (item 51) and the first fourteen measures of the *Fantasy* from the *Eight Etudes and a Fantasy* (item 53). Etude VII is also cited as an example of monophony.

648. Derby, Richard. "Carter's *Duo for Violin and Piano*." *Perspectives of New Music* 20, nos. 1–2 (Fall–Winter 1981/Spring–Summer 1982): 149–68.

In this especially detailed analysis Derby explores the relationship between expression and compositional technique in the *Duo for Violin and Piano* (item 52). Numerous examples are given of Carter's use of polyrhythms, fixed octave schemes, and intervallic partitioning between the two instruments, as means to a variety of expressive ends.

649. Derrien, Jean-Pierre. "Elliott Carter aujourd'hui" (Elliott Carter today). *Entre temps* 4 (June 1987): 51–53.

This brief laudatory essay introduces a special issue of *Entre temps* devoted to Carter's music. Derrien combines a biographical sketch with commentary emphasizing Carter's originality and his close connection to European musicians (Pierre Boulez and Sir William Glock) and musical concerns.

Doering, William T. *Elliott Carter: A Bio-Bibliography.* Listed above as item 609.

650. Downes, Edward. "Elliott Carter." In *The New York Philharmonic Guide to the Symphony*, 246–51. New York: Walker and Co., 1976. ISBN 0-8027-0540-5.

This anthology of program notes written for concerts of the New York Philharmonic contains three on pieces by Carter. "*Concerto for Orchestra*" (item 422) and "*Variations for Orchestra*" (item 565) contain lengthy excerpts of Carter's own notes on these pieces; "*Holiday Overture*" is shorter, with a musical example of the theme from the opening bars.

651. Dreier, Ruth. "The Composers String Quartet." *Musical America*, September 1986, 6–7, 38–40.

This profile of the Composers String Quartet on the occasion of their twentieth anniversary includes brief comments by group members and Carter on his *String Quartet No. 4* (item 91), which they premiered.

652. Durieux, Frédéric. "*A Mirror on Which to Dwell:* Domaines d'une écriture." *Entre temps* 4 (June 1987): 55–67.

This essay is primarily concerned with Carter's rhythmic practice in the first three songs of his 1975 song cycle, *A Mirror on Which to Dwell* (item 72). Related issues, such as textural stratification, metric modulation, and literary analogs, are also addressed.

653. *Elliott Carter: A 70th Birthday Tribute.* London: G. Schirmer, 1978.

This fifteen-page booklet published by G. Schirmer in honor of Carter's seventieth birthday contains an essay by Bayan Northcott (item 725) and brief tributes from William Glock, Paul Fromm, Pierre Boulez, Peter Maxwell Davies, Robert Ponsonby, and members of the Composers String Quartet (Anahid Ajemian, Mark Schuman, Jean Dane, and Matthew Raimondi). There is also a short bibliography and list of works.

Elliott Carter: Sketches and Scores in Manuscript. Listed above as item 610.

654. Fend, Michael. Review of *The Music of Elliott Carter*, by David Schiff. *Neue Zeitschrift für Musik* 148, no. 9 (September 1987): 76.

Review of item 769. In contrast to many other reviewers, Fend praises Schiff's analyses of Carter's music for their exactness and the extent to which they point to connections between Carter and other twentieth-century composers. This makes his book "as instructive as it is entertaining" (so lehrreich wie unterhaltsam).

655. Fennelly, Brian. Review of *String Quartet No. 4* (item 91), by Elliott Carter. *Notes* 48, no. 2 (December 1991): 689–90.

Fennelly mentions some of the twelve-note chords not identified by David Schiff (see item 772) and praises the quartet as "testimony to how one of our most creative American composers can find striking new ways of working within a traditional medium."

656. Frank, Andrew. "Elliott Carter: *In Sleep, in Thunder.*" *Notes* 43, no. 2 (December 1986): 408.

A descriptive overview of the composition (item 68), together with a plea for the adequate rehearsal of Carter's music and a wry comment on the price of the score ("Perhaps Carter's music might be more accessible to more people if it weren't so expensive!").

657. Gamer, Carlton. Review of *Flawed Words and Stubborn Sounds,* by Allen Edwards (interview with Elliott Carter). *Perspectives of New Music* 11, no. 2 (Spring–Summer 1973): 146–55.

Review of item 584. Gamer casts his review in the form of an interview between "C.G." and "myself," thus—in spite of his disclaimer—parodying the format of the book under review (and perhaps the similarly formatted "dialogues" of Stravinsky and Robert Craft as well). Gamer acknowledges that the interview format "helps to convey rather vividly a sense of Carter's personality" but suspects that Carter's responses have been revised for publication. Although he is bothered by "the lack of specificity and the analytical inadequacy" of Carter's descriptions of the more technical aspects of his compositional methods, Gamer concludes that "this is a fascinating, unique, and valuable contribution to the growing literature on Carter and his work."

658. Garrison, Leonard L. "Elliott Carter's *Scrivo in vento*. I: Historical and Analytical Notes." *The Flutist Quarterly* 19, no. 4 (Summer 1994): 86–92.

Garrison's historical notes on the genesis of *Scrivo in vento* (item 84) are particularly valuable. He was present at the Centre Acanthes symposium during July 1991 and attended both the premiere and the numerous master classes given by the dedicatee of the piece, Robert Aitken. His article includes extensive quotations from letters between Carter and Aitken written as the piece was taking shape and several examples of revisions made as various performance practice difficulties were encountered. The analytical notes provide useful information about various regular pulses found in the piece; the pitch analysis is limited to the observation of recurring pitches in the extreme registers of the instrument. Part II of the article is listed below as item 659.

659. ———. "Elliott Carter's *Scrivo in vento*. II: Performance Notes." *The Flutist Quarterly* 20, no. 1 (Fall 1994): 75–80.

This article (part II of item 658) is a performance guide for flutists and provides fingerings for various difficult notes and multiphonics found in the piece, as well as the useful admonition "One should not play the offbeat accents as 'syncopations' but as articulations of independent pulses." To this end Garrison provides several exercises in an alternate notation that aligns the pulse accents with the notated meter.

660. Gass, Glenn. "Elliott Carter's *Second String Quartet*: Aspects of Time and Rhythm." *Indiana Theory Review* 4, no. 3 (Spring 1981): 12–23.

Gass begins with a good summary of the most significant features of Carter's *String Quartet No. 2* (item 89), including the characters and intervals assigned to each instrument and the way their interaction determines the large-scale form of the piece. He then describes Carter's use of "recurring pulse rates" as thematic elements, noting the contrast between the "countless number of different pulse rates" used in the *String Quartet No. 1* (item 88) and their substantially reduced number in the *String Quartet No. 2:* "Carter has limited the number of different pulse rates employed, perhaps in order to help make their recurrences and interrelations audibly recognizable." Musical examples are provided for most of the passages discussed.

661. Glock, William. "'Greatness in Our Time Can Only Be Solitary': An Appreciation." See Glock, William, "Laudatio auf Elliott Carter" (item 662).

662. ———. "Laudatio auf Elliott Carter." In *Ernst-von-Siemens-Musikpreis*. Munich: Kastner & Callwey for Ernst-von-Siemens-Stiftung, Zug, Switzerland, 1981. Reprinted as "'Greatness in Our Time Can Only Be Solitary': An Appreciation." *Sonus* 19, No. 1 (Fall 1998): 3–11.

A speech in praise of Carter given on 8 April 1981 at the award ceremony at which Carter received the Ernst-von-Siemens-Musikpreis. Glock compares the multi-layeredness of Carter's music to Robert Musil's *Der Mann ohne Eigenschaften* (The man without qualities) and his unique conception of musical time to Proust's *A la recherche du temps perdu* (A remembrance of things past). Glock hears Carter's "most revolutionary statements" in his string quartets and briefly describes other works by Carter, including *Night Fantasies* (item 74), which is discussed in language startlingly close to that used by David Schiff in the first edition of *The Music of Elliott Carter* (item 769).

663. ———. "A Note on Elliott Carter." *The Score and I.M.A. Magazine* 12 (June 1955): 47–52.

Glock begins with a strong endorsement of Carter's music, identifying the *Piano Sonata* (item 80) as a major turning point in his career. His primary purpose, though, is to describe the workings of metric modulation, using examples from the *Sonata for Violoncello and Piano* (item 87) and the *String Quartet No. 1* (item 88).

664. ———. *Notes in Advance: An Autobiography*, 181–86. Oxford and New York: Oxford University Press, 1991. ISBN 0-19-816192-1. ML423.G645A3 1991.

Glock, whose friendship with Carter dates to 1948, here offers a profile of Carter, laced with anecdotes, the most interesting of which involve Carter's participation in classes at the Dartington School in 1957. In a letter quoted here, Carter responds to the suggestion that he include Schoenberg's *Variations,* op. 31, in his classes: "I was at first taken aback by your suggestion. Still, the idea has acted as a challenge to me and I must say that I welcome the stimulus to find my way around in the 12-tone literature, much of which I have enjoyed without bothering to count to a dozen."

665. Godfrey, Daniel. "A Unique Vision of Musical Time: Carter's String Quartet No. 3." *Sonus* 8, no. 1 (Fall 1987): 40–59.

Godfrey begins with a summary of Carter's ideas about musical time as he expresses them in "Music and the Time Screen" (item 485). The remainder of the article is a compilation of statistics about the constitution and arrangement of movements and movement fragments played by the quartet's two duos. These include "average movement duration," "average fragment duration," "average pause duration," and so on.

666. Goldet, Stéphane. "Distant Music" (in French). *Entre temps* 4 (June 1987): 69–75.

Goldet compares Carter's first three string quartets with the novels of James Joyce. The quasi-independent instrumental parts in Carter's *String Quartet No. 2* (item 89) are said to be analogous to the quasi-independent paths of Bloom and Stephen Dedalus as they move through Dublin in *Ulysses.* The contrast between literal movement divisions and the underlying music that spans them in Carter's *String Quartet No. 1* (item 88) is said to resemble Joyce's narrative technique in *Portrait of the Artist As a Young Man.* There, a series of passages describing Stephen's sexual awakening cuts across the book's chapter divisions. (See item 807 for another comparison of Joyce and Carter.)

667. Goldman, Richard Franko. "Current Chronicle." *Musical Quarterly* 37, no. 1 (January 1951): 83–89. Reprinted in Richard Franko Goldman, *Selected Essays and Reviews 1948–1968,* ed. Dorothy Klotzman, 69–74. (Brooklyn: Institute for Studies in American Music, 1980. ISBN 0-914678-13-2. ML60.G592.)

A rave review, with musical examples, of Carter's *Sonata for Violoncello and Piano* (item 87), which Goldman describes as "one of those rare works that tempt one to extremes of praise." This important early article is also the source of the term *metrical modulation*, which is coined here by Goldman.

668. ———. "The Music of Elliott Carter." *Musical Quarterly* 43, no. 2 (April 1957): 151–70. Reprinted in Richard Franko Goldman, *Selected Essays and Reviews 1948–1968*, ed. Dorothy Klotzman, 33–47. (Brooklyn: Institute for Studies in American Music, 1980. ISBN 0-914678-13-2. ML60.G592.)

An early and important survey of Carter's compositions from his earliest student works through the *Variations for Orchestra* (item 106). Goldman begins by lamenting the passing of an "Age of Innocence" in American music represented by the League of Composers and the WPA. Writing toward the end of a decade he describes as "uneventful," Goldman identifies Carter's music as "perhaps the most significant American development of the last ten years."

669. ———. "Current Chronicle." *Musical Quarterly* 46, no. 3 (July 1960): 361–67. Reprinted in Richard Franko Goldman, *Selected Essays and Reviews 1948–1968*, ed. Dorothy Klotzman, 119–25. (Brooklyn: Institute for Studies in American Music, 1980. ISBN 0-914678-13-2. ML60.G592.)

An enthusiastic review of Carter's *String Quartet No. 2* (item 89), which Goldman calls "the work of an assured master who has created an idiom completely his own." Goldman's brief overview of the piece is garbled in the original article by the inclusion of the incorrect musical illustrations in examples 2 and 3. The second part of the article is a eulogy for the Swiss composer and pianist Jacques de Menasce.

670. ———. "Current Chronicle." *Musical Quarterly* 48, no. 1 (January 1962): 93–99. Reprinted in Richard Franko Goldman, *Selected Essays and Reviews 1948–1968*, ed. Dorothy Klotzman, 135–41. (Brooklyn: Institute for Studies in American Music, 1980. ISBN 0-914678-13-2. ML60.G592.)

Goldman reviews Milton Babbitt's *Vision and Prayer*, Leon Kirchner's *Concerto* for violin, cello, ten winds, and percussion; and

Carter's *Double Concerto* (item 51). His comments about the last are guardedly favorable: "What comes out of Carter's preoccupation with his premises is interesting to listen to, so that one is not forced to limit one's praise to a grudging admiration of the constructive intelligence involved."

671. Gratzer, Wolfgang. "Wahlverwandter des Expressionismus: Über Elliott Carters Traditionsverständnis" (A relative of expressionism: Elliott Carter's understanding of tradition). In *Die neue Musik in Amerika: Über Traditionslosigkeit und Traditionslastigkeit,* ed. Otto Kolleritsch, 113–32. Studien zur Wertungsforschung 27 (1994): Vienna and Graz: Universal, 1994. ISBN 3-7024-0207-1. ML55.S92 Bd. 27.

A summary of the European reception history of Carter's music prefaces a discussion of his *Oboe Concerto* (item 75). Unlike Berg, Schoenberg, Hindemith, and Krenek, Carter chose to break with the nineteenth-century concerto tradition and wrote instead what Gratzer calls a "Detail-composition" (Detailkomposition), in which coherence is achieved by continuous development of details of rhythm, accent, instrumental color, and so on. This is understood as an expansion of Schoenberg's idea of "developing variation" (entwickelnden Variation). In a final section, Gratzer investigates Carter's understanding of tradition by analyzing the composer's own writings, particularly the article "Expressionism and American Music" (item 442). Here, Gratzer finds another connection between Carter and Schoenberg: the desire to go down in history as a composer at the forefront of twentieth-century musical development.

672. Griffiths, Paul. "Variation 2: Cage or Carter." In *The String Quartet: A History,* 194–209. London: Thames and Hudson, 1983.

Griffiths presents a brief overview of Carter's first three string quartets (items 88, 89, and 90) in the context of the two string quartets of Ives.

673. Groth, Renate. "Über die Konzerte Elliott Carters. In *Amerikanische Musik seit Charles Ives,* 177–90. Laaber: Laaber Verlag, 1987. ISBN 3-89007-117-1.

A summary of Carter's career precedes descriptions of his three major works in the concerto form in the 1960s: the *Double Concerto* (item 51), the *Piano Concerto* (item 79), and the *Concerto for Orchestra* (item 49).

674. Harvey, David [I. H.]. Review of sound recording of *A Symphony of Three Orchestras* (item 95) and *A Mirror on Which to Dwell* (item 72), by Elliott Carter (CBS Masterworks 76812). *Tempo* 143 (December 1982): 30–31.

In what is ostensibly a record review, Harvey is primarily interested in refuting David Schiff's claim of salience (see item 765) for the forty-five-note pitch collection that Carter metaphorically calls the "tonic" of *A Symphony of Three Orchestras*. Schiff responded with a letter to the editor (item 768). Harvey's review also contains a brief descriptive overview of *A Mirror on Which to Dwell* and a short paragraph praising the recordings.

675. ———. "Guide to Carter." Review of *The Music of Elliott Carter*, by David Schiff. *The Musical Times* 124, no. 1685 (July, 1983): 426.

Review of item 769. Harvey first points out the connection between Carter and Sir William Glock, a long-time champion of Carter's music and the general editor of Schiff's book. His review is double-edged. On the one hand, "Schiff's fluent and persuasive writing makes a strong impression." On the other, "[t]he analytical coverage of individual works is not particularly penetrating."

676. ———. "New Ground at 80: The Changing Styles of Elliott Carter's Lifework." *The Listener* 120, no. 3092 (1988): 52–53. Title listed in table of contents as "Music: Elliott Carter Improves with Age."

A summary of Carter's life and works through the *Oboe Concerto*, written in honor of his eightieth birthday.

677. ———. *The Later Music of Elliott Carter: A Study in Music Theory and Analysis*. New York and London: Garland, 1989. ISBN 0-8240-0199-0. ML410.C3293H4 1989.

A reprint of the author's 1986 dissertation (Worcester College, Oxford). The "Later Music" here consists principally of three works: the *String Quartet No. 2* (item 89), the *Double Concerto* (item 51), and the *Concerto for Orchestra* (item 49). There are also brief discussions of the *Sonata for Violoncello and Piano* (item 87) and the song "O Breath" from *A Mirror on Which to Dwell* (item 72). The analyses, which are preceded by a quite technical "Sketch of an Analytical Method," "do not constitute an explication of the composers' techniques, but rather of the phenomenological result of the application of those techniques." Also of interest is the discussion in chapters 1–3 of Carter's aesthetics in the context of various trends in twentieth-century music and thought. The volume occasionally suffers from careless editing and/or proofreading (Carter's name is misspelled in the first sentence of the preface, for example). For reviews see items 618 and 775.

678. Heaton, Roger. Review of *The Music of Elliott Carter*, by David Schiff. *Soundings* 11 (Winter 1983–84): 65–68.

Review of item 769. A largely negative review in which Heaton expresses disappointment with Schiff's "lack of analytical detail and true seriousness." According to Heaton, "it is necessary for a critic to come to terms with the technique of the music before he can begin to say anything meaningful about . . . what, if anything, this particular language communicates."

679. Henderson, Robert. "Elliott Carter." *Music and Musicians* 14, no. 5 (1966): 20–23.

In this profile of Carter's life and works through the *String Quartet No. 2*, Henderson is wary of Carter's "unusually taxing demands . . . on the listener's patience and concentration," but concludes that "[Carter's] music belongs rightly with the most important and most challenging of our time."

680. Hitchcock, H. Wiley. Review of *The Music of Elliott Carter*, by David Schiff. *American Music* 6, no. 4 (Winter 1988): 469–71.

Review of item 769. An unusually warm-hearted and largely favorable review: "nothing I have read in the extensive literature on Carter's music approaches the helpfulness of Schiff's discussion in exposing its nerve centers, circulation system, and musculature— and in turn making more intense, comprehensible, and satisfying the auditory experience of it." Hitchcock's goal is to "accentuate the positive," and his chastizing is gentle: "[Schiff's] claims for Carter's primacy in various modernist techniques occasionally border on the embarrassing."

> 681. Hudson, Richard. *Stolen Time: The History of Tempo Rubato*. Oxford and New York, NY: Clarendon Press (Oxford University Press), 1994. ISBN 0-19-816169-7.

See pages 417–24, under the subheading "Carter and the Concertato Style." Hudson cites Carter as the most refined example of what he calls "the new concertato style" that developed in the 1950s and 1960s, in which composers "developed the concept of contrast into a complex aesthetic philosophy involving many other musical elements in addition to rhythm." Echoing Bernard (item 616), Hudson distinguishes between simultaneous and successive presentation of contrasting musics (which he calls "concertato *counterpoint*" and "concertato *alternation*," respectively [italics in original]), and identifies both types in a number of works by Carter.

> 682. Jacobs, Paul. Notes for sound recording of Elliott Carter, *Night Fantasies* (item 74) and *Piano Sonata* (item 80), Nonesuch 79047-1.

This valuable commentary by one of the four pianists who commissioned *Night Fantasies* contains brief anecdotes about the perception of Carter's music in Paris in the 1950s and the premiere of the *Double Concerto* (item 51) in 1961 (at which Jacobs turned pages for harpsichordist Ralph Kirkpatrick). There is also an analytical sketch of *Night Fantasies* that provides a firsthand account of the early performance practice of the piece. Also see Carter's note for the same recording (item 504).

> 683. ———. "Paul Jacobs Talks about Carter and Messiaen." Interview with Will Crutchfield. *Keynote*, December 1983, 19–24.

This lengthy interview with one of the finest performers of Carter's music was conducted less than a month before his tragic premature death. Here Jacobs talks about Olivier Messiaen and about his long friendship with Carter. Of particular interest are his comments on the technical and aesthetic difficulties of Carter's *Night Fantasies* (item 74)—a work he, together with Ursula Oppens, Gilbert Kalish, and Charles Rosen, commissioned.

684. Jones, Allan Clive. "Elliott Carter and the Music of Change." *Classical Guitar* 3, no. 3 (November 1984): 23–25.

A summary of Carter's career (with marginally more emphasis on the works that include guitar) published prior to David Starobin's recitals introducing *Changes* (item 46) to the United Kingdom.

685. Jones, Patricia. "Rutgers University: Elliott Carter Lectures." *Current Musicology* 20 (1975): 9–10.

A brief report of Carter's visit to Robert Moevs's graduate seminar in music analysis at Rutgers University on 3 April 1975. The students, who had been studying Carter's *String Quartet No. 3* (item 90), produced a number of charts and other documents that were exhibited at the Alexander Library at Rutgers. These materials are now in the collection of the New York Public Library for the Performing Arts at Lincoln Center.

686. Kerman, Joseph. "American Music: The Columbia Series." *The Hudson Review* 11, no. 3 (Autumn 1958): 420–30.

The compositions in the Modern American Music Series of recordings made by Columbia Records were chosen by a committee that included the composers Virgil Thomson, Aaron Copland, Henry Cowell, and William Schuman. Kerman devotes a large portion of his review of the series to an unusually balanced and detailed discussion of Carter's *String Quartet No. 1* (item 88). Kerman is impressed by the quartet's rhythmic vitality but unconvinced by Carter's melodic ideas: "As far as melody goes, Carter's lines are utterly bland and as alike as shoe-laces." While his admiration is often grudging, his insightful observations about Carter's rhythmic procedures and aesthetic make this essay stand out among the many early reviews of the piece. Kerman also provides an unusually good description of metric modulation.

687. Kliewer, Vernon. L. "Melody: Linear Aspects of Twentieth-Century Music." In *Aspects of Twentieth-Century Music,* ed. Gary E. Wittlich, 270–321. Englewood Cliffs, NJ: Prentice Hall, 1975. ISBN 0-13-049346-5. ML197.A8.

In this survey of twentieth-century melodic practice Etude VII from the *Eight Etudes and a Fantasy* (item 53) is cited as an exmple of a melodic line created "by simply changing from one loudness level to another," and there is a brief motivic analysis of the violin solo in measures 35–42 of the *String Quartet No. 2* (item 89).

688. Koegler, Horst. "Begegnungen mit Elliott Carter." See Koegler, Horst, "Blick in die Welt" (item 689).

689. ———. "Blick in die Welt." *Musica* 12, no. 6 (June 1958): 363. Expanded version reprinted as "Begegnungen mit Elliott Carter," *Melos* 26 (January 1959): 256–58.
    English translation printed as "Salzburg." *Musical Courier* 157, no. 7 (June 1958): 14–15.

Koegler studied with Carter at the Salzburg seminars in 1958, and this brief article is a reminiscence of their conversations there and in Munich and Vienna in the following weeks.

690. Koivisto, Tiina. "Aspects of Motion in Elliott Carter's Second String Quartet." *Intégral* 10 (1996): 19–52.

Koivisto presents a close reading of the harmony of the *Introduction* and the first twenty or so measures of the *Allegro fantastico* from Carter's *String Quartet No. 2* (item 89). Her analyses, which track the two all-interval tetrachords [0,1,4,6] and [0,1,3,7] as they occur individually and in combination, effectively illustrate Carter's use of pitch and pitch-class collections to create a sense of directed harmonic motion over various time spans.

691. Kostelanetz, Richard. "The Astounding Success of Elliott Carter." *High Fidelity* 18, no. 5 (May 1968): 41–45. Revised version reprinted as "Elliott Carter: Effort and Excellence," in Richard Kostelanetz, *Master Minds: Portraits of Contemporary American Artists and Intellectuals*, 289–303. (Toronto: Macmillan Company, 1969. ISBN 0-932360-30-0. CT220.K67.)

Kostelanetz deftly combines a biographical portrait of Carter, a critical summary of his musical career, and excerpts from interviews. The emphasis is biographical: Kostelanetz seems most interested in figuring out what kind of person Carter is and what makes him tick. The result is one of the most interesting and balanced profiles to have appeared.

692. ———. "Elliott Carter: Effort and Excellence." See Kostelanetz, Richard, "The Astounding Success of Elliott Carter" (item 691).

693. Kozinn, Allan. "Elliott Carter's *Changes*." *Guitar Review* 57 (September 1984): 1–4.

A very informative article that covers the collaboration between Carter and David Starobin (the guitarist who commissioned *Changes* [item 46]) in some detail. The work was substantially revised—largely at Starobin's urging—from an initial four-and-one-half-minute sketch into its finished length of around seven minutes. The article also contains several musical examples and a brief analysis together with quotes from both Carter and Starobin.

694. Kramer, Lawrence. "'Syringa': John Ashbery and Elliott Carter." In *Beyond Amazement: New Essays on John Ashbery*, ed. David Lehman, 255–71. Ithaca and London: Cornell University Press, 1980. Revised version reprinted as "Song As Insight—John Ashbery, Elliott Carter, and Orpheus," in Lawrence Kramer, *Music and Poetry: The Nineteenth Century and After*, 203–21. (Berkeley and Los Angeles: University of California Press, 1984. ISBN 0-520-04873-3. ML3849.K7 1983.)

This essay is primarily a close reading of Ashbery's poem "Syringa," combined with an analysis of the "esthetic of simultaneity" that both the poem and Carter's setting (item 96) are found to embody. Kramer identifies two "voices" in Ashbery's poem: a "meditative voice that engages in a tranquil, often playful consideration of the problem of loss as presented by Orpheus" and an "elegiac voice, full of lament and desire, that uses the Orpheus myth to utter 'hidden syllables' of personal sorrow." These voices are personified in Carter's setting by the mezzo-soprano and bass voices, respectively. Both Ashbery's and Carter's *Syringa* are described as "polyvocal," consisting of simultaneous voices, "neither dialectical nor competitive," that "are not *opposed* to each other at all, but *posed against* each other" (italics in original). For Kramer, the most significant consequence of this aesthetic is the transformation of traditional ideas about time. Thus, an Ashbery poem "does not articulate a process, but simply lets a textured consciousness persist shimmeringly for a given duration." Similarly, in Carter's music "the polyvocal whole composed of these voices absorbs their linear impetus into the resonance of a temporal order that persists instead of progressing."

Although much of the content of the original article is retained in the revised version, the differences are significant enough to warrant consulting both versions.

695. ———. "Song As Insight—John Ashbery, Elliott Carter, and Orpheus." See Kramer, Lawrence, "'Syringa': John Ashbery, Elliott Carter, and Orpheus" (item 694).

696. ———. Letter to the Editor, *Perspectives of New Music* 29, no. 1 (Winter 1991): 335.

Kramer feels his discussion of the relationship between the voices in *Syringa* (item 96) has been misinterpreted by Carter in his interview with Jonathan Bernard (item 580).

697. Kroeger, Karl. "Elliott Carter: *Holiday Overture*." *Notes* 20, no. 3 (Summer 1963): 407.

A brief, favorable review of Carter's *Holiday Overture* (item 67), which had recently appeared in a revised edition. "It is an excellent example of what can be done with fairly ordinary material in the hands of a real master."

698. Larrick, Geary H. "Eight Pieces for Four Timpani." *Percussionist* 12, no. 1 (Fall 1974): 12–15.

Brief descriptions and formal graphs (AABC, etc.) of the *Recitative, Improvisation, Adagio*, and *March* movements of Carter's *Eight Pieces for Four Timpani* (item 54), with a few comments about the relative difficulty of the pieces.

699. Lederman, Minna. *The Life and Death of a Small Magazine (Modern Music, 1924–1946)*, 43–46. ISAM Monographs, no.

18. Brooklyn: Institute for Studies in American Music, 1983. ISBN 0-914678-20-5.

Lederman's comments provide a revealing account of how Carter was perceived by his employer and by his older contemporaries during his early career as a reviewer and writer for *Modern Music*. "Because of his youth there seemed to be doubts and hesitations on the Board that so much responsibility should fall on him. But Carter was not only eager, full of curiosity; he was knowledgeable and extremely conscientious. I felt that he acquitted himself with utmost fairness, and I was grateful, too, for the exceptional range of interests which gave his writing a special intellectual dimension."

700. Lewin, David. *Generalized Musical Intervals and Transformations*, 60–81. New Haven and London: Yale University Press, 1987. ISBN 0300034938. ML3809.L39 1987.

Lewin's goal is to model much of our musical experience using the tools of algebra, especially group theory. His book, in many ways the culmination of a life's work, is a cornerstone of American music theory at the end of the twentieth century. In the fourth chapter, the development of an algebraic object to model time spans relies heavily on a detailed analysis of a passage from Carter's *String Quartet No. 1* (item 88). Lewin makes abundant use of the apparatus of mathematical argument (theorems, proofs, etc.), but his frequent digressions into matters of performance practice and loving insight into the music at hand make the discussion worthwhile reading even for the nonspecialist.

701. Link, John F. "The Composition of Elliott Carter's *Night Fantasies*." *Sonus* 14, no. 2 (Spring 1994): 67–89.

A detailed analysis of the process by which Carter composed *Night Fantasies* (item 74), informed by a thorough study of the roughly one thousand pages of sketches that exist for the work.

702. ———. "Note sulla *Sonata* e le *Night Fantasies* di Carter." Trans. Antonietta Cerocchi Pozzi. In *Da Beethoven a Boulez: Il pianoforte in ventidue saggi*, 229–36. Milano: Longanesi, 1994. ISBN 88-304-1259-7. ML700.D2 1994.

An overview of Carter's *Piano Sonata* (item 80) and *Night Fantasies* (item 74), in a volume published in connection with the 1994 International Piano Competition Umberto Micheli in Milan. The two works were among those selected for the third round of the competition.

703. Lochhead, Judy. "Temporal Structure in Recent Music." *Journal of Musicological Research* 6, nos. 1–2 (January 1986): 49–93. Reprinted in *Understanding the Musical Experience*, 121–66 (New York: Gordon and Breach, 1989. ISBN 2-88124-204-9. ML3800.U5 1989.)

In this article Lochhead applies her concept of "Temporal Objects—henceforth, TO's [*sic*]" to several pieces, including the opening of Carter's *Brass Quintet* (item 42). She calls each type of music represented by Carter's expressive indications in the score ("calm," "menacing," etc.) a TO and narrates measures 1–73 as an overlapping sequence of TOs that "do not have boundaries and are delineated by a process of focusing and unfocusing"—moving to the foreground and background of the listener's attention. This distinguishes them from the TOs with "clear or distinct" or "hazy boundaries" in her other analyses.

704. ———. "On the 'Framing' Music of Elliott Carter's First String Quartet." In *Musical Transformation and Musical Intuition: Essays in Honor of David Lewin*, ed. Raphael Atlas and Michael Cherlin, 179–98. Roxbury MA: Ovenbird Press, 1994. ISBN 1-886464-00-6. ML3800.M87 1994.

Carter has frequently cited Jean Cocteau's film *Le sang d'un poète* as one inspiration for his mature style. A chimney begins to collapse in the film's opening scene and completes its fall only at the very end of the film. Lochhead explores the analogy between these scenes and the opening cello and closing violin solos in Carter's *String Quartet No. 1* (item 88). Her highly technical analysis is couched in the theoretical terminology developed by David Lewin in his *Generalized Musical Intervals and Transformations* (item 700).

705. McCormick, Robert M. "*Eight Pieces for Four Timpani* by Elliott Carter: Analysis." *Percussionist* 12, no. 1 (Fall 1974): 7–11.

A biographical sketch, a short list of the performance techniques called for in the pieces, and brief descriptions of the *Canaries, Moto Perpetuo,* and *March* movements of Carter's *Eight Pieces for Four Timpani* (item 54).

706. McGill, Raymond. Review of *The Music of Elliott Carter,* by David Schiff. *Brio* 20, no. 2 (Fall–Winter 1983): 81–82.

Review of item 769. In what is less a review than an overview, McGill nonetheless praises the book highly.

707. Mead, Andrew. "Pitch Structure in Elliott Carter's *String Quartet No. 3.*" *Perspectives of New Music* 22, no. 1 (1983): 31–60.

French translation ("Le 3e quatuor à cordes: Structure des hauteurs"), trans. Hubert Guery, *Entre temps* 4 (June 1987): 55–67.

This very technical article is a thoroughgoing analysis of the pitch structure in one of Carter's most highly regarded compositions (item 90). Mead explores the harmonic connections within and between the ensemble's two duos in great detail, using the language of pitch-class set theory to describe the multiple functions of collections of various sizes.

708. ———. Review of *The Music of Elliott Carter,* by David Schiff. *Notes* 40, no. 3 (March 1984): 544–47.

Review of item 769. Mead praises the "enthusiasm and care with which the author has approached his task" and notes that the book "may serve as a general introduction to the composer and his music for the interested concert-goer." However, as one of the leading theorists of nontonal music, Mead devotes the majority of his review to a critique of the "[i]nsecure theoretical premises [that] weaken most of Schiff's analytical arguments." These lead Schiff to miss "some of the deeper ironies embodied in the underlying structure" and to overlook the many connections between Carter's music and that of his contemporaries. Mead later elaborated on this last point in some detail (see item 711), motivated in part, perhaps, by Carter's heated response to this review (item 480). Also see Mead's response to Carter's letter (item 709).

709. ———. "To the Editor." *Notes* 42, no. 1 (1985): 187.

A reply to Elliott Carter's letter (item 480) attacking Mead's critical review (item 708) of the first edition of David Schiff's book *The Music of Elliott Carter* (item 769). Mead's response is moderate, refuting the accusation that he advocates Allen Forte's methods of analysis exclusively and pointing out that Schiff's book is presented as the author's, not the composer's, thoughts about Carter's music, and so must be critiqued as such.

710. ———. "The Role of Octave Equivalence in Elliott Carter's Recent Music: A Birthday Celebration." *Sonus* 14, no. 2 (Spring 1994): 13–37.

Mead here illustrates the consequences of invoking octave equivalence in the analysis of Carter's music. While Carter frequently preserves the distinction between complementary intervals (like minor thirds and major sixths), Mead points out ways in which he also recognizes their equivalence—in assigning them to different instrumental groups and to opposite halves of all-interval twelve-note chords. Octave equivalence also makes set classes available as an analytical tool, and Mead illustrates their usefulness in brief analyses of the violin cadenza (mm. 35 ff.) from the *String Quartet No. 2* (item 89), the recurring twelve-note "tonic" chord from the *String Quartet No. 3* (item 90), and selected passages from *Riconoscenza per Goffredo Petrassi* (item 102.2).

711. ———. "Twelve-Tone Composition and the Music of Elliott Carter." In *Concert Music, Rock, and Jazz since 1945: Essays and Analytic Studies,* ed. Elizabeth West Marvin and Richard Hermann, 67–102. Rochester, NY: University of Rochester Press, 1995. ISBN 1-878822-42-x. ML160.C737 1995.

Mead "examines certain pitch structures in Carter's music using tools of twelve-tone theory in order to suggest commonalities with other composers' practice, while highlighting the individual and creative ways Carter has enriched and extended certain familiar theoretical ideas." Mead discusses Carter's *String Quartet No. 3* (item 90), *Piano Concerto* (item 79), and *Night Fantasies* (item 74), finding commonalites with Schoenberg, Babbitt, and others in the idea of ordering as a means of creating pitch and pitch-class hierarchies. The use of all possible collections of a given size and the ordering of collections in register are explored as examples of Carter's originality. Mead is especially good at revealing the general properties of Carter's compositional materials and showing how these properties are manifested in a given composition. The usefulness of twelve-tone theory in relation to Carter's music has been the subject of much, sometimes heated, debate. See, for example, the exchange between Carter and Mead in *Notes* (items 480 and 709).

712. Melis, Andrea. "Elliott Carter e l'ordine sensibile." *Musica/Realtà* 15, no. 45 (December 1994): 49–65.

This article introduces several aspects of Carter's compositional technique and aesthetic interests to an Italian audience for whom they are "decidedly little known" (decisamente poco conosciuto). Metric modulation is illustrated by the "Canaries" movement of the *Eight Pieces for Four Timpani* (item 54); all-interval chords are discussed in relation to *Night Fantasies* (item 74) and the *String Quartet No. 4* (item 91). The emphasis throughout is on the "relationship between compositional structure, perception, and expressive result" (rapporto fra strutture compositive, percezione e risultato espressivo).

713. Mellers, Wilfrid. "The Pioneer's Energy and the Artist's Order: Elliott Carter." In *Music in a New Found Land,* 102–21. London: Barrie and Rockliff, 1964. Reprint New York: Oxford University Press, 1987. ISBN 019520526X. ML200.M44 1987.

Italian translation ("L'energia del pioniere e l'ordine dell'artista: Elliott Carter") in *Musica nel nuovo mondo* (Torino, 1975), 104–22.

For Mellers, Carter's music represents the synthesis of "pioneer heroism: Ives's desire to make anew the toughness, power, copiousness, triviality and grandeur of the American scene and the American spirit" and the "search for order from authenticity: Copland's attempt to reintegrate, in a kind of musical cubism, the disintegrated fragments of the present." In this article, he provides substantial analyses of Carter's *Piano Sonata* (item 80) and *String Quartet No. 1* (item 88) and briefly mentions Carter's other works through the *Double Concerto* (item 51).

714. Meyer, Felix. "Klassizistische Tendenzen in der amerikanischen Musik der zwanziger bis vierziger Jahre" (Classicizing tendencies in American music from the 1920s to the 1940s). In *Die klassizistische Moderne in der Musik des 20. Jahrhunderts*, ed. Hermann Danuser, 187–200. Publications of the Paul Sacher Foundation, vol. 5. Winterthur: Amadeus, 1997. ISBN 3-905049-73-2.

Meyer places Carter's early music together with that of several other pupils of Walter Piston's who rejected "Americanism" in favor of a more international neoclassical style, exemplified by Stravinsky and Hindemith. Meyer discusses a number of influences on Carter's generation of American composers, including Harvard University, Nadia Boulanger, and the wave of important European composers who arrived in America as refugees from the Nazi regime. The neoclassical aspects of Carter's early music are illustrated by several passages from his ballet *The Minotaur* (item 71).

715. Mili, Isabelle Dominique. "Elliott Carter: la lucidité de la critique sociale et de la conception musicale" (Elliott Carter: The lucidity of the social critique and the musical conception). *Dissonanz • Disonance* 31 (February 1992): 4–9. Includes a German abstract of the article ("Elliott Carter: Klarheit und Vernunft der gesellschaftlichen und musikalischen Konzeptionen").

This thoughtful analysis of Carter's aesthetic contains extensive excerpts from *Flawed Words and Stubborn Sounds* (translated into French by Suzanne Rollier). Also of interest are excerpts from Mili's July 1991 interview with Carter. For example: "I do not agree at all with this widespread idea that 'I found myself in my first string quartet of 1951 and that my earlier works belong under the heading of stylistic aberration'" (Je ne suis pas du tout d'accord avec cette idée assez largement répandue que «je me suis trouvé moi-même dans mon premier quatuor à cordes de 1951 et que mes œuvres antérieures sont placées sous le signe de l'errance stylistique»).

716. Moe, Orin. "The Music of Elliott Carter." *College Music Symposium* 22, no. 1 (1982): 7–31.

Moe divides Carter's music into three stylistic phases—"neoclassicism," "expressionist," and "mature" (the last beginning with the *String Quartet No. 1*)—and defines three characteristics of Carter's style that are attributed to the composer's early interest in vocal music: "lyricism," "a texture of differently and irregularly scanned lines," and "extra-musical inspiration." The remainder of the article is a chronological summary of Carter's compositions.

717. Moevs, Robert. Review of sound recording of *String Quartet No. 2* (item 89) and *String Quartet No. 3* (item 90), by Elliott Carter (Columbia M 32738). *Musical Quarterly* 61, no. 1 (January 1975): 157–68.

Although published as a record review, this article is mainly a sketchy descriptive analysis of Carter's *String Quartet No. 2* and *String Quartet No. 3*.

718. Morgan, Robert P. "Elliott Carter's String Quartets." *Musical Newsletter* 4, no. 3 (Summer 1974): 3–11.

Pointing out that Carter's string quartets have "played a critical role" in his development, Morgan gives descriptive analyses of each of the (then) three quartets (items 88, 89, and 90), focusing on what they reveal about the development of Carter's rhythmic practice. Morgan emphasizes Carter's expansion of the traditional metrical system into a more multi-layered ebb and flow of different pulses, his stratifications of texture, and the various ways he incorporates "movements" into the continuous and constantly changing large forms heard in the quartets. The article concludes with a close reading of measures 37–41 of Carter's *String Quartet No. 3*.

719. ———. Review of *The Music of Elliott Carter*, by David Schiff. *The Journal of Musicology* 2, no. 3 (Summer 1983): 340–42.

Review of item 769. While he chastises Schiff for an uncritical attitude toward Carter's music, for making exaggerated claims about Carter's historical precedence, and for occasionally overdoing the purple prose, Morgan concludes that Schiff's book "offers a very useful basic introduction to Carter's music, and one that will provide a helpful point of departure for those wishing to undertake more extensive studies."

720. Morris, Robert D. Review of *The Music of Elliott Carter*, by David Schiff. *Journal of the American Musicological Society* 38, no. 1 (1985): 183–90.

Review of item 769. Morris has four main objections to Schiff's book: it is often unclear whether the descriptions of the pieces are the composer's or Schiff's own; that his descriptions of Carter's music "sometimes smack of idolatry"; that Schiff slights the achievements of other composers and so "implies that it is primarily Carter alone who has brought new music to where it is today"; and that the book lacks the theoretical rigor necessary to "truly do justice to the connection between pitch relations and Carter's expressive intentions." On the other hand, Morris says he "must emphasize that Schiff has given a fair picture of Carter' work as a whole."

721. Nicholls, David. Review of *Elliott Carter: In Conversation with Enzo Restagno for Settembre Musica 1989*, by Elliott Carter. *Music and Letters* 74, no. 1 (February 1993): 128.

Review of item 597. A mildly enthusiastic review. Nicholls praises the volume as "a welcome, if rather brief, addition to the literature on Carter" but criticizes the uneven coverage of Carter's works, the "European high-mindedness" of Restagno's questions, and the occasionally distracting digressions in the conversation.

722. Northcott, Bayan. "Elliott Carter: Continuity and Coherence." *Music and Musicians* 20, no. 12 (August 1972): 28–39.

A particularly substantial and thoughtful survey of Carter's life and works through the *Concerto for Orchestra*.

723. ———. Review of WEC. *Musical Times* 119, no. 1621 (March 1978): 238–39.

Review of item 399. A very brief review, dividing Carter's writings into the period before his international success, when he wrote mainly reviews, and the later period during which he wrote about his own music, about other composers, and about contemporary music's place in society.

724. ———. "Carter in Perspective." *Musical Times* 119, no. 1630 (December 1978): 1039–41.

This rather disorganized article begins with a lengthy discussion of how little Carter has in common with Messiaen and ends with a brief summary of Carter's then recent works. In between, the article touches on Carter's musical influences, including Stravinsky, Scriabin, and Debussy.

725. ———. "Carter the Progressive." In *Elliott Carter, A 70th Birthday Tribute*, 4–11. London: G. Schirmer, 1978.

Although its title echoes Schoenberg's famous essay "Brahms the Progressive," the scope of this seventieth birthday tribute is much more modest. Here Northcott simply retells the story of Carter's compositional development as a "lonely individualist," making his own way rather than following the various trends in composition in the twentieth century.

726. ———. "Fascinatin' Modulation." Review of *The Music of Elliott Carter*, by David Schiff. *New York Review of Books* 31, no. 9 (31 May 1984): 18–20.

Review of item 769. Northcott prefaces his review with a biographical sketch, which includes the story that while at the War Information Office, Carter "found himself orchestrating national anthems ever more desperately as more and more countries came over to the Allies." In his review Northcott criticizes Schiff for not placing Carter's music in relation to that of his contemporaries, but he defends the nontechnical approach of Schiff's analyses. The last part of the review is a meditation on contemporary music, specifically "the absence, or at any rate crisis, of identifiable musical statement—whether conceived as idea, theme, musical object, gestalt, or whatever."

727. ———. "Elliott Carter at 80." *Musical Times* 129, no. 1750 (December 1988): 644–47.

Here Northcott observes three characteristics of Carter's music in his seventies: The use of structural polyrhythms, an abundance of textures dominated by long melodic lines ("structural monody"), and a large number of short compositions.

728. Pappastavrou, George C. "Carter's *Piano Sonata* and *Night Fantasies*." *American Music Teacher* 38, no. 2 (November–December 1988): 18–19.

In this brief article Pappastavrou quotes Donald Francis Tovey, Pablo Picasso, Roger Sessions, and Walt Whitman and also makes a few descriptive observations about Carter's *Piano Sonata* (item 80) and *Night Fantasies* (item 74).

729. Piencikowski, Robert. "Fonction relative du timbre dans la musique contemporaine: Messiaen, Carter, Boulez, Stockhausen" (The relative function of timbre in contemporary music). *Analyse musicale* 3 (April 1986): 51–53.

Piencikowski writes about a twentieth-century shift from thinking of timbre as subordinate to the more important elements of harmony and rhythm to integrating it thoroughly into musical structure. He relates Carter's practice to that of Boulez and Stockhausen and analyzes two passages from the opening section of Carter's *Double Concerto* (item 51). These examples illustrate the changing function of the piano, as it first articulates a single layer of the polyphonic texture, then combines multiple layers to produce an accelerando toward the climax at measure 45.

730. Pollack, Howard. *Harvard Composers: Walter Piston and His Students, from Elliott Carter to Frederic Rzewski.* Metuchen, NJ, and London: Scarecrow Press, 1992. ISBN 0810824930. ML390.P745 1992.

See especially chapter 6 (pp. 104–30), "Expanding the Modernist Tradition: Elliott Carter and Leonard Bernstein." Pollack points out a number of similarities between the two composers in the course of tracing their careers from about 1940 to 1969 (when Bernstein conducted the premiere of Carter's *Concerto for Orchestra* [item 49]). Pollack attributes these similarities to "a basic orientation toward . . . an American modernist tradition as represented, above all, by Stravinsky, Hindemith, Copland, and Piston," which Carter and Bernstein developed as Piston's students at Harvard (Carter in the 1920s; Bernstein in the 1930s).

731. Porter, Andrew. "Mutual Ordering." In *A Musical Season: A Critic from Abroad in America*, 139–46. New York: Viking Press, 1974. ISBN 670-49650-2. First published in *The New Yorker*, 3 February 1973.

A review of the first performance of Carter's *String Quartet No. 3* (item 90). Porter concludes "I am prepared to affirm that Carter's

Third Quartet is a major new composition, a piece that is passionate, lyrical, and profoundly exciting."

732. ———. "Marvelous Performers." In *Music of Three Seasons: 1974–1977*, 26–30. New York: Farrar Straus Giroux, 1978. ML60.P895 M88. First published in *The New Yorker*, 11 November 1974.

A review of a Composers' Showcase concert at the Whitney Museum in New York featuring Carter's *Double Concerto* (item 51), played by Paul Jacobs, harpsichord, Ursula Oppens, piano, and Speculum Musicae, conducted by Gerard Schwarz; *String Quartet No. 3* (item 90), played by the Composers String Quartet; and *Sonata for Violoncello and Piano* (item 87), played by Michael Rudiakov, cello, and Ursula Oppens, piano.

733. ———. "Boris Redivivus." In *Music of Three Seasons: 1974–1977*, 60–65. New York: Farrar Straus Giroux, 1978. ML60.P895 M88. First published in *The New Yorker*, 30 December 1974.

Between reviews of Mussorgsky's *Boris Godunov* and operas by Britten and Holst, Porter notes the premiere of Carter's *Brass Quintet* (item 42), calling it "a major addition to the brass chamber literature."

734. ———. "Duo." In *Music of Three Seasons: 1974–1977*, 127–30. New York: Farrar Straus Giroux, 1978. ML60.P895 M88. First published in *The New Yorker*, 7 April 1975.

Porter reviews the premiere of Carter's *Duo for Violin and Piano* (item 52), praising the piece and Gilbert Kalish's piano playing, but saying of violinist Paul Zukofsky "there are melodies in the work that cry for the warm, emotional tones of a Kreisler, and his tone tended to be thin and keen."

735. ———. "Reflections." In *Music of Three Seasons: 1974–1977*, 306–9. New York: Farrar Straus Giroux, 1978. ML60.P895 M88. First published in *The New Yorker*, 8 March 1976.

A thoughtful review of Carter's song cycle *A Mirror on Which to Dwell* (item 72) and its premiere performance, given by Susan

Davenny Wyner and Speculum Musicae, at the Hunter College Playhouse in New York.

736. ———. "Great Bridge, Our Myth." In *Music of Three Seasons: 1974–1977,* 527–32. New York: Farrar Straus Giroux, 1978. ML60.P895 M88. First published in *The New Yorker,* 7 March 1977.

In the course of this review of the premiere of Carter's *A Symphony of Three Orchestras* (item 95), Porter comments on the piece, on Hart Crane's poem "The Bridge," which inspired it, and also on other works inspired by the Brooklyn Bridge.

737. ———. "Introductions." In *Music of Three More Seasons: 1977–1980,* 157–63. New York: Alfred A. Knopf, 1981. ISBN 0-394-51813-6. ML60.P894. First published in *The New Yorker,* 24 April 1978.

This review of radio broadcasts devoted to contemporary music is useful for its synopsis of a ninety-minute radio interview with Carter conducted by Ben Miller and broadcast on WKCR in New York.

738. ———. "Famous Orpheus." In *Music of Three More Seasons: 1977–1980,* 277–84. New York: Alfred A. Knopf, 1981. ISBN 0-394-51813-6. ML60.P894. First published in *The New Yorker,* 8 January 1979.

A review of the festivities in New York surrounding Carter's seventieth birthday on December 11, 1978. The centerpiece is a substantial discussion of Carter's newly premiered *Syringa* (item 96).

739. ———. "Music in the Silence of the Night." In *Musical Events,* 165–69. New York: Summit Books, 1987. ISBN 0-671-63538-7. ML60.P8955 1987. First published in *The New Yorker,* 30 November 1981.

This lengthy review of Carter's *Night Fantasies* (item 74) quotes Mozart and Beethoven on "nocturnal inspiration" and discusses the role the night has played in the works of other composers. Carter's work, says Porter, "may well be our century's next pianistic landmark after Pierre Boulez's *Second Sonata.*"

740. ———. "Thought-Executing Fires." In *Musical Events,* 435–40. New York: Summit Books, 1987. ISBN 0-671-63538-7. ML60.P8955 1987. First published in *The New Yorker,* 9 May 1983.

In this review of concerts given by the Fires of London, Porter gives high marks to Carter's *Triple Duo* (item 105), which received its first performance.

741. ———. "Songs with a Mind." *The New Yorker,* 2 January 1984, 84–86.

Porter here reviews a concert given by Speculum Musicae in celebration of Carter's seventy-fifty birthday. Porter discusses the then recent *In Sleep, in Thunder* (item 68), commenting on Lowell, his poetry, and Carter's other vocal works of the 1970s (*A Mirror on Which to Dwell* [item 72] and *Syringa* [item 96]) and comments briefly on *Triple Duo* (item 105) and *Changes* (item 46).

742. ———. "Riches in Little Room." *The New Yorker,* 24 December 1984, 62–65.

Riconoscenza per Goffredo Petrassi (item 102.2) and *Canon for 4* (item 44) are discussed and their New York premieres reviewed, as are performances by the New York Philharmonic under Zubin Mehta of *A Symphony of Three Orchestras* (item 95) and by Ursula Oppens and the Cincinnati Symphony, conducted by Michael Gielen, of Carter's *Piano Concerto* (item 79). The Cincinnati concerts were recorded for commercial release (see item 253).

743. ———. "Discourse Most Eloquent." *The New Yorker,* 28 April 1986, 96–99.

A review of the U.S. premiere of *Penthode* (item 78) played by the Ensemble InterContemporain, conducted by Pierre Boulez. Porter praises the performance and describes the piece as "like conversation at All Souls on a night when the country's best brains are there."

744. ———. "Quaternion." *The New Yorker,* 24 November 1986, 114–21.

A detailed critique of Carter's *String Quartet No. 4* (item 91), its place in Carter's oeuvre, and the premiere performance given by the Composers String Quartet at Festival Miami.

745. ———. "Fanfarrado." *The New Yorker*, 20 July 1987, 71–73.

Among the twenty-one fanfares commissioned by the Houston Symphony in honor of the 150th anniversary of Texas's statehood is Carter's *A Celebration of Some 100 × 150 Notes* (item 100.1). Porter, who was invited to listen to all twenty-one fanfares on tape, here reviews several, including Carter's, and gives a brief summary of the flourish of new works Carter produced in the mid-1980s.

746. ———. "Fancy's Rainbows, Wit's Momentary Fires." *The New Yorker*, 23 December 1991, 96–98.

A brief but substantive critique of Carter's *Violin Concerto* (item 107) and a review of its New York premiere, together with reviews of works by several other composers.

747. Price, Harry E., Cornelia Yarbrough, and Michael Kinney. "Eminences of American Composers: University Faculty Attitudes and Symphony Orchestra Programming." *Council for Research in Music Education Bulletin, USA* 106 (Fall 1990): 37–48.

The authors surveyed 574 music composition and theory faculty at major American universities in 1985–86 and found Carter the third most frequently mentioned composer (behind Copland and Crumb) on a list of "the top 10 living composers in the United States at that time." When the programming of twenty-nine major U.S. orchestras was surveyed, it was found to consist of 11 percent works by American composers. "Of the 51 living composers whose works were performed, only three were programmed more than four times or by more than four orchestras (Copland, Schuman, Druckman)." Carter's music was heard on three programs (ten performances total), placing him ninth on the list of most frequently performed American composers in this survey.

748. Reis, Claire. "Elliott Cook Carter, Jr." In *Composers in America*, 57. New York: Macmillan, 1938. Reprinted with annota-

tions in David Schiff, *The Music of Elliott Carter,* 72. (New York: Eulenburg and London: Da Capo, 1983. ISBN 0903873060. ML410.C3293 S34 1983.)

One of the only surviving records of Carter's earliest works, most of which he destroyed.

749. Rochberg, George. Review of sound recording of *String Quartet No. 1* (item 88), by Elliott Carter (Columbia ML 5104). *Musical Quarterly* 43, no. 1 (January 1957): 130–32.

An unusually balanced and perceptive critique of Carter's quartet. Rochberg notes the influence of Berg, Ives, and others, but stresses Carter's "uncommon musical vision" in assimilating the works of his predecessors. The *Adagio* movement is singled out for the highest praise, while the last movement "lacks the excitement and power of the first two" and relies too much on "rapid scale-like figurations."

750. Rockwell, John. *All American Music: Composition in the Late Twentieth Century.* New York, NY: Alfred A. Knopf, 1983. ISBN 0-394-51163-8. ML198.5.R6 1983.

See chapter 3, "American Intellectual Composers and the 'Ideal Public'" (pp. 37–46). In this excursive overview of Carter's career, Rockwell (a former music critic for the *New York Times*) seems to be trying to reach a "thumbs up" or "thumbs down" conclusion about Carter's music. It comes at the end, after considerable soul-searching: "For me, Carter's achievement, for all its demonstrable magnitude, seems curiously constrained, flawed by a lack of inner clarity and expressive directness."

751. Roeder, John. "Voice Leading As Transformation." In *Musical Transformation and Musical Intuition: Essays in Honor of David Lewin,* ed. Raphael Atlas and Michael Cherlin, 41–58. Roxbury, MA: Ovenbird Press, 1994. ISBN 1-886464-00-6. ML3800.M87 1994.

Roeder follows David Lewin in applying mathematical group theory to musical structures. One of his examples refers to brief passages from Carter's *String Quartet No. 4* (item 91). Roeder uses a group to model the succession of intervals within each instrument's part. The other examples are drawn from the music of Schoenberg, Berg, and Webern.

752. Rorem, Ned. "Ned Rorem on Music: Elliott Carter." Review of *Flawed Words and Stubborn Sounds*, by Allen Edwards (interview with Elliott Carter). In *Pure Contraption: A Composer's Essays*, 23–26 (New York: Holt, Rinehart and Winston, 1974). ISBN 0-03-011021-1. ML60.R784P9. First published in *New Republic*, 26 February 1972.

Review of item 584. Rorem's review begins with an overview of Carter's place in the twentieth-century pantheon of American composers. "Carter is the only composer after Bartók who can make a convincing Big Statement in non-vocal mediums, particularly in the otherwise atrophied string quartet." His review of *Flawed Words and Stubborn Sounds*, however, is withering: "From the painful ejection of the very first question the book sags, for the protagonists lack the Craft-Stravinsky gift of gab. . . . Mr. Edwards depicts the two of them in an ivory tower of Babel satirizing a situation which Carter in reality deplores."

753. ———. "Messiaen and Carter on Their Birthdays." *Tempo* 127 (December 1978): 22–24. Also printed as "Messiaen and Carter at 70," *The Listener* 100, no. 2590 (14 December 1978): 806–7.

This chatty birthday greeting to the two composers contains some interesting comments about Carter's music ("Not the diffuse necessity of didactic wisdom but the clean-cut urgency of an epileptic fit"), his personality and "sly Burgess Meredithean glance," and the role of Helen Carter in his career. The two versions of this essay differ in a few minor details (the quote about the epileptic fit, for example, is not in *The Listener*).

754. Rosen, Charles. "One Easy Piece." *New York Review of Books* 20, no. 2 (22 February 1973): 25–29. Reprinted in *Composer* 69 (Spring 1980): 1–8. Also reprinted in Charles Rosen, *The Musical Languages of Elliott Carter*, 21–31. (Washington: Library of Congress, 1984.)

French translation of excerpts ("Un morceau facile: le *Double Concerto* d'Elliott Carter"), trans. Pierre-Etienne Will, *Critique* 36, no. 408 (May 1981): 496–505.

Rosen begins by taking the New York Philharmonic to task for neglecting Carter's music, then discusses the slippery concept of the "difficulty" of contemporary music. His main topic, however, is Carter's *Double Concerto* (item 51) and its early performance history. Rosen, an influential writer about music and one of the great pianists of the twentieth century, was a participant in "more than a third" of the "hundreds of performances" the *Double Concerto* had received by the time the article was written. Thus his account, which emphasizes the "simplicity and directness" of Carter's music, has a special authority. Of particular interest are Rosen's comments about Carter's rhythmic language and use of cross-rhythms that "do not cross, but proceed independently."

755. ———. "Les langages musicaux d'Elliott Carter." See Rosen, Charles, "The Musical Languages of Elliott Carter" (item 758).

756. ———. "I linguaggi musicali di Elliott Carter." See Rosen, Charles, "The Musical Languages of Elliott Carter" (item 758).

757. ———. "Un morceau facile: le *Double Concerto* d'Elliott Carter." See Rosen, Charles, "One Easy Piece" (item 754).

758. ———. "The Musical Languages of Elliott Carter." In *The Musical Languages of Elliott Carter*, 1–20. Washington: Library of Congress, 1984.
   French translation ("Les langages musicaux d'Elliott Carter"), trans. Thierry Baud, *Contrechamps* 6 (April 1986): 123–39.
   Italian translation ("I linguaggi musicali di Elliott Carter") in *EC*, 503–27.

Rosen's thesis here is that unlike their eighteenth- and nineteenth-century predecessors, who could rely on "all kinds of scales, arpeggios, and commonly accepted devices with which to write," contemporary composers must "reinvent a language" for each new composition. Rosen illustrates Carter's success at doing so with a lengthy analysis of his *Piano Sonata* (item 80) and some comments about the *Double Concerto* (item 51), *Piano Concerto* (item 79), *Concerto for Orchestra* (item 49), and *String Quartet No. 3* (item 90).

759. ———. "Happy Birthday, Elliott Carter." *New York Review of Books* 35, no. 19 (1988): 24–25.

This tribute, written on the occasion of Carter's eightieth birthday, contains a brief summary of the composer's career and the observation that, in his music, Carter organizes "conflicting subjective perceptions of time into a dramatic form in which they each simultaneously find free and individual play."

760. Rosenfeld, Paul. "The Newest American Composers." *Modern Music* 15, no. 3 (March–April 1938): 153–59.

See pages 157–58 on Carter. Rosenfeld alludes to the "lyrical and romantic" treatment of Carter's not-yet-completed *Pocahontas* (item 81) and gives brief overviews of two pieces to texts by Robert Herrick (*Harvest Home* [item 65] and *To Music* [item 103]) and a third by John Gay (*Let's Be Gay* [item 69]). "All three pieces are fresh, unpretentious and sincere, charming and light and clear in sonority, and have much rhythmic life." Hearing a disguised political message in Carter's setting of Herrick's line from *Harvest Home*, "To the rough sickle and crooked scythe," Rosenfeld concludes, with tongue in cheek, "I feel that by virtue of the poem and the musical values of the setting, the work constitutes one of the best of leftist chants."

761. Rossiter, Frank. R. *Charles Ives and His America*. New York: Liveright, 1975. ISBN 0-87140-610-1. ML410.I94R68.

In this biography of Ives, Rossiter discusses the composer's various contacts with Elliott Carter.

762. Routh, Francis. "An Enriching Study." Review of *The Music of Elliott Carter*, by David Schiff. *Composer* 80 (Winter 1983): 28.

Review of item 769. In sharp contrast to reviewers such as Mead (item 708), Morris (item 720), Wuorinen (item 821), and others who fault Schiff's book for being analytically weak, Routh calls it a "a technical book, written more for the musician than the general public," and discerns "the peculiarly American qualitites of analytical thoroughness, breadth of cultural viewpoint, and a certain naive East Coast directness." He also criticizes the "not quite complete" bibliography and worries that "Carter is much more talked about than performed."

763. Saez, Richard. "To Regain Wholeness: The Many and the One in Elliott Carter's Songs." *Parnassus* 10, no. 2 (Fall–Winter 1982): 289–329.

This long and loosely organized essay deals primarily with melody and text setting in post-tonal music. Carter's *A Mirror on Which to Dwell* (item 72) and *Syringa* (item 96) are the principal works discussed, although his *Duo* [sic] *Concerto* (item 51), *Concerto for Orchestra* (item 49), and *Canaries,* from *Eight Pieces for Four Timpani* (item 54), are also cited (the last to illustrate metric modulation). Saez's aim is to contrast Carter's text setting with that of earlier traditions, particularly the nineteenth-century lied, but his essay is marred by frequent digressions, often on topics of questionable relevence ("The church, which is at the center of the development of Western music, periodically issued *dicta* ordering a cessation to dancing in the aisles"), and by analyses that rely too heavily on unsupported generalizations ("In the articulation of several staccato sixteenths throughout *Mirror* there is something—in its very difference—like the images of Schubert's songs").

764. Saminsky, Lazare. *Living Music of the Americas,* 91–95. New York: Howell, Soskin and Crown Publishers, 1949.

An early appreciation of Carter's music. Saminsky places Carter together with Normand Lockwood and praises both for their "outstanding creative gift and independent stand" and for their "new direction in American craft." Irritated that Carter's "ballets and vocal composition brought him only a short spell of notice in our lazy-minded, impatient and irresponsible cosmopolis," Saminsky surveys a number of Carter works including *Pocahontas* (item 81), *Heart Not So Heavy As Mine* (item 66), *The Harmony of Morning* (item 64), and *Symphony No. 1* (item 94). There is also a musical example, reproduced from Carter's manuscript, of *The Harmony of Morning,* from two measures before to two measures after letter *M.*

765. Schiff, David. "Carter in the Seventies." *Tempo* 130 (September 1979): 2–10.

Descriptive analyses of three of Carter's compositions from the 1970s—*A Mirror on Which to Dwell* (item 72), *Syringa* (item 96), and *A Symphony of Three Orchestras* (item 95)—with musical examples and several charts of musical materials adapted from Carter's sketches. Schiff emphasizes Carter's return to his earlier interest in vocal music after a long period of writing only instrumental works.

766. ———. "Carter for Winds." *Winds Quarterly* 1 (Fall 1980): 2–6.

Descriptive analyses of Carter's *Eight Etudes and a Fantasy* (item 53) and *Brass Quintet* (item 42). Much of the article was incorporated in revised form into the first edition of Schiff's book *The Music of Elliott Carter* (item 769).

767. ———. "*In Sleep, in Thunder:* Elliott Carter's Portrait of Robert Lowell." *Tempo* 142 (September 1982): 2–9.

This substantial and informative essay on Carter's 1981 song cycle (item 68) also contains a chronology of Carter's friendship with Robert Lowell and addresses the overlapping aesthetic concerns of poet and composer. The musical commentary and writing style are similar to the first edition of Schiff's book *The Music of Elliott Carter* (item 769).

768. ———. Letter to the Editor, *Tempo* 147 (December 1983): 45.

Schiff here defends the relevence of the "45-note tonic chord" used by Carter in *A Symphony of Three Orchestras* (item 95) from David Harvey's charge that the chord "cannot be described as a referential configuration" (see item 674). Schiff responds that the chord is "gradually, but explicitly, revealed throughout the work" and that in his experience "listeners familiar with [Carter's] music invariably identify each work by the sound of its tonic chord."

769. ———. *The Music of Elliott Carter.* London: Eulenburg Books; New York: Da Capo Press, 1983. ISBN 0903873060. ML410.C3293 S34 1983. Revised second edition, London: Faber; Ithaca, NY: Cornell University Press, 1998. ISBN 0-8014-3612-5.

The two editions of this book, which are dramatically different from each other, are essential sources for research on Carter, and scholars will want to consult both. The first edition includes brief analyses of all of Carter's compositions, arranged chronologically from his earliest student works through *Night Fantasies* (1980), together with three introductory chapters: "An Overview: Family, Education, Creative Method," "Musical Time: Rhythm and Form," and "Musical Space: Texture and Harmony." The revised second edition is arranged by genre, with chapters on "Chamber Music," "Vocal Music," "Piano Music," and "Orchestral Music." It adds coverage of Carter's works from 1981 up to and including *Symphonia* (completed 1997), as well as a substantially enlarged catalog of works, bibliography, and discography. The additional material required the omission of many of the first edition's musical examples (particularly of the early works) and a great deal of "the prose of my younger self," as Schiff puts it.

The Music of Elliott Carter was written originally at the behest of Carter and Sir William Glock (who also served as the first edition's editor) and with the composer's encouragement and support. It is thus a sympathetic, even "authorized," critique of Carter's oeuvre. Schiff is especially good at connecting the music with the extramusical poetic concerns to which Carter has often alluded. The analyses, which closely follow Carter's own, are an important window on the composer's aesthetics and creative methods, though they are often too general to pass muster with music analysts. For reviews see items 654, 675, 678, 680, 706, 708, 719, 720, 726, 762, 813, and 821.

———. *Elliott Carter: edizione italiana aggiornata dall'autore.* Listed above as item 401.

770. ———. "Musical Time in Elliott Carter's *Night Fantasies.*" Booklet published for the Arnold Schoenberg Institute's Elliott Carter Festival, Spring [11–14 April] 1983, 4–22. Portions reprinted in David Schiff, *The Music of Elliott Carter,* 313–21. (New York: Da Capo Press, 1983. ISBN 0903873060. ML410.C3293 S34 1983.)

Schiff begins with a discussion of different philosophical classifications of time and concludes with an examination of the technical and aesthetic ideas that underlie Carter's 1980 work for solo piano, *Night Fantasies* (item 74).

771. ———. "Elliott Carter, America's Much-Honored Composer Is Still Creating Challenging Music at Age 75," *Ovation* 4, no. 11 (December 1983): 12–15, 50–52.

This excellent introduction to Carter's music provides an especially thoughtful discussion of the composer's aesthetic sensibilities, laced with a number of revealing anecdotes about Carter himself. For musicians, the article is a useful supplement to the first edition of Schiff's *The Music of Elliott Carter* (item 769), but its nontechnical language makes it a valuable source for nonspecialists wishing to learn more about Carter's music.

772. ———. "Elliott Carter's Harvest Home." *Tempo* 167 (December 1988): 2–13.

Following the format of the first edition of *The Music of Elliott Carter* (item 769), Schiff discusses Carter's *Triple Duo* (item 105), *Changes* (item 46), *Riconoscenza per Goffredo Petrassi* (item 102.2), *Esprit rude/Esprit doux* (item 58), *Penthode* (item 78), *String Quartet No. 4* (item 91), *A Celebration of Some 100 × 150 Notes* (item 100.1), *Oboe Concerto* (item 75), *Enchanted Preludes* (item 57), and *Remembrance* (item 100.2).

773. ———. "Carter's New Classicism." *College Music Symposium* 29 (1989): 115–22.

A substantial and provocative article by one of the foremost writers on Carter's music. Schiff critiques Carter's large-scale works of the 1980s—*Triple Duo* (item 105), *Penthode* (item 78), *String Quartet No. 4* (item 91), and *Oboe Concerto* (item 75)—in terms of Roland Barthes's classification of "classic" and "modern" texts, as expounded in his book *S/Z*. Carter's music is said to fall into the "modern" category, "exploding illusions" of unified and continuous space and time that exemplify the "classic" text and requiring a "writerly reader" who will be "'no longer a consumer but a producer of the text.'" Although the connections Schiff makes between music and literary criticism are sometimes tenuous, his readings of Carter's compositions are insightful. Best is his discussion of Carter's changing use of diverse materials. In the works of the 1960s and 1970s "the diversity of elements became an emblem of freedom while their convergence appeared as a form of tyranny. The recent works reverse this relationship . . . by making the possibility of connection both explicit and desirable—if never entirely attainable." Carter has publically disagreed with the description offered here of his music (see item 598, pp. 90–91). See also items 628, 815, and 817a.

774. ———. "First Performances: Carter's *Violin Concerto*." *Tempo* 174 (September 1990): 22–24.

Very little is said about the premiere of Carter's *Violin Concerto* (item 107) given by Ole Böhn and the San Francisco Symphony conducted by Herbert Blomstedt on 2 May 1990. Instead, Schiff provides an analytical overview of the composition, with a brief musical example and a chart of the work's all-interval twelve-note chords. Most interesting is Schiff's anecdotal account of Carter's perspective on the work's genesis.

775. ———. Review of *The Later Music of Elliott Carter: A Study in Music Theory and Analysis*, by David I. H. Harvey. *Notes* 47, no. 3 (March 1991): 767–69.

Review of item 677. An entirely hostile review. Schiff berates Harvey for his misleading title (the book is about "middle period" rather than "later" works), his "pious" writing style, and especially for "claiming to talk about meaning" while focusing on "a narrow area of syntax." For Schiff, this is most clearly manifested by Harvey's attempt to apply hierarchical pitch structures to Carter's nontonal compositions. Schiff detects "the implication, call it theory hubris, that the author has discovered an objective test that can determine musical quality." Also see the clash between Harvey and Schiff in items 674 and 768.

776. ———. Review of *Oboe Concerto* (item 75), by Elliott Carter. *Notes* 48, no. 3 (March 1992): 1094–95.

Recalling that Carter played the oboe as a student, Schiff proceeds with a summary of Carter's use of the instrument in various pieces, quotes a selection of reviews of the concerto, and describes the music's dramatic scenario.

777. ———. "A Paper Mountain: Elliott Carter's Sketches." In the catalog of the exhibition *Settling New Scores: Music Manuscripts from the Paul Sacher Foundation,* at the Pierpont

Morgan Library 13 May–30 August 1998, ed. Felix Meyer, 115–18. Mainz: Schott, 1998. ISBN 3-7957-0347-6.

A brief overview of Carter's working methods as revealed in his sketches. Schiff describes the various types of sketches Carter makes, notes the enigmatic relationship between sketches containing abstract charts of chords and those containing musical passages, and considers the influence on Carter's methods of Joseph Schillinger, Henry Cowell, Charles Seeger, and Nadia Boulanger. Also of note is Schiff's comment that the last movement of the *Violin Concerto* by Felix Mendelssohn may have been a source for the last movement of Carter's own *Violin Concerto* (item 107).

778. Schiffer, Brigitte. "New York: Elliott Carter." *Music and Musicians* 27, no. 8 (April 1979): 61–62.

Schiffer surveys Carter's career and the many performances of his works in New York in honor of his seventieth birthday and comments on the world premiere of *Syringa* (item 96), performed by Speculum Musicae on 10 December 1978.

779. Schmidt, Dörte. "Das 'bemerkenswerte' Interesse an Alois Hába: Anmerkung zu Elliott Carters 'Harmony Book'" (The "remarkable" interest in Alois Hába: A Comment on Elliott Carter's "Harmony Book"). *Mitteilungen der Paul Sacher Stiftung* 6 (March 1993): 38–42.

In this brief article Schmidt cites primary sources having to do with the origins of Carter's *Harmony Book*. These include sketches from the *String Quartet No. 2* (item 89) (two of which are reproduced as examples), a typescript of a lecture, prepared in 1960 for presentation in Tokyo, and a typescript of an undated note, in which Carter explains that he began working on the *Harmony Book* "after studies of the Alois Hába *Neue Harmonielehre* (see my copy pp. 95–119) J. M. Hauer's *Vom Melos zur Pauke* (see my copy p. 12) and of the 12-tone technique by Schoenberg, Richard Hill, Leibowitz, Babbitt, Martino, Allen Forte, and George Perle."

780. ———. "Emanzipation des musikalischen Diskurses: Die Skizzen zu Elliott Carters zweitem Streichquartett und seine theoretischen Arbeiten in den späten 50er Jahren" (Emancipation of musical discourse: The sketches for Elliott Carter's

String Quartet No. 2 and his theoretical works in the late 1950s). In *Jahrbuch des Staatlichen Instituts für Musikforschung Preußischer Kulturbesitz,* ed. Günther Wagner, 209–48. Stuttgart: J. B. Metzler, 1995.

An exceptionally detailed study of Carter's fundamental reexamination of his compositional materials in the 1950s as revealed in the sketches for his *String Quartet No. 2* (item 89). Schmidt contrasts Carter's research into the "emancipation of musical discourse" with Schoenberg's development of the twelve-tone method and its extension by postwar serial composers. In this context she quotes at length from an unpublished preface and list of exercises that Carter wrote circa 1959 for a never-completed composition textbook. Schmidt notes that these exercises, in which students are encouraged to try many different ways of realizing an idea, bear a striking resemblance to the sketches for Carter's *String Quartet No. 2*. Schmidt divides the sketches into three categories: sketches of general harmonic organization, musical sketches of several evolving versions of a passage, and a small group of analytical sketches, probably made later. She also discusses the order of composition of the movements and provides extensive analyses of sketches related to the harmonic organization, the dramatic scenario, and the rhythmic plan of the quartet. For Schmidt, the sketches reveal a method of composition not based on prefabricated motives or themes but on a discursive process in which the function of structural elements is in a state of continuous evolution.

781. ———. "'The practical problems of the composer': Der schwierige Weg vom Auftrag zur Uraufführung von Elliott Carters zweitem Streichquartett" (The difficult road from commission to premiere of Elliott Carter's *String Quartet No. 2*). *Die Musikforschung* 48, no. 4 (October–December 1995): 400–403.

A documentary history of the commissioning, composition, and early performance history of Carter's *String Quartet No. 2* (item 89), based on unpublished correspondence found in the Carter Collection of the Paul Sacher Foundation in Basel, Switzerland. Schmidt also discusses an upublished lecture, "The Practical Problems of the Composer," written for the Princeton Seminar in Advanced Musical Studies in 1959, and a copy of Carter's course description for the Salzburg Seminars, given in 1958, on the topic "The Amerian Composer, His Cultural, Social and Economic Situation Today."

782. Schonberg, Harold C. "Are Reports of Its Death Greatly Exaggerated?" *New York Times,* 29 September 1968, sec. 2 (Arts and Leisure).

Schonberg disagrees with Carter's point that contemporary music sheds new light on the music of the past. Schonberg feels that the two have nothing to do with each other. He also chides Carter for his claim that "they had the habit of living in the present in Beethoven's time" (Carter). Schonberg responds: "This is nothing but wishful thinking. Carter should look up a few history books and discover who the popular composers were in Beethoven's day." Carter responded with a letter to the editor (item 437).

783. Schreiner, Martin. "Expansion As Design in the *Fantasia* of Elliott Carter's *String Quartet No. 1.*" *Sonus* 12, no. 2 (1992): 11–26.

This article develops Schreiner's contention that "The process of expansion on several levels is what propels and gives shape to the *Fantasia.*" Schreiner describes sections of various durations as expansions of earlier sections and postulates a two-part division of the movement as a whole, with the second part an expansion of the first. Accompanying examples graph changes in the "rate of attacks/minute" over time.

784. Schwartz, Lloyd. "Elliott Carter and the Conflict of Chaos and Order." *Harvard Magazine,* November–December 1983, 57–62.

A summary of Carter's life and works through *Changes* (1983), with most quotations drawn from secondary sources. A sidebar quoting at length from Carter's entry in the *25th Anniversary Report of the Harvard Class of 1930* (item 438) provides the most interesting reading.

785. ———. "Elliott Carter—The Vocal Works (1975–1981)." *Sonus* 19, no. 1 (Fall 1998): 12–25.

A reprint of the author's notes for a recording of Carter's vocal works (Bridge BCD 9014, 1989).

786. Seay, Albert. Review of *Eight Pieces for Four Timpani*, by Elliott Carter. *Notes* 26, no. 3 (March 1970): 623.

A brief review of the recently issued *Eight Pieces for Four Timpani* (item 54). Seay calls them "a tour de force for a medium that is all too often afflicted with a repertory that shows little more than manual dexterity" and adds, "It is fascinating music as well."

787. Shreffler, Anne. "'Give the Music Room': Elliott Carters 'View of the Capitol from the Library of Congress' aus *A Mirror on Which to Dwell*" (in German). In *Quellenstudien II*, ed. Felix Meyer, 255–83. Winterthur: Amadeus Verlag, 1993.

A detailed analysis of the fifth song from Carter's song cycle *A Mirror on Which to Dwell* (item 72) and its autograph sources, including a catalog of sketches and several photographic reproductions of materials in Carter's hand. Shreffler provides an excellent introduction to the composer's working methods in this period and an exceptionally clear and insightful reading of the ways in which his music responds to and interprets Bishop's poem.

788. ———. "Elliott Carter and His America." *Sonus* 14, no. 2 (Spring 1994): 38–66.

In this article, with a title alluding to Frank R. Rossiter's *Charles Ives and His America* (item 761), Shreffler explores "Carter's connections to a particular moment in American musical modernism, the 20s and 30s avant-garde led by Edgard Varèse and Henry Cowell." Other composers involved with this group include Charles Seeger, Ruth Crawford, Conlon Nancarrow, and Charles Ives. Shreffler points out ways these musicians influenced a number of Carter's compositions, including the *String Quartet No. 1* (item 88), *String Quartet No. 2* (item 89), *A Symphony of Three Orchestras* (item 95), and "View of the Capitol from the Library of Congress" from *A Mirror on Which to Dwell* (item 72).

789. Skulsky, Abraham. "Elliott Carter." *Bulletin of American Composers Alliance* 3, no. 2 (Summer 1953): 2–16.

This profile of Carter's life and music up to the *String Quartet No. 1* (item 88) is one of the more substantial early articles that helped to bring him greater renown. It includes a generous selection of musical examples, as well as a five-page "Chronological List of Carter Works with Reviews." The latter contains a detailed listing of premieres, together with long quotes from many reviews of Carter's pieces, dating back to 1937.

790. ———. "The High Cost of Creativity: The Plight of American Composers." *HiFi Review* 2, no. 5 (May 1959): 31–36.

Skulsky, who came to the United States in 1948, here offers his survey of the American compositional scene and the difficulties faced by American composers. In spite of these difficulties, there are a few who rival their European counterparts. "Pride of place," in Skulsky's opinion, goes to Carter, whose *String Quartet No. 1* (item 88) and *Variations for Orchestra* (item 106) "may well mark him as one of the most important composers anywhere in the world today."

791. Steinberg, Michael. "Elliott Carter's Second String Quartet." *The Score and I.M.A. Magazine* 27 (July 1960): 22–26.
    Elaborated German translation ("Elliott Carters 2. Streichquartett"), *Melos* 28, no. 2 (February 1961): 35–37.

The English version is essentially a review of the New York premiere of Carter's *String Quartet No. 2* (item 89) given by the Juilliard String Quartet on 25 March 1960. The German translation is expanded somewhat and contains several new musical examples, including the chords Carter sent to Steinberg on a postcard illustrating the harmonic basis of the quartet. This postcard is reproduced in *Elliott Carter: Sketches and Scores in Manuscript*, 29 (item 610).

792. ———. "Elliott Carter: An American Original at Seventy." *Keynote* 2, no. 10 (December 1978): 8–14.

This profile of Carter and his music through *A Symphony of Three Orchestras* also includes program listings for a series of broadcasts on New York City's WNCN radio in honor of the composer's seventieth birthday.

793. ———. "Celebrating the Music of Elliott Carter." *Symphony Magazine*, January–February 1989, 24–27, 98–99.

A summary of Carter's life and works published in honor of his eightieth birthday.

794. Stewart, Robert. "Serial Aspects of Elliott Carter's *Variations for Orchestra*." *Music Review* 34, no. 1 (1973): 62–65.

The "serial aspects" Stewart reveals in this extremely brief selection of examples include retrograde and inversion statements of portions of the theme and two ritornelli of the *Variations* (item 106) and the presence of all twelve pitch classes in a brief span of time. For more on the relationship between Carter's music and twelve-tone theory, see item 711.

795. Stone, Kurt. "Current Chronicle." *Musical Quarterly* 55, no. 4 (October 1969): 559–72.

After an introduction intended to defend Carter against charges of being a composer of serial music, this article presents a fairly brief but quite useful analysis of Carter's *Piano Concerto* (item 79). Also described in passing are the *String Quartet No. 1* (item 88), *String Quartet No. 2* (item 89), and *Double Concerto* (item 51).

796. Stravinsky, Igor, with Robert Craft. "Some Composers." *Musical America* 82, no. 6 (June 1962): 6–11. Reprinted in Igor Stravinsky and Robert Craft, *Dialogues and a Diary*, 99–101. (Garden City, NY: Doubleday, 1963; London: Faber and Faber, 1968. ML410.S932 A335 1968.)

Responding to Robert Craft's question, "What composition by an American-born composer has most attracted you to date?" Stravinsky replies "Elliott Carter's *Double Concerto*, I think, but you would have to know what other music I have heard to evaluate the preference." Later he says, again in reference to the concerto (item 51), "There, the word is out. A masterpiece, and by an American composer."

797. Sykes, James. "The Music of Elliott Carter." *The Listener* 67, no. 1731 (31 May 1962): 969.

A summary of Carter's life and works.

798. Thomas, Gavin. "Crashing through the Picturesque." *Musical Times* 136, no. 1828 (June 1995): 285–88.

In this article Thomas presents an informal analysis of two then new works by Carter. Although he is skeptical of the "anti-representational and non-illustrative" vocal writing in Carter's cycle of John Hollander poems *Of Challenge and of Love* (item 76), Gavin concludes that "each song is a little miracle of structural ingenuity, of poetry into music, of substance over style" and coins the term *structural pictorialism* to describe Carter's approach to text setting. His observations about the individual songs of the cycle are insightful, with one notable exception: he chastises Carter for setting the word *rises* to a falling minor seventh but fails to observe that Carter's setting follows the pitch descent of the word as it is pronounced. The discussion of *Adagio tenebroso* (item 93.2) is short and rather sketchy.

799. Thomson, Virgil. "Fulfillment Experienced." In *Music Reviewed*, 244–45. New York: Vintage Books (Random House), 1966. First published in the *New York Herald Tribune*, 13 March 1948.

Review of a Webster Aitken recital at Town Hall on 12 March 1948. "Elliott Carter's *Piano Sonata*, written in 1945 and 1946, might just possibly be a work for the repertory. This is a sustained piece full of power and brilliance."

800. ———. "A Powerful Work." In *Music Reviewed*, 370–71. New York: Vintage Books (Random House), 1966. First published in the *New York Herald Tribune*, 5 May 1953.

Review of an early performance of Carter's *String Quartet No. 1* (item 88) by the Walden Quartet of the University of Illinois. Thomson says, "It is an original and powerful piece, and the audience loved it."

801. ———. "Choral Conference." In *Music Reviewed*, 373–75. New York: Vintage Books (Random House), 1966. First published in the *New York Herald Tribune*, 16 August 1953.

Thomson reviews music from a two-day conference, "The American Composer and Choral Music," held at Harvard University in

August 1953. "Elliott Carter's *Musicians Wrestle Everywhere* partly displays and partly conceals its fanciful Emily Dickinson text in a deliciously complex contrapuntal texture modeled, if I guess rightly, after the madrigals of Orlandus Lassus. It is a gay and busy piece, at once airy and compact in sound, and marked by the very great precision of workmanship that is characteristic of Carter."

802. Tingley, George Peter. "Metric Modulation and Elliott Carter's *First String Quartet.*" *Indiana Theory Review* 4, no. 3 (1981): 3–11.

Tingley describes two types of metric modulation: "single-line," involving a single instrument, and "polyphonic," involving more than one instrument. He gives an example of "metric modulation in three parts," meaning three instruments are involved, and, in the section called "Metric Modulation and the Larger Design," provides a graph of the entire quartet showing the return of various tempos.

803. Trimble, Lester. "Elliott Carter." *Stereo Review* 29, no. 6 (1972): 64–72.

Trimble here presents one of the more substantial biographical portraits of Carter in print. It contains a number of quotations from interviews and an observant description of Carter's person and manner. The coverage of Carter's experiences in the 1920s and 1930s is particularly good.

804. Truniger, Matthias. "Elliott Carter's *Esprit rude/Esprit doux.*" *Sonus* 19, no. 1 (Fall 1998): 26–52.

Truniger's analysis of Carter's *Esprit rude/Esprit doux* (item 58) is divided into three sections. In "Time and Rhythm" he describes the two streams of pulsations (one played by the flute, one by the clarinet) that underlie the piece's rhythmic structure and observes that all faster rhythmic values are multiples of these slow pulse rates. "Musical Language" is devoted to describing the "three opposing characters" played by both instruments and a harmonic structure based on the two all-interval tetrachords [0,1,4,6] and [0,1,3,7]. In the section on form, Truniger uses a spectrographic analysis of a performance to illustrate a division of the piece into six "stanzas" that are symmetrically "situated around the point of the Golden Section."

805. Uno, Yayoi. "The Tempo-Span GIS As a Measure of Continuity in Elliott Carter's *Eight Pieces for Four Timpani*." *Integral* 10 (1996): 53–91.

Uno uses David Lewin's concept of a "generalized interval system" (GIS) to examine the temporal continuity (specifically the changes in pulse groupings and speed) in the *Canaries* and *March* movements of Carter's *Eight Pieces for Four Timpani* (item 54). The analyses describe readily audible characteristics of the music in the formal language of algebra.

806. Vlad, Roman. "Recensioni: Musica." *La rassegna musicale* 24, no. 4 (October–December 1954): 369–71.

Vlad surveys a number of early Carter pieces.

807. Warburton, Thomas. "A Literary Approach to Carter's *Night Fantasies*." *Music Review* 51, no. 3 (August 1990): 208–20.

A comparison of the developmental processes in Carter's *Night Fantasies* (item 74) and James Joyce's short story *Clay*. Although clearly motivated by Carter's many references to literature in his published writings, Warburton does not say why he chose *Clay* to compare with *Night Fantasies*, and the analyses of both works, as well as the connection between them, will strike many readers as superficial. (See item 666 for another comparison of Joyce and Carter.)

Weber, Jerome. F. *Carter and Schuman*. Listed above as item 611.

808. Weirich, Robert. "Who's Afraid of Elliott Carter?" *American Music Teacher* 38, no. 2 (November–December 1988): 14–17, 59.

This summary of Carter's musical career, published in honor of his eightieth birthday, is most interesting for its quotations of comments by Earl Carlyss—the second violinist of the Juilliard String Quartet—about the rehearsals for the premiere of Carter's *String Quartet No. 3* (item 90).

Whipple, Harold. "An Elliott Carter Discography." Listed above as item 612.

809. White, John R. "Elliott Carter: Symphony No. 1." *Notes* 22, no. 1 (Fall 1965): 820–21.

A somewhat dismissive review, occasioned by the recent publication of a new edition of the *Symphony* (item 94). White calls it "a perfectly good symphony of a class, a large class right below Piston, Harris, and Copland of the thirties."

810. Whittall, Arnold. "Post-Twelve-Note Analysis." *Proceedings of the Royal Music Association* 94 (1967–68): 1–17.

Whittall devotes four pages to an analysis of Carter's *Double Concerto* (item 51), focusing on Carter's handling of motivic development. In contrast to Webern, whose "motivic manipulation contained a high degree of connective repetition . . . Carter's permutations submerge motivic identity in their sheer evolving energy." Also of interest is the connection between motive and form: "By reducing his thematic material to a number of intervals which can be freely used in different permutations, Carter is able to proceed from motif to melody and back again as the arch-shaped structure he has chosen provides."

811. ———. "Elliott Carter." In *First American Music Conference, Keele University, England, April 18–21, 1975,* 82–98. Keele: Keele University, 1975.

A largely descriptive summary of Carter's career, emphasizing his changing feelings about European musical thought and the development of his later style, which Whittall calls "neo-expressionist."

812. ———. Review of *WEC*. *Tempo* 124 (March 1978): 40–43.

Review of item 399. An enthusiastic review with abundant short quotations from Carter's writings. "[T]he greatest interest for admirers of Carter the composer is to see the extent to which his reactions and opinions reflect and affect his own development."

813. ———. Review of *The Music of Elliott Carter,* by David Schiff. *Music and Letters* 65, no. 3 (July 1984): 276–77.

Review of item 769. Whittall praises certain of the metaphors Schiff uses to describe Carter's music but is unhappy with the "well-informed but inevitably rather superficial, selective approach to the individual compositions."

814. ———. Review of *In Sleep, in Thunder* (item 68); *Triple Duo* (item 105); and *Esprit rude/Esprit doux* (item 58), by Elliott Carter. *Music and Letters* 68, no. 1 (January 1987): 102–3.

Whittall is most interested in Carter's text setting in *In Sleep, in Thunder* and how it compares with Carter's other vocal works of the 1970s. There is also a brief overview of *Triple Duo* and an even briefer paragraph about *Esprit rude/Esprit doux*, which Whittall calls "a pendant to *Triple Duo*."

815. ———. Review of *Penthode* (item 78); *String Quartet No. 4* (item 91); and *Enchanted Preludes* (item 57), by Elliott Carter. *Music and Letters* 72, no. 2 (May 1991): 344–45.

This review becomes a platform for Whittall to debate David Schiff's description of these works as "classical" (see item 773). "If this [music] is 'classic' anything, it is classic atonality, using the resources of the governing system in an authoritative, definitive manner, and in which 'resolution' is still resisted." Whittall develops this point further in item 817a.

816. ———. Review of *Oboe Concerto* (item 75), by Elliott Carter. *Music and Letters* 73, no. 2 (May 1992): 339–40.

A brief analysis of Carter's *Oboe Concerto*, in terms of its place in Carter's oeuvre and its dramatic scenario and form. Whittall hears the concerto as divided into two main stages, the first emphasizing conflict, the second reconciliation between the soloist and concertino on the one hand and the orchestra on the other.

817. ———. "Summer's Long Shadows." *The Musical Times* (April 1997): 14–22.

A descriptive overview of Carter's recent compositions, including *Trilogy* (item 104), *Symphonia* (item 93), *Quintet for Piano and Winds* (item 83), *String Quartet No. 5* (item 92), *Gra* (item 63), *Figment* (item 61), *Of Challenge and of Love* (item 76), and *Clarinet Concerto* (item 47).

817a. ———. "Modernist Aesthetics, Modernist Music: Some Analytical Perspectives. In *Music Theory in Concept and Practice*, ed. James M. Baker, David W. Beach, Jonathan W. Bernard, 157–80. Rochester and Suffolk: University of

Rochester Press, 1997. ISBN 1-878822-79-9. MT6.M962078 1997.

Whittall presents Carter and Harrison Birtwistle as case studies of musical modernism. Although he invokes Adorno early on, Whittall's primary interest (in the section on Carter) is to dispute David Schiff's interpretation of the terms "classic" and "modernist" (see item 773). Examples from *Penthode* (item 78) and *Enchanted Preludes* (item 57) are used to show that Carter's music is not classic because it resists "the siren call of decisively resolving convergence" and because it lacks "classic music's most powerful structural quality" (the structural levels of Schenkerian theory). The article concludes with a brief comparison of Carter and Birtwistle.

818. ———. Review of *CEL*, by Elliott Carter. *Music and Letters* 78, no. 4 (November 1997): 627–29.

Review of item 402. Whittall here summarizes several of Carter's main concerns in the writings under review, including the differences between American and European musical culture, the relationship between Carter's writings and his music, and the influence of Charles Ives. The emphasis throughout is on those writings not previously published in *WEC*.

819. Wolfthal, Marvin Allen. "Elliott Carter (le opere dal 1946 al 1971)." *Musica/Realtà* 4, no. 11 (August 1983): 107–22.

A summary of Carter's ideas about temporal organization in his works from the *Piano Sonata* (item 80) through the *String Quartet No. 3* (item 90).

820. Wuorinen, Charles. "The Outlook for Young Composers." *Perspectives of New Music* 1, no. 2 (Spring–Summer 1963): 54–61.

Notable for its section on Carter, in which Wuorinen says, "The music of Carter is of importance to young composers not only because of his interesting treatment of rhythmic detail, but more importantly for his conceptions of larger form and gesture." On the other hand, "it is doubtful that his pitch treatment will have very wide application. The commitment of most young composers to serialized pitch is probably too great."

821. ———. Review of *The Music of Elliott Carter*, by David Schiff. *Musical Quarterly* 69, no. 4 (Fall 1983): 606–7.

Review of item 769. An especially harsh critique. "Reading like nothing so much as a nightmarishly long program note, [Schiff's book] substitutes adoring panegyrics for objective criticism."

822. Zimmerman, Robert. "The Poetics of Polyrhythm in Elliott Carter's *Anaphora*." *Sonus* 19, no. 1 (Fall 1998): 67–85.

In his analysis of the first song of Carter's cycle *A Mirror on Which to Dwell* (item 72), Zimmerman discusses the way a long-range polyrhythm is used to dramatize the poetic ideas of Elizabeth Bishop's poem. Many of his observations echo those made by Craig A. Weston in a 1992 dissertation (item 876).

Films and Video Recordings

823. *Elliott Carter*. A film by Chris Hegedus and D. A. Pennebaker. Produced by Programs in the Arts of SUNY and Pennebaker Inc. Center of Creative and Performing Arts at the State University of New York at Buffalo. © 1980. Ca. 45 minutes.

A documentary film of Elliott Carter's visit to the State University of New York at Buffalo on 14 October 1979. It begins with Carter's arrival at the Buffalo airport and concludes with a performance of his *Double Concerto* (item 51) by Paul Jacobs (hps), Ursula Oppens (pno), and an ensemble (including flutist Robert Dick and cellist Fred Sherry) conducted by Jan Williams. Other scenes include Fred Sherry and Ursula Oppens rehearsing Carter's *Sonata for Violoncello and Piano* (item 87), a small group discussion including Carter and Morton Feldman, Carter holding a lecture demonstration and question-and-answer session with a class of students, and Carter with several of the performers having dinner at a Chinese restaurant.

824. *Elliott Carter*. The South Bank Show, London Weekend Television. Produced and directed by Alan Benson. Edited and presented by Melvyn Bragg. © 1986. Ca. 53 minutes. Video recording.

This documentary includes biographical information and performances of excerpts of Carter's compositions *A Symphony of Three Orchestras* (item 95), *Holiday Overture* (item 67), and *Concerto for Orchestra* (item 49) by the London Sinfonietta with leader Nona Liddell and conductor David Atherton; *String Quartet No. 2* (item 89) by the Arditti Quartet; and *Piano Sonata* (item 80) and *Night Fantasies* (item 74) by Charles Rosen (who also comments on Carter's music). The biographical material draws on lengthy interviews with Carter and stresses his life in New York City as one source of the theme of constant change in his music. There is some background information about Carter's family and childhood and a good discussion of the influence of jazz, cinema, and literature (Joyce's *Ulysses* and Proust's *A la recherche du temps perdu*) on his compositions. (Charles Ives is not mentioned, however.) Also of interest are Carter's comments on the changes in his style after World War II.

825. *Elliott Carter: Partita.* Chicago Symphony Orchestra, Daniel Barenboim, conductor. Recorded in performance, Cologne, Germany, 1994. Ca. 20 minutes. Video recording.

A video recording of Carter's composition (item 93.1) made for German television.

826. *Speculum Musicae.* Bath Festival Series, Program no. LMA R138D. Produced by Jonathan Fulford. Directed by Peter Maniura. St. George's, Brandon Hill, Bristol, England. British Broadcasting Corporation © 1988. Ca. 77 minutes. Video recording.

A video recording of the New York new music ensemble Speculum Musicae performing at the 1988 Bath Festival in Bristol, England. Also included is an interview with Michael Berkely in which Carter discusses the influences of Ives and Copland and the idea of "accessibility." The film concludes with a performance of Carter's *Triple Duo* (item 105) by members of the group: Susan Palma (fl), Allen Blustine (cl/ebcl/bcl), Aleck Karis (pno), Daniel Druckman (perc), Curtis Macomber (vn), Eric Bartlett (vc), William Purvis (cond).

827. *Time Is Music: Elliott Carter and John Cage.* Produced by Henk Pauwels. Directed by Frank Scheffer. Sine Film/Video,

June 1988. Ca. 60 minutes (30 minutes on Carter; 30 minutes on Cage).

In this film Carter comments on a variety of topics, including his parents (who he says stopped buying insurance from Charles Ives when Carter decided to become a composer) and the influence on his music of Cocteau, Picasso, Schoenberg, Stravinsky, jazz, and Joyce. There is also a brief interview with Pierre Boulez (who admires Carter's perseverance in a not always supportive milieu) and a conversation between Carter and Conlon Nancarrow about metric modulation and writing for the player piano. The film also features excerpts of performances of Carter's first four string quartets (played by the Arditti Quartet) and his *Sonata for Violoncello and Piano* (item 87), *A Symphony of Three Orchestras* (item 95), and *Double Concerto* (item 51).

828. "Are My Ears on Wrong?—A Profile of Charles Ives." Motion Picture. Produced by David M. Thompson. BBC-TV/Open University. Solana Beach, CA: Media Guild, 1982.

Doctoral Dissertations

829. Adams, Daniel Clifford. "Striking Implement and Surface Specification in Unaccompanied Multiple Percussion Solos: Its Compositional Significance." D.M.A. thesis, University of Illinois at Urbana–Champaign, 1985. Includes a section on Carter's *Eight Pieces for Four Timpani* (item 54).

830. Anderson, Bruce Clarke. "The Solo Piano Music of Elliott Carter: A Performance Guide." Ph.D. diss., New York University, 1988. Includes sections on Carter's *Piano Sonata* (item 80) and *Night Fantasies* (item 74).

831. Arlton, Dean Luther. "American Piano Sonatas of the Twentieth Century: Selective Analyses and Annotated Index." Ed.D. diss., Columbia University, 1968. Includes a section on Carter's *Piano Sonata* (item 80).

832. Bals, Karen Elizabeth. "The American Piano Concerto in the Mid-Twentieth Century." D.M.A. thesis, University of

Kansas, 1982. Includes a section on Carter's *Piano Concerto* (item 79).

833. Beckstrom, Robert Allen. "An Analysis of Elliott Carter's *Variations for Orchestra* (1955)." Vol. 1 of Ph.D. diss., University of California at Los Angeles, 1983.

834. Breedon, Daniel Franklin. "An Investigation of the Influence of the Metaphysics of Alfred North Whitehead upon the Formal-Dramatic Compositional Procedures of Elliott Carter." D.M.A. thesis, University of Washington, 1975.

835. Browner, Tara Colleen. "Transposing Cultures: The Appropriation of Native American Musics, 1890–1990." Ph.D. diss., University of Michigan, 1995. Includes a section on Carter's *Pocahontas* (item 81).

836. Coonrod, Michael McGill. "Aspects of Form in Selected String Quartets of the Twentieth Century." D.M.A. thesis, Peabody Conservatory of Music, 1984. Includes a section on Carter's *String Quartet No. 3* (item 90).

837. Corbett, Richard Dean. "Simultaneity in Twentieth-Century Music." D.A. diss., University of Northern Colorado, 1987.

838. Danner, Gregory Guy. "Theoretical Construct for the Analysis of Acoustic Dissonance Fluctuation." Part I of Ph.D. diss., Washington University, 1984.

839. DeLio, Thomas. "Structural Pluralism." Ph.D. diss., Brown University, 1979.

840. Detweiler, Greg Jeffrey. "The Choral Music of Elliott Carter." D.M.A. thesis, University of Illinois at Urbana–Champaign, 1985.

841. Garrison, Leonard L. "Three Late Works by Elliott Carter: An Analysis and Flutist's Performance Guide." D.M. diss., Northwestern University, 1992.

842. Geertsema, Anita. "The Tonal Chamber Music of Elliott Carter." D.Mus. diss., University of South Africa, 1989.

843. Geissler, Fredrick Dietzmann. "Considerations of Tempo as a Structural Basis in Selected Orchestral Works of Elliott Carter." Part II of D.M.A. thesis, Cornell University, 1974.

844. Grau, Irene Rosenberg. "Compositional Techniques Employed in the First Movement of Elliott Carter's *Piano Concerto*." Ph.D. diss., Michigan State University, 1973.

845. Haberkorn, Michael. "A Study and Performance of the Piano Sonatas of Samuel Barber, Elliott Carter, and Aaron Copland." Ed.D. diss., Columbia University, 1979.

846. Hamilton, Jim (James Howard). "A Video-Assisted Instructional Program for Bass Drum and Selected Accessory Percussion Instruments." D.M.A thesis, University of Southern Mississippi, 1988. Includes text of a lecture recital on *Canaries* from *Eight Pieces for Four Timpani* (item 54).

847. Harris, Jane Duff. "Compositional Process in the String Quartets of Elliott Carter." Ph.D. diss., Case Western Reserve University, 1983. Includes sections on Carter's first three string quartets (items 88, 89, and 90).

848. Headrick, Samuel Philip. "Thematic Elements in the Variations Movement of Elliott Carter's *String Quartet No. 1*." Ph.D. diss., Eastman School of Music, 1981.

849. Heritage, Lee. "Hearing Elliott Carter's *Changes*." Part I of "Two Essays on Music Theory and Composition." D.M.A. thesis, University of Illinois at Urbana–Champaign, 1990.

850. Higginbotham, Diane. "Performance Problems in Contemporary Vocal Music and Some Suggested Solutions." Ed.D. diss., Columbia University, 1994. Includes a section on "Dolphins" [sic] from Carter's song cycle *In Sleep, in Thunder* (item 68).

851. Johnson, Lilla Joyce Finch. "Rhythmic Techniques in Twentieth-Century Music including Those Employed in the Piano Sonatas of Elliott Carter and Leon Kirchner." Part III of Ph.D. dissertation, Northwestern University, 1972.

852. Kies, Christopher. "A Discussion of the Harmonic Organization in the First Movement of Elliott Carter's *Sonata for Violoncello and Piano* in Light of Certain Developments in 19th and Early 20th-Century Music." Ph.D. diss., Brandeis University, 1984.

853. Kinney, Michael. "Perceptions of Developmental Influences As Contributing Factors to the Motivation for Musical Creativity of Eminent Twentieth-Century Living American Composers." Ed.D diss., Syracuse University, 1990.

854. Kujawsky, Eric. "Double-Perspective Movement: Formal Ambiguity and Conducting Issues in Orchestral Works by Schoenberg, Sibelius and Carter." D.M.A. thesis, Stanford University, 1985.

855. Link, John F. "Long-Range Polyrhythms in Elliott Carter's Recent Music." Ph.D. diss., City University of New York, 1994.

856. McManus, James Michael. "Rhetoric and Resistance in the Music of Elliott Carter." D.M.A. thesis, University of Illinois at Urbana–Champaign, 1988.

857. Meckna, Robert Michael. "The Rise of the American Composer-Critic: Aaron Copland, Roger Sessions, Virgil Thomson, and Elliott Carter in the Periodical *Modern Music*, 1924–1946." Ph.D. diss., University of California at Santa Barbara, 1984.

858. Nauert, Paul Charles. "Timespan Formation in Nonmetric, Post-tonal Music." Ph.D. diss., Columbia University, 1997.

859. Neil, Mary Oberlander. "The Carter *Piano Sonata* (1945–46): Organizational Elements and Their Effect on Performance Choices." D.M.A. thesis, University of Iowa, 1987.

860. Nelson, John Christopher. "Compositional Technique in Elliott Carter's *Penthode:* A Study in Phraseology and Formal Design." Ph.D. diss., Brandeis University, 1991.

861. Perkyns, Jane E. Gormley. "An Analytical Study of Elliott Carter's *Piano Sonata.*" D.M.A. thesis, University of British Columbia, 1990.

862. Pflugradt, William C. "Elliott Carter and the Variation Process." Ph.D. diss., Indiana University, 1984.

863. Rao, Nancy Yunhwa. "Elucidating Stylistic Difference in Post-Tonal Compositions from a Trichordal Perspective: Commonality and Individual Styles in Selected Compositions of Milton Babbitt, Arnold Schoenberg, Ruth Crawford Seeger, and Elliott Carter." Ph.D. diss., University of Michigan, 1994.

864. Ravenscroft, Brenda. "Texture in Elliott Carter's *A Mirror on Which to Dwell.*" Ph.D. diss., University of British Columbia, 1992.

865. Resanovich, Nikola. "An Analytical Study of Rhythmic Functions in the Carter String Quartets." D.M.A. thesis, Cleveland Institute of Music and Case Western Reserve University, 1981. Includes sections on Carter's first three string quartets (items 88, 89, and 90).

866. Sallmen, John Mark. "A Flexible Approach to Ordering and Grouping in Atonal Music in General: Text-Music Relationships in Elliott Carter's *In Sleep, in Thunder* in Particular." Ph.D. diss., University of Rochester, Eastman School of Music, 1998.

867. Scedrov, Igor. "A Study of the Reciprocal Relationship between the Composer and the Performer in Selected Works

for the Cello by Samuel Barber, Elliott Carter, and Charles Wuorinen." D.M.A. thesis, Temple University, 1994.

868. Schweitzer, Eugene W. "Generation in String Quartets of Carter, Sessions, Kirchner, and Schuller: A Concept of Forward Thrust and Its Relationship to Structure in Aurally Complex Styles." Ph.D. diss., University of Rochester, 1966.

869. Sevice, Alfred Roy, Jr. "A Study of the Cadence as a Factor in Musical Intelligibility in Selected Piano Sonatas by American Composers." Ph.D. diss., Iowa State University, 1958.

870. Shinn, Randall Alan. "An Analysis of Elliott Carter's *Sonata for Flute, Oboe, Cello, and Harpsichord* (1952)." D.M.A. thesis, University of Illinois at Urbana–Champaign, 1975.

871. Smith, Steven H. "The Piano Concerto after Bartók." D.M.A. thesis, Eastman School of Music, 1978. Includes a section on Carter's *Piano Concerto* (item 79).

872. Soskin, Eileen. "Cadences and Formal Structure in Four American String Quartets: Elliott Carter, *String Quartet No. 3*; Andrew Imbrie, *Fourth String Quartet*; Fred Lerdahl, *First String Quartet*; Seymour Shifrin, *Fifth String Quartet*." Ph.D. diss., University of California at Berkeley, 1986.

873. Start, Elizabeth Jane. "Some Unifying and Structural Elements in Elliott Carter's *String Quartet No. 2*." Ph.D. diss., University of Chicago, 1992.

874. Stein, Don Allan. "The Function of Pitch in Elliott Carter's *String Quartet No. 1*." Part I of Ph.D. diss., Washington University, 1981.

875. Vamos, Roland. "An Analysis and Comparison of Elliott Carter's Three String Quartets." Ph.D. diss., Juilliard School, 1975. Includes sections on Carter's first three string quarterts (items 88, 89, and 90).

876. Weston, Craig A. "Inversion, Subversion, and Metaphor: Music and Text in Elliott Carter's *A Mirror on Which to Dwell.*" D.M.A. dissertation, University of Washington, 1992.

877. Wilhite, Carmen Irene. "*Piano Sonata* by Elliott Carter: A Foreshadowing of His Later Style." D.M.A. thesis, North Texas State University, 1977.

878. Wilson, Donald Malcolm. "Metric Modulation." Part II of D.M.A. thesis, Cornell University, 1965.

879. Woods, Benjamin. "The North American Piano Sonata in Transition from Tonal to Atonal Styles." D.M.A. thesis, University of South Carolina, 1991. Includes a section on Carter's *Piano Sonata* (item 80).

880. Wyatt, Lucius Reynolds. "The Mid-Twentieth-Century Orchestral Variation, 1953–1963: An Analysis and Comparison of Selected Works by Major Composers." Ph.D. diss., University of Rochester, 1974. Includes a section on Carter's *Variations for Orchestra* (item 106).

Related Writings about Music

In order to limit the potentially enormous number of "related writings," I have listed only those sources that have a direct connection to some aspect of Carter's life and work. Most either deal with Carter directly or are sources he has cited in his own writings. I have also included Gardner Read's article on notation (item 890), to which Carter responded with a letter to the editor (item 478), and more general theoretical writings on two topics of particular relevence to Carter's recent works: all-interval rows and the all-trichord hexachord.

881. Barbirolli, Sir John. "Quote–Unquote." Interview with Michael Brozen. *Musical America* 84, no. 6 (July 1964): 30.

In the course of this interview, Barbirolli explains why he does not program contemporary music: "I feel it's my duty to perform only the best music, the music I really love. There is no great orchestral music being written today." Carter responded to these remarks with a scathing letter to the editor (item 479).

882. Bauer-Mengelberg, Stefan, and Melvin Ferentz. "On Eleven-Interval Twelve-Tone Rows." *Perspectives of New Music* 3, no. 2 (1965): 93–103.

An "eleven-interval twelve-tone row" is a sequence of all twelve pitch classes arranged so that between consecutive notes each of the eleven intervals from minor second to major seventh occurs exactly once. This article presents an algorithm by which all possible rows of this type may be generated. Using a computer, the authors found 1,928 such rows and offered to send a printout of them to interested readers. Carter, who knew Bauer-Mengelberg, obtained a copy, which he used during the composition of *Night Fantasies* (item 74) and a number of later pieces.

883. Boros, James. "Some Properties of the All-Trichord Hexachord." *In Theory Only* 11, no. 6 (September 1990): 19–41.

The "all-trichord hexachord" is the only hexachord that contains all twelve trichords among its subsets. Boros uses a taxonomy of the hexachord's trichord subsets to generate several examples of trichord networks in which each pair of adjacent nodes forms an instance of the all-trichord hexachord. He then builds several larger networks of all-trichord hexachords in which adjacent nodes share three common tones.

884. Brelet, Gisèle. *Le Temps musical: Essai d'une esthétique nouvelle de la musique*. Paris: Presses Universitaires de France, 1949.

Discussed by Carter in "Time Lecture" (item 559).

885. Cohen, David. "A Re-examination of All-Interval Rows." *Proceedings of the American Society of University Composers* 7, no. 8 (1972–73): 73–74.

A response to the article by Bauer-Mengelberg and Ferentz (item 882). Cohen notes several operations that can be used to make the list of all-interval rows more compact and briefly describes his extension of the all-interval concept to rows of sixteen intervals.

886. Cowell, Henry. *New Musical Resources*. New York: Knopf, 1930.

Cowell's book is a collection of suggestions for rethinking the basic harmonic and rhythmic materials of musical composition. Carter has said the book "furnished me with many ideas" (item 505).

887. Forte, Allen. "Pitch-Class Set Genera and the Origin of Modern Harmonic Species." *Journal of Music Theory* 32, no. 2 (Fall 1988): 187–270.

Forte provides a table of the "pitch-class set genera" found in Carter's *Concerto for Orchestra* (item 49), together with a brief comment.

888. Koechlin, Charles. "Le Temps et la musique." *Revue musicale* 7, no. 3 (January 1926): 45–62.

Cited by Carter (with his own English translation of an excerpt) in "Music and the Time Screen" (item 485).

889. Morris, Robert, and Daniel Starr. "The Structure of All-Interval Series." *Journal of Music Theory* 18, no. 2 (Fall 1974): 364–89.

Following the algorithm of Bauer-Mengelberg and Ferentz (see item 882), the authors present a computer program (written in FORTRAN) for generating eleven-interval twelve-tone rows (here called "all-interval series"). In addition, Morris and Starr compile a list of operations (inversion, multiplication by five or seven, etc.) that transform one all-interval series into another and discuss the properties of various types of all-interval series, such as those whose initial sequence is the same as their inversion read backwards.

890. Read, Gardner. "Some Problems of Rhythmic Notation." *Journal of Music Theory* 9, no. 1 (Spring 1965): 153–62.

In this response to Carter's letter to the editor (item 478), Read explores the problems involved in notating complicated beat divisions (groups of four in compound meter, quintuplets, septuplets, etc.).

891. Roeder, John. "A Calculus of Accent." *Journal of Music Theory* 39, no. 1 (Spring 1995): 1–46.

The end of the vocal melody in Carter's song "Insomnia" from *A Mirror on Which to Dwell* (item 72) is one example analyzed using Roeder's mathematical method for assigning weights to accents.

892. Rosenfeld, Paul. *Musical Portraits: Interpretations of Twenty Modern Composers.* New York: Harcourt, Brace, and Howe, 1920; Freeport, NY: Books for Libraries Press, 1968. ML390.R78 1968.

Mentioned by Carter in his eulogy for Rosenfeld (item 455).

893. Schillinger, Joseph. *The Schillinger System of Musical Composition.* New York: Carl Fischer, 1946.

Reviewed by Carter in *Modern Music* (see item 443).

894. Stone, Kurt. "Problems and Methods of Notation." *Perspectives of New Music* 1, no. 2 (Spring 1963): 9–31.

A survey of contemporary notational practices in the areas of pitch, tempo, rhythm, conducting aids, score setups, dynamics, tone clusters, and vocal notation. Carter's works are frequently cited in the sections on tempo and rhythm.

895. Stravinsky, Igor. *La Poétique musicale* (Cambridge, MA: Harvard University Press, 1942).

Cited by Carter in "Music and the Time Screen" (item 485).

896. Suvchinsky, Pierre. "La Notion du temps et la musique: Réflexions sur la typologie de la création musicale." *Revue musicale* 191 (May–June 1939): 70–80.

Cited by Carter in "Music and the Time Screen" (item 485) and "Time Lecture" (item 559). Suvchinsky describes two different approaches to musical time: as exemplified by Wagner ("chrono-amétrique") on the one hand and by Bach, Haydn, Mozart, and Verdi ("chronométrique") on the other. He reprimands those who criticize Stravinsky for a lack of emotion, saying, "they must *listen* to the music with an ear that not only perceives the music as 'sonorities,' but also as music 'in time'" (ils doivent *écouter* la musique avec une oreille qui, non seulement perçoit la musique comme "sonorités," mais aussi comme musique "dans le temps").

Appendix 1
A Chronology of Elliott Carter's Compositions

Juvenilia and Unpublished Works

ca. 1920s	*Piano Sonata*
	String Quartet
pre-1928	Settings of Joyce's *Chamber Music*
1928	*My Love Is in a Light Attire*
1931	*Incidental Music and Choruses for Sophocles' Philoctetes*
ca. 1932–35	*Musical Studies No. 1–4*
ca. 1933–35	[Counterpoint Exercises]
	Invention on Prout's Subject
	Labyrinth
	Trio
1934	*Flute Sonata*
	Tom and Lily
1935	*First String Quartet*
1936	*Incidental Music and Choruses for Plautus's Mostellaria*
1937	*The Ball Room Guide*
	Oratorio
	Concerto for English Horn and Orchestra

	Incidental Music and Choruses for Shakespeare's Much Ado about Nothing
	Madrigal Book
	One Act Opera
	Second String Quartet
	Symphony
ca. 1940	*Canon from Easy Piano Pieces*
ca. 1940s?	*Five Fanfares*
1944	*The Difference*
date unknown	*Double Piano Sonata*
	Folk Dance No. 2
	I Am Rose, My Eyes Are Blue
	Sonatina
	String Quartet in C
	Symphony No. 2
	Trio

Published Works

1936	*Tarantella* (finale to Mostellaria)
1936–39	*Pocahontas*
1937	*Let's Be Gay*
	Harvest Home
	To Music
1938	*Prelude, Fanfare, and Polka*
	Tell Me Where Is Fancy Bred
	Heart Not So Heavy as Mine
1939	*Canonic Suite.* Revised 1956 and 1981
1939–42	*Elegy.* Revised 1946, 1952, and 1961
1940	*Pastoral.* Revised 1942, 1945, 1987–88, and 1993
1941	*The Defense of Corinth*
1942	*Symphony No. 1.* Revised 1954
	Three Poems of Robert Frost. Revised 1974 and 1980

Appendix 1

1942–43	*Voyage*. Revised 1974–75 and 1979
1943	*Warble for Lilac Time*. Revised ca. 1954
1944	*Holiday Overture*. Revised 1960–61
	The Harmony of Morning
1945	*Musician's Wrestle Everywhere*
1945–46	*Piano Sonata*. Revised 1982
1947	*The Minotaur*
	Emblems
1948	*Woodwind Quintet*
	Sonata for Violoncello and Piano
1949–50	*Eight Etudes and a Fantasy*
1950	*Eight Pieces for Four Timpani*. Revised 1966
1950–51	*String Quartet No. 1*
1952	*Sonata for Flute, Oboe, Cello, and Harpsichord*
1953–55	*Variations for Orchestra*
1959	*String Quartet No. 2*
1961	*Double Concerto*
1961–65	*Piano Concerto*
1969	*Concerto for Orchestra*
1971	*Canon for 3: In Memoriam Igor Stravinsky*
	String Quartet No. 3
1972–74	*Duo for Violin and Piano*
1974	*Brass Quintet*
	A Fantasy about Purcell's Fantasia upon One Note
1975	*A Mirror on Which to Dwell*
1976	*A Symphony of Three Orchestras*
1978	*Birthday Fanfare*
	Syringa

1978–80	*Night Fantasies*
1981	*In Sleep, in Thunder*
1982–83	*Triple Duo*
1983	*Changes*
1984	*Canon for 4* *Riconoscenza per Goffredo Petrassi* *Esprit rude/Esprit doux*
1985	*Penthode*
1985–86	*String Quartet No. 4*
1986	*A Celebration of Some 100 × 150 Notes* (from *Three Occasions for Orchestra*)
1987	*Oboe Concerto*
1988	*Enchanted Preludes* *Remembrance* (from *Three Occasions for Orchestra*) *Birthday Flourish*
1989	*Anniversary* (from *Three Occasions for Orchestra*)
1990	*Violin Concerto* *Con leggerezza pensosa*
1991	*Scrivo in vento* *Quintet for Piano and Winds*
1992	*Trilogy*
1993	*Partita* (from *Symphonia—Sum Fluxae Pretiam Spei*) *Gra*
1994	*90+* *Fragment* *Of Challenge and of Love*
1994–95	*Adagio tenebroso* (from *Symphonia—Sum Fluxae Pretiam Spei*)
1995	*Esprit rude/Esprit doux II* *Figment* *String Quartet No. 5*

Appendix 1

1996	*Clarinet Concerto*
	A 6 Letter Letter
1996–97	*Allegro scorrevole* (from *Symphonia—Sum Fluxae Pretiam Spei*)
1997	*Shard*
	Luimen
	Quintet for Piano and String Quartet
1998	*What Next?*
1998–99	*Tempo e tempi*
1999	*Statement—Remembering Aaron* (from *Three Recollections*)
	Fantasy—Remembering Roger (from *Three Recollections*)

Appendix 2
A Note about Primary Sources

Over the course of his long career, Carter has produced an enormous documentary legacy including sketches, scores, recordings, letters, photographs, concert programs, newspaper and journal articles, interviews, films, memorabilia, and so forth. Before 1988 much of this material was housed at the Music Division of the New York Public Library and at the Library of Congress in Washington, D.C. A substantial number of items were given to these libraries as gifts and remain there today. Other materials (including almost all materials at the New York Public Library) were left on deposit until 1988, at which time Carter sold them to the Paul Sacher Foundation in Basel, Switzerland. The foundation now owns the majority of the Carter materials, including most everything pertaining to Carter's career from 1988 to the present. For Carter's earlier career, the materials are divided among several institutions. The largest collection is in Basel, but a substantial number of items still may be found at the Library of Congress.

I have provided the location of autograph materials relating to specific pieces in the alphabetical list of Carter's compositions earlier in this book. Below is a list of pieces with materials still in the Library of Congress.

Adagio for Viola and Piano
Concerto for Orchestra
The Defense of Corinth
Double Concerto
Eight Etudes and a Fantasy
Elegy for String Quartet

Emblems
Holiday Overture
Let's Be Gay
The Minotaur
Musicians Wrestle Everywhere
Pastoral
Piano Concerto
Piano Sonata
Pocahontas
Sonata for Flute, Oboe, Cello, and Harpsichord
Sonata for Violoncello and Piano

String Quartet No. 1
String Quartet No. 2
Suite for Quartet of Alto Saxophones
Suite for Timpani
Symphony No. 1
Tell Me Where Is Fancy Bred
Variations for Orchestra
Warble for Lilac Time
Woodwind Quintet

Index

Numbers in roman type are item numbers; italicized numbers are page numbers.

List of Works: items
  1–111
Discography: items
  112–398
Bibliography: items
  399–896
92nd St. Y, 46

Abbey of Fossanova,
  Priverno, Italy, 102
Abbey Road Studios,
  117, 267
Abosch, David, 111
Achron, Isidor, 457
Adam, Claus, 89, 90,
  312, 314, 317
Adams, Daniel Clifford,
  829
Adams, John, 236, 237,
  268
Adelson, Robert, 332
Adirondack Chamber
  Orchestra, 355, 379,
  383
Adler, Karl-Theo, 160,
  395
Adler, Samuel, 349
Adorno, Theodor, 487,
  817
aleatoric composition,
  477, 586

Aeschylus, 96
Agee, James, 1
Aitken, Robert, 84, 658
Aitken, Webster, 80,
  799
Ajemian, Anahid, 91,
  166, 309, 313, 318,
  323, 653
Albany (recordings), 172,
  174, 351, 380
Albera, Philippe, 360
Alberman, David, 167,
  168, 310, 315, 320,
  322
Aldeburgh Foundation,
  76
Alder, Christopher, 376
Alexandria Choral Society, 209
Alice Tully Hall, 43, 90,
  550
Allard, Robert, 139
All Hallows, Gospel Oak,
  London, 193
all-interval tetrachords,
  619, 638, 690, 804
all-interval twelve-tone
  rows, 710, 712, 774,
  882, 885, 889
All Saints Church, London, 114, 149, 194,
  195, 305, 325

All Saints Church, Peterham, England, 244,
  348, 353, 378, 382,
  385
all-trichord hexachord,
  883
*Amacadmy: The Newsletter of the American
  Academy in Rome*,
  588
Amati Quartett, 169
Ambassador Auditorium,
  Pasadena, CA, 173
AmCam Recordings,
  209
American Academy and
  Institute of Arts and
  Letters, New York,
  136, 146, 311, 316,
  321, 324, 342, 349,
  460, 466, 533; *4, 5*
American Academy in
  Rome, 49, 91, 106,
  588; *3, 5*
American Brass Quintet,
  42, 60, 116, 191
American Composers
  Alliance, 45, 53, 462,
  568, 789; *2*
American Composers
  Orchestra, 210, 274,
  328

307

American Lyric Theatre, New York, 81
American Music, 680
American Music Center, 74
American Music Center Newsletter, 448
American Musicological Society Journal, 720
American Music Teacher, 728, 808
American Recording Society, 255, 293
American Society of University Composers Proceedings, 885
American Symphony League Newsletter, 526
Amlin, Martin, 139, 177, 200, 207, 216, 230, 340
AMS (recordings), 284
Amsterdam Paradiso, 70
Analyse musicale, 729
Anchutina, Leda, 81
Anderer, Joseph, 393
Anderson, Allen, 303
Anderson, Bruce Clarke, 830
Andrade, Levine, 167, 310, 315, 320, 322
Andriessen, Louis, 122, 179, 184
Anfinrud, Annette, 366
Antheil, George, 203
Apostel, Hans Erich, 121
Arabesque (recordings), 304
Arabic music, 30; 1
Archilochus, 96
Arditi, Didier, 185, 224, 240, 251, 356
Arditti, Irvine, 149, 167, 168, 195, 310, 315, 320, 322, 325, 360
Arditti String Quartet, 82, 92, 167, 168, 168a, 195, 310, 315, 319, 320, 322, 325, 824, 827
Arends, André, 124
Argento, Dominick, 291, 380
Aristotle, 486

Arlton, Dean Luther, 831
Arne, 457
Arner, Leonard, 155
Artaud, Antonin, 456
Arte Nova Classics (recordings), 134, 254, 345
ASCAP Festival of American Music, 502
Ashbery, John, 96, 623, 644, 694
Aspen Center for Compositional Studies, 583; 5
Atherton, David, 824
Atkins, David, 396
Atlas, Raphael, 704, 751
Aubort, Marc J., 170, 173, 287, 295, 309, 313
Auden, W. H., 469
Aulos Woodwind Quintet, 160, 395
Aurelia Saxophone Quartet, 124
Auvidis Montaigne (recordings), 114, 149, 168, 168a, 190, 194, 195, 217, 305, 325, 360, 367
avant-garde, 411, 441, 442, 477, 788
Avery Fisher Hall, New York, 95, 331
Avery Memorial, Hartford, CT, 574
Ayrey, Craig, 621

Babbitt, Irving, 498
Babbitt, Milton, 126, 281, 290, 323, 349, 376, 561, 670, 711, 779, 863
Bach, J. S., 155, 156, 181, 187, 192, 193, 261, 297, 357, 371, 436, 437, 487, 572, 573, 603, 896
Bacon, Ernst, 555
Baerwald, Helmut, 108, 109
Baker, James M., 817a
Balanchine, George, 483, 527, 620
Balinese gamelan, 505
Ballentine, Allan, 312

Ballet Caravan, 81, 527, 574; 2
Ballet Society, 71
Bals, Karen Elizabeth, 832
Banff Center, 591
Barber, Samuel, 135, 136, 152, 160, 173, 192, 193, 226, 267, 272, 277, 303, 351, 389, 391, 395, 397, 475, 499, 500, 845, 867
Barbirolli, Sir John, 479, 501, 511, 881
Barcellona, John, 396
Barenboim, Daniel, 93, 110, 326, 825
Barlow, Samuel, 468
Baron, Samuel, 151, 285
Barrows, John, 152, 397
Barthes, Roland, 773
Bartlett, Eric, 826
Bartók, Béla, 411, 437, 495, 515, 547, 603, 617, 752, 871
Barzin, Leon, 71
Basie, Count, 517
Bath Festival, 44, 74, 826
Gregory Battcock, 625
Bätzing, Hans Bernhard, 121
Baudoin, Nathalie, 240
Bauer, Vincent, 240
Bauer, Wolfgang, 121
Bauer-Mengelberg, Stefan, 466, 613, 882, 885, 889
Bax, Arnold, 457, 511
BBC (British Broadcasting Corporation), 42, 93, 105, 410, 487, 600, 826, 828
BBC Symphony, 93, 100
Beach, David W., 817a
Beaser, Robert, 351
Beauregard, Lawrence, 58
Beckstrom, Robert Allen, 833
Beckwith, John, 478
Beethoven, Ludwig van, 155, 387, 392, 437, 484, 702, 739, 782
Bellan, Jean-Pierre, 291a
Below, Robert, 614

Index

Benjamin, Barry, 388, 389
Bennett, Richard Rodney, 268
Bennett, Robert Russell, 509, 537
Bennington Series, 475
Benson, Alan, 824
Benson, Warren, 349
Berezowsky, Nicolai, 67
Berg, Alban, 456, 475, 497, 547, 589, 603, 671, 749, 751
Berger, Arthur, 389, 397
Bergman, Erik, 298
Bergsma, William, 171, 197, 396, 537
Berio, Luciano, 112, 243, 326, 389, 563, 603
Berkely, Michael, 826
Berlin, Pamela S., 610
Berman, Lawrence, 97
Bernard, Jonathan W., 402, 580, 615–622, 696, 817a
Bernsohn, Lorin, 282
Bernstein, Leonard, 49, 129, 132, 136, 169, 226, 422, 555, 730
Biddlecome, Robert, 42, 60, 116, 191
Bigelow, Edward, 71
Biggs, John, 396
Billings, William, 351, 475
Bindzus, Erwin, 371
Birdwell, Edward, 42, 60, 116, 191
Birtwistle, Harrison, 112, 168a, 243, 817
Bishop's Gate Hall, London, 266
BIS (recordings), 164, 165
Bishop, Elizabeth, 72, 644, 787, 822
Black, Robert, 215, 372, 623
Blackheath Concert Hall, 344
Bland, William K., 125, 126, 281, 342
Bliss, Arthur, 407
Blitzstein, Marc, 468, 517, 538
Bloch, Ernest, 502, 547
Blomstedt, Herbert, 41, 107, 774
Blumenfeld, Harold, 342, 343
Blumer, Hans, 67
Blustine, Alan, 43, 826
BMI Publication Prize, 45; 2
Boatwright, Helen, 108, 109
Bobo, Elizabeth, 386
Bobo, Pinson, 111
Boehm Quintette, 393
Böhn, Ole, 102, 107, 148, 361, 377, 774
Bolcom, William, 236, 237, 349, 351
Boletin interamericano de música, 632
Boretz, Benjamin, 442, 581, 624
Boris, Ruthanna, 81
Bornkamp, Arno, 124
Boroda, M. G., 617
Boros, James, 883
Boston Pops Orchestra, 97
Boston Records, 300
Boston Skyline (recordings), 152
Boston Symphony Chamber Players, 289, 387
Boston Symphony Orchestra, 79, 95, 252, 413, 475, 517, 583
Boulanger, Nadia, 19, 111, 411, 436, 449, 470, 529, 583, 597, 603, 714, 777; 1
Boulez, Pierre, 47, 58, 59, 78, 95, 112, 185, 221, 224, 240, 242, 243, 251, 279, 331, 427, 447, 449, 514, 554, 603, 607, 623, 649, 653, 729, 739, 743, 827
Bowdoin College, 558
Bowles, Paul, 499, 500, 517, 538, 555, 574
Boykan, Martin, 624
Bradley Hills Presbyterian Church, Bethesda, MD, 209
Bragg, Melvyn, 824
Brahms, Johannes, 135, 155, 204, 225, 387, 725
Brancart, Evelyne, 300
Brandeis University, 852, 860
Brandes, Bernard E., 72
Brandt, William E., 625
Brant, Henry, 118, 290, 407, 411, 537, 547, 634
Brecht, Bertolt, 456
Breedon, Daniel Franklin, 834
Brelet, Gisèle, 559, 620, 884
Breuer, Harry, 392
Bridge, Frank, 423
Bridge (recordings), 113, 125, 126, 127, 128, 147, 182, 196, 215, 223, 233, 235, 265, 278, 281, 301, 336, 354, 359, 785
Brieff, Anabel, 282
Brieger, Nicolas, 110
Brio, 706
Britten, Benjamin, 117, 170, 413, 500, 603, 733
Brody, Alan, 139
Broekman, David, 55
Brook, Claire, 577
Brooklyn Bridge, 736
Brooklyn College, 197, 210, 274, 328, 512, 577
Brooks, Richard, 626
Browner, Tara Colleen, 835
Brown, Earle, 578
Brown, Harold, 411
Brown, Silas, 139, 202, 216, 340, 366
Brown University, 839
Bruck, Jerry, 118
Brunswick, Mark, 547
Bryn-Julson, Phyllis, 224, 352, 381, 384
Budd, Harold, 120
Buxtehude, Dietrich, 572
Bye, Antony, 627–629

Cadman, Charles Wakefield, 349, 457

Cage, John, 160, 165, 168, 238, 269, 342, 343, 348, 349, 367, 376, 378, 395, 537, 672, 827
Cagney, James, 444
California EAR Unit, 122, 179, 184
California Institute of the Arts, 122, 179, 184
Caltabiano, Ronald, 630
Calvert, Michael, 127, 128, 147, 182, 196, 278, 301, 359
Calvino, Italo, 48
Cambria (recordings), 159
Campbell, David, 105, 369
Campion Center, Weston, MA, 174, 303
Canady, Alice, 55
Canby, Edward Tatnall, 204, 225
Canby Singers, 204, 225
Candide (recordings), 153, 388
Capitol Records Studio B, 153
Caplan, Stephen, 159
Capriccio (recordings), 121, 192
Capuzzo, Guy, 628, 631
Caras, Tracy, 586
Carewe, John, 75
Carey, 457
Carillon (recordings), 337
Carl, Robert, 358
Carleton College, 584; 4
Carlyss, Earl, 90, 314, 317, 808
Carnegie Hall, New York, 511
Carnegie Recital Hall, New York, 60, 86
Carpenter, Dr. Hoyle, 271
Carpenter, John Alden, 407
Carse, Adam, *The Orchestra from Beethoven to Berlioz,* 437
Carter, Elliott
 analysis of his music, 614, 615, 616, 617, 619, 621, 626, 628, 636, 637, 638, 643, 645, 646, 647, 648, 652, 658, 660, 663, 665, 666, 677, 681, 686, 687, 690, 693, 694, 698, 700, 701, 703, 704, 707, 710, 711, 713, 717, 718, 727, 729, 749, 751, 754, 758, 765, 766, 767, 769, 770, 772, 773, 774, 783, 787, 794, 795, 798, 802, 804, 807, 810, 816, 830, 831, 832, 833, 836, 841, 843, 844, 845, 847, 848, 851, 852, 854, 855, 858, 859, 860, 861, 862, 863, 864, 865, 868, 869, 870, 872, 873, 874, 875, 876, 877, 880, 891
 as performer, 77, 776
 as reviewer for *Modern Music,* 406, 407, 411, 413, 419, 423, 443, 444, 457, 468, 474, 475, 483, 486, 493, 501, 502, 509, 511, 515, 517, 524, 537, 538, 539, 540, 543, 547, 555, 556, 573, 574, 635, 699, 857, 893; 2
 as teacher, 580, 588, 591, 604, 664, 685, 780
 autograph materials by, 602, 608, 610, 622, 644, 701, 764, 765, 777, 779, 780
 compositional development, 580, 583, 584, 586, 593, 594, 595, 597, 604, 616, 629, 644, 677, 714, 715, 716, 725, 727, 730, 748, 769, 771, 772, 773, 778, 780, 784, 788, 789, 792, 793, 797, 803, 806, 808, 811, 812, 817, 824
 compositional methods, 580, 582, 583, 584, 585, 592, 600, 603, 616, 619, 622, 625, 644, 701, 712, 727, 758, 765, 766, 767, 769, 772, 773, 777, 780, 791, 817, 844, 847, 860
 extra-musical influences, 580, 591, 605, 620, 621, 769, 771, 807, 824, 827, 834
 Harmony Book, 580, 779
 neoclassical music of, 586, 714, 715, 716, 764, 769
 performance of his music, 580, 582, 589, 590, 592, 606, 608, 609, 611, 636, 651, 658, 659, 682, 683, 698, 700, 705, 731–746, 754
 percussion in the music of, 606, 698, 705, 786, 805, 829, 846
 piano music of, 596, 701, 702, 728, 754, 758, 769, 770, 795
 rhythm in the music of, 586, 604, 616, 637, 638, 645, 648, 652, 658, 659, 660, 663, 665, 667, 681, 686, 700, 703, 718, 754, 769, 783, 802, 804, 819, 822, 843, 851, 855, 858, 865, 878, 894
 sound recording notes by, 129, 131, 133, 138, 139, 140, 142, 143, 144, 145, 146, 162, 166, 173, 176, 178, 180, 185, 191, 199, 201, 202, 206, 208, 216, 222, 224, 226, 228, 231, 234, 240, 249, 251, 262, 287, 295, 306, 309, 311, 313, 316, 321, 323, 324, 326, 327, 331, 333, 335, 339, 340, 355, 365, 366, 373, 374, 377, 379, 383, 386

Index

surveys of life and
  works, 400, 401,
  583, 584, 597, 625,
  627, 629, 630, 632,
  649, 668, 671, 673,
  676, 679, 684, 691,
  716, 722, 724, 725,
  750, 759, 760, 764,
  765, 766, 769, 771,
  772, 778, 784, 789,
  792, 793, 797, 803,
  808, 811, 817, 824
vocal music of, 580,
  586, 607, 642, 644,
  652, 694, 716, 741,
  763, 765, 769, 785,
  787, 798, 814, 822,
  840, 850, 864, 866,
  876
Carter, Helen, 41, 52, 94,
  100, 753; 2
Casella, Alfredo, 261,
  501
Case Western Reserve
  University, 847, 865
Castelnuovo-Tedesco,
  Mario, 247, 502
Cazden, Norman, 411
CBS (Columbia Broadcasting System), 103
CBS (recordings), 130,
  142, 153, 222, 331,
  374, 388, 674. See
  also Columbia
  Records
CBS Recording Studios.
  See Columbia
  Recording Studios,
  New York
Cedille (recordings), 291
Centaur (recordings),
  188, 303
Central High School of
  Needle Trades, New
  York, 71
Central Islip High School
  Auditorium, Islip,
  NY, 175, 338
Centre Acanthes festival,
  Avignon, France, 84,
  604, 658; 6
Centre Georges Pompidou, 115, 185, 221,
  224, 239, 240, 251,
  356, 449
Cerutty, Michel, 240

Chaloff, Herman, 411
Chamber Music Society
  of America, 539
Chamber Music Society
  of Lincoln Center,
  155
Changes in the Arts, 590
Chanler, Theodore, 347
Chant du monde (recordings), 269
Charles Ives Festival,
  London, 42
Chase, Gilbert, 453, 633
Chastain, Kathleen, 277,
  280
Chávez, Carlos, 475, 537
Cheng, Gloria, 250
Cherin, Milt, 222, 331
Cherlin, Michael, 704,
  751
Cherney, Brian, 390
Cherney, Lawrence, 390
Cherrier, Sophie, 185
Chicago Daily News, 441
Chicago Pro Musica, 59
Chicago Symphony
  Orchestra, 93, 95,
  326, 376, 825
Chiesa della Misericordia, Turin, Italy, 158,
  394
Chihara, Giuseppe, 197
Childs, Barney, 541, 634
Chisholm, Malcolm, 151
Chomsky, Noam, 581
Chopin, Frederic, 235,
  428, 559
Chou Wen-Chung, 120,
  577
Christ, Peter, 396
Christensen, Harold, 81
Christensen, Lew, 81
Ciesinski, Katherine,
  336
Cincinnati Symphony
  Orchestra, 41, 253,
  375, 742
Cioffi, Gino, 387
Cité de la Musique, Paris,
  47
Citkowitz, Israel, 539
City of Birmingham
  Symphony Orchestra, 346
City University of New
  York, 577, 855

Clair, René, 444
Clais, Tristan, 291a
Clarke, Rebecca, 349
Classical Guitar, 684
Classic Editions (recordings), 386
Classics Record Library
  (recordings), 155
Cleemann, Paul, 371
Clementi, Muzio, 501
Clements, Andrew, 635
Cleveland Institute of
  Music, 865
Cleveland Orchestra, 93,
  95
Club Harmonie, Toronto,
  390
Cocteau, Jean, 704, 827
Cogan, Robert, 636–638
Cohan, George M., 444
Cohen, David, 885
Cohen, Isidore, 89, 312
Coker, Wilson, 639
Coldstream Guards'
  Band, 509
Coleman, Dan, 174
Colgate College Singers,
  56
Colgrass, Michael, 252
College Music Symposium, 418, 716, 773
Collegium Musicum
  Zürich, 75
Col Legno (recordings),
  242
Collins Classics (recordings), 117
color organs, 456
Columbia Auditorium,
  Louisville, KY, 106
Columbia Broadcasting
  System. *See* CBS
  (Columbia Broadcasting System)
Columbia Odyssey
  (recordings), 116,
  162, 191
Columbia Recording
  Studios, New York,
  116, 162, 191, 222
Columbia Records, 103,
  129, 142, 222, 282,
  283, 306, 307, 308,
  314, 317, 331, 341,
  374, 507, 508, 554,
  686, 717, 749; 2

Columbia University, New York, 88, 537, 555, 831, 845, 850, 858, 861; 3; Men's Glee Club, 136
Commissiona, Sergiu, 100
Community Center, Davis, CA, 392
Composer, 754, 762
Composers' Forum Laboratory. *See* WPA Composers' Forum Laboratory
Composers' Showcase concert, 732
Composers String Quartet, 91, 166, 309, 313, 318, 323, 550, 651, 653, 732, 744
Conant, Robert, 282
Concert-Disc (recordings), 151
Concordia College, Bronxville, NY, 171
Concours international de quatour à cordes, Liège, Belgium, 88, 521; 3
Cone, Edward T., 442, 624
Connolly, Justin, 640
Conservatoire de Musique, Liège, Belgium, 360
Constable, John, 76, 244, 353, 382, 385
Constant Nymph, 556
Contemporary Chamber Ensemble, 143
Contemporary Music Newsletter, 581
Continuum (recordings), 268
Contrechamps, 530, 600, 758
Convegno Internazionale di Studi sull'Espressionismo, Maggio Fiorentino, 442
Cook, Deborah, 221
Coolidge, Elizabeth Sprague, 423
Coolidge Auditorium, Library of Congress, 82

Coonrod, Michael McGill, 836
Cooper Union, New York, 52, 55
Copland, Aaron, 67, 102, 130, 136, 165, 169, 192, 226, 229, 259, 260, 267, 268, 269, 271, 272, 277, 323, 348, 349, 378, 387, 411, 413, 423, 457, 499, 500, 509, 511, 517, 524, 529, 530, 537, 538, 539, 556, 578, 641, 686, 713, 730, 747, 809, 826, 845, 857
Corbett, Richard Dean, 837
Corigliano, John, 174
Corliss, Frank, 139, 216, 340
Cornell University, 843, 878
Coroniti, Joseph A., 642
Cortese, Paul, 171
Cowell, Henry, 12, 77, 136, 166, 193, 220, 226, 351, 380, 386, 442, 478, 479, 499, 547, 634, 686, 777, 788, 886
cpo (recordings), 161, 183, 189, 292, 398
Craft, Robert, 584, 657, 752, 796
Crane, Hart, 9, 108, 417, 736
Crawford, Ruth, 148, 349, 361, 442, 788, 863
Creston, Paul, 165, 172, 547
CRI (Composers Recordings Inc.), 131, 138, 150, 176, 199, 206, 210, 211, 212, 228, 274, 275, 328, 329, 330, 333, 334, 335, 339, 355, 362, 365, 379, 383
Critique, 754
CRS Master Recordings, 246
Crumb, George, 165, 349, 747

Crutchfield, Will, 683
Crystal (recordings), 120, 171, 250, 396
Cullerier, Jean, 160, 395
Cundiff, Morgan, 608
Cuniot, Laurent, 291a
Cunningham, Merce, 537
Current Musicology, 685
Currier, Donald, 248

Da Capo Chamber Players, 57, 123, 180, 186, 249
Daghlian, William, 235
Dahl, Ingolf, 386
Dalton, Joseph R., 138, 176, 199, 206, 228, 339, 355, 365, 379, 383
Damiens, Alain, 47, 58
Dance International festival, New York, 574
Dane, Jean, 91, 166, 318, 653
Danmarks Radio, 164
Danner, Gregory Guy, 643, 838
Danuser, Hermann, 498, 644, 714
Darbellay, Etienne, 645
Dario, Tina di, 386
Darmstadt school, 477, 580
Dartington School, 593, 664; 3
Dash, Patricia, 59
Davidovsky, Mario, 349, 362, 389
Davidson, John, 245, 246
Davies, Philippa, 105, 369
Davis, Andrew, 93
Davis, Anthony, 237
Dawson, Lynne, 110
De Boer, Harmen, 190
Debussy, Claude, 453, 557, 724
Decca (recordings), 285
Decker, Wolfgang, 121
DeGaetani, Jan, 96, 333, 349
DelGiorno, Susan Napodano, 139, 202, 216, 340, 366

Index 313

Delio, Thomas, 358, 646, 839
Delius, Frederick, 517
Dellheim, Peter, 312
Dello Joio, Norman, 271
DeLone, Richard P., 647
Del Tredici, David, 125
Demenga, Thomas, 61, 181, 371
Denis, Ruth St., 574
Denisov, Edison, 298
Derby, Richard, 648
De Rode Hoed, Amsterdam, 124
Derrien, Jean-Pierre, 221, 649
DesRoches, Raymond, 54
Dessau, Paul, 547
Desto (recordings), 118, 256, 294
Detweiler, Greg Jeffrey, 840
Deutsche Grammophon, 229, 289, 376
Deutsche Staatsoper Unter den Linden, 110
Devienne, François, 245, 246
Diamond, David, 159, 173, 407, 423, 500, 524, 540
Dibdin, 457
Dick, Robert, 823
Dickinson, Emily, 66, 73, 349, 801
Dickinson, Meriel, 348, 378
Dickinson, Peter, 193, 348, 378
Diehl, Ted, 124
Die Musikforschung, 781
Dillon, James, 360
Diry, Roland, 63
Dissonanz • Disonance, 589, 715
Doering, William T., 609
Dohnányi, Christoph von, 93
Donatoni, Franco, 158, 360, 394
Donaueschinger Musiktage, 242
Dorfman, Mrs. Ralph I., 107

Dorian Woodwind Quintet, 153, 388
Dosso, Leonardo, 158, 394
Doué, Jean, 291a
Dougherty, Celius, 351
Dover (recordings), 259
Downes, Edward, 422, 565, 650
Dreier, Ruth, 122, 179, 184, 582, 651
Drew, David, 43, 556
Druckman, Daniel, 372, 826
Druckman, Jacob, 197, 229, 372, 389, 747
Drury, Stephen, 238
Duarte, John, 281
Dudley Recital Hall, University of Houston, 172
Dufallo, Richard, 108, 583
Dufay, Guillaume, 135
Duke, Erika, 122, 179
Duke, John, 351
Duke, Vernon. *See* Dukelsky, Vladimir
Dukelsky, Vladimir (pseud. Vernon Duke), 411, 517
Dunkel, Paul, 210, 274, 328
Dupouy, Jean, 309, 313
Durieux, Frédéric, 652
Dusapin, Pascal, 168a
Dusek, Robert, 246
Dutilleux, Henri, 93; 7
Dutt, Hank, 62
Dwyer, Doriot Anthony, 289, 387

Earplay, 188
Eastman-Rochester Symphony Orchestra, 219
Eastman School Festival of American Music, 94, 524
Eastman School of Music, 848, 866, 871. *See also* University of Rochester
Eaton, John, 578
Ebell, Hans, 1

Eckert, François, 114, 149, 194, 195, 305, 325
ECM (recordings), 170, 181, 187, 357, 371
Editiones Roche (recordings), 112, 243
Ed Landreth Auditorium, 272
Edwards, Allen, 401, 575, 584
Eglise Luthérienne Saint-Pierre, Paris, 269
Eicher, Manfred, 170, 181, 187, 357
Eisenstein, Sergei, 456, 620
Eisler, Hanns, 509, 538
electronic music, 526, 541, 586, 587, 591, 596
Elektra Nonesuch (recordings), 144, 218, 263, 288, 296, 309, 313, 349, 350. *See also* Nonesuch (recordings)
Elektra Sound Recorders, 173
Elite Recordings, Inc., 173
Ellington, Duke, 517
Emelianoff, André, 57, 123, 180
Emerson, Roy, 167, 310, 315, 320, 322
EMI (recordings), 141, 258, 346
Emmanuel Church, Boston, 139, 177, 200, 202, 207, 216, 230, 340, 366
Enesco, Georges, 475, 517
Engel, Lehman, 65, 103
English Chamber Orchestra, 140, 142
Ensemble Contrasts, 161, 183, 189, 292, 398
Ensemble InterContemporain, 47, 58, 78, 185, 221, 224, 240, 243, 251, 743
Ensemble Recherche, 367
Entre temps, 485, 649, 652, 666, 707

Epic (recordings), 140, 257, 273
Erato (recordings), 163, 185, 224, 240, 241, 251
Ernst-von-Siemens Musikpreis, 430
Escot, Pozzi, 358, 638
Esham, Faith, 108
Eskin, Jules, 289
Esser, Franz-Peter, 161, 183, 189, 292, 398
Estrada, Julio, 360
Etcetera (recordings), 167, 232, 264, 310, 315, 320, 322
Etler, Alvin, 537
Everist, Mark, 621
Evett, Robert, 209
expressionism, 442, 594, 671

Factory (recordings), 266
Falla, Manuel de, 285, 291
Farkas, Ferenc, 392
Fauré, Gabriel, 155, 156, 454, 572
Faust, Georg, 183
Faust, Karl, 289
Faust, Michael, 161, 183, 189, 292, 398
Feder, Susan, 236, 330
Feghali, José, 272
Feigen, Irving, 538
Feldman, Morton, 168, 367, 578, 823
Fend, Michael, 654
Fennell, Frederick, 109
Fennelly, Brian, 655
Ferentz, Melvin, 882, 885
Ferneyhough, Brian, 168a, 319, 360
Festinger, Richard, 188
Festival Miami, 91, 744
Festival of American Music, Rochester. *See* Eastman School Festival of American Music
Fetler, Paul, 203
Fima, Louis, 240
Finckel, Chris, 372
Fine, Irving, 136, 151, 169, 173, 174, 226, 349, 387, 389, 391, 393, 397
Fine, Michael, 177, 200, 207, 230
Fine, Vivian, 271
Finlandia (recordings), 298
Fiorillo, Dante, 540
Fires of London, 105, 369, 740
First Presbyterian Church, Mt. Pleasant, MI, 157
First United Methodist Church, Evanston, IL, 291
Fitton, Ellen, 132
Fitz, Richard, 72, 222
Fitzgerald, Robert, 26
Fitzwilliam Virginal Book, 479
Fizdale, Robert, 347
Flanagan, William, 351, 380
Flax, Laura, 123, 186, 249
Flower, David, 117
The Flutist Quarterly, 658, 659
folk music, 449, 509
Foote, Arthur, 501
Forbes, Elliot, 135, 337
Ford, Andrew, 585
Ford Foundation, 79; 4
Forst, Rudolph, 511
Forte, Allen, 709, 779, 887
Foss, Lukas, 136, 226, 236, 237, 389, 500, 538, 579
Foster, Stephen, 349, 351
Françaix, Jean, 157, 411
Frank, Andrew, 188, 656
Frankfurt Radio Orchestra Brass Ensemble, 192
Frankfurt Symphony Orchestra, 67
Free, Karl, 81
Friedmann, Jane, 140
Friedrich, Reinhold, 121
Frohne, Vincent, 247
Fromm Music Foundation, 51, 100, 420
Fromm, Paul, 51, 100, 464, 653
Frost, Robert, 101, 300
Frost, Thomas, 116, 162, 191
Frost-Jones, Helen, 2; *See also* Carter, Helen
Fuente, Louise de la, 132
Fuleihan, Anis, 501
Fulford, Jonathan, 826
Fuller, Donald, 413
Funkhaus Köln, 161, 183, 189, 292, 398
Furniss, Rosemary, 105, 369
Fürstliche Reitbahn, Arolsen, 299

Gable, David, 464
Gaburo, Kenneth, 203
Gagne, Cole, 586
Galilei, Galileo, 486
Gallagher, Maureen, 323
Gamer, Carlton, 581, 657
Gann, Kyle, 168
García-Lorca, Federico, 555
Garcin, Michel, 185, 224, 240, 251
Garfield, Bernard, 53, 150
Garrison, Jon, 215
Garrison, Leonard L., 658, 659, 841
Garvey, John, 88, 306
Gass, Glenn, 660
Gauthier, André, 587
Gawthrop, Daniel, 209
Gay, John, *The Beggar's Opera,* 69, 760
Geer, E. Harold, 567
Geertsema, Anita, 842
Geissler, Fredrick Dietzmann, 843
Gelles, George, 588
Gerber, Steven R., 362
Gershwin, George, 136, 226, 271, 348, 378
Gesualdo, Don Carlo, 204, 225
Giannini, Vittorio, 509
Gielen, Michael, 134, 242, 253, 254, 345, 375, 742
Gilbert, Henry Franklin Belknap, 406
Gilly, Cécile, 604
Gimpel, Bronislaw, 411

Index

Ginsburg, James, 291
Glanville-Hicks, Peggy, 150
Glass, Philip, 193
Glasow, Glenn, 203
Glasunov, Alexander, 170
Glazer, David, 53, 150, 151
Glickman, Loren, 155
Glock, Lady, 96
Glock, Sir William, 40, 44, 96, 306, 649, 653, 661–664, 675, 769
GM Recordings, 123, 180, 186, 249, 372
Godfrey, Daniel, 665
Goeb, Roger, 386
Golden Crest Records, 166, 248, 290, 297
Goldet, Stéphane, 485, 666
Goldman, Richard Franko, 53, 448, 667–670
Goldray, Martin, 147
Goldsmith, Harris, 155
Goldstein, Perry, 372
Gomberg, Ralph, 289, 387
Goodman, Benny, 411
Goodman, Bernard, 88, 306
Goodman, Joseph, 391
Goodman, Paul, 145
Goodman, Saul, 54
Goossens, Eugene, 457
Gordon, Joel, 238
Gordon, Ricky Ian, 380
Gottschalk, Louis Moreau, 269
Gottschalk, W., 160, 395
Gould, Morton, 407
Gow, David, 291a
Grace Rainey Rogers Auditorium, New York, 51
Graef, Richard, 59
Graham, Bud, 116, 162, 191, 222, 331
Graham, Edward T., 314, 317
Graham, Martha, 537, 574

Grainger Ballroom, Orchestra Hall, Chicago, 59
Gramophone Award, 107; 6
Gramophone magazine, 611
Grande Auditório Gulbekian, Lisbon, Portugal, 345
Gratzer, Wolfgang, 671
Grau, Irene Rosenberg, 844
The Great Mr. Handel, 556
Green, Edward, 136
Greenhouse, Bernard, 86, 87, 293
Greenwich House Music School, New York, 103
Greenwich Orchestra, 423
Gregg Smith Singers, 175, 197, 205, 226, 338, 364
Grenadilla (recordings), 247
Grewel, Volker, 398
Grice, Paul, 390
Griffes, Charles, 351
Griffiths, Paul, 110, 276, 368, 672
Grofé, Ferde, 509
Grolimund, Rolf, 112, 243
Gronarz, Christoph, 326
Gronemeyer, Gisela, 168
Grosser Tonhallesaal, Zürich, 75
Groth, Renate, 673
Group for Contemporary Music, 127, 128, 147, 182, 196, 278, 301, 333, 359
Grubbs, John W., 485
Gruenberg, Louis, 423, 444
GSS Recordings, 137, 175, 198, 205, 227, 338, 364
Gualda, Sylvio, 163
Guarneri, Mario, 120
Guerriere, John, 129
Guitar Review, 693
Gutheil, Thomas G., 135

Hába, Alois, 779
Haberkorn, Michael, 845
Hadley, Henry, 502
Haffner, Barbara, 291
Hahn, Stefan, 168
Hahn, Stephan, 292
Haieff, Alexei, 327
Hair, Graham, 270
Hakkila, Tuija, 298
Halewijn, Herman, 190
Hall, David, 219
Hall, Juanita, 509
Hamilton, David, 376
Hamilton, Jim (James Howard), 846
Hamline A Cappella Choir, 203
Hammond Novachord, 509
Hammond organ, 509
Hancock, David, 125, 137, 175, 198, 199, 205, 210, 227, 228, 235, 274, 328, 333, 338, 355, 364, 379, 383
Handel, G. F., 192, 475, 556, 559, 573; 5
Hanson, Howard, 94, 219, 407, 524, 537
Hans Rosbaud Studio. *See* SWF Hans Rosbaud Studio
Hanusch, Helmut, 254, 345
Harbison, John, 237, 362
Harbutt, Charles, 146, 311, 316, 321, 324
Hargail (recordings), 347
Harman, Carter, 210, 274, 328, 333
Harpsichord Quartet of New York, 86
Harrington, David, 62
Harris, Jane Duff, 847
Harris, Roy, 193, 407, 413, 423, 502, 530, 538, 809
Harris, Russell, 203
Harrison, Bob, 114, 149, 194, 195, 305, 325
Harrison, Carl, 246
Harrison, Lou, 197, 342
Hart, Mary Ann, 380
Hartman, Steven, 393

Hartmann, Karl
  Amadeus, 242
Harvard Classical Club,
  25, 26, 30
Harvard Glee Club, 50,
  56, 97, 135, 337; *1*
Harvard Magazine, 784
Harvard University, 100,
  433, 438, 439, 464,
  559, 583, 714, 730,
  784, 801; *1, 4, 5*
Harvey, David I. H., 167,
  310, 315, 320, 322,
  618, 674–677, 775
Harvey, Jonathan, 281,
  319
Harvey, Michael Kieran,
  270
Haskell, Martin, 167,
  310, 315, 320, 322
Hassler, Hans Leo, 135,
  204, 225
Haubiel, Charles, 511
Hauer, Josef Matthias,
  779
Häusler, Josef, 242, 447
Hawkins, Erick, 81, 537
Haydn, Joseph, 155, 156,
  484, 509, 896
Headrick, Samuel Philip,
  848
Heaton, Roger, 678
Hegedus, Chris, 823
Heidegger, Martin, 485
Heiden, Bernhard, 172,
  390, 413
Heilig Geist Kirche, Bad
  Vilbel, Germany, 121
Heininen, Paavo, 298
Heiss, John, 290
Helm, Everett, 373
Helmrich, Dennis, 380
Hemphill, Julius, 236,
  237
Henderson, Robert, 679
Henigman, Willa, 397
Hennagin, Michael, 197
Hennigar, Harcus, 390
Henry Wood Hall, London, 133, 319, 377
Henze, Hans Werner,
  121, 126, 153, 388
Henze, Sheryl, 393
Heritage, Lee, 849
Hermann, Richard, 637,
  711

Hermanns, Günter, 289
Herrick, Robert, 65, 103,
  760
Herrmann, Bernard, 413
Hersh, Ralph, 77
Hesiod, 96
Hess, William, 347
HiFi Review, 790
Hi-Fi/Stereo Review, 526
Higginbotham, Diane,
  850
High Fidelity, 441, 602,
  691
High-Low concerts, 7,
  517
Hilbish, Thomas, 363
Hill, Edward Burlingame,
  407; *1*
Hill, Manfred, 168
Hill, Martyn, 213
Hill, Richard, 779
Hill Auditorium, University of Michigan, 363
Hillyer, Raphael, 89, 312,
  314
Hind, Rolf, 266
Hindemith, Paul, 120,
  121, 204, 225, 248,
  250, 411, 423, 475,
  498, 499, 500, 517,
  537, 538, 539, 572,
  671, 714, 730
Hines, Robert Stephan,
  516
Hitchcock, Alfred, 444
Hitchcock, H. Wiley,
  680
Hitler, Adolph, 436
Hogue, C. Jacqueline,
  245
Hohn, Mark, 161, 183,
  189, 292, 398
Hollander, John, 76, 798
Holliday, Robert, 203
Holliger, Heinz, 38, 75,
  83, 99, 104, 112,
  181, 187, 240, 242,
  243, 276, 357, 368,
  371, 575, 589
Holliger, Ursula, 104,
  368
Holm, Hanya, 574
Holst, Gustav, 583,
  733; *1*
Holy Trinity Episcopal
  Church, New York,

125, 205, 226, 235,
  333, 364
Homer, 96
Hommel, Christian, 161,
  292, 398
Honegger, Arthur, 121,
  261, 501, 539, 547
Horgan, Paul, 555
Horowitz, Israel, 285
Horowitz, Vladimir, 607
Houston Symphony
  Orchestra, 100, 745
Hovaness, Alan, 171
Hove, Carolyn, 250
Howard, Al, 54
Huber, Gerhard, 371
Hudson, Richard, 681
Hudson Review, 686
Huffman, Mark, 209
Hull, Garrison, 209
Hume, Paul, 579
Humphrey, Doris, 574
Humphrey, George, 55
Humphries, John, 117
Hundley, Richard, 380
Hunter College Playhouse, 72, 469,
  735
Huntley, David, 62
Hurnik, Ilja, 291, 291a
Hürth-Knapsack, Feierabendhaus der
  Hoechst AG, 161,
  183, 189, 292, 398
Hurwitz, Robert, 314,
  317, 590
Husa, Karel, 389
Huscher, Phillip, 326
Hush, David, 246
Hüsserl, Edmund, 485
Hyperion (recordings),
  193

Ibert, Jacques, 468
Ibycus, 96
Ignacio, Lydia Walton,
  245
*Il saggiatore musicale:
  Rivista semestrale di
  musicologia*, 645
Imbrie, Andrew, 197,
  342, 343, 358, 872
improvisation, 453, 456
Independent Music
  Publishers Contest,
  67; *2*

Index

Indiana Theory Review, 43, 646, 660, 802
Indiana University, 300, 862
Intégral, 690
International Piano Competition Umberto Micheli, 702
International Society for Musicology: Eighth Congress of, 51
International Society for Performing Arts, 6
In Theory Only, 883
Iowa State University, 869
IRCAM (Institut de Recherche et Coordination Acoustique/ Musique), Centre Georges Pompidou, Paris, 115, 185, 221, 224, 239, 240, 251, 356
ISAM (Institute for Studies in American Music) monographs, 406, 448, 511, 512, 577, 597, 667, 699
ISCM (International Society for Contemporary Music), 77, 403. ISCM Festival, 427, 471, 542, 605; *3* Istituto di Studi Musicali, Latina, Italy, 48
Ivanov, V., 271
Ives, Charles, 10, 14, 132, 136, 168, 193, 203, 226, 229, 267, 289, 349, 405, 410, 411, 414, 433, 437, 442, 455, 474, 521, 529, 530, 541, 547, 583, 589, 594, 597, 635, 644, 672, 713, 749, 761, 788, 818, 826, 827, 828; *1. See also* Charles Ives Festival, London
Ives, Harmony, 433

Jackson, Richard, 610
Jacobi, Frederick, 423, 502, 537, 538
Jacobs, Paul, 74, 142, 143, 234, 262, 287, 295, 504, 562, 682, 683, 732, 823
Jacobs-Bond, Carrie, 349
Jacquinot, Alain, 185, 224, 240, 251
Jaffe, Stephen, 279, 281
Jaggard, David, 236, 237
Jahrbuch des Staatlichen Instituts für Musikforschung Preußischer Kulturbesitz, 780
Jäkel, Gisbert, 110
James, Philip, 501
Jar Church, 148, 361
Jara, Jorge, 110
Järvenpää Hall, Järvenpää, Finland, 298
Jarvinen, Arthur, 122, 179, 184
jazz, 441, 495, 511, 530, 824, 827
Jeanrenaud, Joan, 62
Jennings, Graeme, 195, 325
Jensen, Dag, 161, 398
Jenstad, Anita, 148, 361
Jesus-Christus-Kirche, Berlin, Germany, 160, 395
Johanson, Bryan, 281
John Oliver Chorale, 139, 177, 200, 202, 207, 216, 230, 340, 366
Johns, Gloria, 290
Johnson, Brett, 139
Johnson, Hunter, 411, 413
Johnson, Lilla Joyce Finch, 851
Johnston, Ben, 578
Johnston, Robert, 591
Jonas, Diethelm, 160, 395
Jones, Allan Clive, 684
Jones, Patricia, 685
Jones, W. James, 397
Jones Hall, Houston, TX, 100
Jordan Hall, New England Conservatory, Boston, 238
Jörns, Helge, 160, 395

Josheff, Peter, 188
Journal of Aesthetics and Art Criticism, 639
Journal of Musicological Research, 703
Journal of Musicology, 719
Journal of Music Theory, 478, 619, 887, 889, 890, 891
Journal of the American Musicological Society. See American Musicological Society Journal
Joyce, James, 10, 12, 30, 620, 666, 807, 824, 827
Joyner, William, 110
Juilliard Ensemble, 108
Juilliard Foundation, 81
Juilliard Publication Award, 81; 2
Juilliard School, 89, 90, 428, 475, 875; *4*
Juilliard String Quartet, 89, 90, 311, 312, 314, 316, 317, 321, 324, 791, 808
Julius, Ruth, 577
Junyer, Joan, 71
Justinuskirche Hochst, 192

Kagel, Mauricio, 168a
Kagen, Sergius, 349
Kaipainen, Jouni, 298
Kalish, Gilbert, 52, 74, 143, 145, 304, 349, 683, 734
Kalitzke, Johannes, 242
Kamien, Roger, 259
Kandell, Leslie, 380
Kandinsky, Wassily, 456
Kaplan, Melvin, 386
Kaplan Fund, 74
Karchin, Louis, 352
Karis, Aleck, 235, 826
Karttunen, Anssi, 298
Kashkashian, Kim, 170
Kasmets, Udo, 478
Kazdin, Andrew, 142, 222, 331, 374
Keats, Sheila, 289
Keeley, Michael, 156
Keene State College, 81

Kerman, Joseph, 686
Kerner, Leighton, 592
Kernis, Aaron Jay, 349
Keville, Bernard, 252
Keyes, Larry, 222, 331
Keynote, 683, 792
Khrennikov, Tikhon, 475
Kies, Christopher, 290, 852
Killough, Richard, 129, 314
Killmayer, Wilhelm, 121
Kingsley, Sidney, 444
Kinney, Michael, 747, 853
Kirchner, Leon, 140, 579, 670, 851, 868
Kirkbride, Jerry, 389
Kirkpatrick, Hope, 108
Kirkpatrick, John, 108, 413
Kirkpatrick, Ralph, 51, 140, 407, 567, 682
Kirstein, Lincoln, 17, 71, 81, 527; 2
Kitzinger, Fritz, 81
Kleinsinger, George, 407
Klibonoff, Jon, 171
Kliewer, Vernon. L., 687
Klotzman, Dorothy, 448, 667–670
KM Records, 392
Knowles, Gregory, 105, 369
Knox, Garth, 168, 195, 240, 325
Knussen, Oliver, 68, 93, 100, 133, 213, 344, 369, 377
Knussen, Sue, 593
Knuth Hall, San Francisco State University, 188
Koch (recordings), 139, 160, 177, 178, 200–202, 207, 208, 216, 230, 231, 244, 272, 340, 353, 366, 382, 385, 395
Kodály, Zoltán, 170, 539
Koechlin, Charles, 485, 620, 888
Koegler, Horst, 689
Köhler, Lutz, 192
Koivisto, Tiina, 690

Kolb, Barbara, 125, 126, 342, 343
Kolbe, Helmuth, 143
Kolisch String Quartet, 475
Kolleritsch, Otto, 671
Kölner Philharmonie, Cologne, 83
KölnMusik, 83
Kopperud, Jean, 372
Korde, Shirish, 279, 358
Korngold, Eric, 556
Kostelanetz, Richard, 691
Kouguell, Alexander, 285
Koussevitzky, Serge, 67, 475, 501, 517, 583
Kozinn, Allan, 693
Kraber, Karl, 153, 388, 389
Kramer, Edward, 142, 374
Kramer, Lawrence, 694, 696
Krasner, Louis, 475
Krebill, Kerry, 209
Krenek, Ernst, 671
Krieger, Arthur, 279
Kroeger, Karl, 697
Kronos String Quartet, 62
Krosnick, Joel, 295, 304, 311, 316, 321, 324
Kubik, Gail, 499
Kujawsky, Eric, 854
Kurtág, György, 158, 168a, 394
Kuskin, Charles, 153, 287, 388, 389
Kutulas, Janet, 188

Lachenmann, Helmut, 168a, 242
Laenger, Peter, 181, 187, 357
La Flute traversière (recordings), 277
La Musica Théâtre, La Chaux-de-Fonds, Switzerland, 276, 368
Lang, Morris, 54, 162
Lang, Paul Henry, 541
Lange, Hans, 501
Langer, Suzanne, 485
Lanier String Quatet, 55
Lanini, Phyllis, 393

Lansky, Paul, 281
Lanzillotta, Luigi, 48
La Rassegna Musicale, 806
Larkin, Christopher, 193
Larrick, Geary H., 698
Laskey, Charles, 81
La Sonore Wind Quintet, 157
Lassus, Orlandus, 801
Lateiner, Jacob, 79, 252
Lattman, Robert, 143
Lauréat du Prix de Composition Musicale, 93; 7
Lauridsen, Morton, 351
Lavista, Mario, 281
Lawson, Peter, 267
League of Composers, 108, 109, 403, 413, 539, 547, 668; 2
Leavitt, Michael, 393
LeClerq, Tanaquil, 71
Ledbetter, Steven, 139, 177, 178, 201, 202, 208, 216, 231, 300, 340, 366
Lederman, Minna, 406, 511, 699
Le Dizes-Richard, Maryvonne, 356
Lee, Noël, 148, 260, 269, 277, 361
Lefebvre, Gilles, 578
L'Eglise du Liban, Paris, 163
Lehman, David, 694
Lehman Engel Madrigal Singers, 65, 103
Leibowitz, René, 779
Leinsdorf, Erich, 79, 252
Le monde de la musique, 441, 603
Lennon, John Anthony, 125, 126, 281
Leroux, Germaine, 547
Les nouvelles littéraires, 587
Lester, Joel, 123
Levin, Harry, 26
Levin, Robert, 170, 289
Levine, James, 376
Lévy, Ernst, 407
Lewin, David, 700, 704, 751, 805
Lewis, Lolly, 188

Index

Lewis, Robert Hall, 120
Lewis, William, 153, 388
Library of Congress, 52, 82, 608; *305*
Liddell, Nona, 824
Lieberman, Carol, 358
Lieberson, Goddard, 475, 538, 539
Lieurance Woodwind Quintet, 397
Ligeti, György, 158, 221, 242, 266, 394, 603
Lincoln Theatre, Mount Vernon WA, 396
Linden, Johan van der, 124
Link, John F., 701, 702, 855
Lipka, Stefan, 134, 254, 345
Liptak, David, 247
Listen: The Guide to Good Music, 405, 454
The Listener, 676, 753, 797
Liszt, Franz, 170, 261
Little Bridges Auditorium, Pomona College, 250
Littlefield Ballet, 573, 574
Littlefield, Catherine, 543
Lochhead, Judy, 703, 704
Lockwood, Normand, 764
Lolya, Andrew, 386
London Gabrieli Brass Ensemble, 193
London Intimate Opera Company, 457
London Sinfonietta, 44, 68, 133, 213, 344, 377, 824
London Weekend Television, 824
Long Island Symphonic Choral Association, 175
Longoni, Maurizio, 158, 394
Loon, Hendrik Willem van, 411
Lopatnikov, Nikolai, 547
Lopes, Joe, 215, 354
Lopez-Cobos, Jesus, 41
Lorentz, Robin, 122

Loring, Eugene, 81
Los Angeles Chamber Orchestra, 173
Los Angeles Philharmonic, 95
Louisville Orchestra, 106, 327, 373
Louisville Philharmonic Society, 106
Lowell, Robert, 68, 642, 741, 767
Lucier, Alvin A., 168
Ludewig-Verdehr, Else, 247
Luening, Otto, 407, 475
Lully, Jean Baptiste, 392
Lussier, Henry, 139
Lutes, Nancy E., 397
Lutosławski, Witold, 63, 117, 607

Maazel, Lorin, 565
MacDonald, Calum, 268
MacDowell, Edward, 269, 501, 517; 6
MacDowell, John Herbert, 502
Mâche, François-Bernard, 168a
Machover, Tod, 356
Macintyre, Bruce, 577
Mackey, Steve, 281
Mackie, Neil, 68
Macomber, Curtis, 362, 826
Madison, Carolyn, 197
Maggio Fiorentino, 442
Mahler, Gustav, 572
Makas, Anthony, 87, 293
Malipiero, Gian Francesco, 475, 540
Mallet, Franck, 168
Mamlock, Ursula, 188
Manhattan Center, New York, 218
Maniura, Peter, 826
Mann, Robert, 89, 90, 146, 311, 312, 314, 316, 317, 321, 324
Mannoni, Gerard, 163
Manziarly, Marcelle de, 500
Marcard, Micaela von, 110
Markham, Mark, 352, 381, 384

Marlowe, Sylvia, 86, 285, 286
Martin Beck Theater, 81
Martino, Donald, 779
Martinů, Bohuslav, 547
Martirano, Salvatore, 279
Martland, Steve, 266
Marunas, Raymond, 137, 175, 198, 205, 227, 338, 364
Marvin, Elizabeth West, 637, 711
Marvin, John, 250
Marx, Joseph, 77, 282
Mary Duke Biddle Foundation, 74
Mase, Raymond, 42, 60, 116, 191
Mason, Daniel Gregory, 457, 511
Mason, Francis, 527
Mason, Patrick, 354
Massachusetts Institute of Technology. *See* MIT
MasterSound, Astoria, NY, 113, 127, 128, 147, 182, 196, 278, 301, 336, 359
Matthews, Colin, 133, 344, 377
Maxwell Davies, Peter, 105, 372, 578, 653
Mayer, Roger, 173
Mayer, William, 197
Maylone, Bill, 291
Mazzeo, Rosario, 247
McBride, Robert, 407, 457, 537, 574
McCabe, John, 268
McCormick, Robert M., 705
McDonald, Harl, 540
McGill, Raymond, 706
McKim Fund, Library of Congress, 52
McKinley, William Thomas, 177, 200, 207, 230
McManus, James Michael, 856
McMillan Theater, Columbia University, New York, 88
McPhee, Colin, 219

Mead, Andrew, 480, 707–711
Meckna, Robert Michael, 857
Media Guild, 828
Mehta, Bejun, 332
Mehta, Zubin, 742
Meier, Gustav, 51, 140
Melbourne Records, 390
Melby, John, 356
Melis, Andrea, 712
Mellers, Wilfrid, 267, 713
Mellon Foundation, 72
Mellquist, Jerome, 455
Melodiya (recordings), 271
Melos, 542, 689, 791
Menasce, Jacques de, 669
Mendelssohn, Felix, 777
Menting, Evert, 276, 368
Mercury (recordings), 219, 220
Mercury Theater, 98, 341
Meredith, Burgess, 753
Merkin Concert Hall, New York, 61, 62, 123, 186
Merrill, David, 113, 281
The Merry Widow, 556
Merwijk, Willem van, 124
Messiaen, Olivier, 221, 242, 266, 603, 617, 683, 724, 729, 753
Messinis, Mario, 594
Mester, Markus, 121
Metamorphosen Chamber Orchestra, 174
metric modulation, 541, 586, 603, 652, 663, 667, 686, 712, 763, 802, 827, 878
Meurer, Christian, 161, 183, 189, 292, 398
Meyer, Andreas, 132
Meyer, Felix, 442, 622, 714, 777, 787
Meyer, Joseph, 396
Miaskovsky, Nikolai, 299
Micheli, Umberto. *See* International Piano Competition Umberto Micheli
Michigan State University, 844

Milhaud, Darius, 468, 499, 501, 547
Miller, Ben, 737
Miller, Curt, 159
Millet, Florence, 115, 239
Mili, Isabelle Dominique, 715
Mills, Charles, 537
Mimnermus, 96
MIT (Massachusetts Institute of Technology), 456; 4
Mitropoulos, Dimitri, 568
Mitteilungen der Paul Sacher Stiftung, 779. *See also* Paul Sacher Foundation
Moe, Orin, 716
Moevs, Robert, 685, 717
Mohr, Richard, 387
Mönch, Georg, 102
Montale, Eugenio, 99
Monteaux, Pierre, 459
modern dance, 574
Modern Music, 1, 6, 7, 13, 406, 407, 411, 413, 419, 423, 443, 444, 457, 468, 474, 475, 483, 486, 493, 501, 502, 509, 511, 515, 517, 524, 537, 538, 539, 540, 543, 547, 555, 556, 573, 574, 635, 699, 760, 857, 893; 2
Molinari, Ernesto, 187, 371
Monod, Jacques, 273
Monteux, Claude, 86
Monteverdi, Claudio, 204, 225, 468
Moore, Douglas, 499, 547
Moore, Lisa, 302
Moore, Ray, 116, 129, 162, 191, 314, 317
Morel, Jorge, 281
Moretto, Gustavo, 188
Morgan, Robert, 259
Morgan, Robert P., 146, 311, 316, 321, 324, 363, 577, 718, 719
Morgan, Sandra, 291

Morgan Library. *See* Pierpont Morgan Library
Morley, Thomas, 486
Morris, Robert D., 720, 889
Mortenson, Gert, 164
Moryl, Richard, 118
Mosolov, Alexandr, 547
Moszkowski, Moritz, 155, 156
Mouret, Jean Joseph, 392
Mowrey, Tom, 289
Mozart, W. A., 155, 387, 468, 475, 484, 487, 559, 589, 603, 739, 896
Mozart String Sinfonietta, 475
Muller, David, 396
Müller, Wolfgang, 161, 183, 189, 398
Müller-Brachmann, Hanno, 110
Muñoz, Frédéric, 291a
Museum of Modern Art, New York, 53, 54, 108, 109, 555
Musica, 607, 689
Musical America, 479, 582, 651, 796, 881; 6
Musical Art Quartet, 511
Musical Heritage Society (recordings), 154, 156, 203, 318, 391
Musical Newsletter, 529, 584, 718
Musical Quarterly, 426–429, 541, 569, 620, 667–670, 717, 749, 795, 821
Musical Times, 484, 627, 675, 723, 724, 727, 798, 817
Music Analysis, 615, 618
Music and Artists, 578
Music & Arts (recordings), 236, 237, 323, 352, 381, 384
Music and Letters, 721, 813, 814, 815, 816, 818
Music and Musicians, 635, 641, 679, 722, 778

Musica/Realtà, 594, 712, 819
Music Educators Journal, 625
Music Hall, Cincinnati, 253, 375
"Music in the Making" concert, 55
Music Journal, 558
Music Magazine, 591
Music Perception, 643
Music Review, 614, 794, 807
music theater, 602, 607
Musikproduktion Dabringhaus und Grimm, 299
Musiksaal des Stadt-Casinos, Basel, Switzerland, 38, 112, 243
Musikszene Schweitz (recordings), 169
Musil, Robert, 662
Musto, John, 351

Nabokov, Nicholas, 69, 426, 457
Najera, Edmund, 197
Nancarrow, Conlon, 168, 236, 237, 521, 530, 634, 788, 827
National Association for American Composers and Conductors, 111
National Endowment for the Arts, 91, 95, 96
National Institute of Arts and Letters. *See* American Academy and Institute of Arts and Letters, New York
National Music Council, 6
National Music Council Bulletin, 421
Nauert, Paul Charles, 858
Naumburg Musical Foundation Award. *See* Walter W. Naumburg Musical Foundation Award
Negro Melody Singers, 509

Neidich, Charles, 99, 128, 196
Neidich, Irving, 386
Neil, Mary Oberlander, 859
Nelson, John Christopher, 860
Neue Zeitschrift für Musik, 589, 654
Neuma (recordings), 238, 279, 358
Neves, Madeira, 345
New Albion (recordings), 122, 179, 184
New Art Wind Quintet, 386
New England Conservatory, Boston, 238; 4
New England Conservatory Chamber Players, 290
New England Conservatory (recordings), 166, 290
New England Conservatory Scholarship Woodwind Quintet, 636
Newlin, Dika, 577
New Music, 12, 77
New Philharmonia Orchestra, 374
New Republic, 752
New School, New York, 411
New World Records, 253, 356, 363, 375
New York Chamber Symphony, 218
New York City Ballet, 71, 527
New Yorker, 731–746
New York Herald Tribune, 462, 567, 799–801
New York Music Critics' Circle Award, 51, 89; 4
New York New Music Ensemble, 372
New York Philharmonic, 49, 52, 95, 129, 331, 407, 413, 422, 475, 514, 515, 517, 539, 554, 565, 568, 613, 650, 742, 754

New York Philharmonic Symphony Society, 49
New York Public Library, 423, 475, 498, 602, 610, 612, 685; 305–306
New York Review of Books, 726, 754, 759
New York Times, 437, 542, 579, 750, 782
New York Times Hall, New York, 73, 111
New York University, 830
New York Woodwind Quintet, 53, 150, 151, 152
New York World's Fair, 509
Nguyen Thien Dao, 163
Nicholls, David, 721
Nickrenz, Joanna, 143, 145, 170, 173, 309, 313
Nicolet, Christiane, 371
Nielen, Otto, 326
Nielsen, Carl, 152
Niemöller, Klaus Wolfgang, 644
Nieuw Ensemble, 70, 190, 217
Nilsson, Bo, 427
Nold, Simone, 110
Nonesuch (recordings), 143, 145, 173, 204, 213, 225, 234, 262, 287, 295, 309, 313, 369, 434, 503, 504, 505, 506, 682. *See also* Elektra Nonesuch (recordings)
Nono, Luigi, 168a, 242, 607
Nordoff, Paul, 475, 538
Nørgård, Per, 164, 281
Notes, 480, 626, 633, 634, 655, 656, 697, 708, 709, 775, 776, 786, 809
North, Alex, 538
North German Radio, Hamburg, 441
Northcott, Bayan, 114, 133, 149, 194, 195,

Northcott, Bayan (*continued*)
305, 325, 344, 377, 722–727
North Texas State University, 877
Northwestern University, 841, 851
Noubel, Max, 115, 239
Nounou, Marie-Paule, 291a
NYSCA (New York State Council on the Arts), 72, 74

Ober, William B., 153, 388
Oldfather, Christopher, 146
Oliver, John, 139, 177, 200, 201, 202, 207, 216, 229, 230, 340, 366
Olivieros, Pauline, 578
Ollu, Franck, 115, 239
Opalach, Jan, 136, 336
Opéra Berlioz Le Corum, Montpellier, 291a
Oppens, Ursula, 74, 82, 114, 149, 236, 253, 254, 297, 305, 683, 732, 742, 823
Orchestra Hall, Chicago, 59, 376
Orenstein, Martin, 111
Orion (recordings), 245, 261
Ormandy, Eugene, 475, 517
Orpheus, 96, 342, 343, 351, 694, 738
Österreichische Musikzeitschrift, 571
Ostrow, Elizabeth, 356
Otto, Peter, 122, 179, 184
Ovation, 464, 771
Ovid, *Fasti*, 25, 97
Owings, John, 272

Pablo, Luis de, 360
Padmore, Elaine, 487
Page, Tim, 132, 356
Palma, Donald, 223
Palma, Susan, 826

Palmer, Robert, 413, 499, 537, 538
Panebianco, Sebastiano, 394
Panitz, Murray, 53, 150
Pappastavrou, George C., 728
Paraskevas, Apostolos, 281
Parnassus, 433, 763
Parris, Robert, 362
Parry, Milman, 26
Petazzi, Paolo, 157, 394
Paul, Louis, 111
Paul, Thomas, 96, 333
Paul Sacher Foundation, 498, 608, 609, 622, 714, 777, 779, 781; 16, 305. *See also* Sacher, Paul; *Mitteilungen der Paul Sacher Stiftung*
Pauwels, Henk, 827
Peabody Conservatory of Music, 836
Pearson, Kathleen Funk, 567
Penderecki, Krzysztof, 242
Pennebaker, D. A., 823
Percussionist, 698, 705
Percussive Notes, 606
Pereira, David, 302
Perkyns, Jane E. Gormley, 861
Perle, George, 123, 180, 186, 279, 779
Perlea, Jonel, 509
Perlis, Vivian, 414
Perse, Saint-John, 514, 580, 621
Persichetti, Vincent, 171, 250, 386, 393, 397
Perspectives of New Music, 411, 441, 442, 459, 466, 477, 534, 561, 580, 581, 612, 616, 623, 624, 648, 657, 696, 707, 820, 882, 894
Petazzi, Paolo, 157, 158, 394
Peterson, Wayne, 188
Petrassi, Goffredo, 39, 102, 427, 563, 583, 605

Peyer, Gervase de, 155
Pflugradt, William C., 862
Philadelphia Orchestra, 95, 475, 517, 539
Philharmonic Chamber Orchestra, 475, 501
Philharmonic Hall, New York, 49
Philips (recordings), 276, 368
Phillips, Burrill, 500, 524
Phoenix (recordings), 119
Piano Time, 596, 605
Pianovox (recordings), 115, 239
Picasso, Pablo, 728, 827
Picker, Tobias, 237
Piencikowski, Robert, 729
Piern, Paul, 152
Pierpont Morgan Library, 622, 777
Piston, Walter, 136, 148, 159, 169, 226, 277, 361, 386, 387, 393, 407, 413, 423, 479, 500, 517, 538, 547, 569, 572, 583, 714, 730, 809; 1
Plato, 96, 486, 559
Plaut, Fred, 129, 314, 317
Plautus, *Mostellaria*, 25
Pleasants, Henry, *The Agony of Modern Music*, 403
Pleshakov-Kaneko Music Institute, Palo Alto, CA, 261
Plog, Anthony, 396
Poirier, Alain, 276, 368
Pollack, Howard, 730
Pomarico, Francesco, 158, 394
Pomona College, Claremont, CA, 250
Pompidou Center. *See* Centre Georges Pompidou
Ponsonby, Robert, 653
Pontino music festival, 39, 63, 104, 594, 596
Pope, Alexander, 503
Poper, Roy, 120

Index

Popkin, Mark, 111
Porter, Andrew, 731–746
Porter, David, 428
Porter, Quincy, 150, 248, 289, 423, 475, 511, 547
Posthuma, Klaas A., 113, 232, 264
Potrel, Yves, 291a
Poulenc, Francis, 299, 304, 457, 573
Powell, Mel, 323
Pozzi, Raffaele, 99, 459, 460, 584, 595, 596, 605
Prausnitz, Frederik, 142, 374
Premiere (recordings), 393
Preuves, 497
Previn, André, 268
Price, Harry E., 747
Price, Paul, 54
Priebe, Cheryl, 290
Princeton Seminar in Advanced Musical Studies, 781
Princeton University, 541, 557; 4
Pro-Arte Quartet, 539
Proceedings of the American Society of University Composers. See *American Society of University Composers Proceedings*
Proceedings of the Royal Music Association. See *Royal Music Association Proceedings*
Program Promotions (recordings), 270
Prokofiev, Sergei, 302, 304, 413, 500, 547
Proms, 93
Proust, Marcel, 620, 662, 824
Prout, Ebenezer, 27
Pruslin, Stephen, 105, 369
Pulitzer Prize for Music, 89, 90; *3, 5*
Purcell, Henry, 60, 192, 457
Purcell, Margaret, 411

Purchase Conservatory of Music Recital Hall, 304
Purvis, William, 336, 826
Pythagorean derivation of musical intervals, 559

Quan, Linda, 372
Quantitative Linguistics, 617
Quasimodo, Salvatore, 99
Quatuor Jean-Marie Leclair, 291a
Quintetto Arnold, 158, 394

Rabelais, François, *Pantagruel*, 50
Rachmaninoff, Sergei, 300
Racine, Philippe, 181, 187, 371
Radio City Music Hall, 543
Radio DRS, Studio Basel, 371
Radio DRS, Studio Zürich, 181, 187, 357
Radio France (ORTF), 512
Radio France/IRCAM (recordings), 221
Radio Portugal, 345
Radiostudio Zürich, 169
Raeburn, Andrew, 363
Raffman, Relly, 203
Raimondi, Matthew, 91, 166, 309, 313, 318, 323, 653
Ran, Shulamit, 343, 362
Randolph, David, 73
Randolph Singers, 73
Ranger, Louis, 42, 60, 116, 118, 191
Rankin, Herbert, 42, 60, 116, 191
Rao, Nancy Yunhwa, 863
Raseghi, Andreas, 242
Rathaus, Karol, 547
Rattle, Simon, 346
Ravel, Maurice, 457, 517, 573
Ravenscroft, Brenda, 864

Raynié, Michel, 291a
RCA (recordings), 252, 312, 319, 387
RCA Recording Studios, New York, 145, 215, 223, 234, 262, 354
Rea, John, 390
Read, Gardner, 478, 515, 890
Rees, Rosalind, 342, 355, 364, 379, 383
Reicha, Anton, 152
Reider, Brent, 253, 375
Reiman, Elise, 71
Reis, Claire, 748
Rembrandt Chamber Players, 291
Renwick, Wilke, 392
Resanovich, Nikola, 865
Restagno, Enzo, 400, 563, 597
Révil, Rudolf, 413
Revue musicale, 888, 896
Rex Foundation, 76
Rhee, Heasook, 299
Rhodes, Samuel, 90, 311, 316, 317, 321, 324
Rider, Rhonda, 303
Riegger, Wallingford, 136, 220, 226, 386, 537, 568
Rihm, Wolfgang, 168a, 242
Rijks, Peter, 160, 395
Risi, Jorge, 48
River City Studios, 157
Rivolta, Renato, 158, 394
Rizzi, Ben, 127, 128, 147, 182, 196, 278, 301, 359
Robinson, Earl, 407
Robinson, Gerald, 390
Robison, Paula, 155
Rochberg, George, 171, 172, 268, 343, 396, 749
Rockefeller Foundation, 49, 106
Rockwell, John, 750
Roeder, John, 751, 891
Roger-Ducasse, Jean-Jules, 501
Rogers, Bernard, 500, 524

Rognan, Arne-Peter, 148, 361
Rohrig, James, 122
Rollier, Suzanne, 715
Rorem, Ned, 197, 209, 285, 349, 351, 752, 753
Rosbaud, Hans, 477
Roseman, Ronald, 151, 285
Rosen, Charles, 51, 74, 113, 140, 142, 232, 257, 264, 273, 401, 484, 575, 600, 683, 754, 758, 759, 824
Rosenfeld, Jayn, 372
Rosenfeld, Paul, 455, 760, 892
Rosenzweig, Stanley, 118
Ross, Anthony, 300
Ross, Hugh, 511, 517
Rosseau, Jean-Jacques, 449
Rossi, Franck, 115, 239
Rossini, Gioacchino, 468
Rossiter, Frank. R., 761, 788
Rosslyn Hill Chapel, London, 213, 268
Roth, Jerome, 53, 150, 151
Rothenberg, Sarah, 249
Roussakis, Nicolas, 330
Roxbury, Ronald, 197
Routh, Francis, 762
Royal Albert Hall, London, 78, 93
Royal Festival Hall, London, 100
Royal Music Association Proceedings, 810
Ruders, Poul, 281
Rudhyar, Dane, 442
Rudiakov, Michael, 166, 297, 309, 313, 732
Ruehr, Elena, 174
Ruggles, Carl, 193, 442, 499, 529
Ruscher, Uta, 276, 368
Russian Ballet, 573
Russian music, 545
Russian State Radio, 271
Russo, John, 245, 246
Rutgers Presbyterian Church, New York, 287, 295

Rutgers University, 685
Rzewski, Frederic, 237, 730

Sabow, Ralph, 160, 395
Sacher, Paul, 38, 75. *See also* Paul Sacher Foundation; *Mitteilungen der Paul Sacher Stiftung*
Saez, Richard, 763
Sahl, Michael, 236, 237
St. Agnes Catholic Church, Lake Placid, NY, 355, 379, 383
St. Andrews Catholic Church, Boulder City, NV, 159
St. George's, Brandon Hill, Bristol, England, 826
St. John's College, 450, 486, 588; 2
St. John's Smith Square, London, 68
St. Luke's Church, Hampstead, London, 369
Saint–Saëns, Camille, 155, 156
St. Silas Church, Kentish Town, London, 167, 310, 315, 320, 322
Saks, Jay David, 317
Salle Beracasa, Opéra Berlioz Le Corum, Montpellier, 291a
Salle Patino, Geneva, 104
Sallmen, John Mark, 866
Salonen, Esa-Pekka, 250
Salter, Lionel, 121
Salzburg Opera Guild, 468
Salzburg seminars, 689, 781; 3
Salzman, Eric, 173, 362
Saminsky, Lazare, 64, 66, 407, 475, 764
Samuel, Claude, 604
Sanders, Robert, 411
Sanders Theatre, Harvard University, 25, 26
Sandner, Wolfgang, 181, 187, 357, 371
San Francisco State University, 188

San Francisco Symphony, 41, 107, 774
Santen, Ann, 57
Santen, Harry, 57
Sappho, 96
Sarah Lawrence College, 545
Saram, Rohan de, 167, 168, 194, 195, 305, 310, 315, 320, 322, 325
Saturday Review, 499, 500, 572, 592
Sauguet, Henri, 285
Scarponi, Ciro, 48
Schadeberg, Christine, 223
Schaefer, Murray, 578
Scedrov, Igor, 867
Scheffer, Frank, 827
Schenkerian theory, 817a
Schenkman, Edgar, 423
Schiff, András, 83, 276
Schiff, David, 127, 128, 131, 147, 154, 182, 196, 210, 213, 253, 274, 278, 301, 318, 319, 328, 329, 333, 334, 335, 359, 369, 375, 401, 480, 655, 662, 674, 709, 748, 765–777, 815, 817a
Schiffer, Brigitte, 778
Schillinger, Joseph, 443, 777, 893
Schmid, Elman, 83, 276
Schmidt, Dörte, 779–781
Schmitt, Florent, 407
Schmitt, Homer, 88, 306
Schneeberger, Hansheinz, 357, 371
Schocker, Gary, 380
Schoenberg, Arnold, 168a, 437, 442, 456, 475, 487, 495, 497, 499, 500, 538, 558, 559, 572, 589, 597, 603, 664, 671, 711, 725, 751, 779, 780, 827, 854, 863
Schola Cantorum, 511, 517
Schöllhorn, Johannes, 367
Schonberg, Harold, 437, 782

Index

School of American
 Ballet, 527
Schrader, David, 291
Schreiner, Martin, 783
Schuller, Gunther, 123,
 151, 159, 160, 166,
 180, 186, 249, 352,
 376, 381, 384, 389,
 395, 396, 428, 478,
 868
Schulte, Rolfe, 102, 128,
 147, 359
Schultz, Gary, 146, 311,
 316, 321, 324
Schuman, Mark, 653
Schuman, William, 129,
 136, 197, 209, 226,
 312, 342, 343, 349,
 351, 396, 407, 423,
 499, 538, 547, 572,
 611, 686, 747
Schumann, Robert, 155,
 235, 527
Schutz, Heinrich, 135
Schwartz, Elliott, 541
Schwartz, Lloyd, 215,
 218, 223, 263, 336,
 350, 354, 784, 785
Schwarz, Gerard, 118,
 173, 218, 732
Schweitzer, Eugene W.,
 868
Scofield, Milton M., 72
*The Score and I.M.A.
 Magazine,* 530, 663,
 791
Scotese, Giuseppe, 39
Scott, Howard, 252
Scriabin, Alexander, 521,
 724
Seay, Albert, 786
Seeger, Charles, 136, 226,
 777, 788
Seeger, Ruth Crawford.
 See Crawford, Ruth
Sequoia String Quartet,
 91
Serenus (recordings), 286
serial music, 453, 477,
 497, 541, 576, 586,
 587, 594, 605, 664,
 711, 779, 780, 794,
 794, 795, 820, 882,
 889
Sermisy, Claude, 204,
 225

Servies, John, 152
Sessions, Roger, 102,
 136, 226, 237, 259,
 260, 407, 413, 423,
 429, 457, 465, 479,
 529, 530, 533, 534,
 538, 539, 547, 578,
 728, 857, 868
Settembre Musica festival, Torino, 400, 597
Severance Hall, Cleveland, 93
Sevice, Alfred Roy, Jr.,
 869
Shafer, Robert, 209
Shakespeare, William, 5,
 98, 341, 468
Shakhnazaryan, E., 271
Shapero, Harold, 282,
 413
Shapey, Ralph, 356
Shapiro, Lois, 303
Shelly, Frances, 397
Shelton, Lucy, 76, 244,
 353, 382, 385
Sheng, Bright, 177, 200,
 207, 230
Shepard, John, 610
Sherba, John, 62
Sherman, Judith, 123,
 180, 186, 236, 249,
 323, 336, 354, 362
Sherry, Fred, 72, 99, 128,
 182, 287, 301, 823
Shifrin, Seymour, 303,
 363, 872
Shinn, Randall Alan, 870
Shostakovitch, Dmitri,
 426, 538
Shreffler, Anne, 291, 787,
 788
Shulman, Henry, 86
Shuman, Mark, 91, 318,
 323
Sibelius, Jean, 502, 854
Siegmeister, Ellie, 351,
 393
Sierra Wind Quintet, 159
Silverman, Stanley, 98
Sine Film/Video, 827
Širola, Božidar, 511
Skalkottas, Nikos, 121
Skarbo (recordings), 280
Skulsky, Abraham, 789,
 790
Sluchin, Benny, 63

Smeyers, David, 161,
 189, 398
Smirnoff, Joel, 311, 316,
 321, 324
Smith, Gregg, 136, 138,
 175, 176, 197, 199,
 205, 206, 226, 228,
 339, 342, 343, 355,
 364, 365, 379, 383.
 See also Gregg Smith
 Singers
Smith, Hale, 209
Smith, Nicholas E., 397
Smith, Patrick J., 602
Smith, Steven H., 871
Smits, Robert, 148, 361
Society for Music in the
 Liberal Arts College,
 450, 462
Society for the Preservation of the American
 Musical Heritage.
 See Musical Heritage
 Society (recordings)
Society for the Publication of American
 Music, 87
Socolof, Murray R., 72
Sollberger, Harvey, 96,
 182, 278, 287, 333,
 358
Somfai, Laszlo, 578
Sondheim, Stephen, 126
Soni Ventorum Wind
 Quintet, 391
Sontag, Wesley, 475
Sonus, 589, 643, 662,
 665, 701, 710, 783,
 785, 788, 804, 822
Sony Classical (recordings), 132, 146, 311,
 316, 321, 324, 332
Sophocles, *Philoctetes,*
 26, 632
Sørensen, Bent, 281
Sorkin, Leonard, 151
Soskin, Eileen, 872
Soule, Richard, 159
Soundings, 678
Sousa, John Philip, 392
South Bank Show, 824
Spanjaard, Ed, 70
Speculum Musicae, 72,
 96, 215, 222, 223,
 333, 336, 354, 732,
 735, 741, 778, 826

Spencer, Patricia, 57, 123, 180, 186, 279
Sperry, Paul, 351
Squires, Gregory K., 393
Stadt-Casinos, Basel, Switzerland, 38, 112, 243
Stagliano, James, 387
Stanford University, 854
Stanley String Quartet, 89
Starobin, Becky, 281
Starobin, David, 46, 85, 113, 125, 127, 128, 147, 182, 196, 215, 223, 278, 281, 301, 342, 354, 359, 684, 693
Starobin, Michael, 281
Starr, Daniel, 889
Starreveld, Harrie, 190
Start, Elizabeth Jane, 873
Stassevitch, Paul, 501
State University of New York at Buffalo, 823
State University of New York at Purchase, 180, 236, 249, 279, 323, 352, 362, 372
Steiger, Rand, 122, 179, 184
Stein, Don Allan, 874
Stein, Leonard, 146, 311, 316, 321, 324
Steinberg, Michael, 229, 252, 282, 312, 610, 791–793
Steiner, Max, 555
Steiner, Ralph, 509
Stereo Review, 803. *See also Hi-Fi/Stereo Review*
Sterne, Teresa, 204, 225, 295, 309, 313, 350
Steuermann, Clara, 428
Steuermann, Edward, 411, 428, 547
Stevens, Thomas, 120, 250
Stevens, Wallace, 505
Stewart, Douglas, 390
Stewart, Robert, 794
Still, William Grant, 457, 509
Stockhausen, Karlheinz, 122, 179, 184, 242, 603, 729

Stone, Dorothy, 122, 179, 184
Stone, Else, 399
Stone, Jerald, 338
Stone, Kurt, 86, 399, 795, 894
Strad, 629
Stradivarius (recordings), 158, 394
Straus, Volker, 276, 368
Strauss, Richard, 392, 539
Stravinsky, Igor, 43, 79, 120, 121, 166, 204, 225, 242, 244, 270, 290, 342, 353, 382, 385, 411, 418, 423, 453, 459, 460, 475, 483, 487, 495, 498, 499, 500, 517, 527, 539, 547, 558, 559, 572, 583, 584, 589, 593, 597, 603, 642, 657, 714, 724, 730, 752, 796, 827, 895
Stubb, James, 43
Stubblebine, Paul, 188
Studien zur Wertungsforschung, 671
Subotnick, Morton, 578
Suits, Paul, 175, 338
Sulem, Jean, 240
Summers, Hilary, 110
Summit (recordings), 397
Suter, Charles, 112, 243
Suttonsmith, Mark, 136
Suvchinsky, Pierre, 485, 559, 620, 896
Sweelinck, Jan, 152
Swenson, Robert, 88, 306
Swenson, Warren, 351
SWF Hans Rosbaud Studio, Baden-Baden, Germany, 134
SWF Symphony Orchestra, 134, 242, 254, 345
Swift, Kay, 524
Swift, Newton, 1
Swift, Richard, 166
swing, 511
Sykes, James, 80, 797
Symphony Hall, Boston, 97, 252
Symphony Hall, Chicago, 93

Symphony Magazine, 793
Symphony Space, New York, 105, 562
synaesthesia, 456
Synthèses, 495
Syracuse University, 853
Szalowski, Antoni, 411
Szersnovicz, Patrick, 603
Szigeti, Joseph, 411, 475
Szymanowski, Karol, 509, 539

Tailleferre, Germaine, 517
Takemitsu, Toru, 125, 126, 326
Tall Poppies (recordings), 302
Talma, Louise, 136, 226, 279, 351
Tamiris, 574
Tanglewood Festival Chorus, 229
Tanglewood Festival of Contemporary Music, 100
Tanglewood Festival Orchestra, 100
Tansman, Alexandre, 556
Taras, John, 71
Tate, Allen, 56
Tati, Jacques, 110
Taylor, Deems, 493
Taylor, Jane, 153, 388, 389
Tchaikovsky, Peter Ilyich, 540, 543
Teldec (recordings), 326
Temple Emanu-El, 64, 66
Temple University, 867
Tempo, 43, 62, 433, 466, 593, 596, 613, 628, 630, 631, 640, 674, 753, 765, 767, 768, 772, 774, 812
Texas Christian University, Fort Worth, TX, 272
Théâtre des Champs-Elysées, 527
Théâtre de la Ville, Paris, 221
Thiery, Daniel, 291a
Thiery-Ballard, Tessa, 291a
Thomas, Gavin, 798

Index

Thomas, John Charles, 413
Thompson, David M., 828
Thompson, Oscar, *Great Modern Composers*, 419
Thompson, Randall, 363, 407
Thomson, Virgil, 136, 193, 226, 348, 378, 457, 468, 499, 572, 574, 576, 686, 799–801, 857
Thorne, Francis, 330
Thouvenel String Quartet, 91
Three Choir Festival, New York, 66
Thunemann, Klaus, 83, 276
time in music, 485, 506, 558, 559, 590, 603, 620, 645, 660, 662, 665, 681, 694, 700, 759, 770, 773, 884, 890, 896. See also Carter, Elliott, rhythm in the music of
Timm, Joel, 43
Tingley, George Peter, 802
Tippett, Michael, 117
Toch, Ernst, 423
Tocqueville, Alexis de, 449
Tomfohrde, Ruth, 172
Tonkel, Stan, 363
Torke, Michael, 122, 179, 184
Tovey, Donald Francis, 728
Town Hall, New York, 87, 411, 413, 799
Travis Chamber Players, 392
Trenkner, Evelinde, 261
Trimble, Lester, 803
Troob, Jolie, 290
Trouttet, André, 185
Truniger, Matthias, 644, 804
Tryggvason, Tryggvi, 133, 244, 344, 353, 377, 382, 385

Tunisia, 30; *1*
Tunnicliff, Theresa, 184
Turnabout (recordings), 342
twelve-tone music. *See* serial music

Ullrich, Dietmar, 160, 395
UNESCO First Prize, 89; *4*
Ungaretti, Giuseppe, 99
Unger, Dr. Anette, 121
Unicorn (recordings), 348, 378
United States bicentennial, 72, 95
University of British Columbia, 861, 864
University of California at Berkeley, 872
University of California at Los Angeles, 833
University of California at Santa Barbara, 857
University of Chicago, 464, 873
University of Houston, 172
University of Illinois, 88, 306, 462, 560, 800, 829, 840, 849, 856, 870
University of Iowa, 859
University of Kansas, 832
University of Michigan, 835, 863; Chamber Choir, 363
University of Northern Colorado, 837
University of Rochester, 866, 868, 880. *See also* Eastman School of Music
University of South Africa, 842
University of South Carolina, 879
University of Southern California, 606
University of Southern Mississippi, 846
University of Texas at Austin, 485
University of Washington, 834, 876

Uno, Yayoi, 805
Urpeth, Peter, 266
U.S. Air Force Band of Golden Gate, 392
Ussachevsky, Vladimir, 524, 526
Ustinov, Peter, 387

Vactor, David van, 411
Vallecillo, Irma, 351
Valois (recordings), 260
Vamos, Roland, 875
Van Doren, Mark, 20, 64
Vanguard Classics (recordings), 124
Vanguard Sound Studio, New York, 318
Van Solkema, Sherman, 512, 577
Vardell, Charles, 524
Varèse, Edgard, 103, 277, 332, 442, 512, 529, 577, 583, 597, 617, 788
Vassar Choir, 567
Vaughan Williams, Ralph, 170
Vayo, David, 188
Veale, Peter, 367
Verdi, Giuseppe, 457, 589, 896
Veress, Sándor, 276, 368
Victoria (recordings), 148, 361
Vieuxtemps, Henri, 170
Villa-Lobos, Heitor, 509
Villa Serbellni, Bellagio, 49
Vine, Carl, 270
Virgin Classics (recordings), 133, 267, 344, 377
Viscuglia, Felix, 159
Vlad, Roman, 605, 806
Vlatković, Radovan, 83, 276
Vossen, Norbert, 134, 254
Vox (recordings), 136, 153, 197, 226, 343, 388, 389

Wadhams, Wayne, 152
Wagenaar, Bernard, 413, 475, 540

Wagner, Günther, 780
Wagner, Richard, 456, 457, 559, 896
Wagner, Robert, 393
Walden, Stanley, 349
Walden String Quartet, 88, 306, 462, 537, 800
Waldrep, Mark, 122, 179, 184
Wallace, John, 117
Walt, Sherman, 387
Walter W. Naumburg Musical Foundation Award, 86; 3
Walt Whitman Auditorium, Brooklyn College, 197, 210, 274, 328
Warburton, Thomas, 807
Warlock, Peter, 204, 225
Warsaw Fetival, 477
Washington University, 838, 874
Waxman, Donald, 197
WDR (Westdeutscher Rundfunk) Köln, 168, 326, 367
Webb, Roy, 555
Weber, Ben, 351, 576
Weber, Jerome. F., 611
Webern, Anton, 168a, 423, 477, 497, 501, 547, 751, 810
Webster, Beveridge, 255, 259, 475
Weidman, Charles, 574
Weill, Kurt, 351, 509, 547, 556
Weinberg, Jacob, 457
Weinberger, Jaromir, 407, 501, 502
Weirich, Robert, 808
Weisberg, Arthur, 143, 151
Weisgall, Hugo, 351
Weiss, Marcus, 104
Welles, Orson, 98, 341
Wells College Glee Club, 69
Wergo (recordings), 213, 214, 369
Wernick, Richard, 281
Wessel, Mark, 511

West, John H., 117
Westdeutscher Rundfunk. *See* WDR
Westminster Choir School Festival, 423
Weston, Craig A., 822, 876
Westwood Woodwind Quintet, 396
We Will Come Back, 556
Wheeler, Lawrence, 172
Whipple, Harold., 612
White, John R., 809
Whitehead, Alfred North, 498, 620, 645, 834
Whiting, John, 213, 369
Whitman, Walt, 109, 728
Whitney, Robert, 106, 327, 373
Whitney Museum, 732
Whittall, Arnold, 810–818
Whittenberg, Charles, 118
Whyte, Bert, 151
Wick, Tilmann, 299
Wiechowich, Stanislaw, 509
Wiese, Lucie, 455
Wilcox, Max, 218, 234, 262, 350
Wilder, Thornton, 444
Wilhite, Carmen Irene, 877
Williams, Jan, 54, 823
Williams, Jonathan, 105, 369
Williams, Laura, 30
Williams, Paul, 578
Wilson, Donald Malcolm, 878
Wilson, Keith, 248
Wilson, Patrick, 606
Wilson, Richard, 244, 353, 382, 385
Winds Quarterly, 43, 646, 766
Winn, James, 372
Witten New Music Days, Witten, Germany, 104

Wittlich, Gary E., 647, 687
Wjuniski, Ilton, 292
WKCR Radio, 737
WNBC Radio "Story of Music," 73
WNCN Radio, 792
Wohlmacher, Johannes, 292
Wolf, Bert vander, 124
Wolfe, Kristin, 159
Wolff, Cristoph, 464
Wolfthal, Marvin A., 607, 819
Wolpe, Stefan, 104, 118, 121, 367, 466, 547, 613
Woods, Benjamin, 879
Woodworth, G. Wallace, 50, 56, 97
Woolen, Russell, 209
World War I, 495, 498
World War II, 304, 411, 413, 453, 497, 498, 499, 583, 824
WPA Composers' Forum Laboratory, 407, 423, 502, 547
WPA (Works Progress Administration), 103, 668; 2
Wright, David, 159
Wright, Simon, 117
Wtorczyk, Wolfgang, 134
Wuorinen, Charles, 237, 301, 352, 381, 384, 820, 821, 867
Wyatt, Lucius Reynolds, 880
Wyner, Susan Davenny, 72, 222, 735

XCP (recordings), 291a
Xenakis, Iannis, 163, 164, 168a, 242

Yaddo Orchestra, 109
Yarbrough, Cornelia, 747
Yeh, John Bruce, 59
Yeston, Maury, 351
Yim, Jay Alan, 168
Yoo, Scott, 174
York Winds, 390
Young, La Monte, 168

Zaferes, Peter, 146, 311, 316, 321, 324
Zemlinsky, Alexander von, 547
Ziegler, Warren P., 139
Zielinsky, Gregor, 376
Zimmermann, Bernd Alois, 242
Zimmerman, Robert, 822
Zimney, Murray, 142, 374
Zinman, Paul, 223, 336
Zukofsky, Paul, 52, 145, 734
Zuponcic, Veda, 271
Zürich Festival, 75
Zürich Radio Orchestra, 273
Zwilich, Ellen Taaffe, 174

About the Author

JOHN F. LINK is active as a composer, teacher, musicologist, and bass player. His compositions for diverse media (including orchestra, chamber and jazz ensemble, rock band, and electroacoustic instruments) have won awards from ASCAP and Meet the Composer. He is also a founding member of the New York City composers' collective, Friends & Enemies of New Music. Dr. Link's writings on music theory and analysis have appeared in *Da Beethoven a Boulez, Il pianoforte in ventidue saggi,* translated by Antonietta Cerocchi Pozzi (Milan: Longanesi & C., 1994), in the American journal *SONUS,* and in the *Institute for Studies in American Music Newsletter.* He has received fellowships from the Paul Sacher Foundation in Basel, Switzerland, for his work on Elliott Carter's sketches. Dr. Link is Assistant Professor of Music at William Paterson University, in Wayne, New Jersey, where he directs the Center for Electroacoustic Music.

Composer Resource Manuals
Guy A. Marco, *General Editor*

1. Heinrich Schütz (1981)
   by Allen B. Skei
2. Josquin Des Prez (1985)
   by Sydney Robinson Charles
3. Sergei Vasil'evich Rachmaninoff (1985)
   by Robert Palmieri
4. Manuel de Falla (1986)
   by Gilbert Chase
   and Andre Budwig
5. Adolphe Adam and Léo Delibes (1987)
   by William E. Studwell
6. Carl Nielsen (1987)
   by Mina F. Miller
7. William Byrd (1987)
   by Richard Turbet
8. Christoph Willibald Gluck (1987)
   by Patricia Howard
9. Girolamo Frescobaldi (1988)
   by Frederick Hammond
10. Stephen Collins Foster (1988)
    by Calvin Elliker
11. Antonio Vivaldi (1988)
    by Michael Talbot
13. Johannes Ockeghem and Jacob Obrecht (1988)
    by Martin Picker
14. Ernest Bloch (1988)
    by David Z. Kushner
15. Hugo Wolf (1988)
    by David Ossenkop
16. Wolfgang Amadeus Mozart (1989)
    by Baird Hastings
17. Nikolai Andreevich Rimsky-Korsakov (1989)
    by Gerald R. Seaman
18. Henry Purcell (1989)
    by Franklin B. Zimmerman
19. G.F. Handel (1988)
    by Mary Ann Parker-Hale
20. Jean-Philippe Rameau (1989)
    by Donald Foster
21. Ralph Vaughan Williams (1990)
    by Neil Butterworth
22. Hector Berlioz (1989)
    by Jeffrey A. Langford
    and Jane Denker Graves
23. Claudio Monteverdi (1989)
    by K. Gary Adams
    and Dyke Kiel
24. Carl Maria von Weber (1990)
    by Donald G. Henderson
    and Alice H. Henderson
25. Orlando di Lasso (1990)
    by James Erb
26. Giovanni Battista Pergolesi (1989)
    by Marvin E. Paymer
    and Hermine W. Williams
27. Claude Debussy (1990)
    by James Briscoe
28. Gustav and Alma Mahler (1989)
    by Susan M. Filler
29. Franz Liszt (1991)
    by Michael Saffle
31. Franz Joseph Haydn (1990)
    by Floyd K. Grave
    and Margaret G. Grave

34. ALLESANDRO AND DOMENICO SCARLATTI (1993)
by Carole F. Vidali

35. HENRICUS ISAAC (1991)
by Martin Picker

36. GUILLAUME DE MACHAUT (1995)
by Lawrence Earp

37. EDWARD ELGAR (1993)
by Christopher Kent

38. ALBAN BERG (1996)
by Bryan R. Simms

39. BENJAMIN BRITTEN (1996)
by Peter J. Hodgson

40. BÉLA BARTÓK (1997)
Second Edition
by Elliott Antokoletz

41. JEAN SIBELIUS (1998)
by Glenda D. Goss

42. GIUSEPPE VERDI (1998)
by Gregory Harwood

43. TOMÁS LUIS DE VICTORIA (1998)
by Eugene Casjen Cramer

44. ZOLTÁN KODÁLY (1998)
by Mícheál Houlahan and Philip Tacka

45. ISAAC ALBÉNIZ (1998)
by Walter A. Clark

46. CARLOS CHÁVEZ (1998)
by Robert Parker

47. SCOTT JOPLIN (1998)
by Nancy R. Ping-Robbins

48. GIACOMO PUCCINI (1999)
by Linda B. Fairtile

49. GABRIEL FAURÉ (1999)
by Edward R. Phillips

50. FRÉDÉRIC CHOPIN (1999)
by William Smialek

52. ELLIOTT CARTER (2000)
by John F. Link